Le Cyclop

Le Cyclop

The Monumental Folly by Jean Tinguely, Niki de Saint Phalle, and their Friends (1969–2024)

jrp|editions

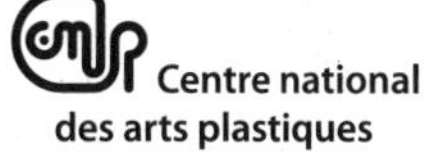

Table of Contents

1

Foreword

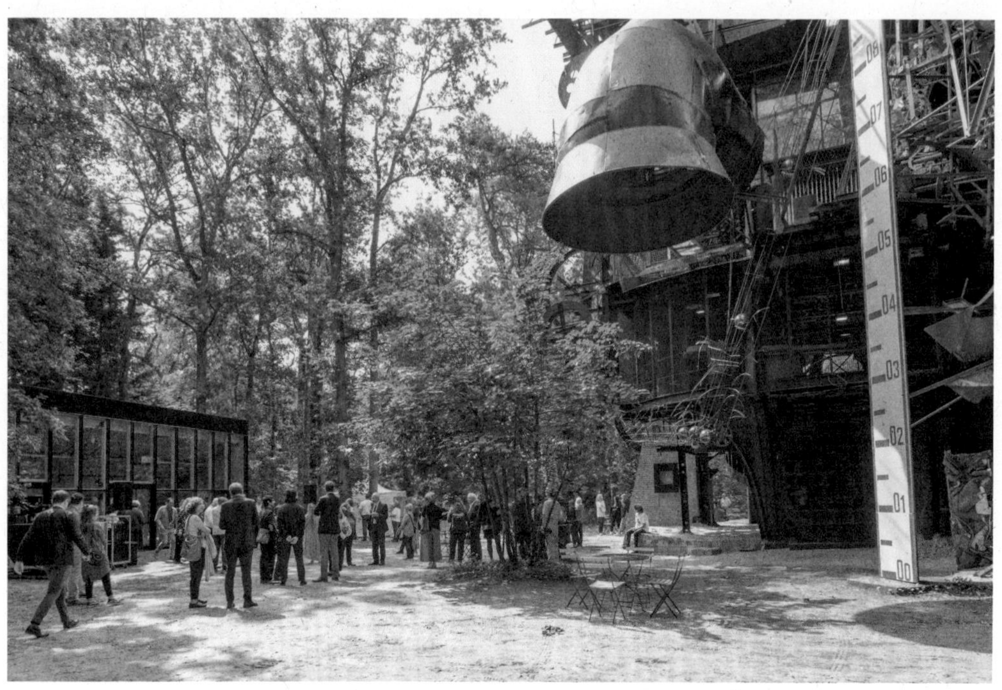

Le Cyclop, Milly-la-Forêt, 2024

Le Cyclop, Always in Motion!
Béatrice Salmon

In May 2022, *Le Cyclop* (The Cyclops) by Jean Tinguely, a mysterious
and monumental artwork hidden deep in the forest of Milly-la-Forêt near
Paris, reopened its doors to the public after two years of restoration.
The Centre National des Arts Plastiques (Cnap) has been responsible for
this masterpiece from the second half of the 20th century since 1987,
following Tinguely and Niki de Saint Phalle's decision to entrust it to the
national collections of the French state. More than 30 years later, major
restoration work was required.

The diversity of materials comprising the totality of this piece, to which
many artists contributed, made the task particularly complex. The thousands
of fragments of Saint Phalle's *La Face aux miroirs* (The Mirrored Face)
were tarnished, and had to be replaced one by one. Eva Aeppli's *Hommage
aux déportés* (Homage to the Deportees), a 1930s railway freight car
similar in every way to those used to transport Jews to concentration
camps under the Vichy regime, suspended in the structure and populated
by fabric sculptures with vacant gazes, received the special care textile
works require. The freight car itself has been carefully renovated, and the
sculptures restored in accordance with the wishes of the artist, who died
in 2015. The aluminum bars of Jesús Rafael Soto's *Le Pénétrable sonore*
(The Resonating Penetrable), which produce a sound somewhat similar to
that of Japanese wind chimes in air currents, have also been treated against

corrosion. At the very top of the construction, the pool designed to reflect the blue of the sky, in tribute to Yves Klein, has been cleaned and waterproofed, and multiple interventions, more or less delicate, on all the works that play their individual part in the overall symphony of *Le Cyclop*, have restored the latter to its original appearance.

The need arose to accompany this reopening with a number of complementary initiatives furthering knowledge about *Le Cyclop*. Available on site, a publication edited by Catherine Francblin, one of the leading specialists in Nouveau Réalisme, offers a particularly sensitive and informed reading of the work, enabling visitors to prolong the magic of their visit.

At the same time, the Cnap has launched the digital platform archivescyclop.fr. Accessible to all, researchers and amateurs alike, there are over a thousand documents to consult: photographs, drawings, letters, sound recordings, etc., evoking the 56 years of *Le Cyclop* adventure. Nourished by numerous archives, notably French and Swiss, from artists, photographers, museum protagonists, and public libraries, this site is, as *Le Cyclop* has long been, a work in progress, destined to expand.

Le Cyclop. The Monumental Folly by Jean Tinguely, Niki de Saint Phalle, and their Friends (1969–2024) is the new opus we wish to deliver. Following on from Virginie Canal's monograph published in 2007, and the films and magazine articles devoted to this truly extraordinary work, the time had come to give a voice not only to those who witnessed the construction first-hand, but also to art historians who, with the benefit of hindsight, can offer new interpretations of this "monument."

Aude Bodet, head of the Cnap's collection department, created the book's architecture by bringing together the superb team of authors she introduces; she was assisted in this task by Stéphanie Fargier-Demergès, Bénédicte Godin, and Gaëlle Guérin. We would like to thank them for their unfailing enthusiasm in this adventure.

Last but not least, we would not have been able to bring these ambitious projects to fruition without the unflagging commitment and support of the French Ministère de la Culture's Direction Générale de la Création Artistique, its director Christopher Miles and his teams at the Délégation aux Arts Visuels, and the warm and fastidious attention of Bloum Cardenas, Saint Phalle's granddaughter, and director of the Niki Charitable Art Foundation, joined here by Tinguely's son, Jean-Sébastien Tinguely.

Of course, I cannot forget the invaluable support of the Association Le Cyclop, its director François Taillade, and its board of directors, who bring *Le Cyclop* to life on a daily basis. My heartfelt thanks to them all.

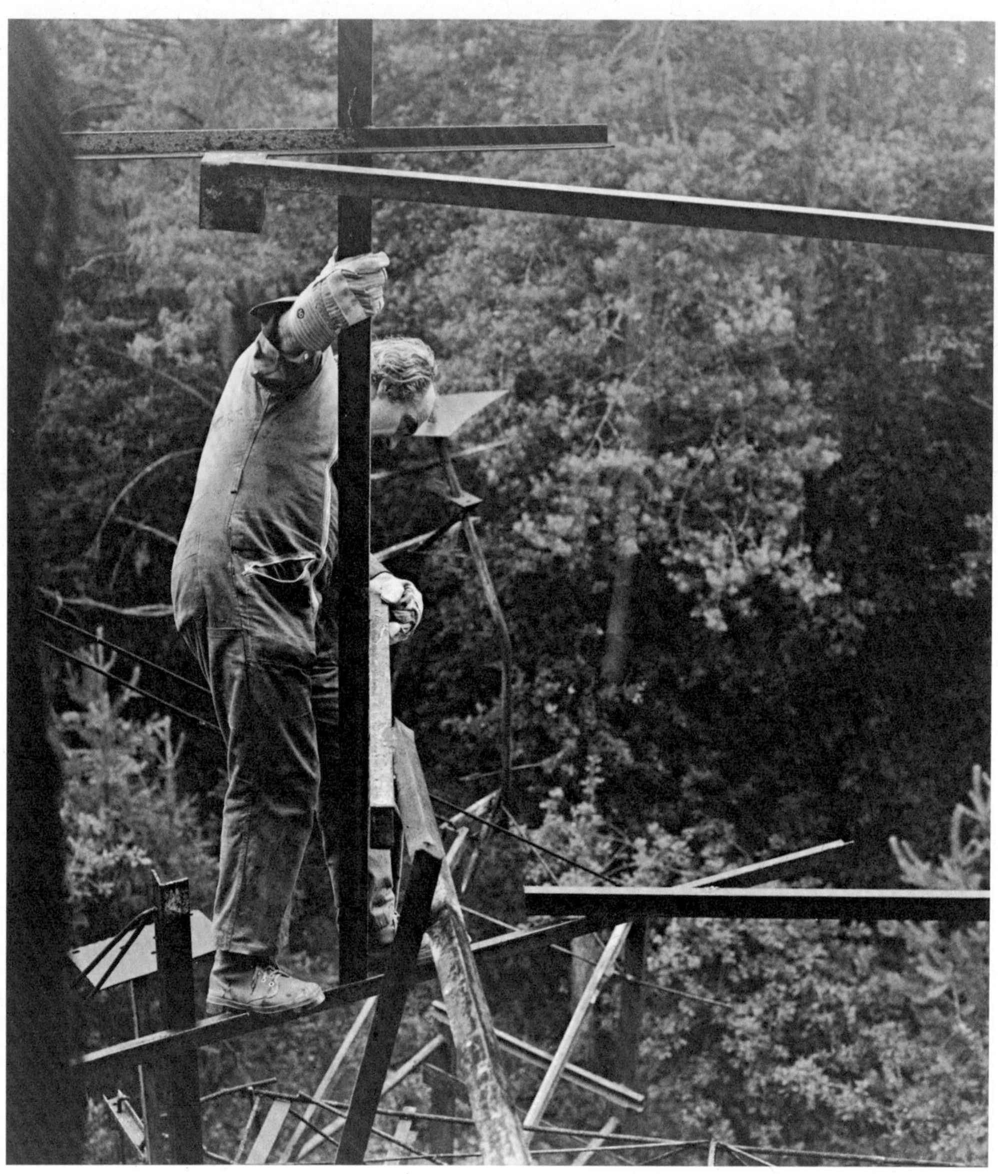

Jean Tinguely during the making of *Le Cyclop*, 1981

"Bigger, Crazier ... "
Aude Bodet

The major exhibition organized by Harald Szeemann at the Kunsthalle
Bern in 1969, considered one of the founding events of contemporary art,
was entitled *When Attitudes Become Form*. Szeemann's title was inspired
by Yves Klein's phrase "my paintings are but the ashes of my art."[1]
But this complex expression was complemented by a simpler injunction,
this one borrowed from Keith Sonnier: "Live in Your Head." Szeemann
was thinking of so-called conceptual art, which does not necessarily need
to be embodied in an object in order to exist.

In the same period, two artists chose to literally live in a head.
In 1969, Jean Tinguely set up home with Niki de Saint Phalle in Soisy-sur-
École, on the edge of the Fontainebleau Forest, and imagined building
a gigantic habitable head hidden in the nearby woods of Milly-la-Forêt.
This monument to dreams and friendship, which kept both artists tirelessly
occupied, would require 25 years of labor, 350 tons of recycled metal,
a not inconsiderable dose of audacity, and a wealth of ingenuity. Tinguely
avoided applying for planning permission for the edifice, which would
no doubt have been refused. He brought together, without hierarchy and
under the same banner, players from all walks of life, from collectors

1   Yves Klein, "6. L'Époque bleue," in *L'Évolution de l'art vers l'immatériel. Conférence de la Sorbonne*, La Sorbonne, June 3, 1959, available online: https://www.yvesklein.com/fr/archives/#/fr/archives/view/audio/4/conference-de-la-sorbonne-6-l-espoque-bleue?sb=_created&sd=desc (last accessed May 2025).

Jean and Dominique de Menil to Guy Duperche, a scrap-metal dealer
based in Essonne, and his wife Françoise, from Marina and Michel de
Grèce to Claude Pompidou, a major patron of artists, and the influential
museum curators Dominique Bozo and Pontus Hultén.

As this last said in 1989, "Tinguely [was] an anarchist," and even
more, "a Swiss anarchist." With *Le Cyclop* (The Cyclops), he pursued
a libertarian dream with rigor and obstinacy.[2] His aim, he said, was to
"escape from museumization," and to achieve this, "there's nothing better
than involving the public, integrating them, providing them with emotions."
Le Cyclop was "a museum for working," as Bernhard Luginbühl put it.
But above all—for Tinguely— it was "the story of a team of mad sculptors
[whose] work is serious, for a purpose that is not."[3]

In addition to the couple's work, the project brings together pieces by
many exceptional artists and artisans—Tinguely and Saint Phalle were not
among those who differentiated between the two—most often friends,
but not necessarily: Eva Aeppli, Arman, Philippe Bouveret and his wife
Dorothée, César, Seppi Imhof, Pierre Marie Lejeune, Luginbühl, Giovanni
Battista Podestà, Jean Pierre Raynaud, Larry Rivers, Jesús Rafael Soto,
Daniel Spoerri, and Rico Weber. In these unusual surroundings, tributes
are paid to personalities who played a decisive role in history, but who are
rarely celebrated in more conventional settings. Among them is Étienne-
Émile Baulieu, inventor of the RU 486 abortion pill.

A close cousin of the Facteur Cheval's *Palais idéal* (Ideal Palace) in
Hauterives, Simon Rodia's *Watts Towers* in Los Angeles, the colossal Olmec
heads in Mexico or the monsters of the Sacro Bosco monumental park
in Bomarzo, Italy, as well as the papier-mâché figures of the Basel carnival
and the three *Merzbau* built by Kurt Schwitters in Germany, Great Britain,
and Norway, and Antoni Gaudí's buildings in Barcelona, *Le Cyclop*
grew up—over 22 meters tall when completed—almost clandestinely,
without the intervention of any art dealer or the French Ministry of
Culture, until 1987.

It was in this year that the work was donated to the French state
and given its definitive title, since for 20 years all those involved in its
construction simply referred to it as the Head or the Monster. It would take

---

2   No doubt Hultén had in mind that the Centre
     International de Recherches sur l'Anarchisme is
     located in Lausanne, Switzerland, where one would
     least expect to find it.
3   Taken from a reportage on Radio-Télévision Suisse
     (Swiss National TV) broadcast in 1989,

these citations are included in a remarkable 2005
documentary realized by Louise Faure and Anne
Julien: *Le Monstre dans la forêt* in *Le Rêve de Jean*,
DVD, Quatre à Quatre films, Paris 2005, 134'.

another seven years after the donation for *Le Cyclop* to be completed
—under Saint Phalle's careful supervision following Tinguely's death
in 1991—protected, and overseen. By the end of the 1970s, the strange
creature had already aroused the curiosity of inconsiderate wanderers
who came to it at night and committed petty thefts of all kinds, or outright
acts of vandalism, to the point of almost discouraging Tinguely, who
referred to these people as "penetrators." Upgraded to public-access
standards, *Le Cyclop* was formally inaugurated in 1994 by President
François Mitterrand and Jacques Toubon, then Minister of Culture.

To his friend Bénédicte Pesle, once director of the Galerie Iolas,
who asked him how to care for his mobile sculptures over time, Tinguely
once jokingly replied that "first and foremost, you need a good mechanic."[4]
He wasn't really joking, as the conservation and restoration of *Le Cyclop*,
just like its construction, requires the skills of every type of artisan,
not just those of professional restorers. The edifice is all the more fragile
as it is exposed to the elements in the heart of a forest whose own integrity
and wild flora and fauna have been preserved as far as possible. These
professionals—and a passionate team, that of the Le Cyclop non-profit
organization created in 1988 to "promote *Le Cyclop*" to the public, which
now welcomes visitors, "while ensuring respect for the artist's moral
rights"[5]—today ensure the artwork's maintenance.

*Le Cyclop. The Monumental Folly by Jean Tinguely, Niki de Saint Phalle,
and their Friends (1969–2024)* is a collective publication that aims to
renew our analysis and view of the artwork. Of course, factual history is
not absent. In it, we discover "A History of Le Cyclop by the People Who
Made It," drawn from archive photographs taken over the years, notably
by Leonardo Bezzola and Laurent Condominas, from the laying of the
first RSJs—those I-shaped steel beams that form the basis of most modern
constructions—to the laying of the last tesserae of mirrors, and the opening
of *Le Cyclop* to the public in 1994. Extracts from interviews with Tinguely,
Saint Phalle, Spoerri, Aeppli, and Raynaud, as well as the writings of
Luginbühl, compiled by the Documentation and Research Department of
the Centre National des Arts Plastiques,[6] shed light on this often-unusual
iconography.

---

4   Conversation with the author, 1985.
5   Clause from the organization's legal foundation
     (1988), Centre National des Arts Plastiques Archives,
     Paris. The association was directed by Annick
     Leroy from 1988 to 2011, and by François Taillade
     since 2011.

6   Stéphanie Fargier-Demergès, Head of the Documen-
     tation and Research Department, assisted by Gaëlle
     Guérin, multimedia documentalist and iconographer,
     have also created the site archivescyclop.fr
     (last accessed May 2025).

But this book also gives historians a greater say. Dominik Müller lucidly situates *Le Cyclop* in the continuity of Tinguely's American sojourns and the tradition of the art of assemblage, celebrated in 1961 at New York's Museum of Modern Art in William C. Seitz's famous exhibition, which bore this title.[7] The failure of the *New Realists* exhibition at the Sidney Janis Gallery, New York, in October–December 1962, meant that Tinguely and his accomplices were for a long time viewed solely from the angle of European history. But this failure was mainly due to commercial and nationalist considerations, since time and the artists' vision know no such boundaries, as Müller brilliantly demonstrates.

Jill Carrick looks in detail at Tinguely's fascination with Marcel Duchamp, and how this is expressed in the Milly-la-Forêt colossus.
[P. 111] The beautifully conserved photograph of Marcel Duchamp experimenting with his younger colleague's drawing machine at an opening at Galerie Iris Clert in 1959 shows that the bonds between the two men are no fiction.

Baptiste Brun pertinently reiterates *Le Cyclop*'s debt to the solitary artists categorized as "bruts" or "outsiders" by Jean Dubuffet. These creators also often embarked on unreasonable and disproportionate ventures— connections not usually highlighted. Saint Phalle, with her painful experience of melancholy and internment, had a hand in reclaiming this reputedly marginal source. But we should also remember that Switzerland, Tinguely's native country, was a pioneer in these matters: the monograph devoted to Adolf Wölfli by Dr. Walter Morgenthaler,[8] his physician at the psychiatric clinic in Bern, can be considered the first book to take the work of mental health patients seriously, its publication in 1921 having preceded by a year the publication of Hans Prinzhorn's famous work *Bildnerei der Geisteskranken: ein Beitrag zur Psychologie und Psychopathologie der Gestaltung* (Artistry of the Mentally Ill: A Contribution to the Psychology and Psychopathology of Configuration).

Camille Paulhan emphasizes the role of the collective in Tinguely and Saint Phalle's Cyclopean project, in a text whose erudition is pleasantly concealed beneath the title of a popular song, "Let's Talk About Love." At a time when the question of working together and inclusion is becoming increasingly acute, Paulhan points to the visionary nature of the couple's work. An ode to the recycling of machines, *Le Cyclop* is indisputably in tune with contemporary society, and with the rejection of individualism professed by today's younger generations, concerned about the very future of humanity, threatened by industrial overproduction.

---

7   *The Art of Assemblage*, The Museum of Modern Art, New York, October 4–November 12, 1961.
8   Walter Morgenthaler, *Adolf Wölfli*, E. Bircher, Bern and Leipzig 1921; republished in *L'Art Brut* [1964], booklet no. 2, second edition, Compagnie de l'Art Brut, Lausanne 1979.

Last but not least, Denys Riout takes stock of these unforgettable monuments—almost a tautology: the roots of the Latin "monumentum," from which "monument" derives, lie in the verb "monere," "to remind," "to bring to the notice of"—which are not the result of any commission, other than those that artists one day gave themselves, under the pressure from what Wassily Kandinsky called an "inner necessity," rather than some lobby wanting to honor memory.

Le Cyclop tells and shapes a long history of friendship, mutual aid and complicity, fantasy and disinterestedness; its future engages the same values. The Cnap would not be faithful to the intentions of Tinguely and Saint Phalle if it did not support the idea of perpetuating the collective spirit borne by the extravagant monument. Since 2011, *Le Cyclop* organization's director, François Taillade, has been proposing an artistic program for each season, based on the principle of joint creation, performance, and correspondences between sound and the visual arts, in particular thanks to the establishment of artist residencies that bring *Le Cyclop* to life through new perspectives and new creations that, of course, are not added to it permanently, but constantly echo it. Babi Badalov, Élisabeth Ballet, Davide Balula, Véronique Joumard, Denis Savary, Virginie Yassef, and many other artists have intervened around the artwork, making a few allusions to early accomplices, including Spoerri, who imagined in June 2014 a *Pique-nique en pagaille* (Dishevelled Picnic) organized at the foot of *Le Cyclop*. This picnic on the grass was a comical invitation to share: everyone brought their own meal, but was obliged to leave it at the entrance, where it was put in a bag. The guests then had to choose at random which mysterious morsel they would savor …

One might wonder whether, secretly, *Le Cyclop* might not be a sacred edifice, dedicated to what our times still sometimes find hard to admit: the gratuitous gesture, love and friendship devoid of ulterior motives, the inventiveness of artists and daydreamer scholars, free work, and whimsical beauty. All the more reason, were it necessary, for the Cnap to take the greatest care of the artwork. This book would then be—and truly is—a tribute to one of the most astonishing secular cathedrals built in Europe today, the fruit of an extraordinary partnership between Tinguely and Saint Phalle,[9] who throughout their lives encouraged each other "to do bigger, crazier things."[10]

---

9   In 1993, Niki de Saint Phalle would write of this bond: "[it] lasted all our lives, through all the storms and problems. The great love of Jean's life and mine was Art," in *Niki de Saint Phalle, Aventure Suisse,* Espace Jean Tinguely–Niki de Saint Phalle, Museum Jean Tinguely, Benteli Verlag, Fribourg/Basel/Bern 1993, second edition revised and updated, 1998, p. 24.

10   Ibid., p. 23.

2

The Works of *Le Cyclop*

The page numbers indicated next to the works refer to
the photographs taken after the restoration of *Le Cyclop*,
and reproduced in the portfolios.

Eva Aeppli
Zofingen, 1925–Honfleur, 2015

[P. 134–135,
304–305,
306–307]

Hommage aux déportés, 1976/1993
(Homage to the Deportees)
Wood, metal, fabric, and kapok; freight car: 391 × 300 × 880 cm,
height of the sculptures: c. 200 cm each
FNAC 95419 (1) and (2)
Outside/Fourth floor

Arman
Nice, 1928–New York, 2005

[P. 204]

L'Accumulation de gants, 1991
(The Accumulation of Gloves)
Installation in *Le Cyclop* in 1993
Heavy-duty leather work gloves (c. 210), Plexiglas and glue,
200 × 300 × 5 cm
FNAC 95419 (2)
Second floor/Second floor mezzanine

Philippe Bouveret
Melun, 1960

[P. 144, 314]

Le Tableau générique, 1994
(The Generic Plaque)
Painted metal, stainless steel, glass, aspirin tablet, Plexiglas,
and PVC, 93 × 87 × 41 cm
FNAC 95419 (4)
Outside/Ground floor

César
Marseille, 1921–Paris, 1998

[P. 140,
142–143]

La Grande Compression, 1994
(The Big Compression)
    Various metals, 200 × 76 × 66 cm
    FNAC 95419 (6-1)
    Outside/Ground floor

[P. 140]

La Petite Compression, 1994
(The Small Compression)
    Various metals, 155 × 71 × 66 cm
    FNAC 95419 (6-2)
    Outside/Ground floor

Josef (Seppi) Imhof
Bern, 1943

[P. 206–207]

La Tour Imhof, 1972
(The Imhof Tower)
    Sections, angles, and painted metal tubes, 312 × 286 × 156 cm
    FNAC 95419 (13)
    Second floor

Pierre Joly
France, 1951–Le Raincy, 1978

Untitled, n. d.
    Newsprint, black ink, and carnauba, 53 × 34.5 cm
    FNAC 95419 (37-1)
    Apartment/Third floor mezzanine/Fourth floor

[P. 302]

Untitled, n. d.
    Newsprint, black thread, white gouache, and black ink, 60 × 83.7 cm
    FNAC 95419 (37-2)
    Apartment/Third floor mezzanine/Fourth floor

Pierre Marie Lejeune
La Celle-Saint-Cloud, 1954

[P. 297,
298–299]
Le Siège-rameur du Petit Théâtre, 1992
(The Little Theater's Rowing Seat)
Installation in *Le Cyclop* in 1993
Forged steel, metal, polyester resin, and photographs by
Laurent Condominas, 122 × 205 × 180 cm
FNAC 95419 (15)
Third floor

Bernhard Luginbühl
Bern, 1929–Langnau im Emmental, 2011

[P. 136–137]
Hommage à Eiffel, 1971
(Homage to Eiffel)
Painted metal, 1300 × 130 × 1600 cm
FNAC 95419 (33)
Outside

[P. 198–199]
Le Tellflipper, before 1973
Subtitle: *Hommage à Guillaume Tell*
(The Tellpinball: Homage to William Tell)
Installation in *Le Cyclop* in 1978
Metal, 135 × 495 × 200 cm
FNAC 95419 (17)
First floor

[P. 134–135]
L'Oreille, 1973
(The Ear)
Painted metal and motor, 632 × 420 × 80 cm
FNAC 95419 (18)
Outside

[P. 142–143]
Boss Tor, 1974–1975
Folded sheet metal and paint, 270 × 290 × 38 cm
FNAC 95419 (16-1)
Outside/Ground floor

[P. 142–143]   *Hommage à Louise Nevelson*, 1978
               (Homage to Louise Nevelson)
                   Concrete, wood, and black paint, 276 × 203 × 40 cm
                   FNAC 95419 (16-2)
                   Outside/Ground floor

Ursula Luginbühl Koelner
Basel, 1936–Bern, 2017

Untitled, n. d.
    Ceramic, 8 × 15.5 × 16.5 cm
    FNAC 95419 (36)
    Apartment/Third floor mezzanine/Fourth floor

Giovanni Battista Podestà
Torre Pallavicina, 1895–Laveno-Mombello, 1976

[P. 164–167,   *Piccolo Museo*, n.d.
208]   (Small Museum)
                   Installation in *Le Cyclop* in 1993
                   Seven parts
                   FNAC 95419 (19-1) à (19-7)
                   Staircase to the third floor
                   L'Écriteau (The Sign)
                   Wooden plywood, papier-mâché, wire, plaster, metallic paper, mirror,
                   paint, fabric, and plastic thread; sculpture: 25 × 24 cm;
                   display case: 65 × 72 cm
                   Pendule aux enfants (Children with Clock)
                   Wood, hardboard, papier-mâché, plaster, metallic paper, paint,
                   plastic thread, and alarm clock; sculpture: 36 × 50 cm;
                   display case: 78 × 91 cm
                   La Terre, l'Espace et Dieu (Earth, Space, and God)
                   Wood, hardboard, papier-mâché, plaster, raw earth, metallic paper,
                   paint, plastic wire, wire, cord, textile, plastic film, copper alloy nails,
                   shells, and acorn; sculpture: 120 × 47.5 × 13 cm;
                   display case: 151 × 86 cm

La Procréation (Procreation)
Wood, mirror, papier-mâché, metallic paper, paint, plastic thread,
string, Ovaltine wrapper, and glitter; sculpture: 55 × 41 × 12 cm;
display case: 86 × 106 cm
La Cure d'amaigrissement (Weight Loss Cure)
Wood, mirror, papier-mâché, plaster, metallic paper, paint, plastic
thread, vegetable fiber, thistle, colored plastic film, poultry feet,
and glitter; sculpture: 75 × 30 × 30 cm; display case: 121 × 78 cm
Le Bien et le Mal (Good and Evil)
Wood, fabric, iron, cardboard, papier-mâché, plaster, metallic paper,
paint, and plastic thread; sculpture: 36 × 25 × 15 cm;
display case: 58 × 67 cm
Grand Buste écaillé aux deux langues
(Large Chipped Bust with Two Tongues)
Wood, cardboard, plaster, metallic paper, paint, plastic thread,
and fabric; sculpture: 50 × 70 cm; display case: 85 × 111 cm

Jean Pierre Raynaud
Courbevoie, 1939

[P. 133, 312] *La Jauge*, 1975–1976/1990
(The Gauge)
Sheet metal, enamel paint, U-profiles, and cement, 2200 × 80 × 3 cm
FNAC 95419 (20)
Outside/Ground floor/Second floor/Fourth floor

Larry Rivers
New York, 1923–Southampton, 2002

[P. 300] *Hommage à Mai 68*, 1978–1979
(Homage to May 68)
Installation in *Le Cyclop* in 1994
Plexiglas and acrylic paint
Sans titre (Liberté), 218 × 140 × 1 cm
Sans titre (La Manifestation), 183 × 145 × 1 cm
Sans titre (C), 93 × 72 × 1 cm
Sans titre (Ni Dieu ni mètre), 149 × 218 × 1 cm
Sans titre (L'Homme à l'écharpe tricolore), 86 × 74 cm
Sans titre (Daniel Cohn-Bendit), 73.5 × 101 × 1 cm

Sans titre (La Charge des CRS), 149 × 218 × 1 cm
Sans titre (Les Pavés), 150 × 200 × 1 cm
Sans titre (Les CRS), 150 × 200 × 1 cm
FNAC 95419 (21-1) to (21-9)
Third floor

Niki de Saint Phalle
Neuilly-sur-Seine, 1930–La Jolla, 2002

[P. 129, 130, 131, 194-195]
La Face aux miroirs, 1987–1991
(The Mirrored Face)
Metallic armature, projected concrete, mirror, paint, water,
motor, and spotlight, 2100 × 1100 × 1380 cm
FNAC 95419 (7)
Outside/Ground floor/First floor/Fourth floor

[P. 298-299]
Le Banc, 1989
(The Bench)
Installation in *Le Cyclop* in 1994
Polyester resin, paint, and mirror, 160 × 142 × 94 cm
FNAC 95419 (10)
Third floor

[P. 194-195]
Le Carrelage au damier, 1992–1993
Subtitle: *Hommage à la course automobile*
(The Checkerboard Tiles: Homage to Car Racing)
Tiles and mirror, 535 × 529 cm
FNAC 95419 (31)
First floor

[P. 201]
La Colonne, 1993
(The Column)
Concrete, ceramic, and mirror, 350 × 140 × 120 cm
FNAC 95419 (8)
Second floor

Jesús Rafael Soto
Ciudad Bolívar, 1923–Paris, 2005

[P. 202–203] *Le Pénétrable sonore*, 1972
(The Resonating Penetrable)
    Installation in *Le Cyclop* in 1993
    800 square tubes, aluminum, polished stainless steel,
    and snap hooks, 232 × 348 × 330 cm
    FNAC 95419 (22)
    Second floor

Daniel Spoerri
Galat, 1930–Vienna, 2024

[P. 301] *La Chambre renversée de l'hôtel de l'Étoile*, 1976
(The Hôtel Étoile's Upside-Down Room)
    Wood, metal, tiles, fabric, wall paper, and linoleum,
    220 × 250 × 400 cm
    FNAC 95419 (24)
    Third floor

[P. 205] *Restaurant Spoerri*, 1994
    Partial reconstruction of the restaurant run by Daniel Spoerri
    in Düsseldorf between 1968 and 1972
    Panels: plasterboard and paper collage (for conservation reasons,
    the panels were reproduced as photographs mounted on Dibond
    in 2024); chairs and tables: wood and metal; sign: Plexiglas and
    paint, overall dimensions: 230 × 397 × 312 cm
    FNAC 95419 (23)
    Second floor mezzanine

Jean Tinguely
Fribourg, 1925–Bern, 1991

[P. 131, 132]   *La Méta-Maxi*, 1972–c. 1977
(The Meta-Maxi)
Metal, straps, and 380-volt engine, 1210 × 630 × 800 cm
FNAC 95419 (30)
Outside/Second floor

[P. 139, 306–307, 309]   *La Tour éphémère*, 1973–1989
(The Ephemeral Tower)
Metal, height: 2250 cm
FNAC 95419 (29)
Outside/Ground floor/Second floor/Fourth floor

[P. 142–143, 144, 303, 306–307]   *La Dégringolade*, 1975–1976
(The Helter-Skelter)
Metal, coppered steel, transmission belt and motor;
diameter of balls: 35 cm, structure diameter: 41 cm
FNAC 95419 (14)
Outside/First to fourth floor

[P. 193, 194–195]   *La Batterie*, c. 1976
(The Battery)
Steel, 241 × 170 × 115 cm
FNAC 95419 (32)
First floor

[P. 310–311]   *Hommage à Yves Klein*, 1976–1979
(Homage to Yves Klein)
Welded sheet metal, paint, and water, 117 × 890 × 950 cm
FNAC 95419 (26)
Fourth floor

[P. 297]   *Le Méta-Merzbau*, 1976–1981
Subtitle: *Hommage à Kurt Schwitters*
(The Meta-Merzbau: Homage to Kurt Schwitters)
Painted metal, 434 × 330 × 555 cm
FNAC 95419 (12)
Third floor

[P. 138]   *La Broyeuse de chocolat*, 1977
Subtitle: *Hommage à Marcel Duchamp*
(The Chocolate Grinder: Homage to Marcel Duchamp)
    Installation in *Le Cyclop* in 1978
    Molded steel and stone, 165 × 190 × 170 cm
    FNAC 95419 (11)
    Outside/Ground floor

[P. 206–207]   *La Méta-Harmonie*, 1980–1981
(The Meta-Harmony)
    Metal, wood, Sandow cable, plastic, clamps, straps, and motors,
    460 × 695 × 700 cm
    FNAC 95419 (25)
    Second floor

[P. 298–299]   *Les Sièges du Petit Théâtre*, 1980–1981
(The Little Theater's Seats)
    Seven parts
    Gray armchair: faux leather, 112 × 77 × 65 cm; stool: metal and
    painted wood, 44 × 39 × 39 cm; stool: folded sheet metal,
    73 × 42 × 21 cm; round stool: metal, diameter: 26 cm; tractor seat:
    metal, 72 × 47 × 48 cm; rocking chair: metal and painted wood,
    80 × 59 × 80 cm; tractor seat: metal, faux leather; 75 × 48 × 50 cm
    FNAC 95419 (5-2)
    Third floor

[P. 298–299]   *Le Petit Théâtre*, 1981/1994
(The Little Theater)
    Collaborator: Philippe Bouveret
    Metal, stainless steel, foam, wood, motor, glass, and fabric,
    3000 × 3100 × 3700 cm
    FNAC 95419 (5-1)
    Third floor

[P. 194–195, 197]   *La Molécule RU 486*, 1991/1994
Subtitle: *Hommage à Étienne-Émile Baulieu*
(The RU 486 Molecule: Homage to Étienne-Émile Baulieu)
    Collaborator: Philippe Bouveret
    Stainless steel and polyester resin, 243 × 183 × 175 cm
    FNAC 95419 (3)
    First floor

[P. 142–143]   *La Porte-levis*, n. d.
                 (The Drawbridge Door)
                         Corrugated iron, 320 × 250 × 32 cm
                         FNAC 95419 (34)
                         Ground floor

[P. 302]   *La Lampe*, n. d.
                 (The Lamp)
                         Metal, plastic, and golden plastic garland, 125 × 142 × 96 cm
                         FNAC 95419 (35)
                         Flat/Third floor mezzanine/Fourth floor

---

Jean Tinguely and Niki de Saint Phalle

[P. 133, 200]   *L'Incitation au suicide*, 1978/c. 1992
                 (Incitement to Suicide)
                         Resin, mirror, gold and red paint, palladium and light bulb;
                         air vent: 430 × 320 × 830 cm, skull: 109 × 89 × 116 cm
                         FNAC 95419 (9)
                         Outside/Second floor

Rico Weber
Hinwil, 1942–Bern, 2004

[P. 141,   *Les Gisants*, 1978
142–143]   (Recumbent Statues)
                         Installation in *Le Cyclop* in 1994
                         Plaster and water repellent, 185 × 83 × 38 cm each
                         FNAC 95419 (27)
                         Ground floor/First floor

[P. 194–195,   *Le Tableau électrique*, 1994
196]   (The Distribution Board)
                         Resin, graphite powder, and wood, 336 × 301 × 15 cm
                         FNAC 95419 (28)
                         First floor

Sketches and Models

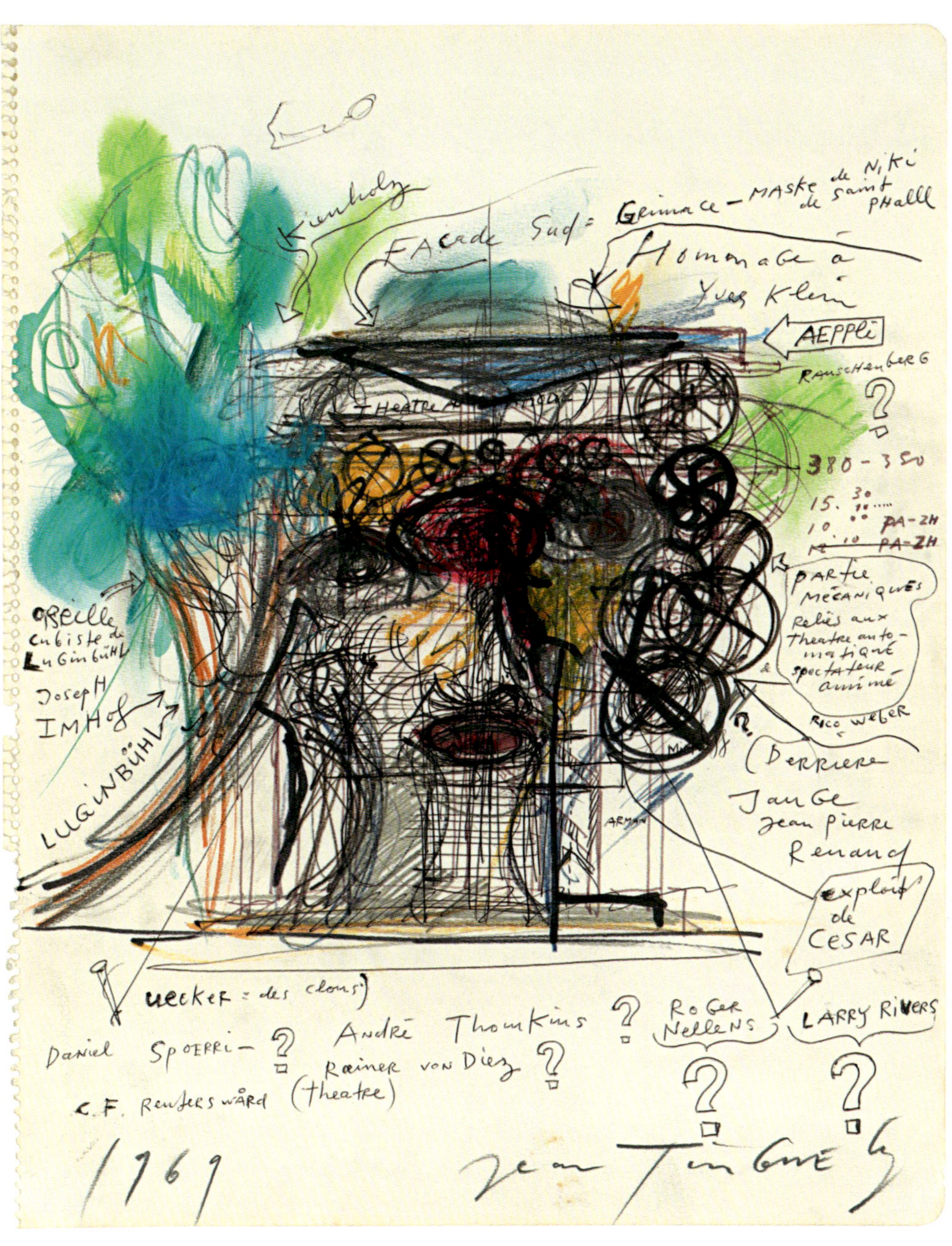

Jean Tinguely
Le Monstre dans la forêt, 1969
Ballpoint, felt-tip, graphite pencil, colored pencil, watercolor, and feather on paper, 41 × 32 cm
Collection Musée d'Art et d'Histoire, Geneva; purchased with the support of Fondation Diday

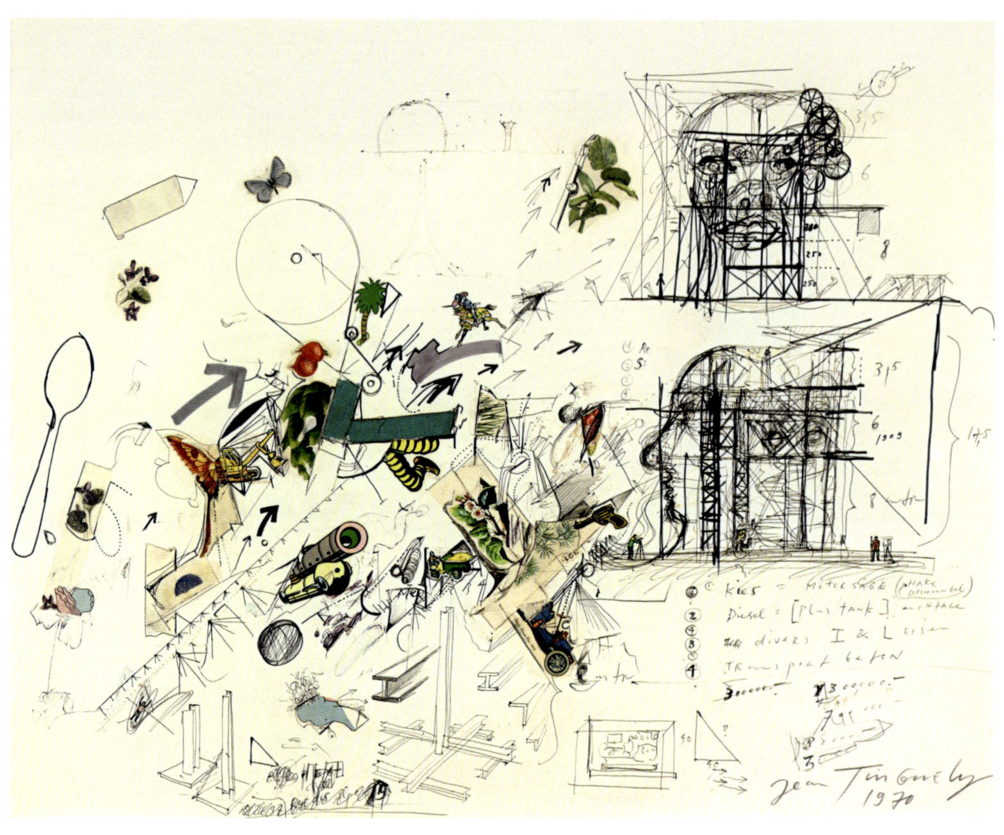

Jean Tinguely
Sketch, 1970
Graphite pencil, ballpoint, felt-tip, and collage on paper, 51.5 × 65.5 cm
Collection Centre National des Arts Plastiques, Paris

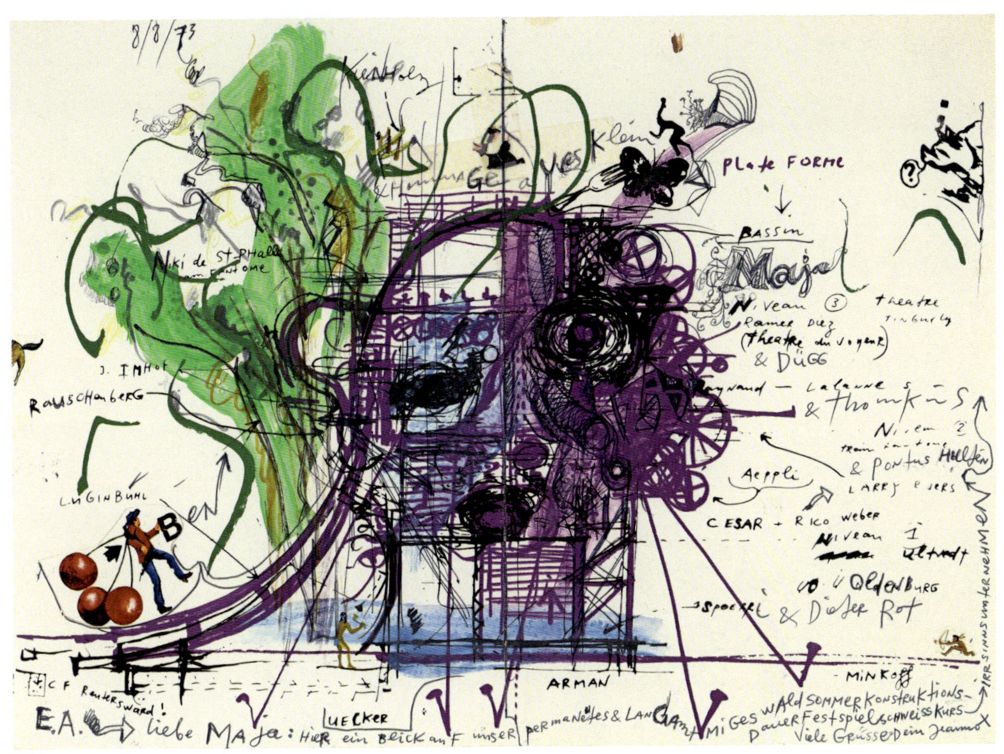

Jean Tinguely
Drawing for Maja Sacher, August 8, 1973
Ballpoint, felt-tip, watercolor, and collage, lithograph on paper, 30 × 42 cm
Collection Museum Tinguely, Basel; bequest of Paul Sacher

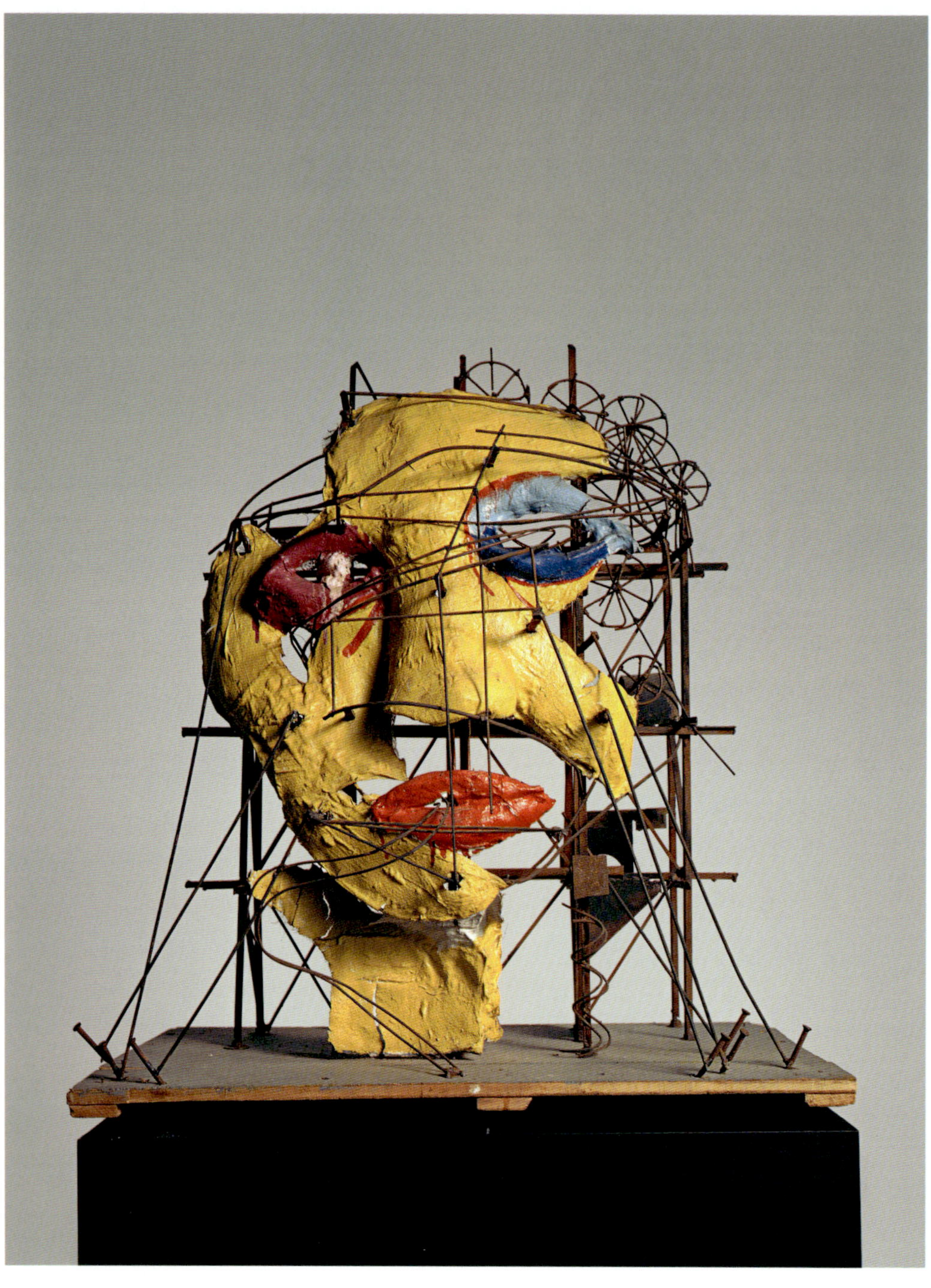

Niki de Saint Phalle and Jean Tinguely
Le Cyclop – La Tête, 1970
Wire, paint, scrap metal, plaster, 82 × 77 × 47 cm
Collection Museum Tinguely, Basel; bequest of Niki de Saint Phalle

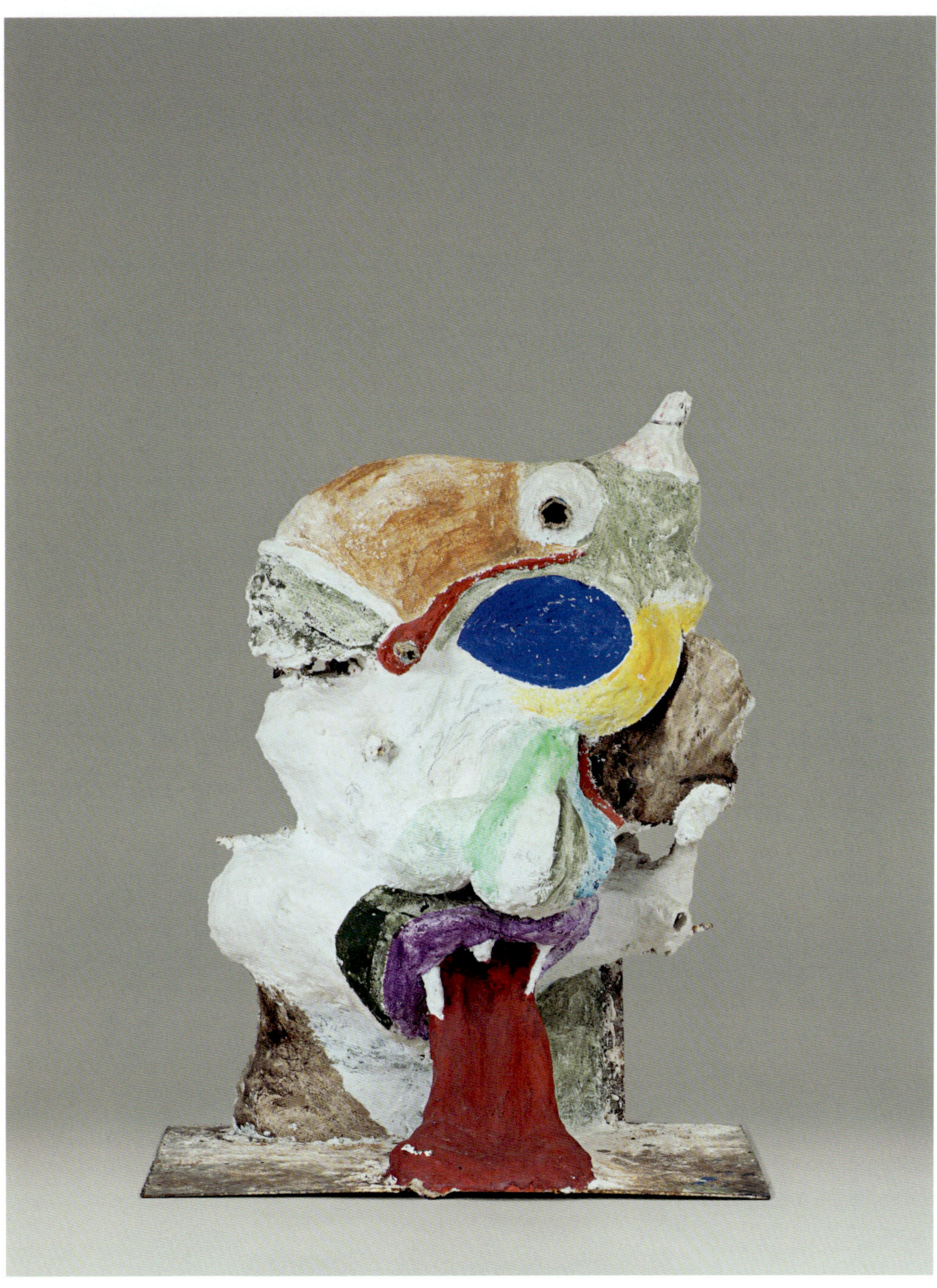

Niki de Saint Phalle and Jean Tinguely
Kopf (Head), c. 1970–1974
Metal, frame for a cast iron model, plaster, pencil, paint, 71 × 51 × 40 cm
Private Collection

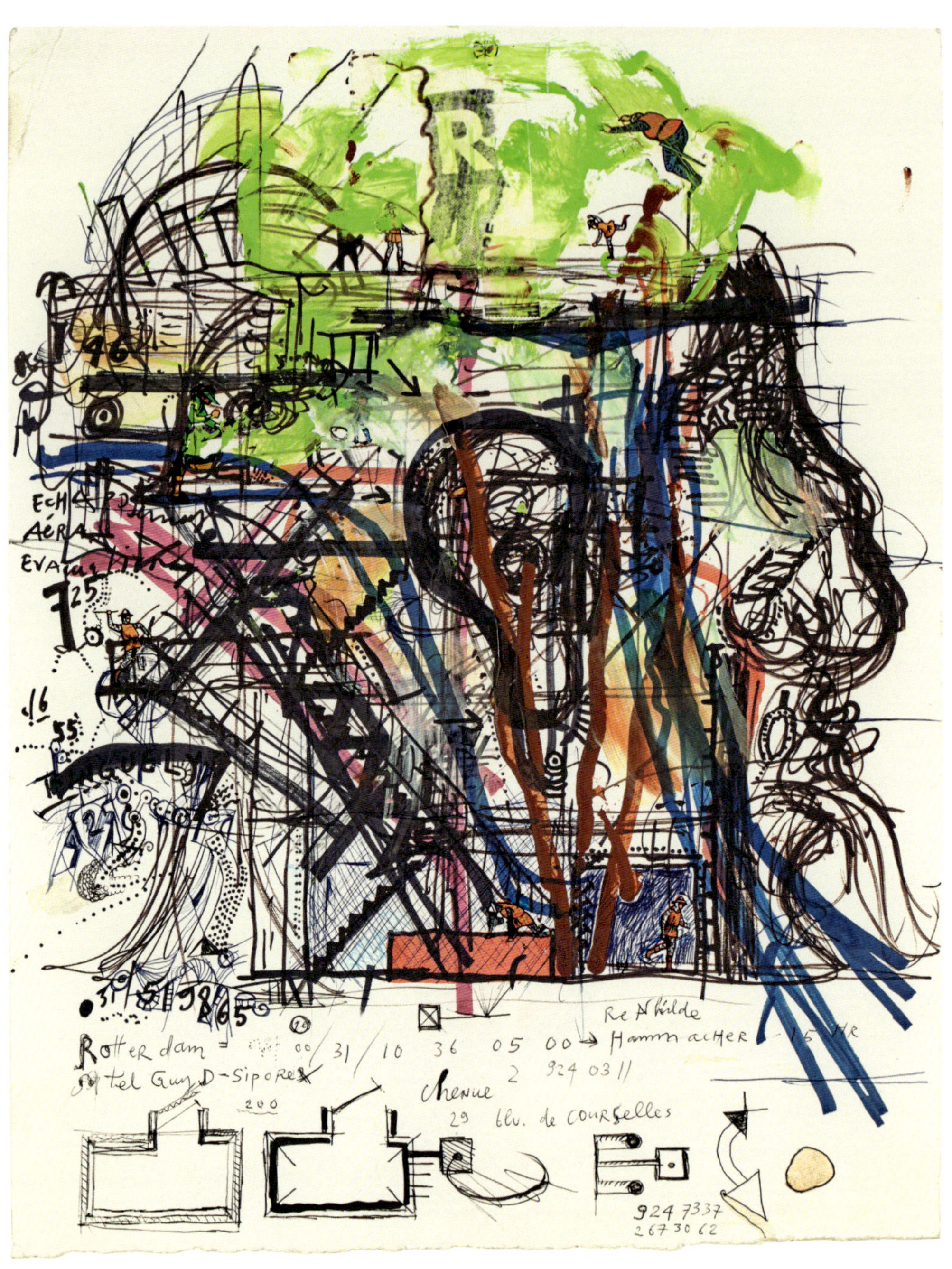

38

Jean Tinguely
Drawing for the west face of *Le Cyclop*, 1971
Watercolor, pencil, felt-tip, ballpoint, and collage on paper, 40 × 30.1 cm
Collection Museum Tinguely, Basel; bequest of Josef Imhof, 2021

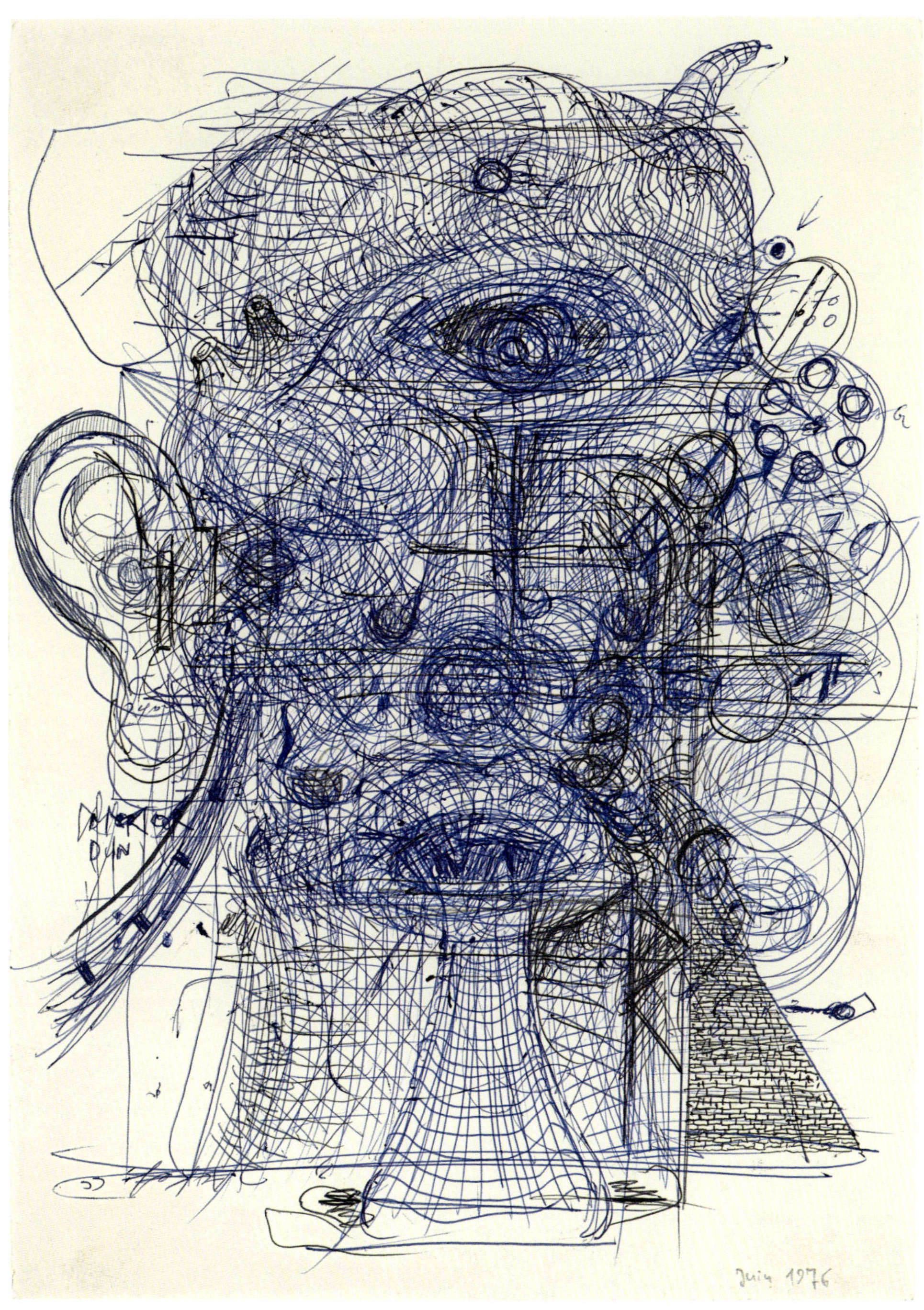

Jean Tinguely
Le Monstre dans la forêt de couleur bleue, 1976
Pencil and ballpoint on paper, 38 × 27.9 cm
Collection Museum Tinguely, Basel

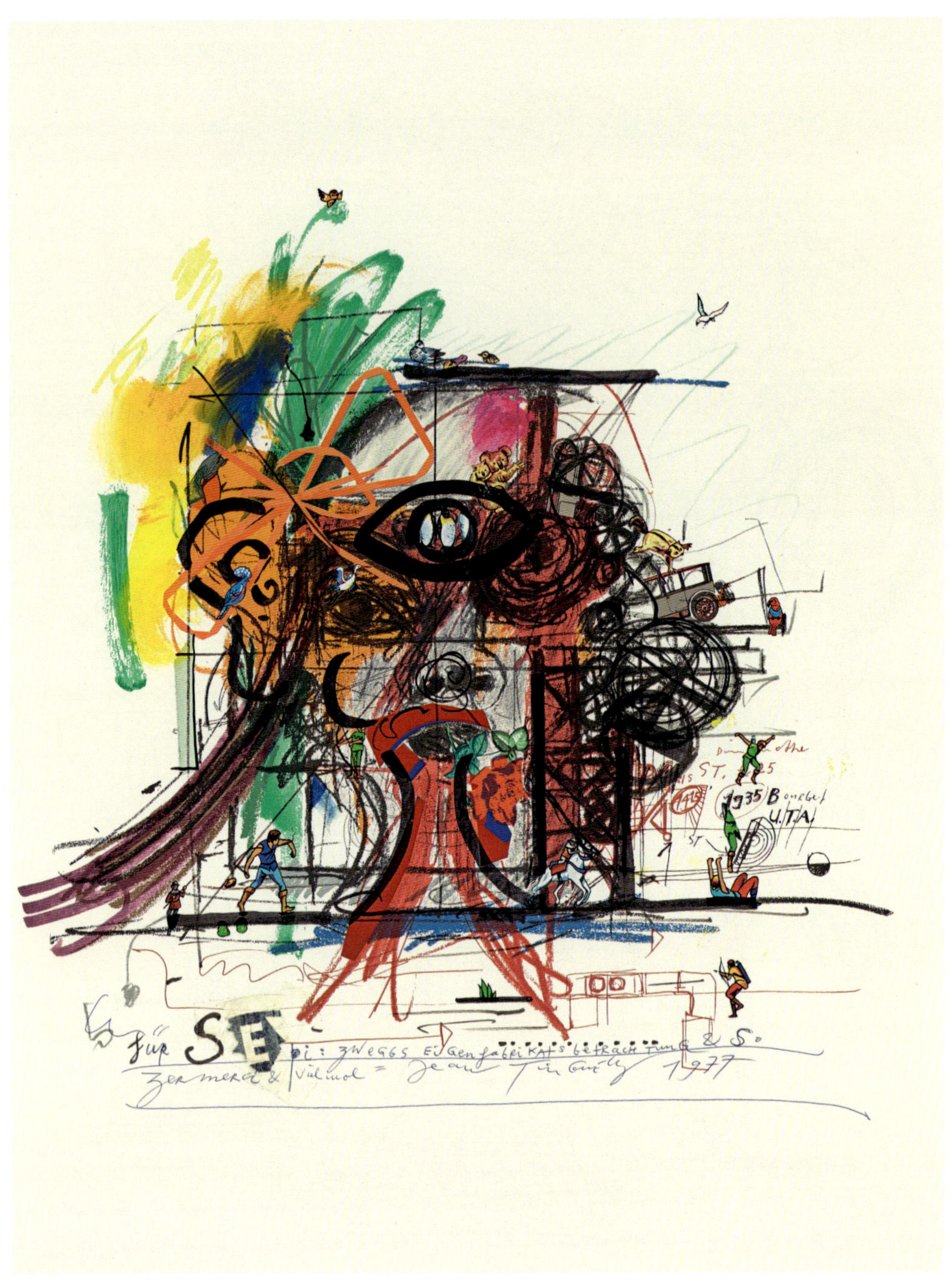

Jean Tinguely
Drawing of *Le Cyclop* for Seppi Imhof, 1977
Transfers, felt-tip, ball point, chalk on silkscreen, 65 × 50 cm
Collection Museum Tinguely, Basel; bequest of Josef Imhof, 2021

3

Essays

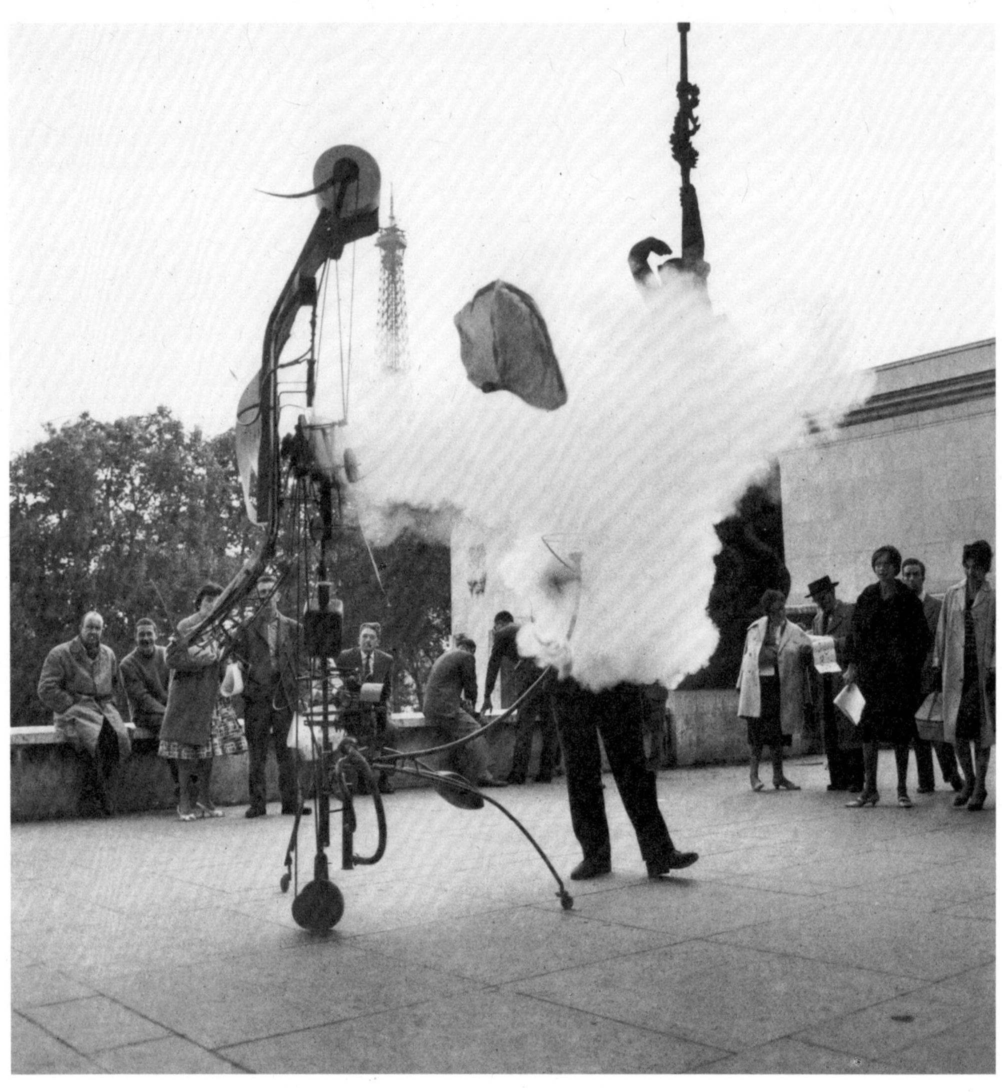

Jean Tinguely behind his *Méta-Matic No. 17*, piazza of the Musée d'Art Moderne de la Ville de Paris, first Paris Biennial, Paris,
October 1959

This Assemblage Is Not (A) Happening
A Pre-History of Jean Tinguely's Magnum Opus,
Le Cyclop
Dominik Müller

Jean Tinguely created his masterpiece, *Le Cyclop* (The Cyclops), in a woodland in Milly-la-Forêt, near Fontainebleau, together with a great number of his artist friends. This essay traces the origins of this collaborative work and situates it in the art genre of assemblage, which emerged prominently around 1960, particularly in the United States. Tinguely spent a lot of time in America in the early 1960s, both in New York and Los Angeles, where he assimilated this new form of art. It was the basis for and the key to the realization of *Le Cyclop*.

Introduction

By the end of 1958, Tinguely had established himself as a sculptor and a figurehead for Kinetic art in Paris and Europe. After his first solo exhibition at the Galerie Arnaud in Paris in the spring of 1954, he exhibited in Sweden, Germany, Italy, Switzerland, and Belgium, either solo or with friends or well-known artists from his homeland, Switzerland, or from elsewhere in Europe or South America. The Denise René and Iris Clert galleries in Paris were successively his most important representatives, and thanks in part to exhibitions such as *Le Mouvement* (The Movement), organized by Denise René in 1955, just a year after his arrival in Paris, Tinguely gained access to important older and contemporary representatives of Kinetic art: Pol Bury, Alexander Calder, Marcel Duchamp, Robert Jacobsen, Jesús Rafael Soto, and Victor Vasarely. Tinguely's rise in the second half of the 1950s was swift—the cogwheels of his career turning as smoothly as those of his reliefs. During the years of reconstruction in Europe after the end of World War II, Tinguely traveled a great deal, always installing his exhibitions in various cities himself—his motorized artworks required this of him—and using these visits to network directly with the protagonists of the local art scenes. Many of these acquaintances then also led to participation in other projects, often in the form of events or, as they were called in New York in the early 1960s, Happenings. But more on that later.

This tireless and deliberate movement brought his work a great deal of visibility, not only among the audience of his exhibitions, but also in the media (print, radio, and television), which closely followed the art world in the mid- and late 1950s, especially in relation to the dialogue between France and Germany. As a native of Switzerland with French roots, Tinguely could easily communicate in German and French, and due to this, as well as his early move from Basel to Paris, he was often not even perceived by the public as a Swiss artist, but rather as a French one.

Two important things happened at the end of 1958. Tinguely collaborated for the first time with the French artist Yves Klein (1928–1962), with whom he was friends. The results were presented in the exhibition *Vitesse pure et stabilité monochrome* (Pure Speed and Monochrome Stability) at the Galerie Iris Clert. In the years that followed, Tinguely and Klein were to become two of the international figureheads of the Nouveau Réalisme movement, both causing a stir in the United States in their own way. Thus it seems to me even more significant that 1958 was the first time Tinguely's work was ever shown in a group exhibition in the United States. Tinguely had submitted one of his dynamic black-and-white "Kinetic Paintings" entitled *Métamorphe III* (1956) to the *1958 Pittsburgh Bicentennial International Exhibition of Contemporary Painting and Sculpture* at the Carnegie Institute through the Lord's Gallery based in London.[1] The work was a wooden panel with painted metal elements on metal rods, which, when the electric cable was plugged in, could be moved by means of rubber belts, wheels, and a motor attached to the back, creating constantly changing forms. In the mid-1950s, this represented an innovation in the art world, though in formal terms Tinguely drew heavily on predecessors in nonrepresentational painting such as Calder, Auguste Herbin, and Wassily Kandinsky. Tinguely's participation in this exhibition in late 1958 marked the start of his interest in and exchange with the art scene in the USA.

---

1   See *The 1958 Pittsburgh Bicentennial International Exhibition of Contemporary Painting and Sculpture,* exh. cat., Carnegie Institute, Pittsburgh, December 5, 1958–February 8, 1959, 1959, no. 436.

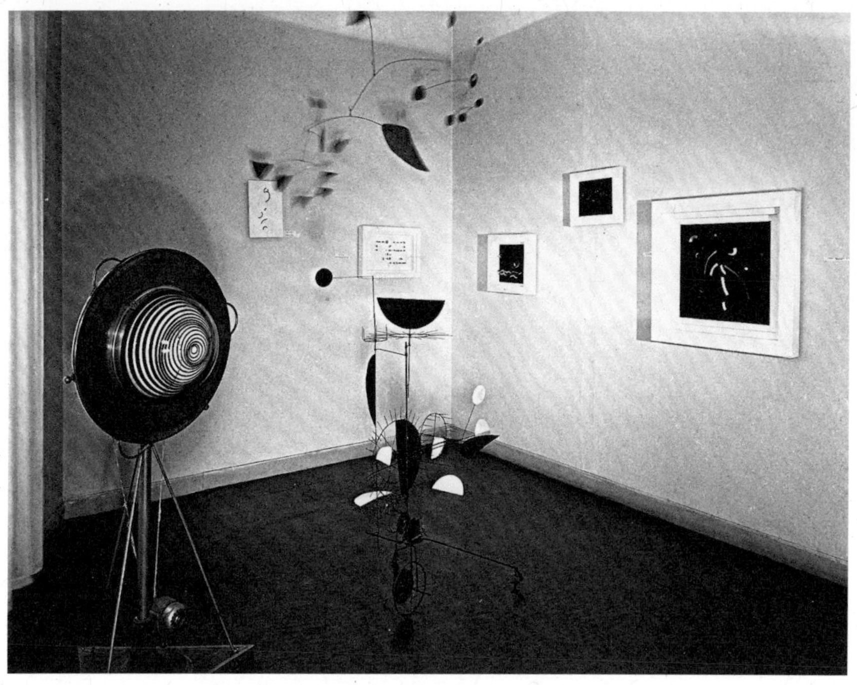

Exhibition view, *Le Mouvement*, Galerie Denise René, Paris, April 6–30, 1955

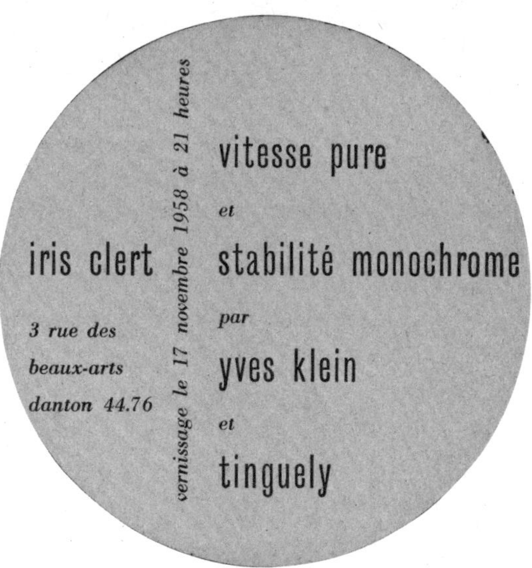

Invitation card to the exhibition *Vitesse pure et stabilité monochrome* by Yves Klein and Jean Tinguely,
Galerie Iris Clert, November 17–30, 1958
Printed cardboard, diameter: 9 cm

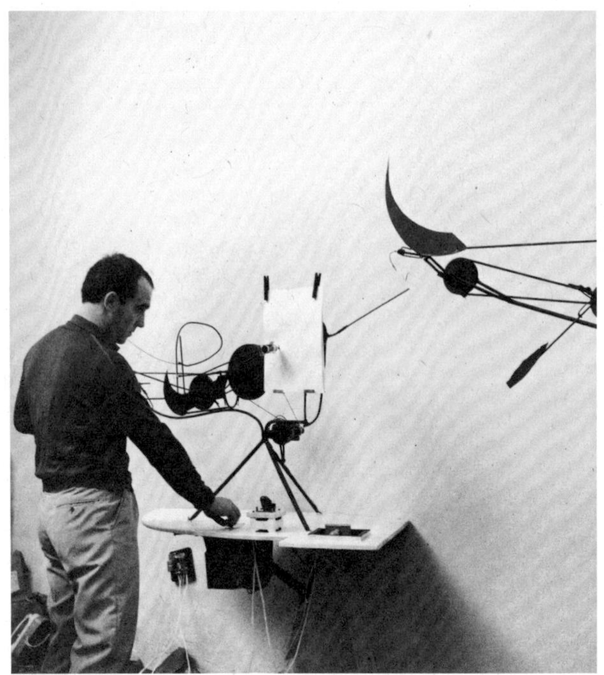

Jean Tinguely and one of his "Méta-Matics," Paris, 1959

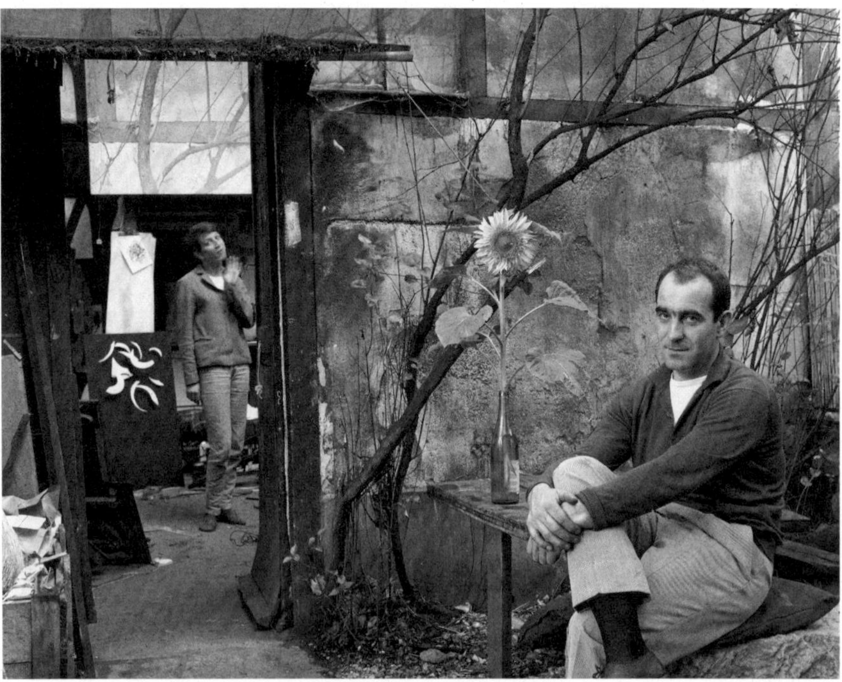

Eva Aeppli and Jean Tinguely, Impasse Ronsin, Paris, July 1959; photograph published in *Point de Vue* in 1959

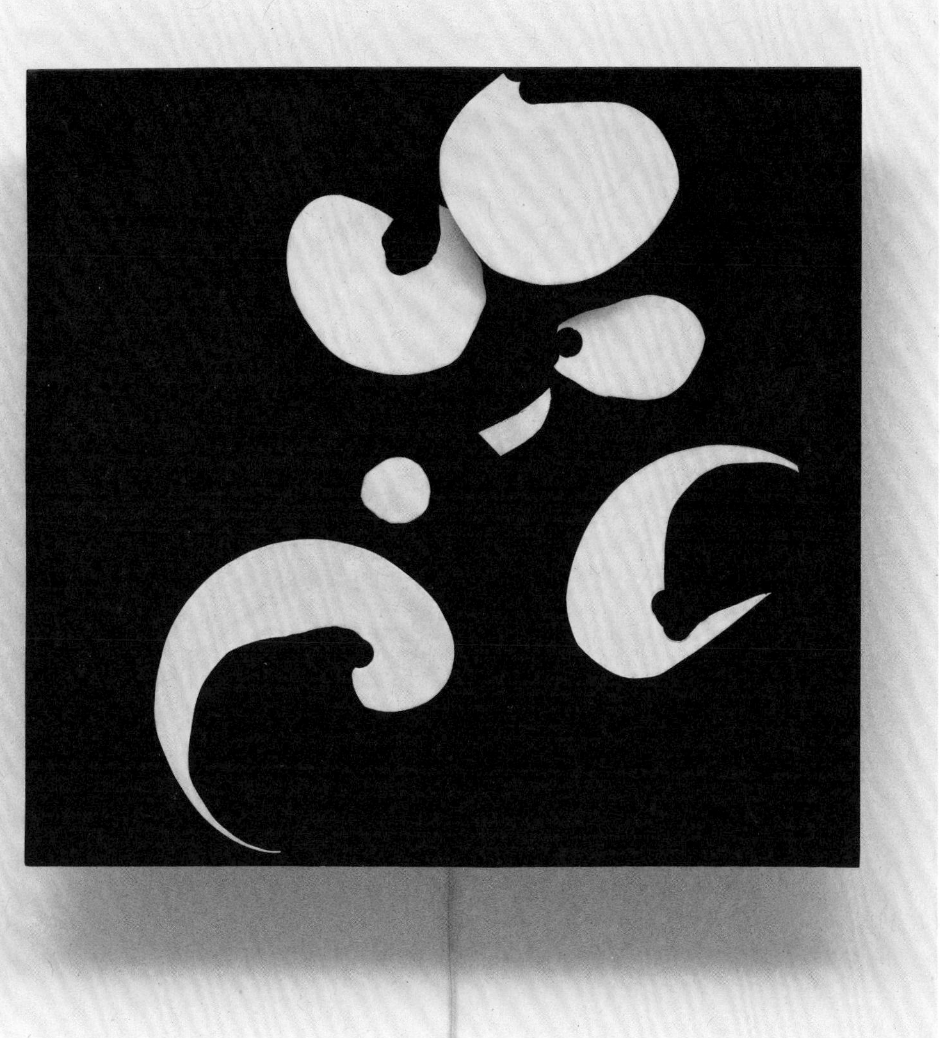

Jean Tinguely
Œuf d'éclosion No. 2 (Hatching Egg No. 2), 1958
Painted metal, plywood, and motor, 77.5 × 82.4 × 22.7 cm
Collection The Museum of Modern Art, New York; gift of Erwin B. Steiner

1959

Then came 1959, "the year everything changed," as Fred Kaplan declared
in the title of his book of 2009.[2] Kaplan's title may have been an
exaggeration, but it was certainly true in terms of the further course of
Tinguely's career. That year, he invented and patented his "Méta-Matics,"
a series of 12 bigger and smaller drawing machines that used pens to
produce scribbled drawings on paper through interaction with the user.
In terms of physical form, these were metal sculptures painted monochrome
black. While his reliefs were an innovation, these new hybrid structures
were a sensation, and the exhibition at Iris Clert was a feast for the press.[3]
That summer, the famous French photographer Robert Doisneau immortal-
ized Tinguely on a double-page spread for the magazine *Point de Vue*.[4]

[P. 111] Photographs also document Marcel Duchamp's visit to the exhibition at
the Galerie Iris Clert, during which he created a drawing with one of the
"Méta-Matics" on display as Tinguely and Clert looked on. The exhibition
generated a great deal of excitement not only among its visitors and in
Paris, but also in Europe and the United States. Interest in Tinguely rose
sharply in 1959, particularly in New York and its Museum of Modern Art.
In the spring of 1959, Tinguely's work *Œuf d'éclosion No. 2* (*Hatching Egg
No. 2*, 1958) entered the MoMA collection as a gift from Erwin B. Steiner.

[P. 42] Another highlight of this eventful year was Tinguely's presentation
in October of his most famous drawing machine, the *Méta-Matic No. 17*,
at the first Paris Biennial held at the Musée d'Art Moderne de la Ville de
Paris. For fire safety reasons, and because the other exhibitors complained
since they did not want a noisy, moving, and smelly sculpture next to
their own works, Tinguely was not allowed to exhibit his machine in the
museum itself. At the opening it plied its devilish trade on the museum's
esplanade. Art historian and curator Jean-Christophe Ammann recalls:
"The sensation of the first Paris Biennial in 1959 was the monumental
drawing machine 'Méta-Matic automobile odorante et sonore' (Meta-Matic
odorous and sonorous automobile). During the exhibition, it created [...]
40,000 multicolored images. The machine was complemented by a balloon
from which emanated a penetrating odor [...] The odorous balloon and
the act of painting are eminently narrative elements, but they do not possess
an emphatic life of their own in the sense that the function does not

---

2   Fred Kaplan, *1959: The Year Everything Changed*,
John Wiley & Sons, New York 2009.

3   *Les Méta-Matics de Tinguely: les sculptures qui
peignent*, Galerie Iris Clert, July 1st–30 1959.

4   "Gens d'images. Le salon permanent de la photo
par Albert Plécy. Un reportage de Robert Doisneau:
Tinguely – anarchiste de la joie," in *Point de Vue*,
Summer 1959, n. p.

identify with the structure."[5] That same month, London's Kaplan Gallery organized Tinguely's first major solo exhibition in England, with over 20 works (including several "Méta-Matics"). The artist was on hand, in part because he had been invited by the Institute of Contemporary Arts to give a lecture. "The Conference-Happening *Art, Machines and Motion* that he […] held at the ICA in London demonstrates his in-depth knowledge of artistic developments in New York, where Allan Kaprow had organized his first Happening a year earlier."

As with the exhibition of the "Méta-Matics" at the Galerie Iris Clert, and Tinguely's participation in the Paris Biennial, the London exhibition, and especially the Happening, were also accompanied by prolific media coverage, this time predominantly in English. Ammann was correct in assuming that Tinguely was intimately familiar with developments in the USA, especially in New York. Tinguely's previous works had produced sounds and smells, moved, or drawn; they had an inherent performative character, and they enacted something, ideally in collaboration with the viewer. Tinguely took advantage of this characteristic of his artworks for his own appearances with them, taking his formal cues from artists such as Allan Kaprow, Jim Dine, and Claes Oldenburg, who were operating within the new art genre of the Happening in New York at around the same time or just a little earlier. Tinguely's actions with the drawing machines in Paris and London exemplified his interest in performative aspects that exceeded the inherent capacities of his machines and required his own additional participation. That this specifically took the form of Happenings—and thus unavoidably engaged with the artist Allan Kaprow—is also significant with regard to another newer art genre that would soon become a passionate interest for Tinguely: assemblage, which was an art form with which Kaprow had also been, and would continue to be, deeply engaged. In 1966, Kaprow published his seminal work *Assemblage, Environments & Happenings*, which he regarded as "an introduction to a recent development in the arts."[6]

Having established an excellent foothold as an artist in Europe by the end of the 1950s, with his focus increasingly turned to the newest trends in art, the leap to the United States seemed a logical development. In contrast to European art, American art after World War II, and especially in the 1950s, was increasingly seeking its own identity, a genuinely American art, independent of European models and precursors. To establish such an American art, a single new direction in painting, such as Abstract Expressionism,

5   Here and following quote: Jean-Christophe Ammann, "Jean Tinguely," in *Das Werk: Architektur und Kunst*, vol. 53, March 1966, p. 113.

6   Allan Kaprow, *Assemblage, Environments & Happenings*, Abrams, New York 1966. According to Kaprow, the text was produced significantly earlier: "This book was largely written in 1959 […] and it was finished in the next year," p. 150.

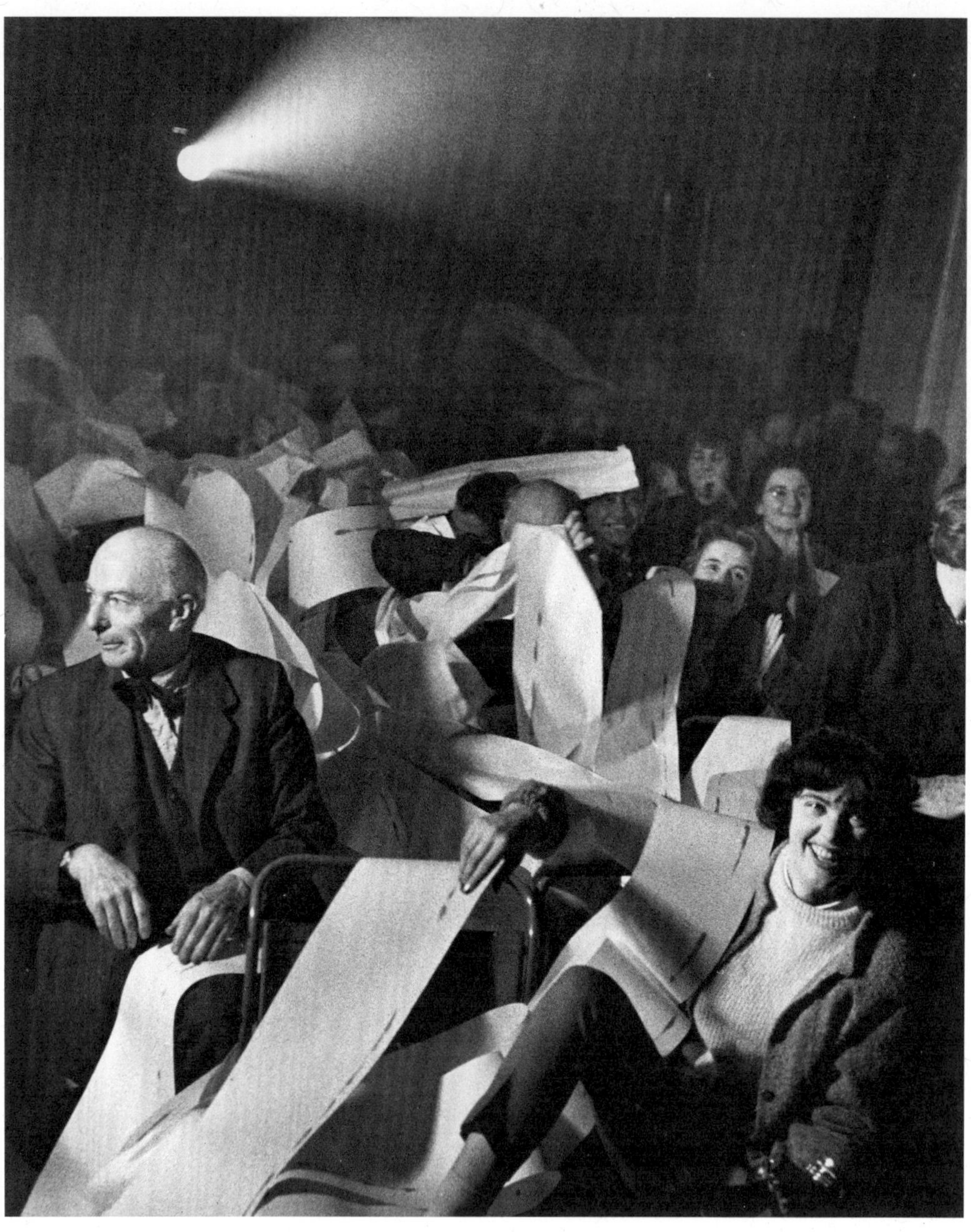

The audience during Jean Tinguely's *Art, Machines and Motion* lecture-Happening, Institute of Contemporary Arts, London,
November 12, 1959
Silver print on Baryté paper, 29.4 × 24.1 cm

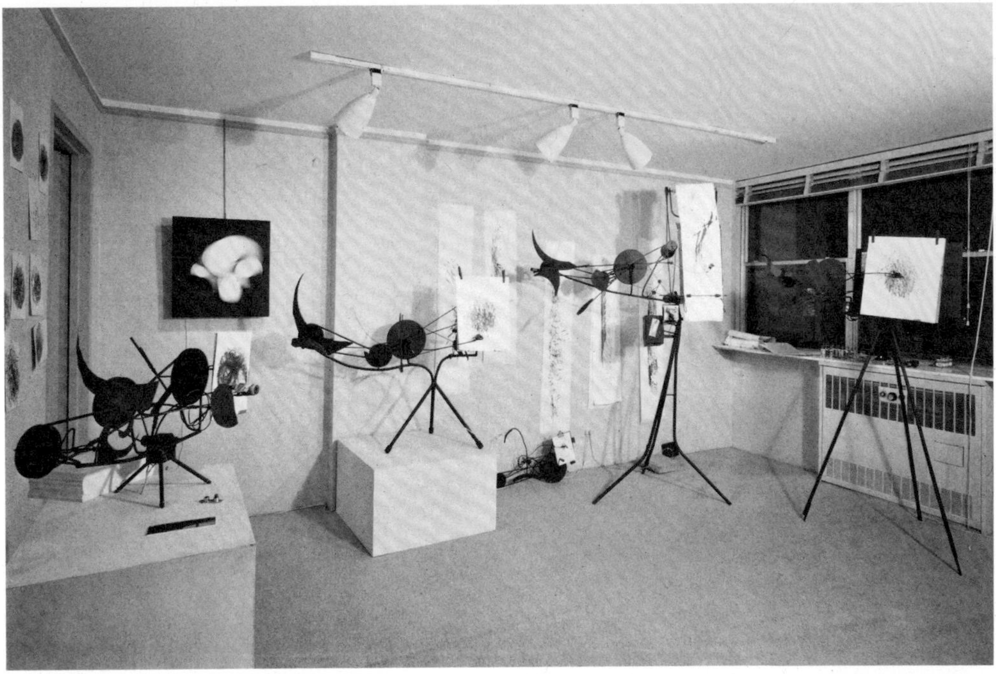

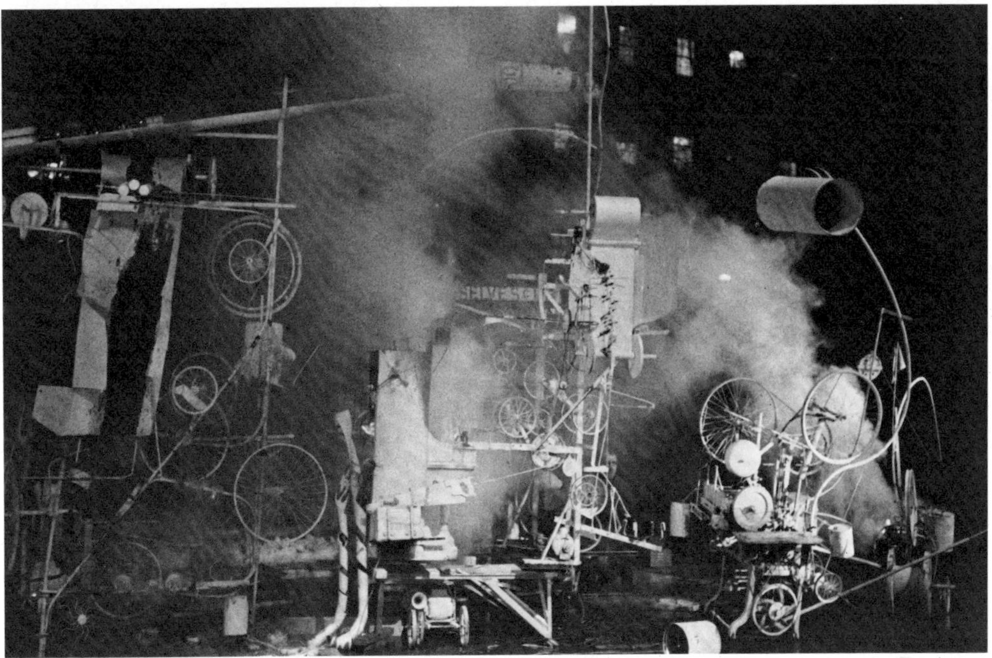

Exhibition view *Jean Tinguely: Kinetic Constructions and Drawing Machines*, Staempfli Gallery, New York, January 25–February 13, 1960

View of the Happening *Homage to New York: A Self-Constructing and Self-Destroying Work of Art Conceived and Built by Jean Tinguely*, The Museum of Modern Art, New York, March 17, 1960

was not enough. Innovative new forms and genres were needed: Happenings, environments, assemblage. These developments occurred mostly in the two centers of New York and Los Angeles, interestingly enough in galleries, artist-run spaces, studios, apartments, lofts, in the open air and in restaurants, as well as in the most important museum of contemporary art at that time, New York's Museum of Modern Art. Consciously or unconsciously, it was this breeding ground, where new art forms were emerging or reviving ("art-in-the-making," "things rapidly evolving"[7]), that Tinguely sought and also needed in order to develop further, and to set the course for the most important and largest project of his career: *Le Cyclop*.

Arrival in the USA and *Homage to New York*

The American art critic Calvin Tomkins described the events of early 1960 as follows: "George Staempfli, a New York gallery owner and art dealer, had met Tinguely in Paris and promised him a New York show, and in January 1960 Tinguely crossed the Atlantic in tourist class on the Queen Elizabeth to be on hand for the first exposure of his art in America."[8] Once again, Tinguely followed up an invitation with a personal appearance and installed 25 works at the Staempfli Gallery for the exhibition *Jean Tinguely: Kinetic Constructions and Drawing Machines*. The success of his "Méta-Matics" in Paris and London was certainly a major reason for Staempfli's initiative. New York far exceeded Tinguely's expectations. His enthusiasm for the city and its architecture was so pronounced that he decided to express it in a homage, described to Calvin Tomkins in 1962: "The skyscraper itself is a kind of machine. The American house is a machine. I saw in my mind's eye all those skyscrapers, those monster buildings, all that magnificent accumulation of human power and vitality, all that uneasiness, as though everyone were living on the edge of a precipice, and I thought how nice it would be to make a little machine there that would be conceived, like Chinese fireworks, in total anarchy and freedom."[9] These impressions are in line with statements made by the art historian and MoMA curator William C. Seitz on the subject of assemblage: "The tradition of assemblage has been predominantly urban in emphasis […] The proper backdrop for recent assemblage is the multifarious fabric of the modern city. The cityscape gives evidence of the

7   Ibid., p.150.
8   Calvin Tomkins, *The Bride and the Bachelors: Five Masters of the Avant-Garde*, Penguin Books, Harmondsworth 1968/1976, p. 166. The five masters of the avant-garde discussed by Tomkins are Marcel Duchamp, John Cage, Jean Tinguely, Robert Rauschenberg, and Merce Cunningham. It should be noted that Staempfli was born in Switzerland.
9   Calvin Tomkins, "Profiles: Beyond the Machine," in *The New Yorker* (February 1962), p. 44–93. This thorough profile of Tinguely was in fact Tomkins' first non-fiction piece for *The New Yorker*.

worldwide collision of moralities and panaceas, facts and propagandas, and sets in relief the countless images of contemporary life […] The city—NYC above all others—has become a symbol of modern existence. The tempo of Manhattan, both as subject and conditioning milieu, has been instrumental in forming the art of our time."[10]

Such considerations and influences were the foundation for Tinguely's most progressive work of art at that time, *Homage to New York*. After his arrival in January, Tinguely promptly connected with representatives of the scene through the New York art critic Dore Ashton and the exiled German Dadaist Richard Huelsenbeck, both of whom he knew from Paris. These connections included not only artists of the older generation such as Marcel Duchamp, who he already knew, but also the new generation of American artists such as John Chamberlain, Jasper Johns, Robert Rauschenberg, and Richard Stankiewicz. The new working environment inspired Tinguely enormously. His foundational ideas for the *Homage* included not only fire, freedom, and anarchy, but above all a working method and art form that had just been newly interpreted in New York by artists such as Rauschenberg and Johns: the assemblage. Along with environments and Happenings, Kaprow considered assemblage to be among the three most important new art genres of his time: "More recently, a large body of diverse compositions referred to as Combines (Robert Rauschenberg's name for his own work), Neo-Dada, or Assemblage employs a variety of materials and objects in an equally varied range of formats, completely departing from the accepted norms required by 'painting' as we have known it."[11] Tinguely's *Homage to New York* is taken up in Kaprow's volume as "Assemblage in motion."[12] The work of art would not only be "assembled," but also have a duration of barely a few minutes and destroy itself in the course of a "Happening" (a presentation, an event). As a venue for this event, Tinguely insisted on The Museum of Modern Art, whose curator of collections Alfred H. Barr was already quite familiar with his work through Erwin B. Steiner's gift. The curator of the exhibited artwork and its processes was the art historian and MoMA's curator Peter Selz. Tinguely was supported not only by assistants, but also by the engineer Billy Klüver, Rauschenberg, who contributed an element to the assemblage,[13] and Robert Breer, who recorded the event in an art film.

---

10 William C. Seitz, in *The Art of Assemblage*, exh. cat., The Museum of Modern Art, New York 1961, p. 73–74.

11 Allan Kaprow, *Assemblage, Environments & Happenings*, p. 155.

12 Ibid., p. 81–82.

13 Rauschenberg's contribution is named the "Money Thrower": "It was a box filled with gunpowder and 12 silver dollar coins which, at some point during the process, exploded, throwing the coins chaotically all over the garden," in Mary Lynn Kotz, *Rauschenberg/Art and Life* [1990], Harry N. Abrams, New York 2004, p. 120.

MoMA issued the official invitation to the event for March 17, 1960. The guests included renowned New York artists such as Barnett Newman and Mark Rothko.[14] After a slight delay, Tinguely began his action in the museum's garden. The assemblage, some 16 meters long and over 8 meters high, made of metal, countless wheels, fan belts, motors, found objects such as a piano and a bathtub, drawing machines, a balloon, etc., set itself in motion, and, due to numerous mishaps and malfunctions, destroyed itself without following the planned sequence. The assemblage had become a Happening, to whose burned and crashed remains the clapping and whistling audience could help themselves at the end. "The idea of participation, that is, a broad public audience accepting and playing along with a reality perceived as theatrical, was," according to Swiss art historian Philip Ursprung, "also one of the central themes of American art in the 1960s."[15] This was undoubtedly the art with which Tinguely had become involved with *Homage to New York*; he was now part of it himself.

The Art of Assemblage

When he returned to Paris from New York, Tinguely's formal language had changed drastically. Shaped by the profound experiences of his barely three-month-long stay, and by the study and assimilation of the new technique of assemblage, and, to a certain extent, the Happening, he developed entirely new structures made of metal, found objects, and industrial waste, using these as before in conjunction with the principle of the fan belt and motor. For the sake of accuracy, I prefer to use the term "assemblage" to refer to the work of this type that Tinguely created from the 1960s on.

In October–November 1961, William C. Seitz and Peter Selz of The Museum of Modern Art in New York organized the exhibition *The Art of Assemblage*—the first time that great academic and art historical effort had been devoted to an overview of this art genre, which had reemerged in New York at the end of the 1950s with greater intensity and in a newly interpreted form.[16] Even then, it was not easy to define this art form, whose roots, as the exhibition clearly demonstrated, lay in early 20th-century Europe. In his introductory text, however, Seitz gave some indication for how he understood the genre: "The physical characteristics that these collages, objects, and constructions have in common can be stated simply:

---

14 See Miranda Fuchs, "'Kunst ist Aufruhr' – Jean Tinguely als Aktionskünstler," in *Museum Tinguely. Die Sammlung,* Museum Tinguely, Basel, Kehrer Verlag, Heidelberg/Berlin 2012, p. 210–243, p. 212.

15 Philip Urpsrung, *Grenzen der Kunst. Allan Kaprow und das Happening, Robert Smithson und die Land Art,* Metzel, Munich 2003, p. 29

16 The exhibition traveled to the Dallas Museum of Contemporary Art and the San Francisco Museum of Art during the first semester of 1962.

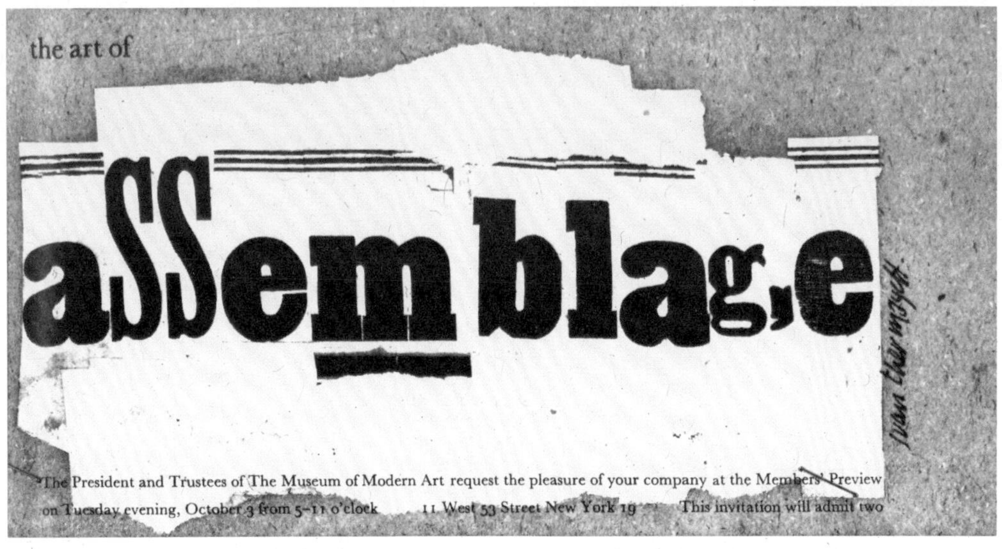

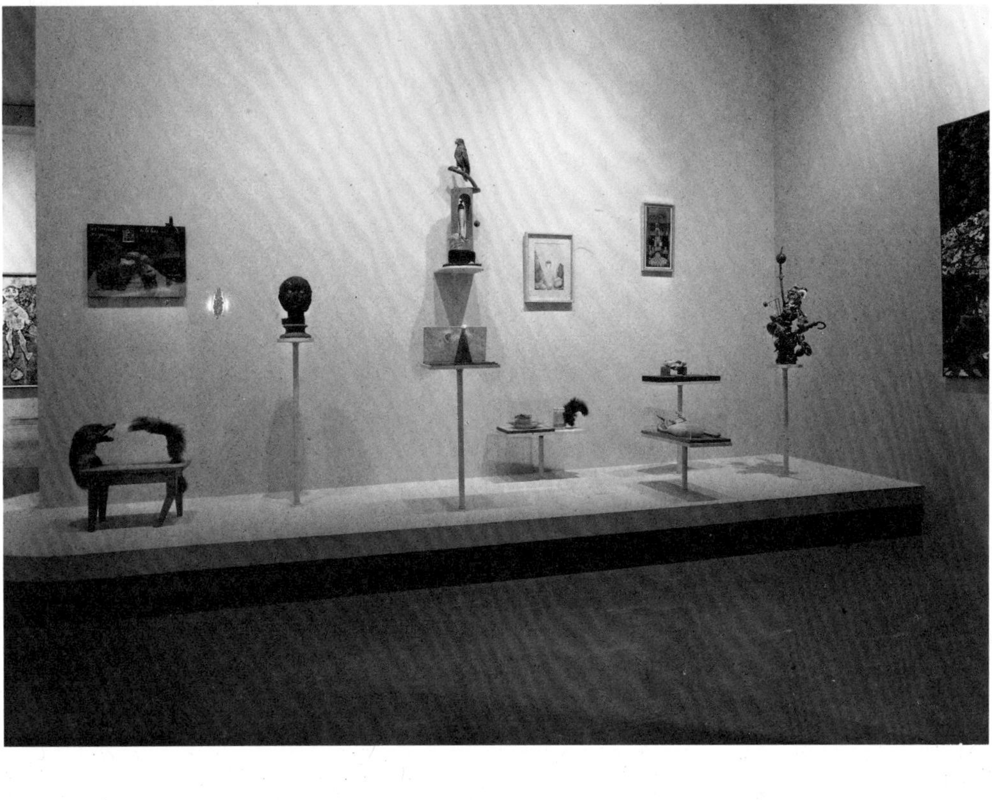

Invitation card and exhibition view of *The Art of Assemblage*, The Museum of Modern Art, New York, October 4–November 12, 1961

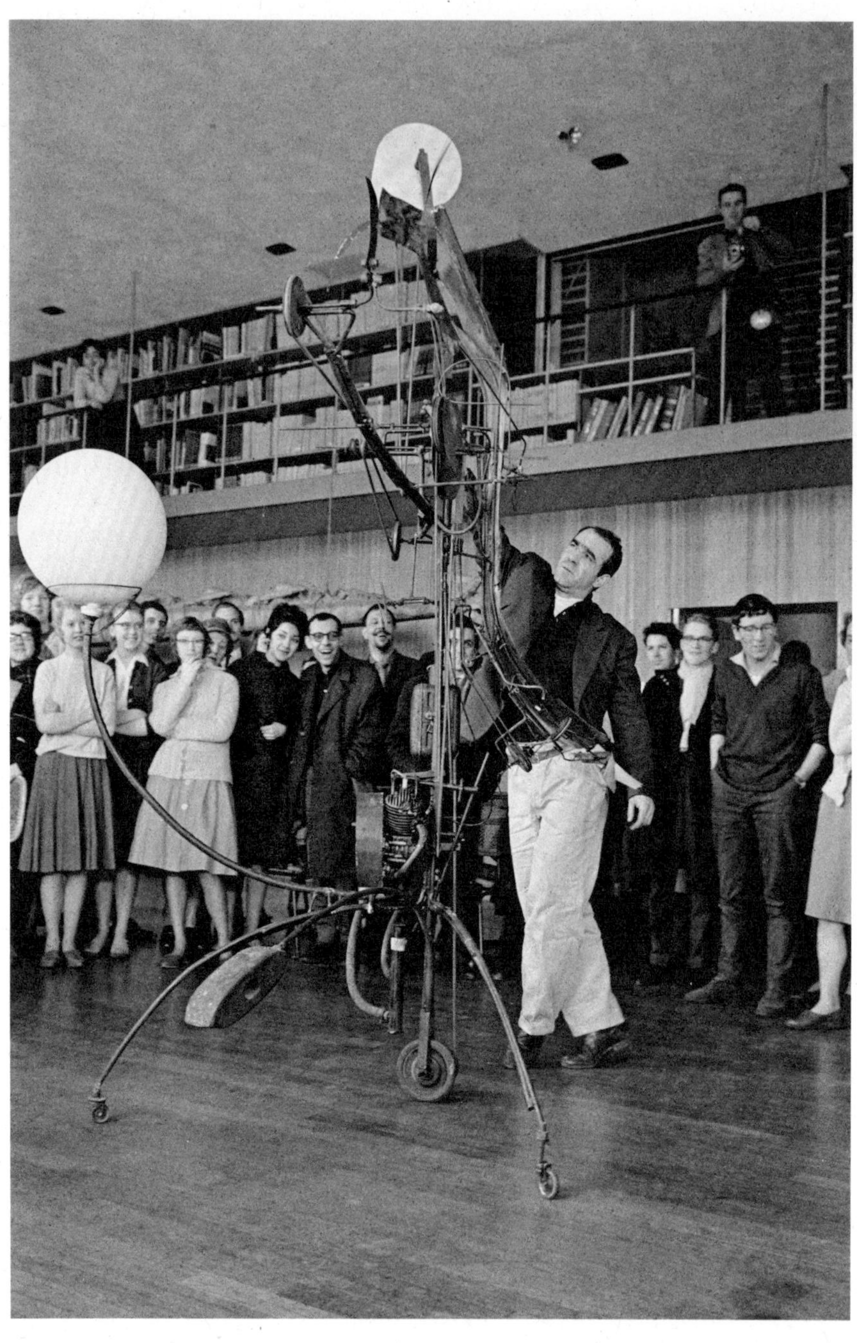

Jean Tinguely at the exhibition *Bewogen Beweging*, Stedelijk Museum, Amsterdam, March 10–April 17, 1961

1. They are predominantly assembled rather than painted, drawn, modeled, or carved. 2. Entirely or in part, their constituent elements are preformed natural or manufactured materials, objects, or fragments not intended as art materials [...] The term assemblage has been singled out to denote not only a specific technical procedure and form used in the literary and musical, as well as the visual arts, but also a complex of attitudes and ideas."[17] Despite the genre's past and its place in art historical tradition, however, Seitz clearly maintained that "Assemblage is a new medium." And it was to this medium that the most important museum of the time devoted a major exhibition, with 252 works including two by Tinguely—*Monstranz*, 1960, and *Marokko* or *L'Araignée* (The Spider), 1961—whose post-New York works were clearly categorized by MoMA as belonging to this (new) genre.

Étude pour une fin du monde No. 1

In 1961, the Stedelijk Museum Amsterdam director Willem Sandberg, with whom Tinguely was acquainted, and Pontus Hultén, the Stockholm Moderna Museet Director, Tinguely's most loyal companion from his first days in Paris, invited Tinguely and his friend Daniel Spoerri to organize a large-scale survey exhibition on movement in art (Kinetic art) entitled *Bewogen Beweging* (Moving Movement). Tinguely was represented at all three exhibition venues with 28 out of a total 233 works, many of them in his new form of assemblage.[18] The exhibition was an attempt to lend this loose stylistic movement from the most recent history of art a certain unity and an academic veneer without seeming to be historicizing. Tinguely, still energized by his experiences in New York, did not miss the opportunity to stage *Étude pour une fin du monde No. 1*—this time together with Niki de Saint Phalle—at the end of the tour in the garden of the Louisiana Museum of Modern Art, Denmark, as a continuation of *Homage to New York*, as it were. They made this work self-destruct at the push of a button and in front of an invited audience. Consisting of five large and several smaller assemblages, again made of mixed materials, it contained considerably more explosive power than in New York. Tinguely took advantage of this last stop and the larger context of the traveling exhibition—whose actual theme was Kinetic, moving art, and not assemblages

---

17 Here and following quote: *The Art of Assemblage*, p. 10 and p. 87. In this catalog, Jean Tinguely's *Marokko* is listed under the incorrect title *Makroko*.

18 *Bewogen Beweging* (Moving Movement), Stedelijk Museum, Amsterdam, March–April 1961; *Rörelse i Konsten*, Moderna Museet, Stockholm, May–September 1961; and *Bewegaelse I Kunsten*, Louisiana Museum of Modern Art, Humlebæk, Denmark, September–October 1961.

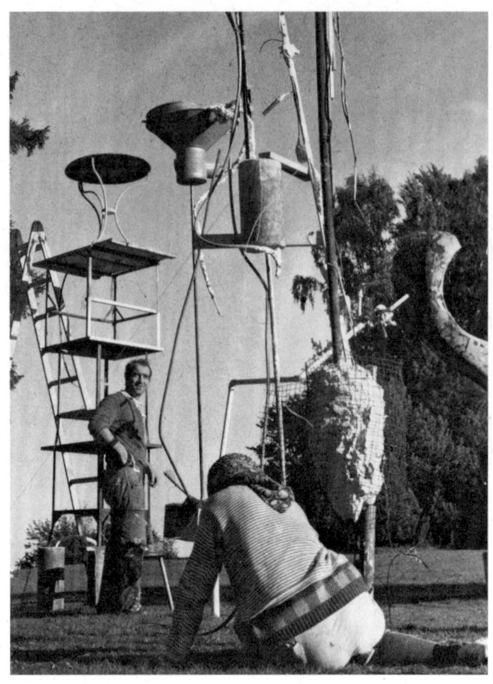

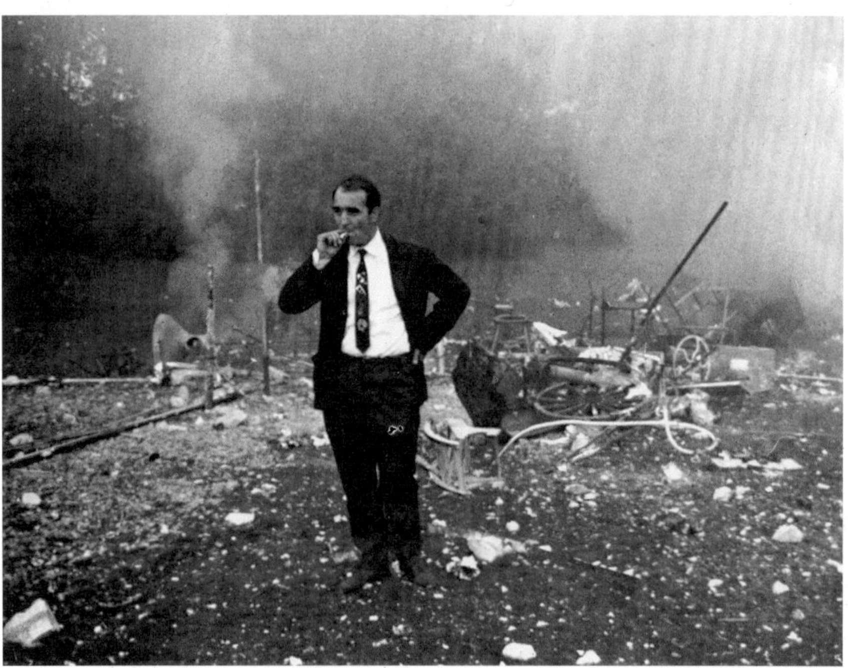

Jean Tinguely
Étude pour une fin du monde No. 1, Louisiana Museum of Modern Art, Humlebæk, September 22, 1961

or auto-destructive art—to present a group of self-destructing assemblages to the public. This was made possible by Tinguely's hybrid form of "assemblage in motion." And, of course, a fair amount of fun—an important factor for the art public of the early 1960s, who were becoming increasingly sensitized to spectacle.

Los Angeles: *Study for End of the World No. 2*

In February 1962, Tinguely traveled to Los Angeles for a solo exhibition at the Everett Ellin Gallery, and another action using an "assemblage in motion." His *Marokko*, already shown at MoMA and now on display at the gallery, graced the cover of the inaugural issue of the prestigious American art magazine *Artforum* in June 1962. A substantial cause of this publicity was the project *Study for End of the World No. 2*, which he carried out with Saint Phalle on the Jean Dry Lake Bed in the Nevada desert on March 21, 1962. This time, he was not filmed by artist friends or documented by photographers hired for the occasion, but accompanied by a camera crew from the US television broadcaster NBC, who filmed the study for *David Brinkley's Journal*. On site was not only the broadcaster, but a whole slew of renowned journalists from major media, just as they had been in MoMA's garden in 1960 on the occasion of *Homage to New York*. Seven assemblages were remotely controlled by the two artists from a control panel, and destroyed following a programmed sequence. It was a great success, in part due to NBC's documentation in color, which was not only seen by a considerable number of viewers on television, but had an almost cinematic character. The film documented the process, the gathering of the materials, and the construction of the individual assemblages at the Flamingo Hotel in Las Vegas, as well as the transport into the desert by truck with a police escort.

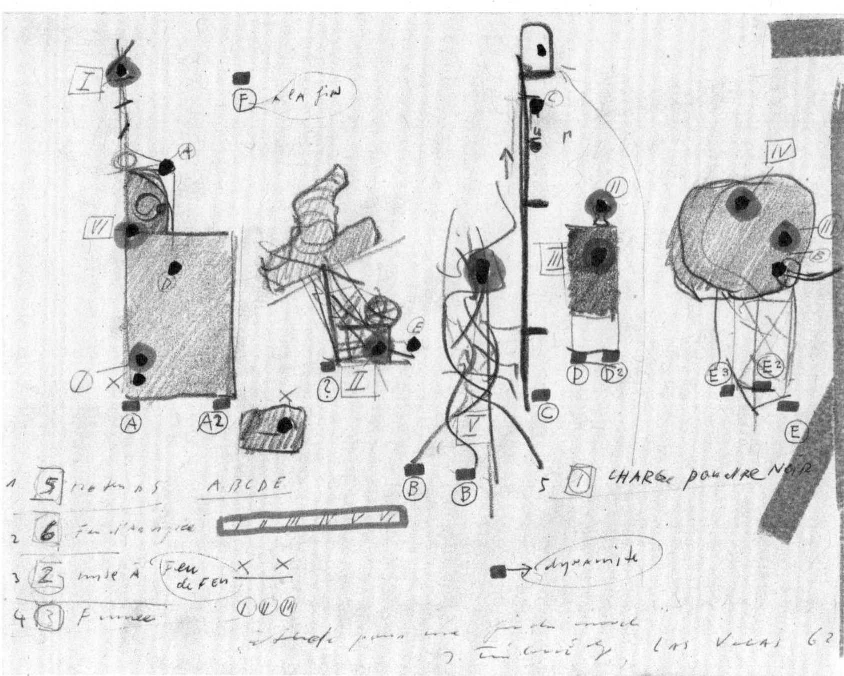

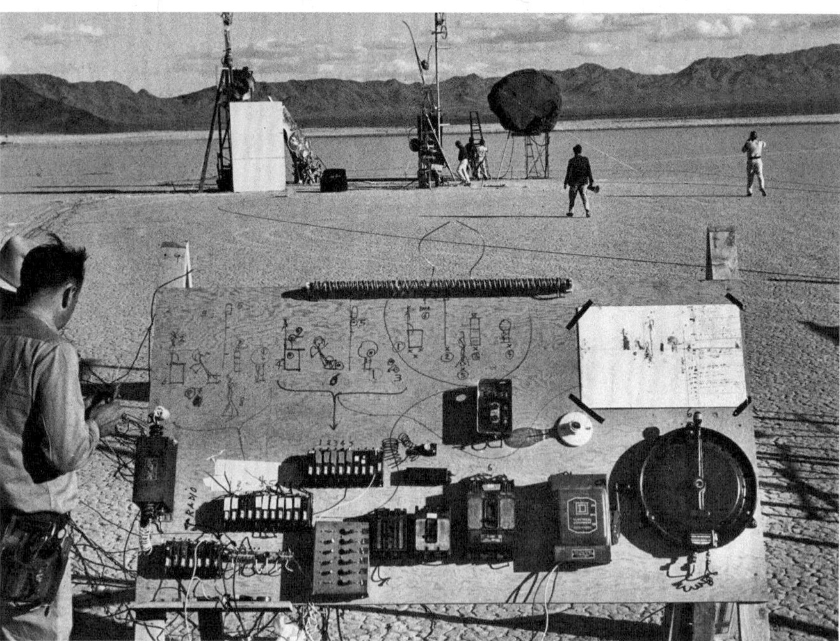

Top: Jean Tinguely
Study for End of the World No. 2, 1962
Pencil, felt-tip, and ballpoint on paper, 22.8 × 30.2 cm; Collection Museum Tinguely, Basel

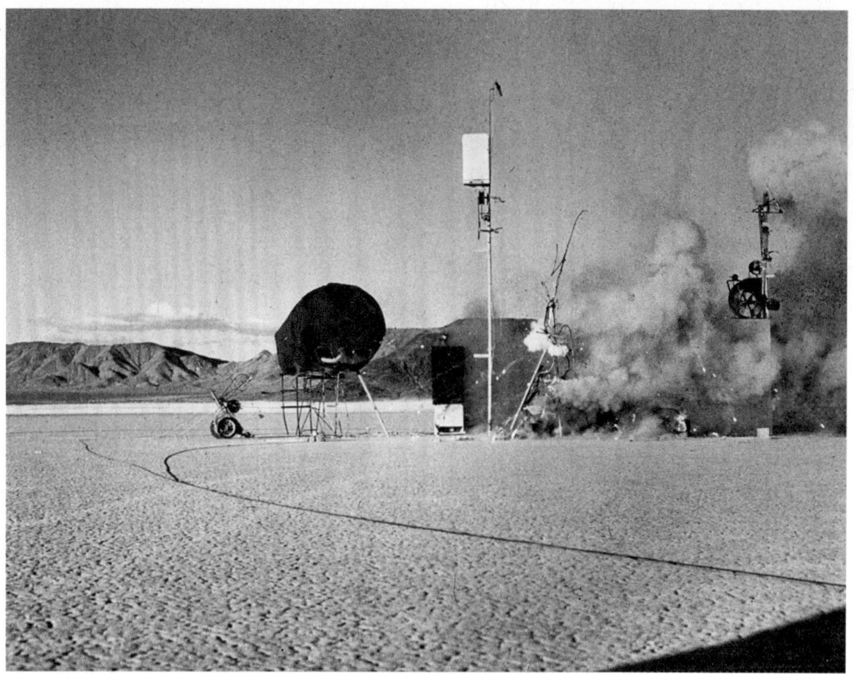

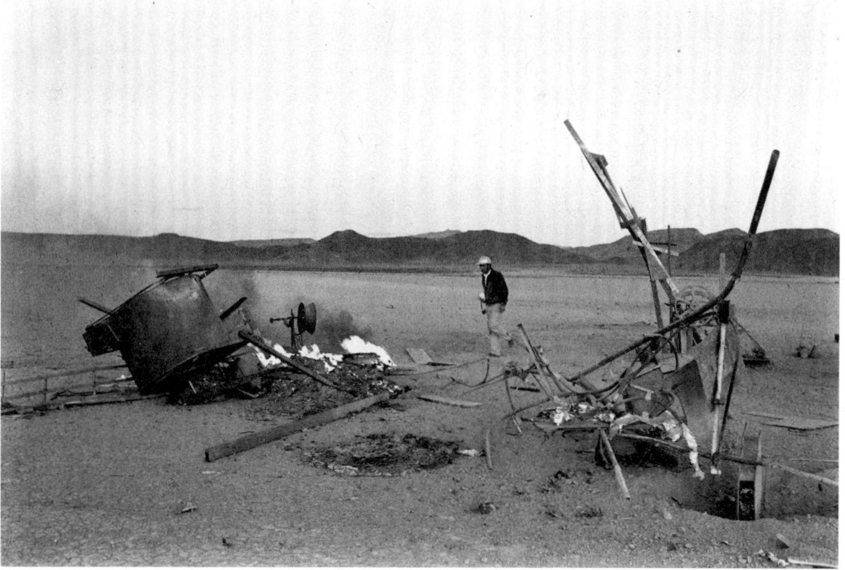

Here and opposite page bottom: Jean Tinguely
Study for End of the World No. 2, Jean Dry Lake, Nevada, March 21, 1962

Dylaby

After his return in France and the shocking news of the unexpected death of his good friend, the artist Yves Klein, Tinguely set about his next exhibition project, based on an idea he had apparently been pursuing with Spoerri and Luginbühl since 1960: the creation of a dynamic labyrinth. There was even a model for it. According to Spoerri, "this fairground model, which was to be presented as a project for the 1964 national exhibition in Lausanne, gathered dust for years in a shed at Bernhard Luginbühl's and is now finally lost."[19] There is however a black-and-white illustration in the Spoerri catalogue just cited, which shows a gigantic architectural structure assembled from various elements. Like Tinguely's later (quasi-) architectural projects—*Heureka*, which he actually showed at the 1964 Schweizer Landesausstellung [Swiss National Exhibition]; *Chaos No. 1* (1974) in Columbus, Ohio; *Le Crocrodrome* (1977) for the opening of the Centre Pompidou; *Grosse Méta Maxi Maxi Utopia*, first shown at the Palazzo Grassi in 1987, and, of course, his most important work, *Le Cyclop* —it was a monumental sculpture. Spoerri and Tinguely realized the idea of the dynamic labyrinth[20] together with Saint Phalle, Per Olof Ultvedt, Martial Raysse, and Rauschenberg, at the invitation of Sandberg in 1962 in the exhibition *Dylaby: Dynamic Labyrinth*. It was a "new exhibition practice whose fundamental characteristic was the reassessment of the space of the museum."[21] Thus, the artists did not create a new monumental architecture-like assemblage within a museum space, but rather hijacked the existing museum spaces: "To this end, each participant was able to design individual sections of the spaces in which the artistic approach of their creator was evident." Central here, again, was the fusion of art with life, with reality, as Tinguely had experienced it in the United States —a principle that also united the members of Nouveau Réalisme. Many elements of this collaborative exhibition, whose origin lay in the idea for a large architectural assemblage,[22] remained present for Tinguely and later culminated in the realization of *Le Cyclop*.

[p. 72–73]

---

19 *Anekdotomania. Daniel Spoerri über Daniel Spoerri*, Hatje Cantz, Ostfildern-Ruit 2001, p. 68.

20 For more on this, see Anna-Sophia Reichelt, *Kunst macht Ausstellung. Das Amsterdamer Stedelijk Museum und die Avantgarde*, Metzel, Munich 2018, p. 160–227.

21 Here and following quote: ibid., p. 224.

22 In the collection of the Museum Tinguely in Basel, there is a portfolio with five works on paper and views of a tower, which Tinguely had designed together with the French architect Claude Parent (see p. 68–69). It was a clear continuation of what Spoerri called the "fairground model," in which Tinguely, Spoerri, and Luginbühl visualized their idea of a dynamic labyrinth. Interestingly, Tinguely deliberately pursued this idea further himself, and specifically in collaboration with an architect.

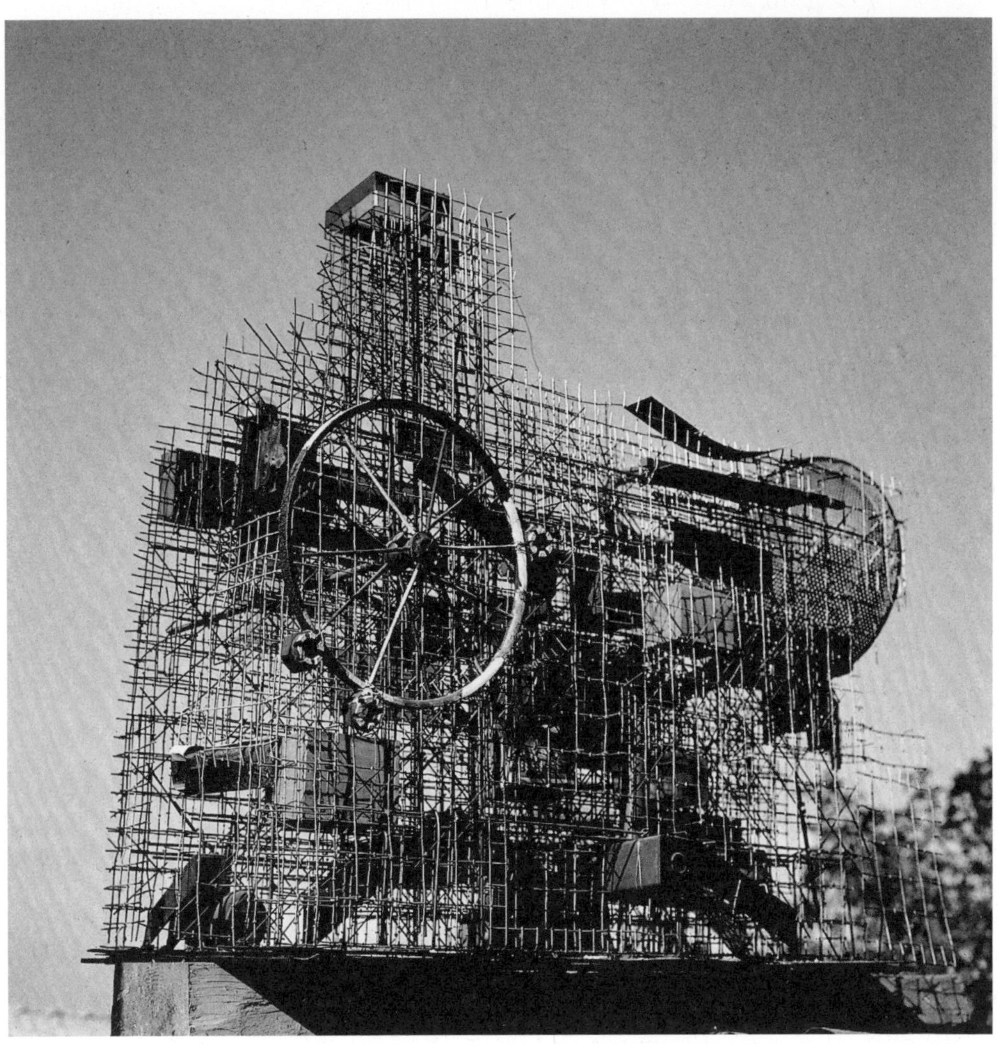

Bernhard Luginbühl, Daniel Spoerri, and Jean Tinguely
Model for *Labyrinthe dynamique*, 1960

DYLABY

I daniel spoerri
1 zoemer
2 fietswiel
3 schuimrubber vloer
4 draaibare zuilen
5 schuine vloer
6 fietsbanden
7 marmer
8 blitzlicht
9 oude kleren
10 bed
11 kippengaas
12 schuine vloer
13 rolschaats (tinguely)
14 fietswiel
15 paspop
16 brandweerhelm
17 draaischijf
18 rubberdraden
19 beweegbare wand
20 "tableau piège"
21 warm paneel
22 natte spons
23 closetpot
24 hagedis op sterk water
25 rood licht
26 ketting
27 vochtige wand
28 groene lamp
29 nooddeur
30 microfoon
31 matras

II per olof ultvedt
A gedesynchroniseerde radio (tinguely)
1 ingang
2 buffet
3 stoel
4 hobbelpaard
5 gebroken stoel
6 contra gewicht (rieten been)
7 deur met kippengaas
8 cyther
9 fietswiel
10 dienblad met aluminium servies
11 aluminium pan
12 ruimte met contra gewichten
13 mangel
14 fauteuilrug
15 gong
16 niet gebruikte meubelen
17 uitgang

III daniel spoerri
1 stoel
2 theekastje
3 beeld
4 lamp
5 schilderij

IV martial raysse
1 jukebox
2 badstoel met baadster
3 meisje met parasol
4 groen gras met vruchten
5 bad met plastic dieren
6 bonte vloer
7 zwarte tegels
8 meisje met zwaan
9 strand
10 strandspelen
11 de rand van het strand
12 zee in het zuiden

V niki de saint phalle
1 diplodocus lentus
2 tyrannosaurus rex
3 hoofdenzuil
4 raket
5 kathedraal
6 paspop
7 wolkenkrabber
8 vrouw met grote slang
9 en 10 mechanieken voor het
monster en verfzakjes (tinguely)
11 geweer
jean tinguely
12 machine/sculptuur
13 "hommage à anton müller"
per olof ultvedt
14 doorloop met spoken

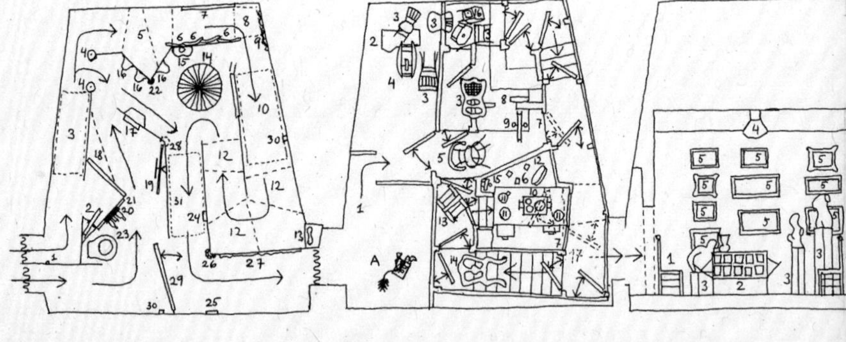

Floor map of the *Dylaby* exhibition, curators: Willem Sandberg and Jean Tinguely, Stedelijk Museum, Amsterdam, August 30–September 30, 1962

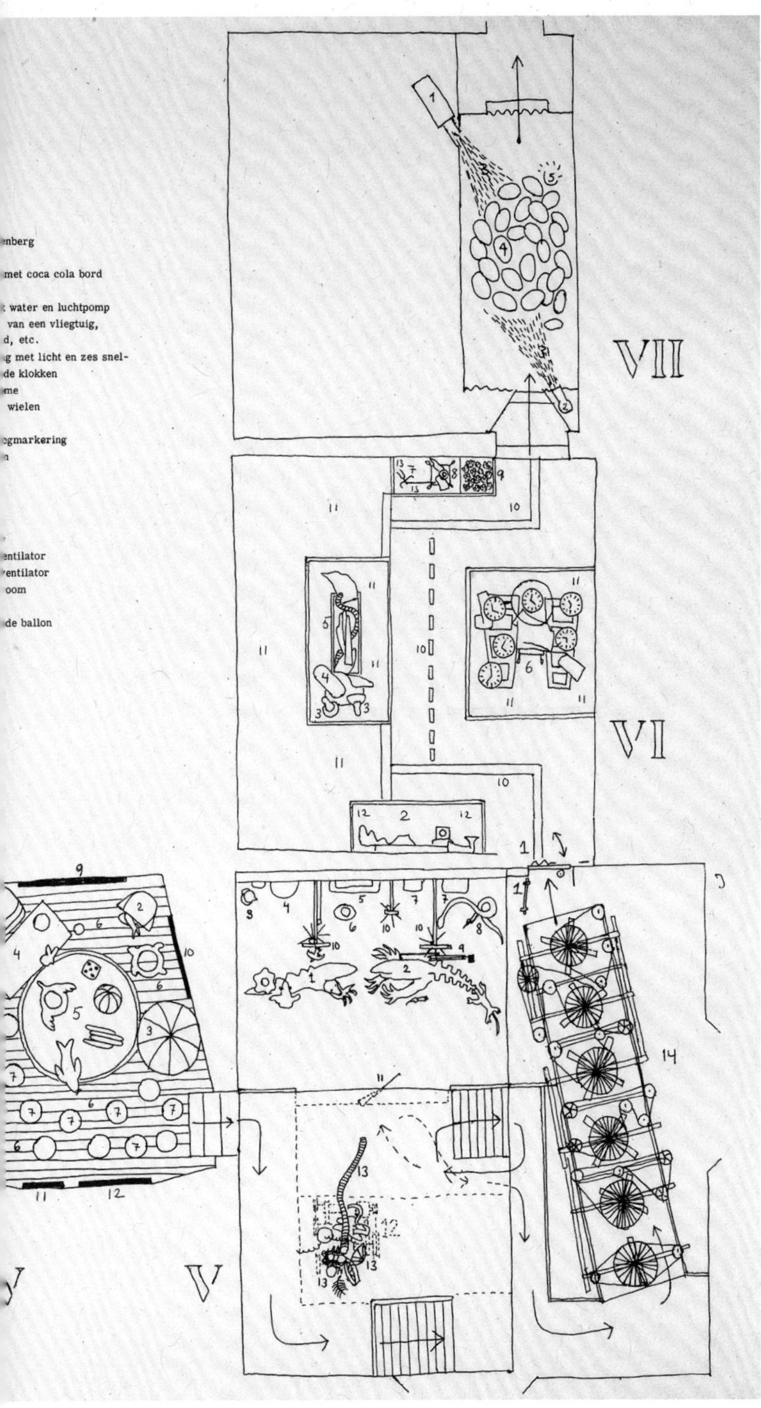

enberg

met coca cola bord

water en luchtpomp
van een vliegtuig,
d, etc.
g met licht en zes snel-
de klokken
me
wielen

gmarkering
n

entilator
entilator
oom

de ballon

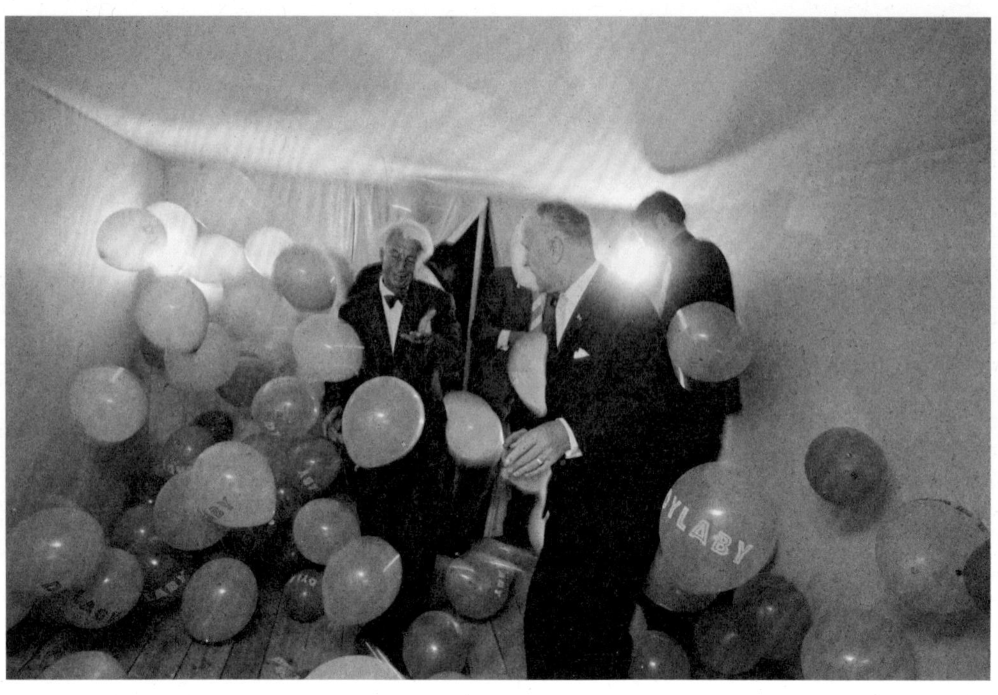

Exhibition views, *Dylaby*, curators: Willem Sandberg and Jean Tinguely, Stedelijk Museum, Amsterdam, August 30–September 30, 1962
Willem Sandberg (center) in Jean Tinguely's "Balloons Room"; Jean Tinguely, *Hommage à Heinrich Anton Müller*, 1962;
Jean Tinguely and Niki de Saint Phalle in one of her installations

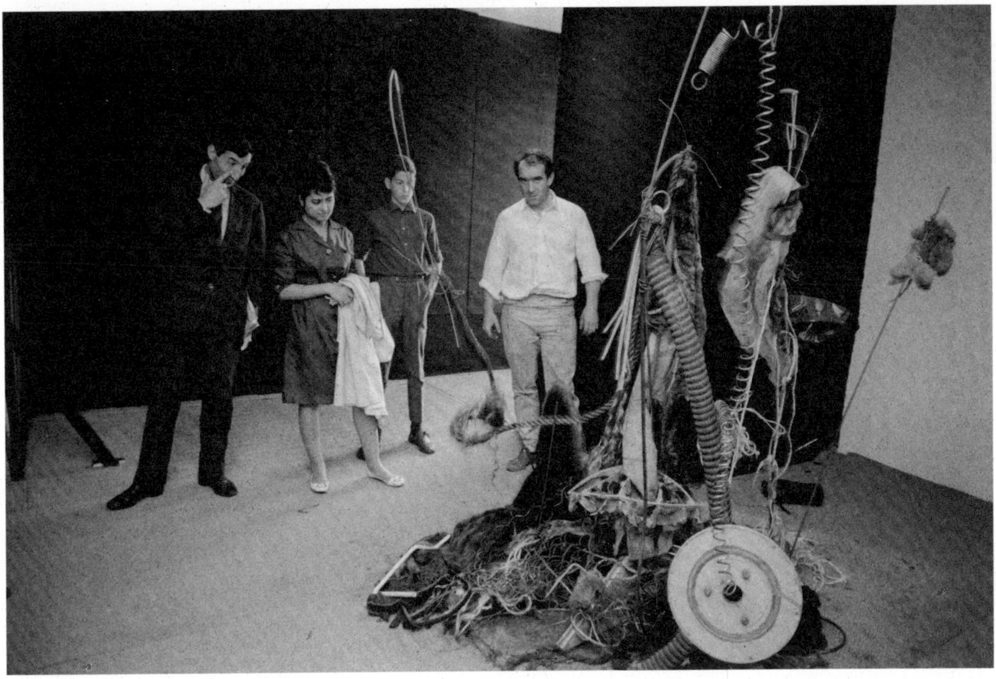

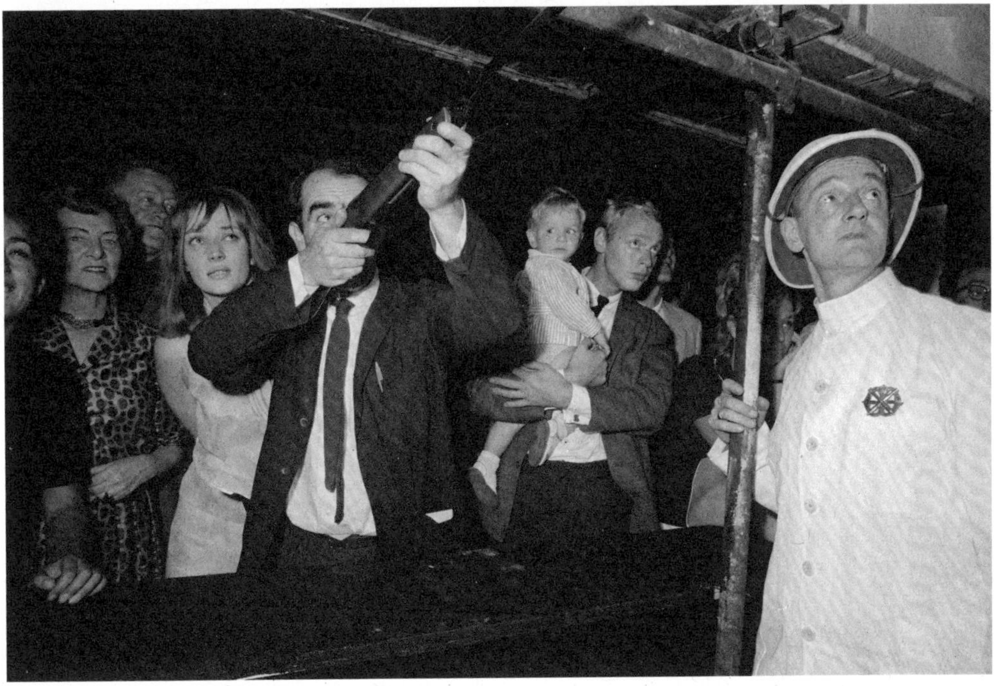

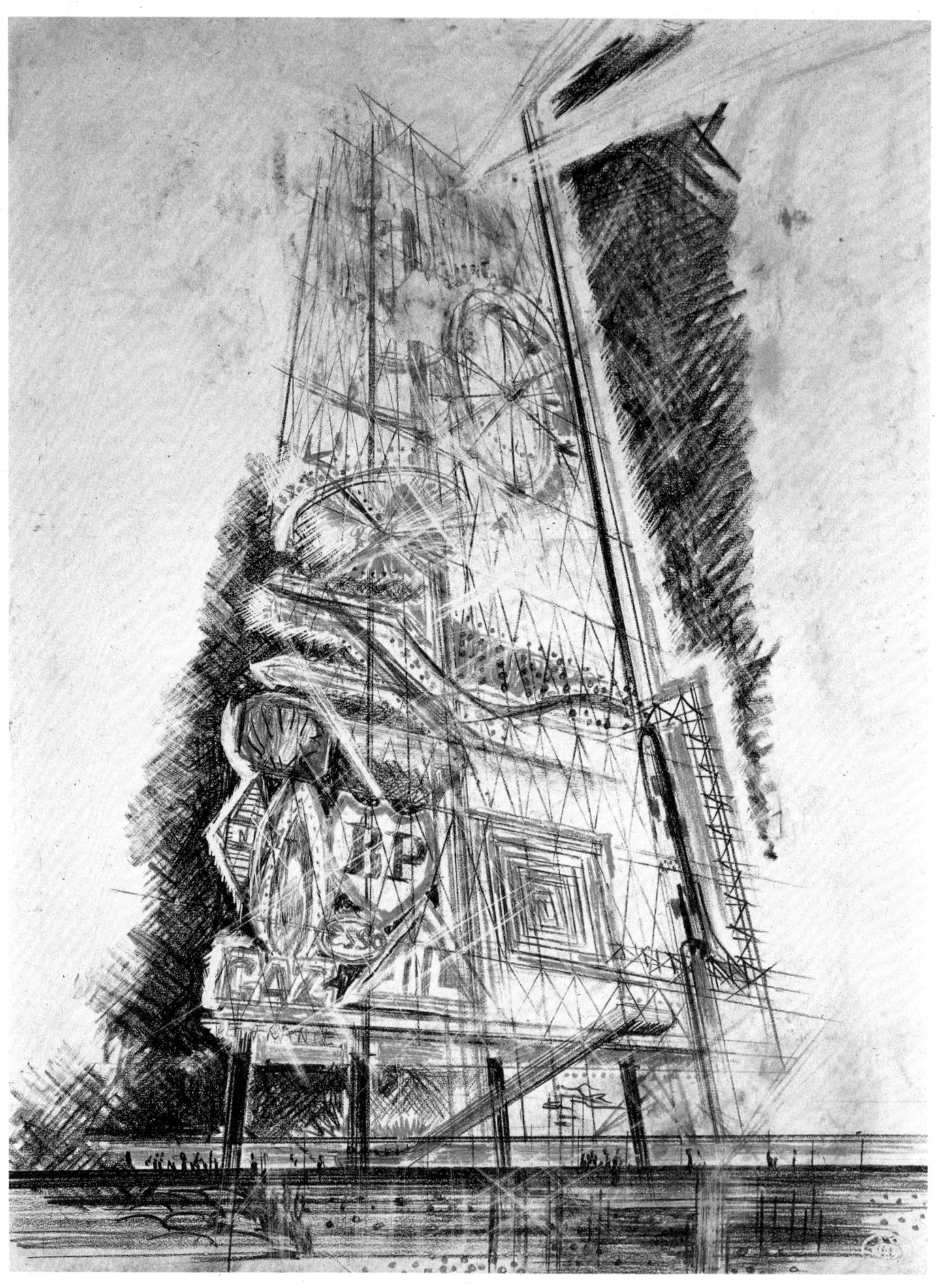

Jean Tinguely and Claude Parent
Lunatrack – Lunatour, 1964
Mixed media on paper, 65 × 50 cm
Collection Museum Tinguely, Basel

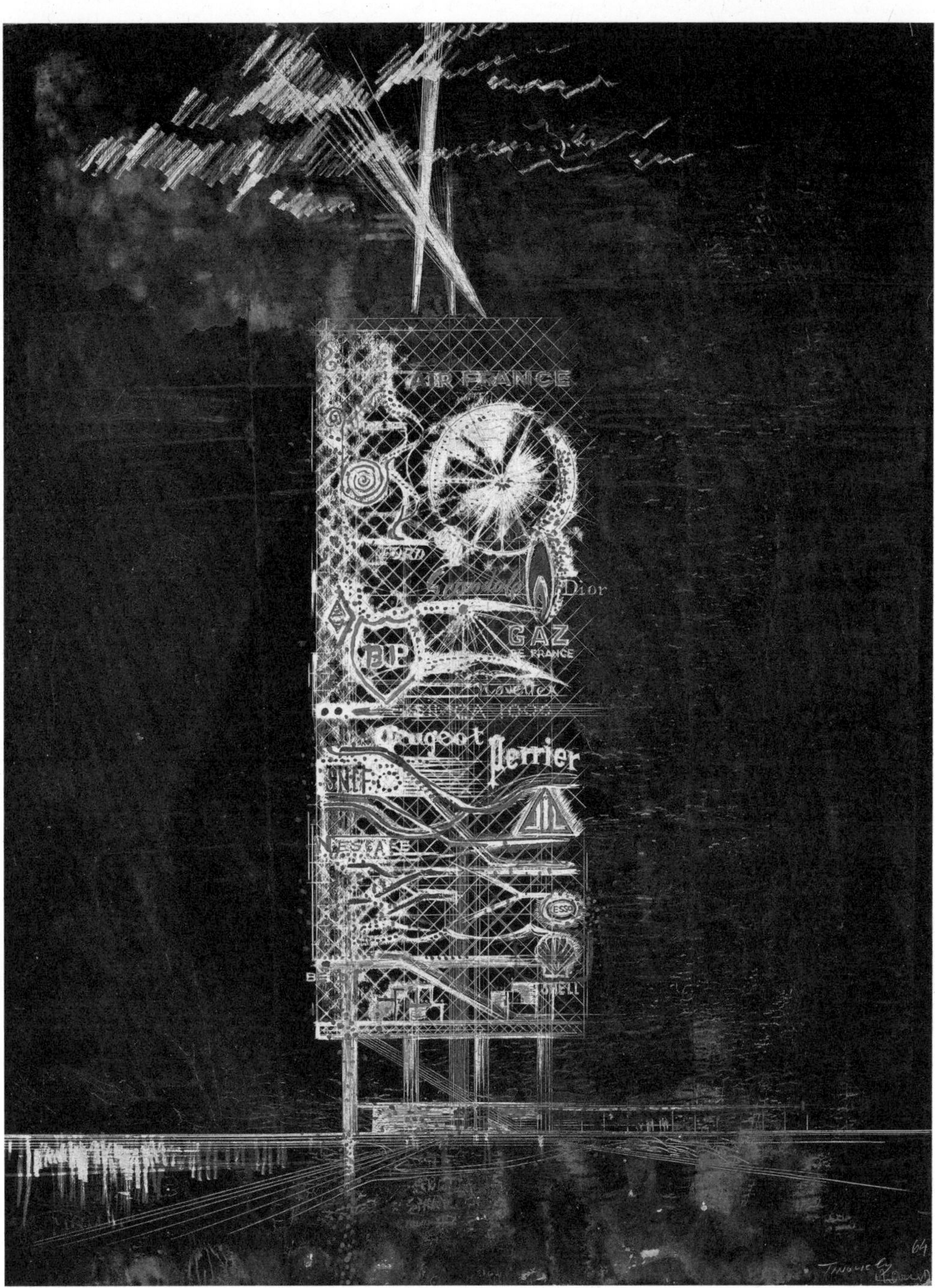

Jean Tinguely and Claude Parent
Lunatrack – Lunatour, 1964
Mixed media on paper, 65 × 50 cm
Collection Museum Tinguely, Basel

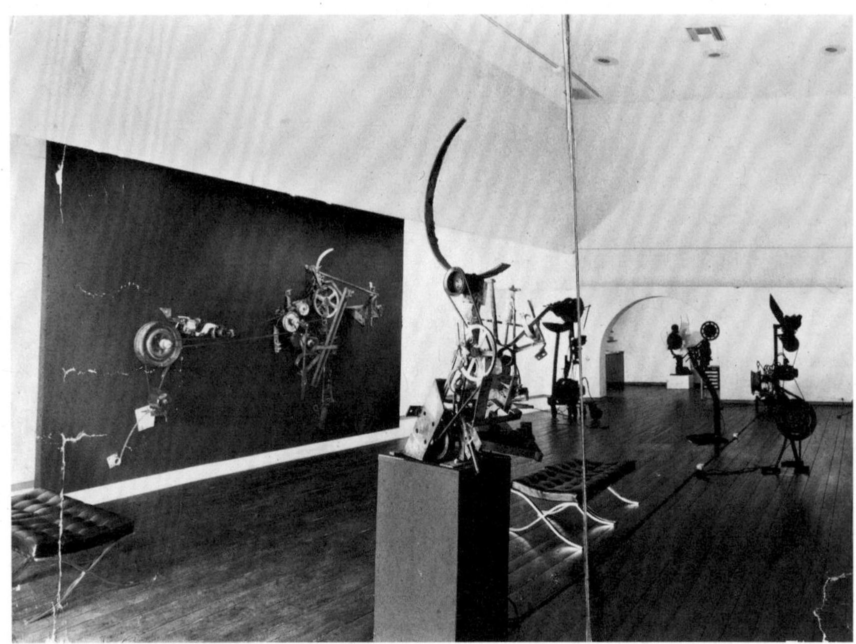

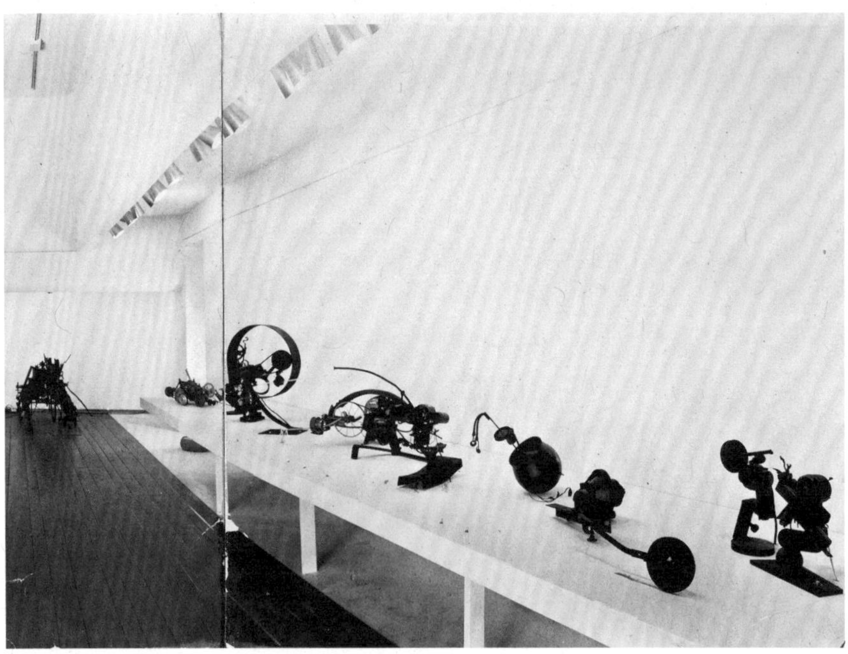

Exhibition views, *Jean Tinguely*, Dwan Gallery, Los Angeles, May–June 1963
Collection Museum Tinguely, Basel

Return to California and *Heureka*

Tinguely became acquainted with a completely different kind of assemblage from that in New York on his second, return trip to California. He arrived in Los Angeles as early as the start of 1963 to prepare his first big solo exhibition there at the Dwan Gallery. Virginia Dwan had already exhibited works by Tinguely in February of that year under the title *Dealer's Choice*, together with works by Arman, Lee Bontecou, Jim Dine, Edward Kienholz, Klein, Roy Lichtenstein, Oldenburg, Rauschenberg, Raysse, Ad Reinhardt, Larry Rivers, and James Rosenquist. An illustrious company—testimony to Dwan's efforts to establish transatlantic dialogue—and above all, encompassing many artists of assemblage, Happening, and environment from both New York and Los Angeles. Tinguely intensified contact in particular with Kienholz, one of the most important assemblage artists on the West Coast. Kienholz also attempted to show his works, some of which were huge, in conventional art galleries and institutions, in stark contrast to many other assemblage artists in the region, who preferred to produce assemblages with an ephemeral spirit; exhibit them in their studios, homes, or the great outdoors; alter them, dispose of them, or simply leave them standing as needed; and above all not release them for commercial sale. This field of tension had a stimulating effect on Tinguely and can certainly be understood as a reference point for the later fixed placement of *Le Cyclop* in a secluded piece of woodland, far away from Paris and the usual exhibition spaces of the city. The exhibition at Dwan, which opened in May, had a museum-like character, not only because of the classical and spacious gallery space, but also because Tinguely had produced a high-quality group of works.

Back in Europe, he immediately began to realize his largest non-self-destructing assemblage to date, *Heureka*, for the Schweizer Landes-ausstellung in Lausanne. It was the most daring project so far, which Tinguely himself described in a 1967 radio interview as "a dimension that goes beyond conventional sculpture. To come into contact with the people who watch TV, who are familiar with cars, who under the influence of modern civilization have developed a new impression of speed, these are the people art should move toward. Modern art in its abstract version no longer really appeals to the ordinary people of our age."[23] *Heureka* was dismantled at the end of the exhibition in Lausanne, but after a long period of uncertainty and difficulties, found a permanent home in Zurich in 1967.

---

23   "Gespräch über die Plastik 'Heureka,'"
       audio document, radio station unknown, 1967,
       Museum Tinguely, Basel, transcript by the author.

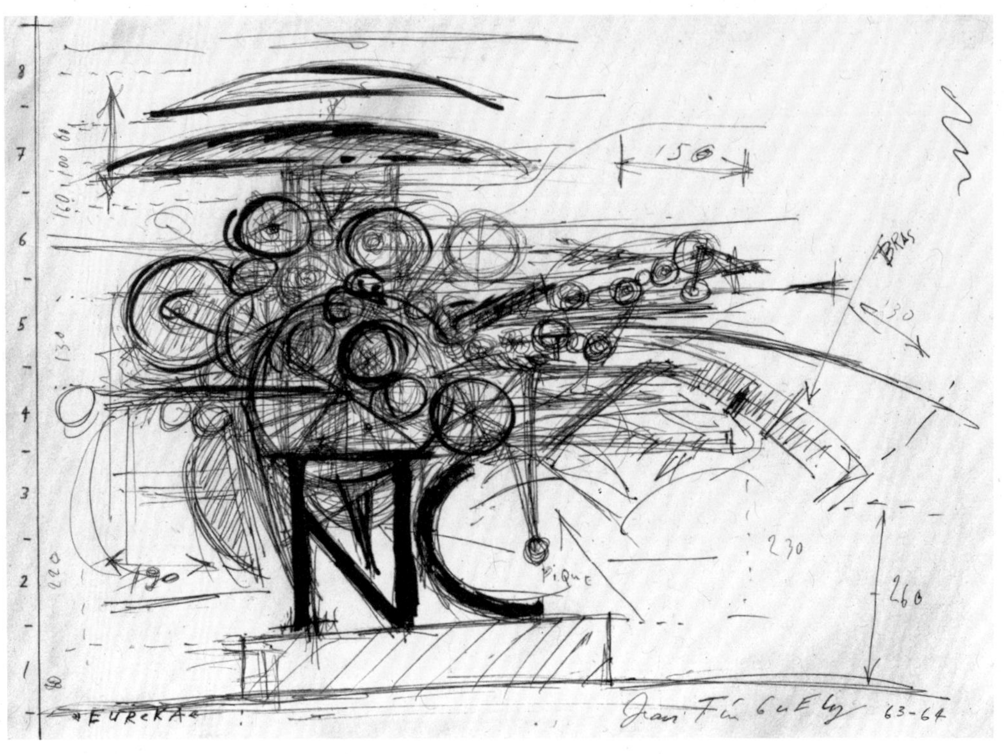

Jean Tinguely
Eureka – Heureka, 1963–1964
Felt-tip on paper, 21 × 29.5 cm
Collection Museum Tinguely, Basel

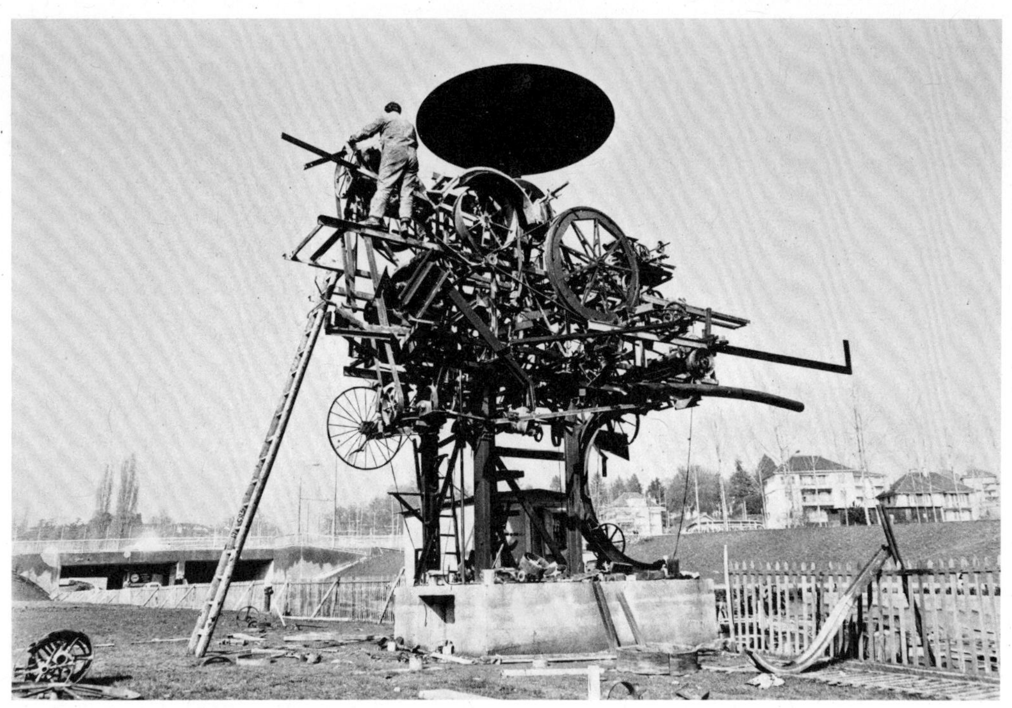

Jean Tinguely during the building of *Heureka* for the Swiss National Exhibition or Expo 64, Lausanne, 1964

Kulturstation, Le Cyclop – La Tête

[P. 68–69]

According to art historian Annja Müller-Alsbach "another drawing attests to one of the predecessor projects of *Lunatour* and to *Le Cyclop*: the unrealized project titled *Kulturstation – Gigantoleum*, which was planned in 1968 for the Weyermannshaus district of Bern as a further development of the idea for Dylaby from 1961."[24] In her essay, Müller-Alsbach mentions a second drawing in connection with the *Kulturstation*: "In a drawing that [...] bears the title *Gigantoleum* and is dated 1968, the formal connection to *Le Cyclop* is already established by the head shown in profile." This sketch was the first concrete reference in artistic form to Tinguely's idea for the monumental assemblage in the forest of Milly-la-Forêt. On paper, the project developed steadily from then on. In 1969 and 1970, a series of sketches emerged—detailed construction plans with descriptions, whereby Tinguely titled his idea alternately as the Monster, the Head, or the Monster in the forest. That this new, long-term project would rely on collaborations with artist friends is evidenced not only by its present form, but by an

[P. 115]

early sketch from 1969–1973, in which Tinguely listed those whose artistic participation he would like to have: "Per Olof Ultvedt – Arman – Niki de Saint Phalle – Spoerri & Kienholz – Rauschenberg – Uecker – Tinguely – Cécar – Lalanne – P. Hultén – J. P. Raynaud – Rico Weber – J. Imhof – Luginbühl & Ben & Minkoff & Oldenburg & Reuterswärd & Eva Aeppli & Ad Petersen & Larry Rivers & Soweiter." Even if in the end not all the people he envisioned participated, and some different ones joined in, this enumeration does precisely reflect Tinguely's development up to the beginning of the 1970s, as described in this text. The participants came from his native Switzerland as well as from his adopted country France, and from Europe and the USA, where he had spent such formative years between 1960 and 1963. Moreover, it was artists working in the new genres such as assemblage, environments, and Happenings that interested Tinguely so particularly and had greatly accelerated his career. Tinguely's intention was therefore not only to assemble material into a monumental work of art, but also to bring together artists from his environment, his companions and encounters from all over the world, and in this way to complete his assemblage in the forest.

---

24   Here and following quote: Annja Müller-Alsbach,
      "Das Medium der Zeichnung im Werk von Jean
      Tinguely," in *Museum Tinguely. Die Sammlung*,
      p. 246–378, p. 308.

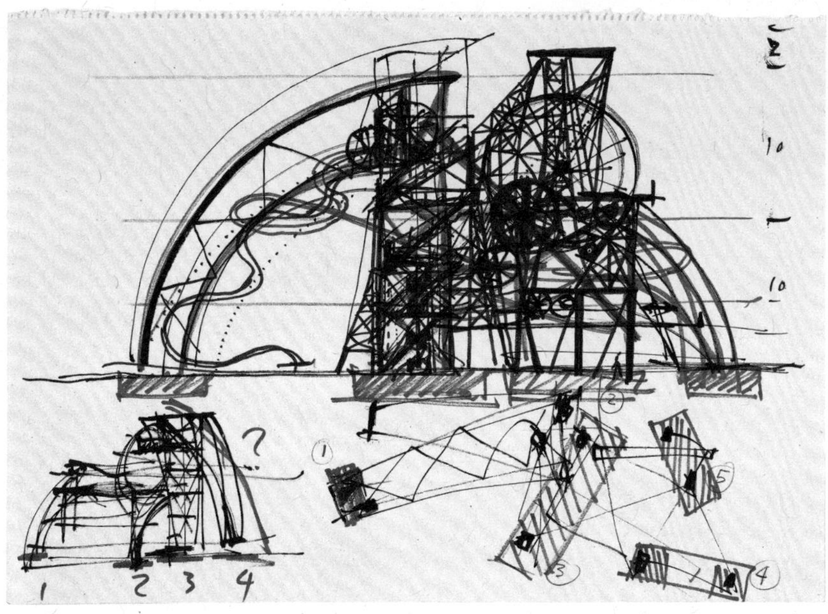

Jean Tinguely
Kulturstation – Gigantoleum, c. 1968
Felt-tip and pencil on paper, 29.5 × 42 cm
Collection Museum Tinguely, Basel

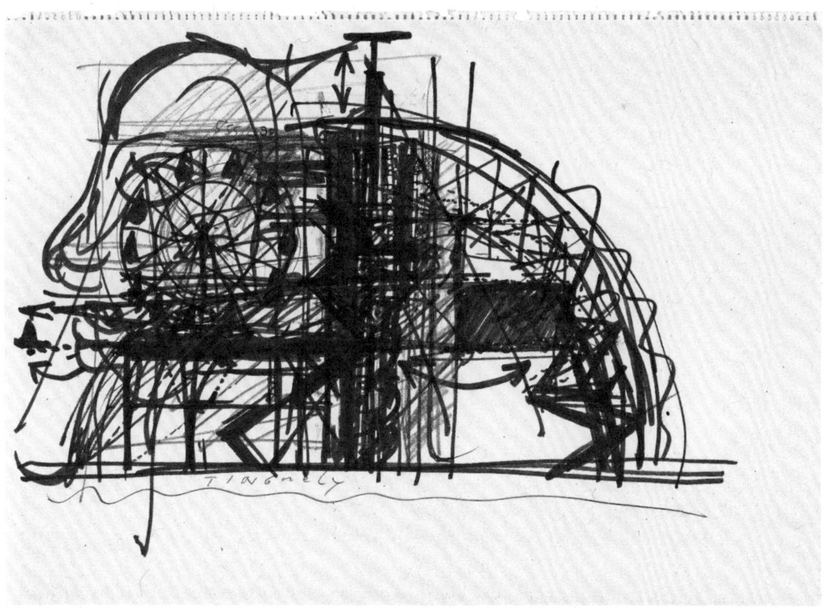

Jean Tinguely
Gigantoleum, c. 1968
Felt-tip, pencil, colored pencil, chalk, and ballpoint on paper, 29.5 × 42 cm
Collection Museum Tinguely, Basel

Construction Begins

Thanks to his exceptional network, Tinguely quickly succeeded in finding two suitable pieces of land in Milly-la-Forêt, which Saint Phalle acquired in May 1970. A few months later, Jean and Dominique de Menil acquired a series of plots of land adjacent, enabling the artists to start building *Le Cyclop*.[25] In 1970, the first three-dimensional models for the object in the forest were created in collaboration with Saint Phalle, and as the photographs by Leonardo Bezzola and Ad Petersen indicate, construction officially began. The earliest images show pieces of iron, scaffolding, and other materials in the forest, and, most significantly, the construction team in conversation. Tinguely had officially begun work on his most important and largest work of art, an assemblage of a scale really comparable only to previous works by non-artists such as Facteur Cheval (*Palais idéal*; Ideal Palace), Simon Rodia (*Watts Towers*), and Clarence Schmidt (*House of Mirrors*). In the visual arts, there is hardly a point of reference to be found. Over the previous 15 years, Tinguely had successively attempted, whether consciously or unconsciously, to put himself in a position where he could begin and also complete such a virtually utopian work (and it actually came to pass with *Le Cyclop*).

Conclusion

In this essay I was not primarily concerned with defining where *Le Cyclop* fits into Tinguely's oeuvre as a work of art (I continue to prefer to call it an assemblage), but rather with showing his artistic development, which provided him with the foundation to be able to develop and realize such a project. In my estimation, the stages and aspects described here belong to this foundation, without claiming to be a complete account. The key elements include his experiences between 1960 and 1963 in the United States, where he came into direct contact with developments in new or rediscovered art genres such as environments, Happenings, and—particularly central for Tinguely—assemblage. This scaffolding enabled his leap into this monumental dimension: the realization of a work of art that had evolved over years and was assembled from countless individual pieces

[P. 36–37]

---

25   The de Menil family were passionate collectors of Tinguely's art. An excerpt from a 1965 American newspaper article reports: "When John de Menil walked into the Alexandre Iolas Gallery in Paris one day in 1964, Jean Tinguely's moving, noisy sculptures stole a part of his heart. He spoke with James Johnson Sweeney, director of The Museum of Fine Arts in Houston, and the two men bought the entire exhibit of 12 "Méta-Mécaniques" for the museum's collection." In "Art Circles: Wild Spasms, Rituals of Tinguely's Sculptures," *The Houston Chronicle*, April 4, 1965, n.p.

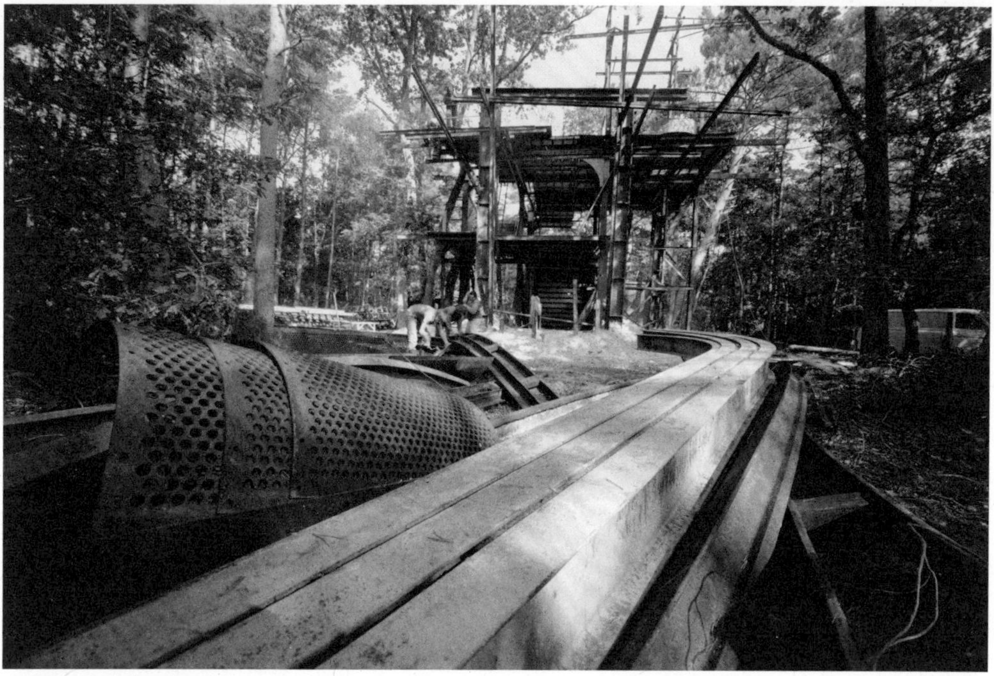

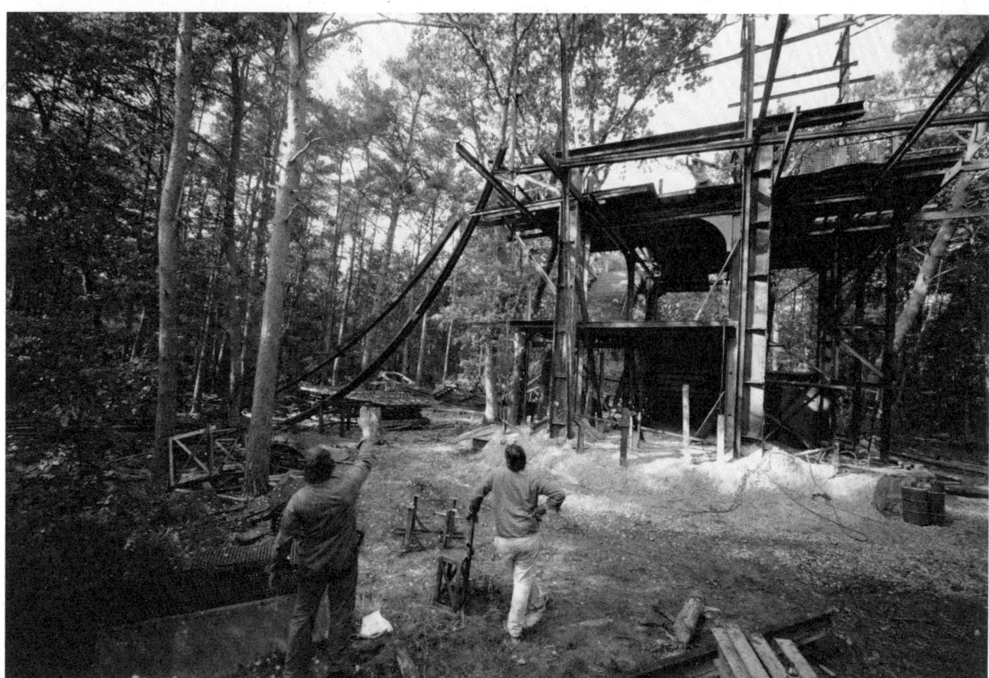

Le Cyclop in progress, 1971–1975

contributed by him and collaborating artists to form a total work of art that could be walked through and experienced.

In conclusion, I will take us to 1982 and to a time when, after nearly 10 years of work on *Le Cyclop*, Tinguely was for various reasons close to losing patience and resorting to drastic means, as one of Luginbühl's diary entries testifies: "latest harebrained idea, cut the head in the forest into pieces and send it to the USA by ship […] The rusty cargo ship was already waiting in Le Havre to pick up the THING. Jeano moans about the vandals who cause ever greater damage to the HEAD."[26] At a time of profound crisis surrounding the condition of his most important work of art, there appeared to its creator to be only one way out: the seemingly impossible relocation of the head, not within France or any other European country, but to the USA, home of unlimited possibilities.[27] This (unrealized) scheme now closes the circle of the USA and the assemblage that I attempted to open with *Homage to New York* in 1960. Today *Le Cyclop* lives more splendidly than ever in the forest of Milly-la-Forêt and delights every art lover who wants to discover, experience, and admire it for itself.

---

26 Bernhard Luginbühl, *JT Tagebuchnotizen von Bernhard Luginbühl oder ein Rezept für Zwiebelfischsuppe No. 2*, Bern 2009, April 24, 1982 entry.

27 In the mid-1980s, Tinguely and Seppi Imhof even produced a portfolio of plans for dismantling, transporting, and reassembling the Head. In principle, this too was only possible because it was a assemblage of multiple parts. On this, see *"Le Cyclop": petite documentation pour le démontage-transport et reconstruction de Jean Tinguely*, Centre National des Arts Plastiques, Paris, here on p. 117, 262. The Museum Tinguely in Basel owns a copy.

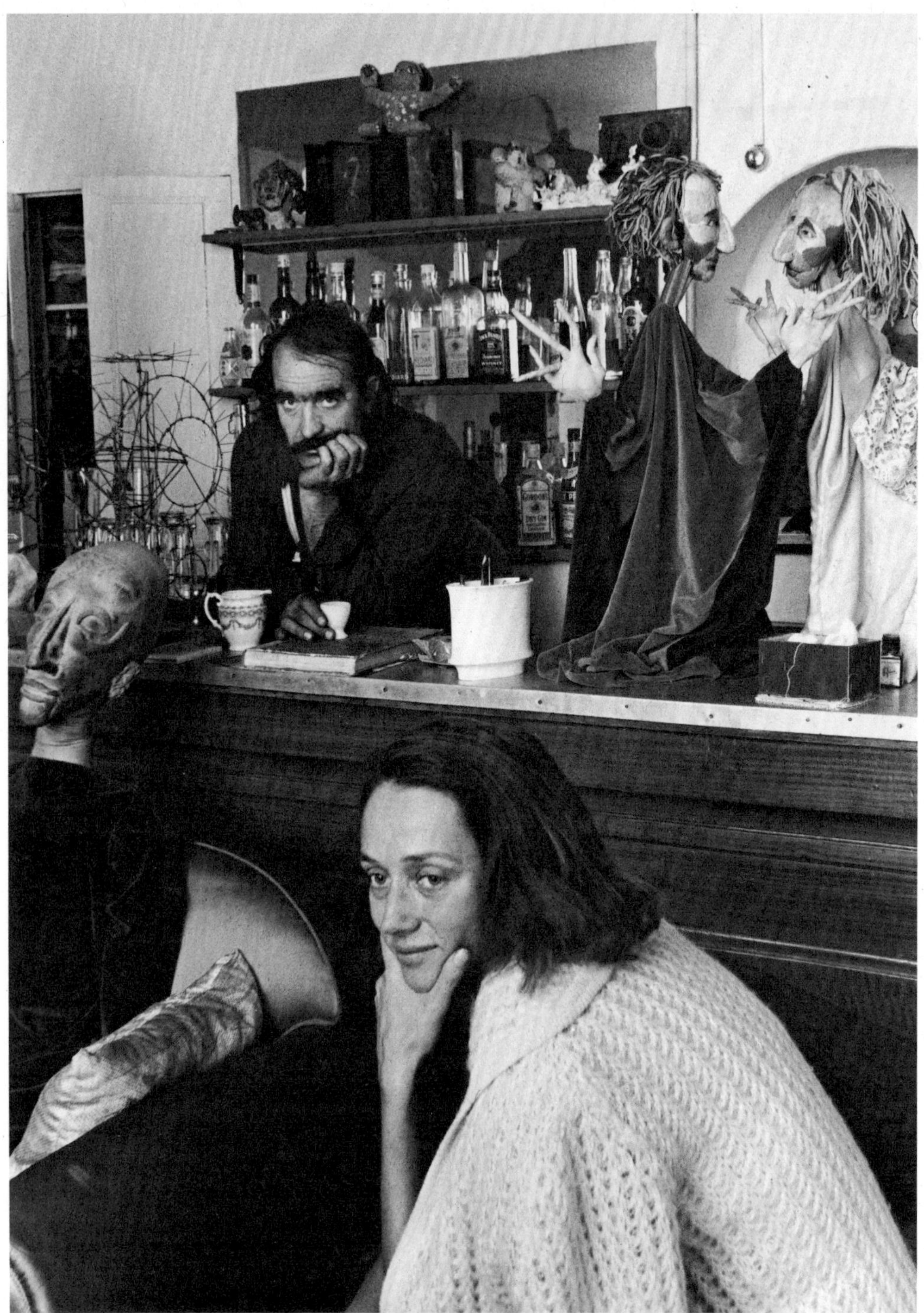

Niki de Saint Phalle and Jean Tinguely, Soisy-sur-École, July 27, 1971

Let's Talk About Love
Camille Paulhan

In a statement about Jean Tinguely and his *Cyclop*, published for the official opening of the project, Niki de Saint Phalle asserted that the artist "had made his amazing dream come true. He felt the time was right, so he did it. And he loves the other artists."[1] Indeed, as soon as we take an interest in the way Tinguely recruited what might be called his accomplices—in order to help him finish a work simultaneously attributable to himself, as well as being a thoroughly collective one—love seems to play a key role. Tinguely stated as much himself in 1988 in a joint interview with Saint Phalle. "Love is always there. Without love, there's nothing to be done—nothing *can* be done. Love is the foundation, the flame, the fire."[2] While the Swiss artist was referring to his collaboration with Saint Phalle, this statement could well apply to *Le Cyclop* (The Cyclops), a more Dantean project he worked on for some 30 years, bringing together a certain number of close friends. Tinguely felt there was "no need to hate other artists. Although I can be jealous, I tend to admire them."[3] Indeed, rivalry proved fertile, spurring him to envisage the creation of a structure that would contain works by all his artist friends who he envied and also esteemed.

1   Niki de Saint Phalle, *Le Cyclop*, A.C.T.E. 91, Évry 1993, p. 14.

2   Jean Tinguely, in "Portrait Chinois," directed by Agnès Delarive, broadcast on French TV (Antenne 2) for the program *Haute Curiosité*, May 29, 1988.

3   Jean Tinguely, interviewed by Heinz-Norbert Jocks, "Ich beschäftige mich mit dem Tod, um ihn zu bekämpfen," *Kunstforum*, no. 115, September/October 1991, p. 275.

The genealogy of *Le Cyclop* is well known and fully discussed in various books, documentaries, broadcasts, and articles devoted to the work.[4] This essay seeks to discuss—beyond the straightforward chronology— the way in which Tinguely's project spurred dozens of people into action, involving them to various degrees in this giant sculpture-installation of indefinite design. These people were not only artists, of course, but also collectors, patrons, technicians, logistical experts, civil servants, funders, children, and families. Over three decades, they contributed to the success of this fascinating "Monstre dans la forêt" (Monster in the forest) (or la Tête (the Head), as it was called until *Le Cyclop* was donated to the French state).[5] Tinguely was not new to collaborative effort, many of his works since the 1960s having been collective. In 1987, regarding *Le Cyclop,* he even wittily commented, "I don't want it to be just the work of a given person—Luginbühl and I are the basis, but then I wanted to bring more and more people into it. Guys who do funny things, you know, sticking mostly with the bizarre, with the unexpected, always messing around, while also not letting the thing get too defined. Once it begins to please everybody, we'll change it all, we'll paint it sugary pink. So that everybody will say, 'That's disgusting!'"[6]

The spontaneous cotton-candy repainting of *Le Cyclop* never took place—perhaps fortunately—but this statement was emblematic of the way the artist viewed collaboration with his peers: namely, a question of friends getting together to forge a skillful alloy that Tinguely described in his own words as "trance, dream, and intuition, from which you get an emulsion called enthusiasm. And those four elements are then mixed with a chemical element that some people call pure madness."[7] A few years later, Pontus Hultén summed it up more simply: "[Tinguely] loved the idea of collaboration, of inspiration, of sharing. It was his dream, an old, private dream."[8]

4   See, notably, Pontus Hultén, "La Tête," in Pontus Hultén, *Une magie plus forte que la mort*, Le Chemin vert, Paris 1987; Niki de Saint Phalle, "La Tête de Jean," 1987–1988, in Margrit Hahnloser-Ingold, *Pandémonium—Jean Tinguely*, Ex Libris, Lausanne/ Zurich 1990; *Le Cyclop*, A.C.T.E. 91, Évry 1993; Pontus Hultén, "Un monument pour une génération," *Connaissance des arts*, no. 506 (May 1994); Jill Johnston, "The Cyclops of Fontainebleau," *Art in America*, vol. 84, no. 6, June 1996; Arne Steckmest, *Le Cyclop de Jean Tinguely*, 1996 (film); Louise Faure and Anne Julien, *Le Monstre dans la forêt*, 2005 (film); "Mais... où est passée l'oreille du Cyclop?," France Culture radio broadcast, Atelier de Création Radiophonique, March 28, 1999; Virginie Canal, *Jean Tinguely: Le Cyclop*, Centre National des Arts Plastiques/Isthme Éditions, Paris 2007; and, more recently, Catherine Francblin, *Le Cyclop de Jean Tinguely*, Centre National des Arts Plastiques/ Association Le Cyclop, Paris/Milly-la-Forêt 2022.

5   Although it would be more accurate, chronologically, to refer to la Tête (the Head), here we have decided to employ the work's final title, *Le Cyclop* (The Cyclops) exclusively, although it was little used by Tinguely's various artists and coworkers.

6   Jean Tinguely in 1987, quoted in Arne Steckmest, *Le Cyclop de Jean Tinguely* (film).

7   Ibid.

8   Pontus Hultén, quoted in Louise Faure and Anne Julien, *Le Monstre dans la forêt*.

The story of *Le Cyclop* began well before the 1960s. It might have started the moment Tinguely met other artists—who subsequently became faithful friends and contributors to a project produced by "crazy sculptors."[9] Back in the 1940s, Tinguely had a relationship with Eva Aeppli, with whom he lived for while in Basel at the end of the decade. It was through Aeppli that he met Daniel Spoerri in 1949. In the 1950s the Aeppli-Tinguely couple moved to Paris and frequented many artists. At 11 Impasse Ronsin —a cul-de-sac where they settled in 1955—Tinguely met Claude and François-Xavier Lalanne, who had worked there since 1949 (and who he briefly considered recruiting for *Le Cyclop*), as well as Niki de Saint Phalle (who first entered the premises in 1955 to visit another artist), and Larry Rivers (who was living there in 1961).

In 1954 a decisive encounter took place in Paris when Tinguely met Pontus Hultén, who had not yet become the dynamic director of Stockholm's Moderna Museet (he would be appointed in 1958), but who was already a young exhibition curator extremely open to contemporary experimentation. The very next year Hultén exhibited works by Tinguely in a group show at the Galerie Samlaren in Stockholm, as well as writing several articles on him.

Yves Klein, who Tinguely met in 1955 at the Salon des Réalités Nouvelles, was one of the first artists to collaborate with him. It was not all smooth sailing: for a show at the Galerie Iris Clert titled *Vitesse pure et stabilité monochrome* (Pure Speed and Monochrome Stability, 1958), a joint work called *Excavatrice de l'espace* (Excavator of Space) posed numerous problems for both artists. Tinguely publicly criticized Klein for appropriating the machine in his own name alone; the latter retorted in a long-winded statement, partly written in capital letters: "I'd like to know whether Jean is ready to state before all the witnesses to our argument at La Coupole that this machine is indeed my invention but made under his influence! And then the collaboration will be officially relaunched in a pure spirit of trust in one another! This may sound childish, but that's the way it is!!!!!"[10] The childish nature of these wrangles will be left to the reader's judgment, but the argument did not prevent the two artists from continuing to work together until Klein's death.

Another decisive encounter occurred in 1957 when Tinguely met Bernhard Luginbühl, a Swiss sculptor who, like Tinguely, worked with iron. The friendship that developed was rock solid. That same year Tinguely became friends with the Venezuelan artist Jesús Rafael Soto.

---

9   Jean Tinguely in 1987, quoted in "Mais… où est passée l'oreille du *Cyclop*?"

10   Yves Klein, "Compte rendu de l'exposition en collaboration avec Jean Tinguely," 1958, typewritten manuscript, Archives Yves Klein, Paris.

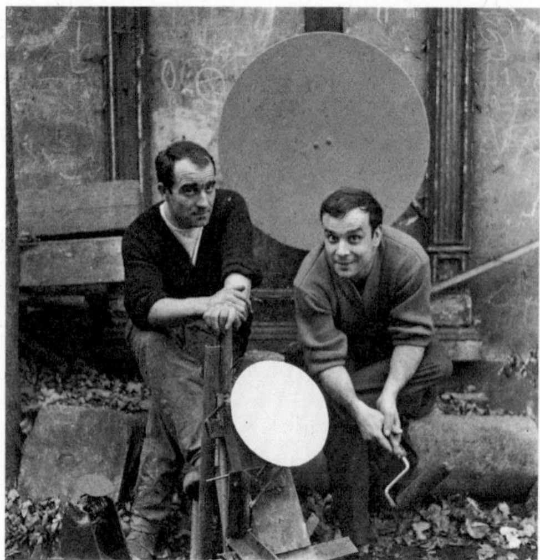

Yves Klein and Jean Tinguely in the courtyard of Impasse Ronsin, Paris, with their works *Excavatrice de l'espace* and *La Vitesse totale*, both 1958

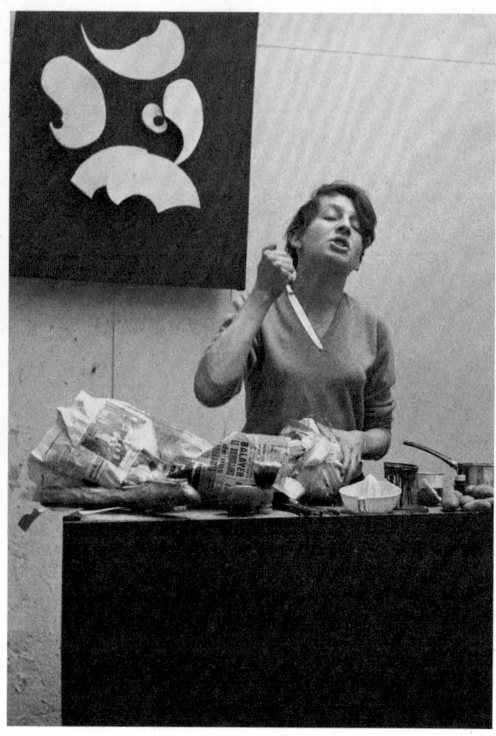

Eva Aeppli in her studio, Impasse Ronsin, Paris, 1959

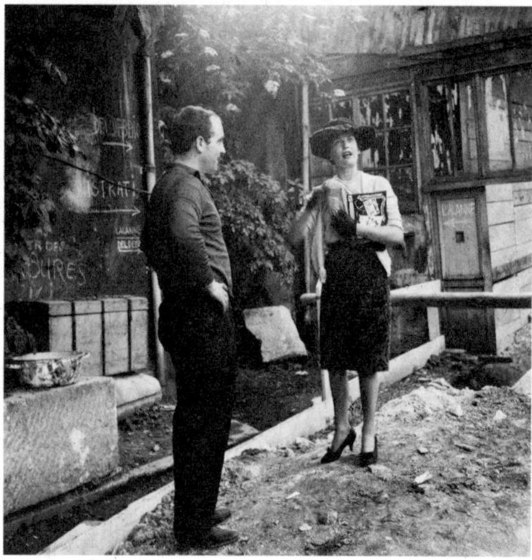

Jean Tinguely and Claude Lalanne, Impasse Ronsin, Paris, c. 1960

In the late 1950s Klein introduced Tinguely to French art critic Pierre Restany, as well as, little by little, the group of artists who Restany labeled Nouveaux Réalistes: Arman, César, and also the *affichistes* artists Mimmo Rotella, François Dufrêne, Raymond Hains, and Jacques Villeglé. Outside Restany's group other friendships sprang up and strengthened—as did animosities. Also in the late 1950s, the workshop on Impasse Ronsin, with its empty lots and easy-going neighbors, swiftly became a workspace for Tinguely alongside other friends. The people who lived and/or worked there, in addition to Aeppli and Saint Phalle (who moved into Tinguely's premises in 1960), included Spoerri (who made his first works there) and Luginbühl. Klein would go there to complete ambitious sculpture projects that were too dirty for his very clean studio in rue Campagne-Première, a 20-minute walk away. And that is where, in 1961, Arman made *NBC Rage: Colère de contrebasse* (NBC Rage: Double Bass Anger). Photographs taken in Impasse Ronsin at the time included other regulars such as Hultén and Restany.[11] Yet neither Hains nor Villeglé seemed to have been invited there, even though they lived in the same neighborhood. As the very artificial Nouveau Réalisme movement petered out, elective affinities determined which members of the group would consort with Tinguely.

Tinguely's artistic network became even more international as the 1960s dawned, abetted by his Franco-German bilingualism. In early 1959, he had a show at the Galerie Schmela in Düsseldorf, when he probably met Günther Uecker, who in February of that year held a masked ball in his honor in his apartment-studio.[12] In January 1960 Tinguely traveled to New York, where he met Louise Nevelson and Robert Rauschenberg. He had long conversations with Marcel Duchamp, who he had met in Paris the previous year. Although none of these artists would produce a work for the future *Cyclop*, all were considered and ultimately incorporated into the project. Uecker's proposal—a huge nail—was dropped. Rauschenberg is mentioned on various drawings and documents by Tinguely, but apparently never proposed anything.[13] Meanwhile, Nevelson (1899–1988) and Duchamp (1887–1968) were the subjects of tributes, to which I will return.

[P. 33, 35]

---

11 See the illustrations in Pontus Hultén's book, *Une magie plus forte que la mort.*

12 On Jean Tinguely's relationship with Germany, see Antje Kramer, *L'Aventure allemande du Nouveau Réalisme, 1957-1963*, Les presses du Réel, Dijon 2012, p 46–47.

13 In 1985, Rauschenberg was still being mentioned on preparatory sketches. See *Le Cyclop* (1993), cover drawing. Rico Weber's 1994 *Le Tableau électrique* (The Distribution Board) still cites Rauschenberg as well as Uecker.

[P. 56]

[P. 64–67]

In the early 1960s Tinguely was involved in various collective projects with some of the artists mentioned above, as well as new-comers. First came a Kinetic art show, *Bewogen Beweging* (Moving Movement) at the Stedelijk Museum in Amsterdam in 1961. Here Tinguely collaborated not on an artwork, but on an entire exhibition, alongside curators Hultén and Willem Sandberg, as well as his artist friend Spoerri. The following year Tinguely worked on an experimental proposal, *Dylaby*, this time exclusively with artists—Spoerri, Rauschenberg, Martial Raysse, Saint Phalle, and Per Olof Ultvedt; Sandberg had invited them to conceive a new show to follow *Bewogen Beweging*, and Tinguely devised a huge, maze-like structure in which each artist would occupy one or several spaces. *Dylaby* was a collective experiment in which every participant retained his or her individuality—no collective artwork was exhibited. But Tinguely was not the only one to envisage participating in a joint action: in 1966 Saint Phalle produced her famous *Hon* (She) for the Moderna Museet. What Hultén called "the Cyclops' mother"[14] was also a kind lab experiment for Tinguely. It required the help of other artists including Tinguely and Ultvedt, as well as assistants like the young artist Rico Weber, who was working as a cook in the museum's restaurant at the time. (In subsequent years Weber would become an important colleague of the Tinguely-Saint Phalle couple.) Also in 1966, Tinguely discussed his plans in an interview with Alain Jouffroy. "I have several ideas, above all *one* idea … [which] concerns something very special—a huge piece I've been imagining, and which I'll do someday. It's a big sculpture that people can move around in. But it's not utopian … I've made a lot of models, a lot of drawings—and one of these days I'm going to start on it, to bring it to life. It will be great, but I don't want to talk about it, because I don't want anyone to swipe so much as a detail or idea—nothing."[15]

Alongside this mysterious statement of intent, Tinguely had made several sketches not yet of a Cyclops, but of a head. During this period he had already been forced to abandon monumental projects such as a cultural amusement park, conceived with Luginbühl and Spoerri. But there was no question, as he stated above, of remaining in a purely utopian realm.

[P. 75]

He and Luginbühl were also working on a culture mall (*kulturstation*) called *Gigantoleum*, an immense structure whose plan turned out to be somewhat chimerical. In a particularly heady text signed by both artists, they speculated on the possibility of creating not just a snack bar, movie theater, shooting gallery, and tactile maze, but also "an aviary with

---

14 Pontus Hultén, "Un monument," p. 82.

15 Alain Jouffroy, "Jean Tinguely," *L'Œil*, no. 136, April 1966, p. 64.

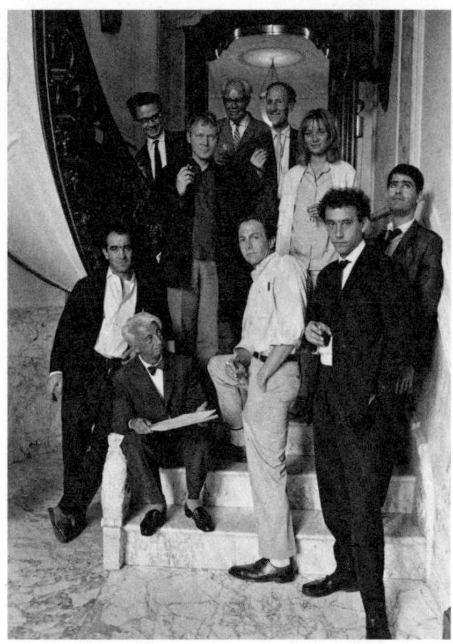

Willem Sandberg, Director of the Stedelijk Museum, Amsterdam, and the artists of the exhibition *Dylaby*, 1962;
foreground: Jean Tinguely, Willem Sandberg, Per Olof Ultvedt, Robert Rauschenberg, Niki de Saint Phalle,
Daniel Spoerri, and Martial Raysse

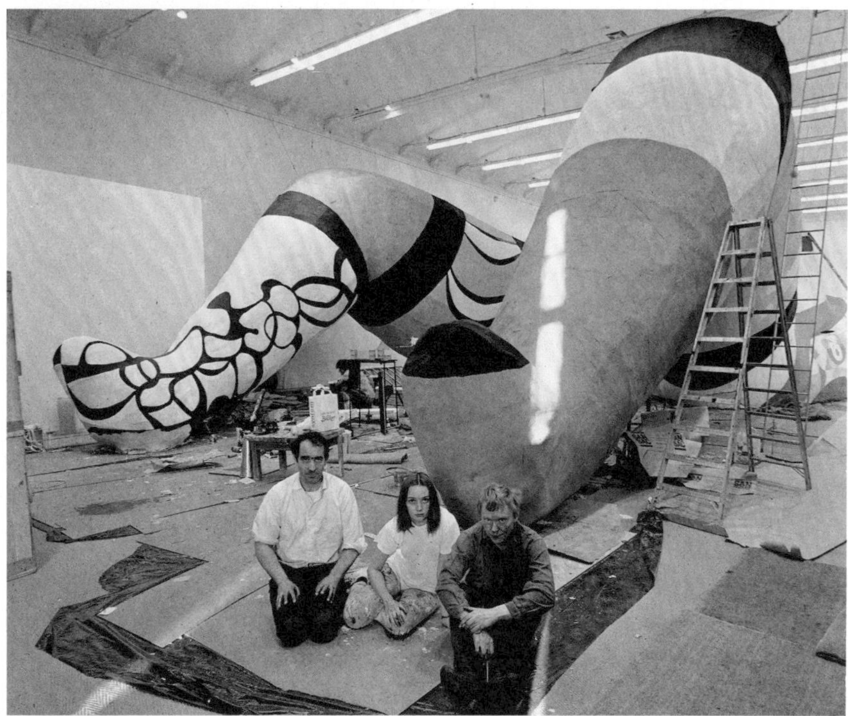

Niki de Saint Phalle, Jean Tinguely, and Per Olof Ultvedt in front of *Hon*, Moderna Museet, Stockholm, 1966

ten thousand sparrows" and a "milk bar with a real cow on grass behind a window with a panoramic view of the Alps," not to mention "a sculptor from Brienz carving life-size bears from wood." In the midst of what seemed like an idealized county fair, there would be "stalls selling ordinary or bizarre things," the "largest slide in the world,"[16] and an "ice-cream factory." Discreetly nestling in this mass of more desirable attractions were "exhibitions of art." It hardly needs pointing out that the call for bids was a flop. What we now call *Le Cyclop* is probably a happy combination of the whimsical amusement park, the impossible-to-produce *Gigantoleum*, and the early Head, all the while following the previous model of *Hon*. The future *Cyclop* was planned to include an initial community of artists and Tinguely's close friends: Saint Phalle, Luginbühl, Spoerri, Ultvedt, Weber, and of course Hultén. When Tinguely and Hultén first met in the mid-1950s, the artist had already spoken to the curator of his desire to build a giant, participatory construction encompassing various fields of art.

In the meantime, Tinguely remained hampered throughout the 1960s by financial and organizational issues concerning the installation of the future *Cyclop*. In 1964 he and Saint Phalle had moved into a former inn, the Auberge du Cheval Blanc, in Soisy-sur-École, a village in the department of Essonne, south of Paris, where he began to seek a site for the project. He and Saint Phalle considered places in various regions of France and abroad—based on friendships and other connections—such as Sicily or Puglia in Italy, North Africa, and Bern, Switzerland. But soon Essonne became a more likely location for a project inevitably so complex to implement. A relative of Saint Phalle who owned an imposing estate in nearby Saint-Vrain, where Aeppli and her husband Samuel Mercer lived, was nearly convinced by the couple to sell them a plot of land. He changed his mind at the last minute, in order to build a zoo.[17] Several accomplices remained very skittish, despite attempts at persuasion.

Ultimately, in May 1970 Saint Phalle bought two small, cheap plots of land in the forest of Milly-la-Forêt, some six miles from Soisy-sur-École. But *Le Cyclop* would only come to fruition if new accomplices were recruited, beginning with the mayor of Milly-la-Forêt, Clovis Lelong. The mayor (from 1968 to 1986) had to agree that Tinguely's mad scheme could be erected on land not zoned for construction. The conciliatory public official granted his permission, even advising the artists not to apply for

[P. 80]

---

16   Here and previous quotes: Bernhard Luginbühl and Jean Tinguely, "Appel d'offre pour la réalisation du *Gigantoleum* par MM. Luginbühl et Tinguely" (July 1968), *Chroniques de l'art vivant,* no. 1 bis, March–April 1969, p. 6.

17   See Niki de Saint Phalle, "La Tête de Jean," p. 306. The logistical details described below are also given by Saint Phalle in her article. Note that the zoo in Saint-Vrain opened in 1974 and closed 25 years later.

official authorization. Other, unanticipated, accomplices became involved in *Le Cyclop*, such as the art collectors Dominique and Jean de Menil, who bought the rest of the plots needed for the project. A modest financial foundation was also required before work could begin: their friend Rainer von Diez—a German prince, art patron, and stage director—provided an initial sum of $10,000. Tinguely and Saint Phalle each sought to contribute an equal amount by selling sculptures. Tinguely, who continued to put money aside, also came up with the idea of a kind of subscription, designing an original lamp that would sell for $10,000. Several collectors committed themselves, in particular Jackie Monnier and Prince Michael and Princess Marina of Greece.

Work began at Milly-la-Forêt, at which point coworkers had to be recruited. Tinguely and Saint Phalle immediately called upon assistants including, obviously, Weber. Tinguely would also be joined from 1987 by Pierre Marie Lejeune, who in the 1980s worked on Saint Phalle's *Fontaine Stravinsky* (Stravinsky Fountain) and *Jardin des Tarots* (Tarot Garden), as well as the couple Philippe and Dorothée Bouveret. Luginbühl brought his assistants into the venture, Rudolf ("Ruedi") Tanner and Paul Wiedmer, the latter a skilled welder. "[Tinguely's] long-armed rico and my long-nosed paul went well together," recalled Luginbühl.[18] In 1970 Tinguely had placed an advertisement in the search for a new assistant, one specialized in welding, and Josef ("Seppi" or "Sepp") Imhof was hired. Unlike most of the other assistants, Imhof had no artistic experience at the time, but worked as a professional welder in a metal factory, after having trained as a locksmith.[19] His skill as an assiduous contributor to *Le Cyclop* was crucial, according to Saint Phalle and Tinguely themselves. Saint Phalle called him "Jean's right-hand man,"[20] while Tinguely referred to the "man of iron" as follows: "[With] my friend Bernhard Luginbühl, and Niki de Saint Phalle, we were a trio, plus Sepp here. He did 99% of the work, I simply provided the advice. I displayed my admiration for the finished piece, I was the No. 1 spectator."[21] Other technicians were subsequently recruited, notably a mason named del Toso (who in 1974 built a brick wall inside the neck of *Le Cyclop*—later called "The del Toso Pillar"), another welder, Martin Bühler, and a man called Big Mike, described by Luginbühl as "a real gladiator straight out of a Hollywood film" who could "spin the girders."[22]

---

18   Letter from Bernhard Luginbühl to Margrit Hahnloser-Ingold, quoted in *Pandémonium*, p. 317 (Luginbühl's lower-case spelling is respected in all excerpts from this letter).

19   My thanks to Seppi Imhof for answering my questions about *Le Cyclop* by email in March 2022. Some additional information comes from this exchange, authorized by Annja Müller-Alsbach, curator of the Museum Tinguely in Basel.

20   Niki de Saint Phalle, "La Tête de Jean," p. 308.

21   Jean Tinguely, 1987, quoted in Arne Steckmest, *Le Cyclop de Jean Tinguely* (film).

22   Letter from Bernhard Luginbühl to Margrit Hahnloser-Ingold, quoted in *Pandémonium*, p. 319.

Perhaps it should be mentioned here that in the 1970s the true core of
Le Cyclop, namely Luginbühl, Spoerri, and Saint Phalle, with their assistants Imhof, Tanner, Weber, and Wiedmer, referred to themselves "Zig and
Puce" after the French comic-book characters.[23] In 1977, when Hultén—
by then director of the Musée National d'Art Moderne—oversaw Tinguely's
installation of his *Crocrodome*[24] in the center's forum, documentation
of the event systematically called it "Zig and Puce's *Crocrodome*."

Tinguely rapidly organized a functioning construction site. For one thing,
contrary to his initial idea of setting the structure straight on the ground,
he allowed himself to be convinced that foundations were required.
Luginbühl, in a letter to Margrit Hahnloser-Ingold, described the chaotic
start.[25] Their assistants would come to work whenever each was able;
in addition, Tinguely and Luginbühl worked with a couple of local scrap
merchants, Guy and Françoise Duperche. In order to avoid conflict,
Tinguely often reduced the team to a minimum: Saint Phalle, Luginbühl,
the assistants, and himself. After the 1980s, the team was apparently often
even smaller, just two or three people.[26] The artists invited to participate
came one by one to install their works.

It should be pointed out that work at Milly-la-Forêt required
complex logistics. There was no water or electricity on the site—Tinguely
had a generator installed. Tinguely and Saint Phalle's apartment on the
third level of *Le Cyclop* was not completed until 1980—sometimes they
had coffee there, scarcely more. Luginbühl mentioned that food was complicated. Tinguely sometimes paid Dutch cooks to arrive with their trucks.
At other times, the couple's friend Roger Nellens—a Belgian artist, patron,
and collector—would bring lunch from Knokke in Belgium (about 400 km
away). Saint Phalle was known to organize lavish picnics. Drinking water,
meanwhile, had to be brought daily. The crucial role of this organization
should not be underestimated. As Luginbühl recalled, "i still hear jeano
asking every day who would bring the water, was there enough water."[27]
People stayed at La Commanderie, a house in Dannemois, near Milly-la-
Forêt, purchased by Tinguely in 1970 in addition to their place in Soisy-sur-
École, which then became a storage. Dannemois also served as a workshop,
for the two towns were just a few miles apart. They were stocked with

23 *Zig et Puce* was a Franco-Belgian comic series
    created by Alain Saint-Ogan in 1925; it ran until
    1969.

24 On the *Crocrodrome*, see *Le Crocrodrome de Zig
    et Puce*, exh. cat., Centre Pompidou, Paris 1977.
    The *Crocrodrome* was accompanied by a *Musée
    Sentimental* and a *Boutique Aberrante*, two works
    by another steadfast friend, Daniel Spoerri.

25 See letter from Bernhard Luginbühl to Margit
    Hahnloser-Ingold, *Pandémonium*, p 316–317.

26 Philippe Bouveret, "Mais… où est passée l'oreille
    du Cyclop?"

27 On all these details, Luginbühl's account can be
    heard in L. Faure and A. Julien, *Le Monstre dans
    la forêt*, as well as read in his letter to Margit
    Hahnloser-Ingold, *Pandémonium*, p 318–319.

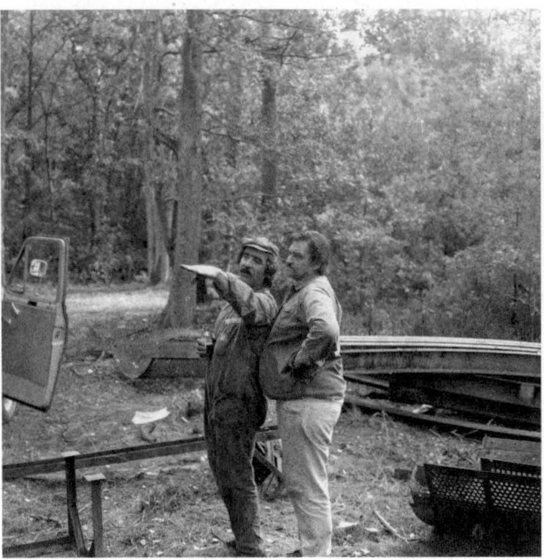

Jean Tinguely and Bernhard Luginbühl at *Le Cyclop*, 1971

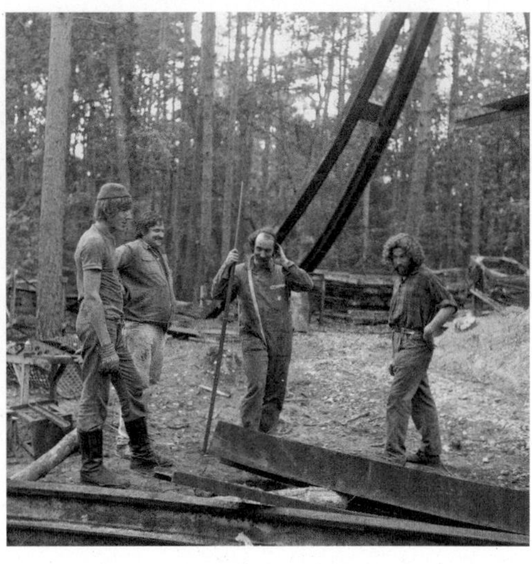

Paul Wiedmer, Bernhard Luginbühl, Jean Tinguely, and Seppi Imhof at *Le Cyclop*, 1971

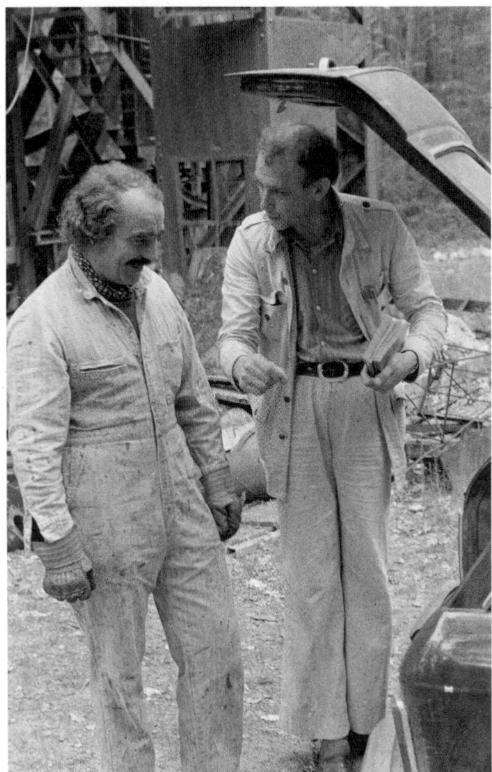

Jean Tinguely and Daniel Spoerri at *Le Cyclop*, 1976

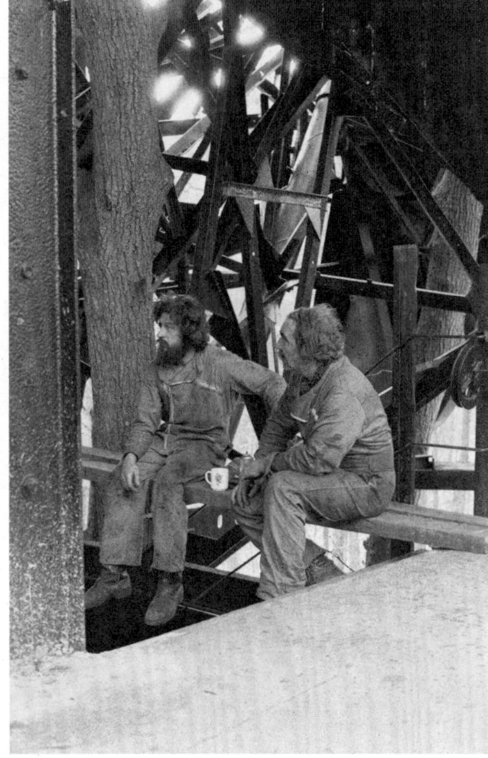

Seppi Imhof and Jean Tinguely at *Le Cyclop*, 1981

supplies in anticipation of the summer's picnics. The partners of some artists also pitched in, such as Wiedmer's wife, Jacqueline Dolder, and Luginbühl's spouse, Ursula. She was herself a potter, and she regularly went to the construction site of *Le Cyclop* with the couple's four children —Brutus, Basil, Jwan and Eva, born in 1958, 1960, 1963, and 1966, respectively—who organized numerous barbecues. As Imhof also explained, the coworkers also improvised a living room on the ground floor, where they made coffee. Finally, when it came to more basic needs, "there were no toilets in the Head, but plenty of trees in the forest."[28] The atmosphere was enthusiastic nevertheless, according to Saint Phalle. "Life … at Soisy and La Commanderie was joyous, we had a lot of fun. They [Tinguely, Imhof, and Weber] spoke Swiss-German in a dreadful dialect I didn't even attempt to understand. I liked to daydream and wasn't bothered by their racket, like cranking gears that reminded me of Jean's machines."[29] Luginbühl remembers "the astonished people who looked at our work with joy, as though it was all perfectly obvious—Pontus Hultén, for instance, laughed with delight on seeing us do it."[30]

Given the situation, it is easy to understand why it was impossible to assemble all the artists at the same time, as well as why work on *Le Cyclop* progressed in intensive stages, usually during the summer. By the end of the 1970s, off-periods would be subject to regular invasions by vandals. Saint Phalle described Tinguely's attitude toward these anti-collaborators. "At first, I had the impression Jean felt it was a game, he tried to be cleverer than the aggressors by making phony doors. Little by little, la Tête became a fortress. But that kind of game doesn't last long. Jean got fed up. He began to think of allowing la Tête to rot in the forest—of abandoning it. He tried to imagine how it might be, all broken and overgrown with vegetation, swallowed up by the forest. So the Sleeping Beauty period began: very little happened on la Tête for several years, just enough to maintain it. La Tête fell asleep."[31]

In fact, it seems that Tinguely initially drew additional energy from the vandalism, countering the unwelcome visitors by devising several entrances, with real and phony doors. But the repetitive, intense damage done in the 1980s led him to consider moving the collective installation piece by piece, temporarily halting work. Potential new sites included the park of Saint-Cloud (outside Paris), Australia, and California. But Tinguely wanted the work to remain linked to the Centre Pompidou.

28   Emails from Seppi Imhof, March 2022.
29   Niki de Saint Phalle, "La Tête de Jean," p. 309.
30   Letter from Bernhard Luginbühl to Margit Hanhloser-Ingold, *Pandémonium*, p. 320.
31   Ibid., p. 310.

It was ultimately donated to the French government in 1987, along with all the complex maintenance it entailed.

But let us now return to the artistic contributions to *Le Cyclop*. How can we attain a global conception of a monumental project designed to be a mélange of the desires of all the artists contacted by Tinguely? The beginnings were a little laborious, even if "right from the start," according to Imhof, "Jean knew exactly what the head would look like." He nevertheless added that "the other elements arrived more or less by chance, there was no real 'blueprint.' The organization of work depended on our whims and on the weather."[32] While sketches show a giant head from the very beginning, which slowly turned into a Cyclops, Tinguely's expectations regarding the artists he hoped would contribute remained fairly vague. Some proposals were swiftly implemented, such as those by Luginbühl and Saint Phalle. In addition, Tinguely initially hoped to show works by Spoerri, Soto, and Rivers. The first and the second levels were built in 1971. Works were grafted onto the metal structure as things progressed, which fascinated Saint Phalle. "For me it was a little like a fairy tale, seeing all those crazy Swiss guys 20 meters off the ground, with no vertigo, carrying iron bars with incredible casualness. It was a terrific show. Jean's dream was coming together little by little."[33]

One thing that is immediately striking to anyone who takes an interest in the work: early on, Tinguely wanted to bring together numerous artists, who were asked to make specific proposals for the project. His preparatory sketches often clearly include names, many of whom did not reappear later, such as Rauschenberg, Uecker, as well as other friends of the artist such as Gérald Minkoff, the Lalannes, Julian Schnabel, Keith Haring, Edward Keinholz, Ben Vautier, and Dieter Roth. Little is known about these non-participations. Did they not happen due to technical complexities, or simply because the artists did not feel like investing in a project that demanded distinct physical and material availability?

[P. 33, 35]

    For that matter, some artists acknowledged reticence about Tinguely's overall plan. Jean Pierre Raynaud, for example, was unsympathetic to the collective nature of *Le Cyclop*. As he later explained, "I remember telling him, 'Listen, Jean, I can carry out a project on my own, but group projects are not my strong point.' But I couldn't refuse."[34] Raynaud went off on a tangent, proposing a huge yardstick (*La Jauge*; The Gauge) at the entrance

---

32   Here and previous quote: Seppi Imhof, quoted in Arne Steckmest, *Le Cyclop de Jean Tinguely* (film).

33   Niki de Saint Phalle, "La Tête de Jean," p. 308.

34   Jean Pierre Raynaud, quoted in Arne Steckmest, *Le Cyclop de Jean Tinguely* (film).

to the structure, which was finally installed in 1975. "So I am there, present and yet absent, like a sort of marker through the red that I had got just right back then … I am there, we are there together. Separate, but together."[35] Other artists did not manage to come up with a fully convincing idea, postponing their contribution for several years. Arman, who finally found a spot for his Plexiglas-encased *L'Accumulation de gants* (The Accumulation of Gloves), dithered for several years, only concretely producing the work in the early 1990s, shortly after Tinguely died, and at Saint Phalle's request. César's project, for that matter, dates from 1994, and consists of two *Compressions* made of scrap metal from *Le Cyclop*. And yet César had expressed enthusiasm: "If Jean Tinguely had asked me to climb up a tree, I would have done it! Because I liked him, I mean because I liked his work."[36] He even admitted that he no longer knew whether the idea was his or Tinguely's. These examples nevertheless demonstrate not only how convincing Tinguely and Saint Phalle were, but also the wide-open dimension of the project, continuing after death of the former thanks to the perseverance of the latter.

Even if technical constraints sometimes slowed progress on *Le Cyclop*, certain works were designed early on. This was the case, for example, with Ultvedt's structure (1973), with Spoerri's reconstruction of a Paris hotel room (1976), and Aeppli's *Hommage aux déportés* (Homage to the Deportees, begun in 1976), whose main complexity resided in suspending a 1930s train carriage. Bought for the occasion by Prince Michael and Princess Marina of Greece, the ten-ton railroad car had two be lifted 15 meters from the ground. Meanwhile, Soto's *Le Pénétrable sonore* (The Resonating Penetrable) had been noticed by Tinguely in the 1970s, and he had asked the artist to reserve it for the future *Cyclop*. "He said, 'I would like to do something that will bring all my friends together,' in a kind of head."[37] Soto's work was installed in 1993, after Tinguely's death. The set of paintings on Plexiglas panels by Rivers, *Hommage à Mai 68* (Homage to May 68), was planned by the artist in the 1970s, but only installed in 1994. *Le Cyclop* as it exists today probably resembles, in part, Tinguely's nebulous wishes of the 1970s, but it would never be seen as such by its originator.

It is worth noting the extent to which Tinguely wished to acknowledge what he owed to his collaborators at the start as well as the end of the project. Most of the assistants who contributed to *Le Cyclop* were

---

35   Ibid.
36   César, quoted in Arne Steckmest, *Le Cyclop de Jean Tinguely* (film).

37   Jesús Rafael Soto, quoted in Philippe Bouveret, "Mais… où est passée l'oreille du *Cyclop*?"

able to sign their work. This point is worth emphasizing, because the project is too often described as a collective work in which "artists" simply had their work installed in place by "assistants" reduced to a purely technical role. We know for certain that Tinguely viewed himself primarily as a "head engineer," an "initiator" who "often turned into the assistant of [his] assistant."[38] Indeed, the assistants were fully integrated into the creative process behind *Le Cyclop*—Imhof made *La Tour Imhof* (The Imhof Tower) as early as 1972. Weber made his *Gisants* (Recumbent Statues) in 1978: plaster casts arrayed outside showing him asleep, decomposing more or less rapidly—the first casts were installed in 1994. Weber also produced *Le Tableau électrique* (The Distribution Board), a trompe-l'oeil electrical panel with the names of the people who helped to build *Le Cyclop*. After Tinguely's death, Philippe Bouveret and Pierre Marie Lejeune produced other works within and around *Le Cyclop*: the former made *Le Tableau générique* (The Generic Plaque) and contributed to *Le Petit Théâtre* (The Little Theater), while the latter produced *Le Siège-rameur du Petit Théâtre* (The Little Theater's Rowing Seat) and transformed a firetruck into a ticket office. Although neither Armin Heusser (another of Tinguely's assistants, if apparently not on this project) nor Paul Wiedmer ultimately created a work for *Le Cyclop*, they at least appear in a sketch dating from the 1980s.[39]

A further singularity in connection with contributions from other artists lies in the incorporation, in various ways, of art world figures Tinguely held to be legendary. During his lifetime, four tributes to artists he admired—living and dead—were installed, making them contributors despite themselves. The execution of some of these can be attributed to Tinguely (usually with help from Imhof), while others were made by Luginbühl. Tinguely first wished to honor two masters who partly shaped his artistic commitment, namely Marcel Duchamp and Kurt Schwitters (1887–1948). The tribute to the former, who died in 1968, consisted of a real chocolate grinder (*La Broyeuse de chocolat*), placed directly onto the forest floor as early as 1978. When it came to the latter, *Le Méta-Merzbau* (The Meta-Merzbau, 1976–1981), devised by Tinguely, is a respectful pastiche in welded metal of the German artist's domestic plaster construction, which had strongly impressed the young Swiss artist when a student. That same year, Tinguely started his *Hommage à Yves Klein* (Homage to Yves Klein) at the top of *Le Cyclop*, in memory of his friend who had died suddenly in 1962. This work is neither a copy nor a parody, but rather

---

38   Jean Tinguely, 1987, quoted in Arne Steckmest, *Le Cyclop de Jean Tinguely* (film).

39   *Le Cyclop*, 1993, p. 37.

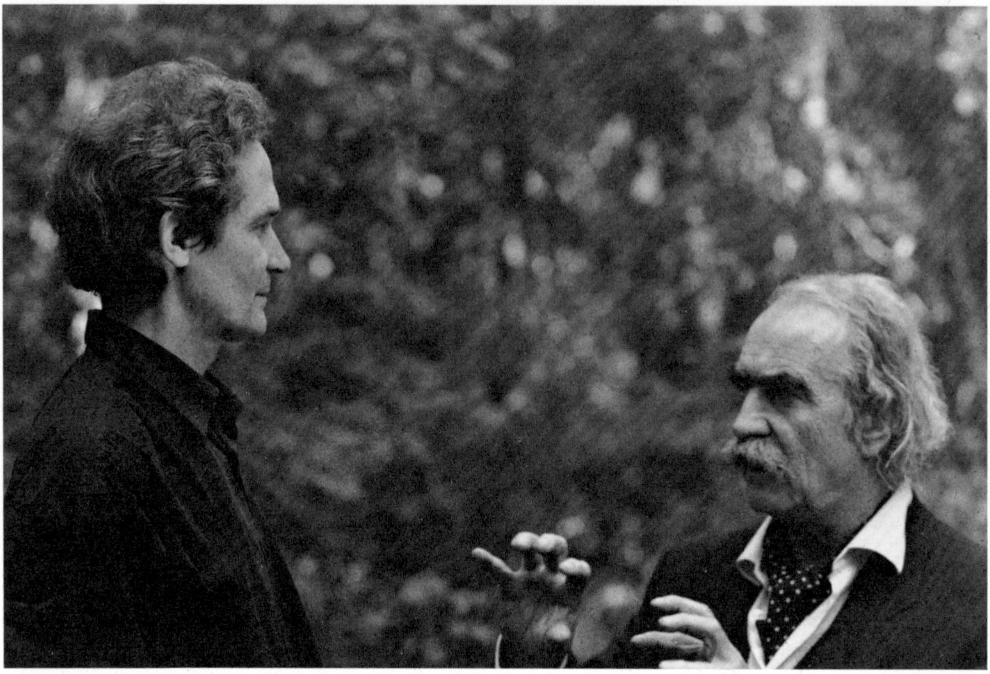

Jean Tinguely and Jean Pierre Raynaud at *Le Cyclop*, 1990

Rico Weber at *Le Cyclop* in front of *Le Tableau électrique*, c. 1994

a way of recalling Klein's fascination with the ever-shifting blue of the sky. Unlike much of *Le Cyclop*, where sound plays a key role—just think of the creaking *La Méta-Harmonie* (The Meta-Harmony), the clashing steel balls of *La Dégringolade* (The Helter-Skelter), and above all the outsized carillon of *Le Pénétrable sonore*—the tribute to Klein is experienced in silence. This meditative work is disturbed only by birdsong and the rustle of leaves in the surrounding trees. Finally, in 1978 Luginbühl completed *Hommage à Louise Nevelson* (Homage to Louise Nevelson), in which the American artist's assemblages of wood are pastiched in a huge relief of cast concrete, employing industrial objects, some of which remained imprisoned in the concrete, which was then painted black.

After Tinguely died, Saint Phalle wanted to complete the tributes anticipated by her husband, and therefore installed two new works, neither of which had been executed during the artist's lifetime. The first was a set of works by Giovanni Battista Podestà (1895–1976), collected by Tinguely. He had no direct connection to the Italian artist, who died in 1976, and apparently the two men never met.[40] Tinguely had wished to give Podestà a place in *Le Cyclop*, and the *Piccolo Museo* (Small Museum), installed in 1993, testifies to that desire to include him in the circle of friends and masters. One final curiosity, ultimately installed in 1994, but also initiated by Tinguely, must be mentioned. On the second floor of the structure, in a niche covered with countless shards of mirror (as is the Cyclops' huge face), a small metallic model is displayed. The model is an enlarged reproduction of the molecule RU 486, used in the abortion pill developed in 1982 by Dr. Étienne-Émile Baulieu (b. 1928) as an alternative to suction curettage. A label signed by the doctor reads, "Jean asked me: place your pill (RU 486) among artists. We, too, deal with intolerance, but for science it is serious." The apolitical aspect of *Le Cyclop* crumbles with this implacable statement by Tinguely, a staunch defender of liberty. Indeed, when this item was installed within the giant work, activists distributed leaflets signed by "anti-abortion artists and pro-life feminists" who protested against the "poison pill" and "the elimination of human beings through abortion." They demanded that "this model of RU 486 be withdrawn from the sculpture of *Le Cyclop* not only because of its message of death, but also because it is not a real artwork."[41] Predictably, the pro-lifers were not asking for the destruction of Tinguely and Saint Phalle's *L'Incitation au Suicide* (Incitement to Suicide, 1978/c. 1992), but just of this model—which,

---

40 On this piece, see in particular Baptiste Brun, "Au Cyclop dessillant: L'antimusée de Jean Tinguely au regard du *Piccolo Museo Podestà*," in François Taillade (ed.), *La Forêt réenchantée: Une saison au Cyclop de Jean Tinguely*, Association Le Cyclop/ Centre National des Arts Plastiques, Milly-la-Forêt/ Paris 2015, p. 49–52.

41 See Arne Steckmest, *Le Cyclop de Jean Tinguely* (film).

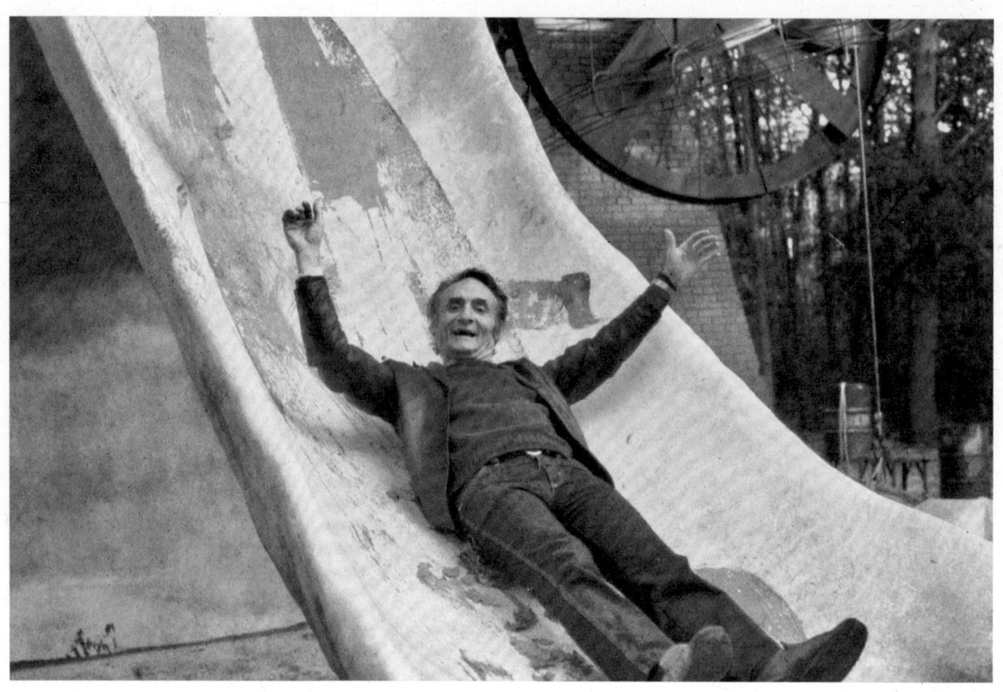

Larry Rivers at *Le Cyclop*, 1978

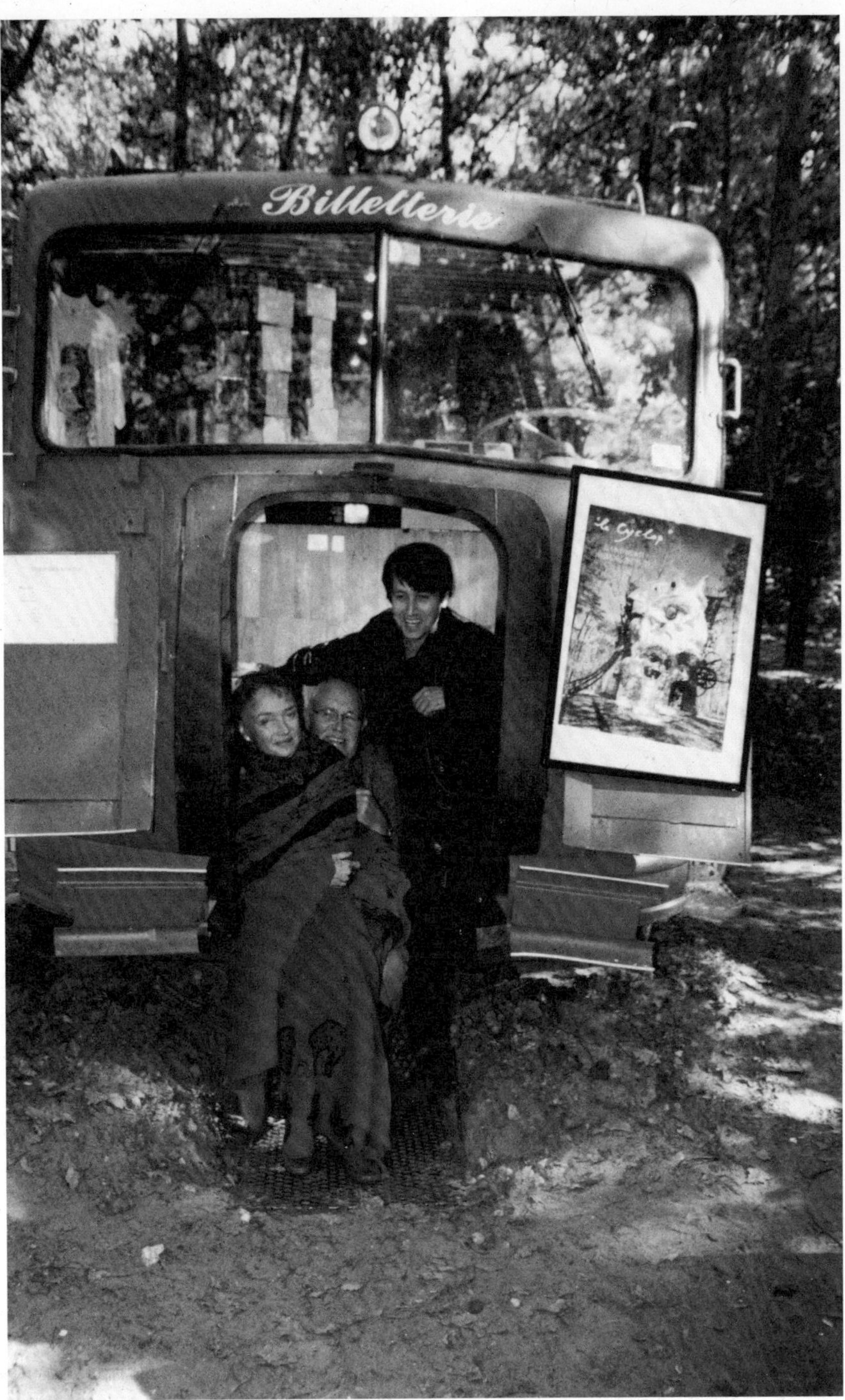

Niki de Saint Phalle, Pontus Hultén, and Pierre Marie Lejeune seated in the fire truck converted into a ticket office by Lejeune, 1997

by the way, is highly abstract and metaphorical. Dr. Baulieu, when questioned about these demonstrations, serenely stated that "intolerant people do not allow others, especially women, to decide whether or not to have a child in a free, responsible, dignified way." But, he went on, "they see that our view of things, which is simultaneously free, bold, realistic, and positive for people, is now winning out, and that their old prejudices—often the product of ignorance, for that matter—are crumbling."[42] There is nothing trivial about the presence of *La Molécule RU 486* in *Le Cyclop*: it probably contributes to the "self-depedestalization" proclaimed by Tinguely.[43]

Le Cyclop as we know it today is a collective symphony, signed by an orchestra conductor named Jean Tinguely yet welcoming multiple collaborations within it, many of them finally completed or installed after his death, in accordance with his wishes. His accomplices worked, one after another, for nearly 30 years to bring this gentle monster to life. It is the fruit of Tinguely's true admiration and love for works by his friends, gathered around a shared project. "We dream of utopia and unlimited action (which is illusory, I know) and we adopt an attitude of Research into Gratuitous and Useless Acts. And we're perfectly happy this way, provided that no one prevents us from working (like mad—it goes without saying)."[44] As Saint Phalle commented, referring to the exchanges and collaborations triggered by Tinguely's project, "everything grew like flowers"[45]—proof, if it were needed, that folly had sewn more than just a few seeds around *Le Cyclop*.

---

42   Ibid.
43   After Jean Tinguely died, his daughter-in-law Laura Duke Condominas had four cushions in the apartment in *Le Cyclop* embroidered with the phrase, *Et ne pas oublier l'autodépiedestalification* (Don't forget self-depedestalization) (see p. 302).
44   Jean Tinguely, *Jean Tinguely. Le Cyclop*, p. 16.
45   Niki de Saint Phalle, *Le Cyclop*, 1993, p. 14.

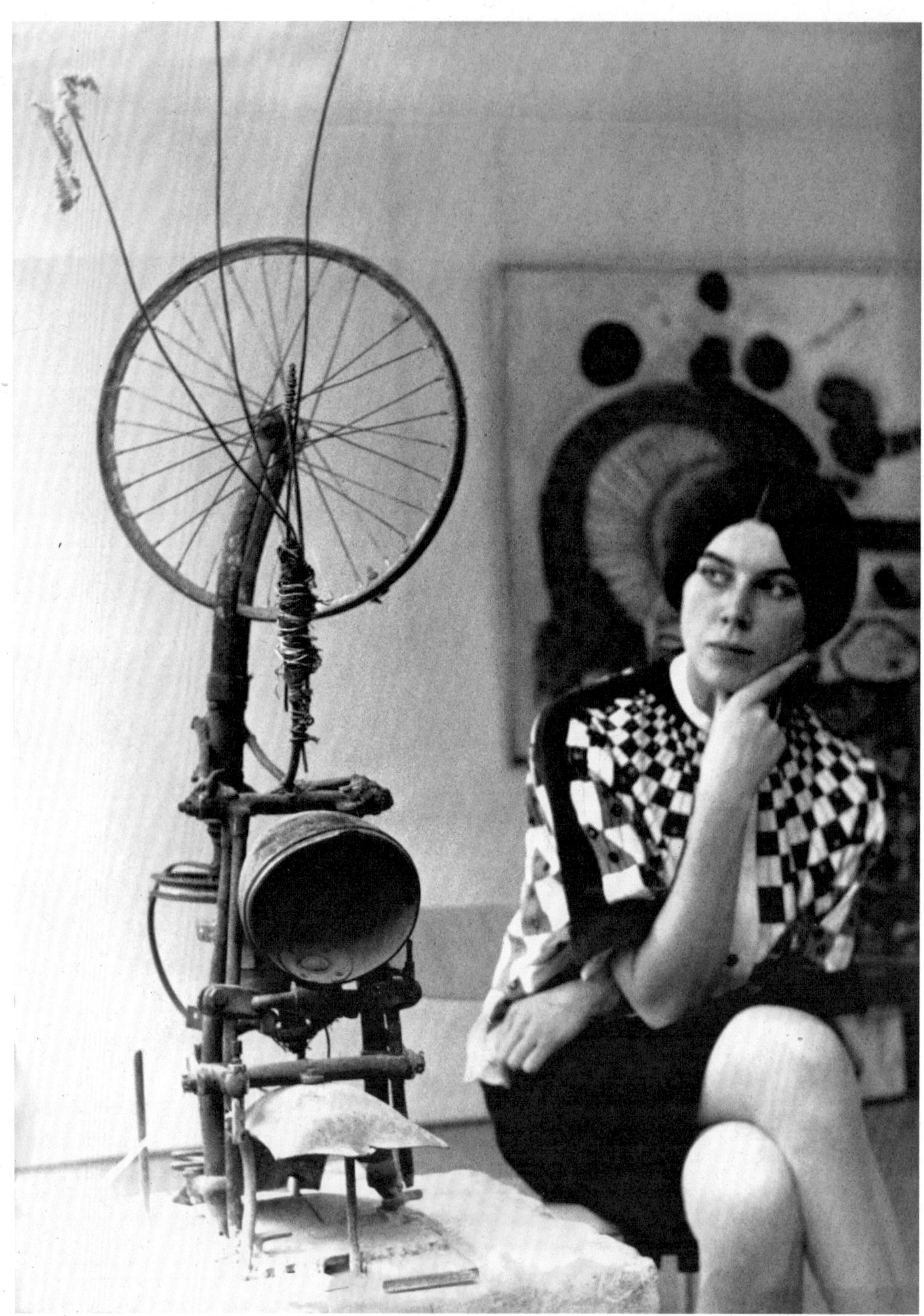

Viewer next to *Hommage à Duchamp* (1960) by Jean Tinguely, Galerie Zwirner, Cologne, June 2, 1965

**Beyond *The Chocolate Grinder*
Jean Tinguely's Homage to Marcel Duchamp
in *Le Cyclop***
Jill Carrick

"We look for the fathers of every astonishing development in art, and Duchamp is always among them. He is Dada, he is also the father of certain forms of Realism, certainly of Nouveau Réalisme. He is always difficult to pigeonhole, and there is a great deal that he foreshadowed."[1]
    —Jean Tinguely, 1987

Jean Tinguely's vast building-sculpture *Le Cyclop* consists in part of homages to major figures of 20th-century art such as Marcel Duchamp (1887–1968), Kurt Schwitters (1887–1948), and Louise Nevelson (1899–1988). Built largely in secret in a forest outside of Paris, it was created collaboratively by Tinguely and a group of artist friends, and its joyous celebration of both collectivity and different artists' individual visions is reflected in its homages to artists past and present.[2] Tinguely's contribution *La Broyeuse de chocolat: Hommage à Duchamp* (The Chocolate Grinder:

---

1   Jean Tinguely in "Often Neglected—But One of the Greats. Interview with Jean Tinguely by Dieter Daniels," Cologne, January 12, 1987, available at www.hgb-leipzig.de/daniels/Dieter-Daniels_Interview-Tinguely_Often-Neglected-But-One-of-the-Greats.pdf, p. 5 (last accessed May 2025). Also published in *Marcel Duchamp*, exh. cat., Museum Tinguely, Basel, Hatje Cantz Verlag, Ostfildern-Ruit 2002.

2   *Le Cyclop*'s official titled homages include tributes to Marcel Duchamp, Kurt Schwitters, Yves Klein, Louise Nevelson, and Gustave Eiffel. Other homages pay tribute to William Tell, Étienne-Émile Baulieu, the events of May 1968 in France, and World War II deportees.

Homage to Duchamp, 1977, installed in 1978) is an acknowledged homage to Duchamp, and it signals his interest in both the earlier artist's work, and Dada more generally. Careful scrutiny of *Le Cyclop*, moreover, reveals that Tinguely's response to Duchamp goes far beyond *La Broyeuse de chocolat*, and may well involve a rethinking of and playful engagement with one of Duchamp's most famous works, *La Mariée mise à nu par ses célibataires, même (Le Grand Verre) (The Bride Stripped Bare by Her Bachelors, Even [The Large Glass]*, 1915–1923).

Le Cyclop*'s articulation of relationships to Duchamp and Dada is far more complex than is generally acknowledged. As the following essay suggests, this engagement stemmed in part from Tinguely's deep and sustained interest in Duchamp, and in part from the work of Pontus Hultén, the former director of the Moderna Museet in Stockholm and first director of the Musée National d'Art Moderne between 1973 and 1981. Hultén, a collaborator on *Le Cyclop*, was, like Tinguely, engaged in rethinking Duchamp's and Dada's legacy and connections to Neo-Dada during the period of *Le Cyclop*'s construction. Tinguely, with input from Hultén, forged a dazzlingly multifaceted contribution to this project with the help of his artist-contributor friends. *La Broyeuse de chocolat: Hommage à Duchamp* offers just one of many possible lenses through which to catch glimpses of *Le Cyclop*'s shifting, multi-layered dialogue with Dada.

The Chocolate Grinder: Homage to Duchamp

Close to the entrance of *Le Cyclop*, near the foot of the building, visitors are likely to encounter Tinguely's homage to Duchamp. It consists of a large old-fashioned machine comprising two heavy millstones on a circular metal base. Visitors may recognize this imposing object as a real machine used in chocolate factories, and indeed, such objects were admired by Tinguely, whose father is reported to have worked in a chocolate factory in Switzerland.[3] The found object, titled *La Broyeuse de chocolat: Hommage à Duchamp*, doubles as a "readymade" sculpture, and references Duchamp's early 20th-century paintings of cocoa mills, namely *La Broyeuse de chocolat I* and *II* of 1913 and 1914. Where Duchamp, however, claimed his works sought to embody a "completely ... *dry* conception of art"[4] based on the

---

3   See Frank Popper, "Tinguely: Inspired Anarchist. Tinguely's Auto-Destructive Period (1960–1962)," in Mario Amaya (ed.), *Art and Artists 1*, no. 5, August 1966, p. 12. Tinguely emphasized his enthusiasm for chocolate grinders: "I really like classic industrial machines, such as packaging machines or chocolate grinders, I'm sensitive to their visual beauty," in Alain Jouffroy, "Jean Tinguely," *L'Œil*, April 1966, p. 39.

4   "I wanted to go back to a completely *dry* drawing, a *dry* conception of art," Marcel Duchamp, interview with James Johnson Sweeney, "Regions which are not ruled by time and space," 1955, in Michel Sanouillet and Elmer Peterson (eds.), *The Writings of Marcel Duchamp*, Da Capo Press, New York 1973, p. 130.

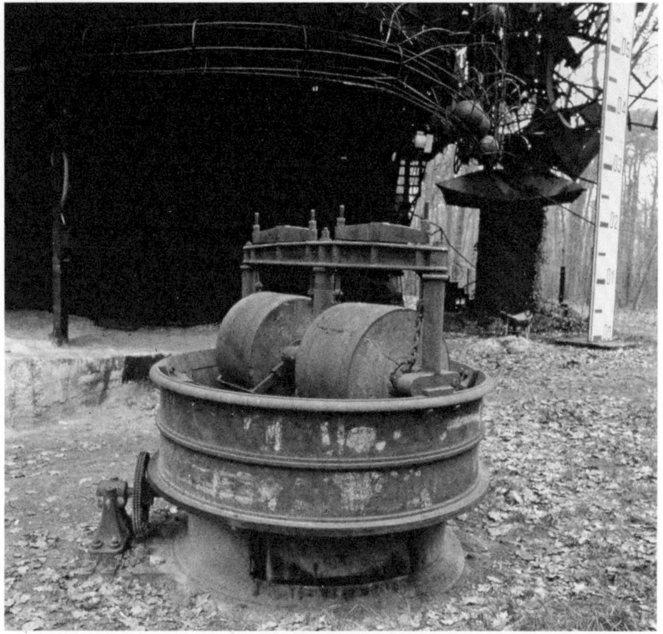

Jean Tinguely, *La Broyeuse de chocolat: Hommage à Duchamp*, 1977 (installed 1978)

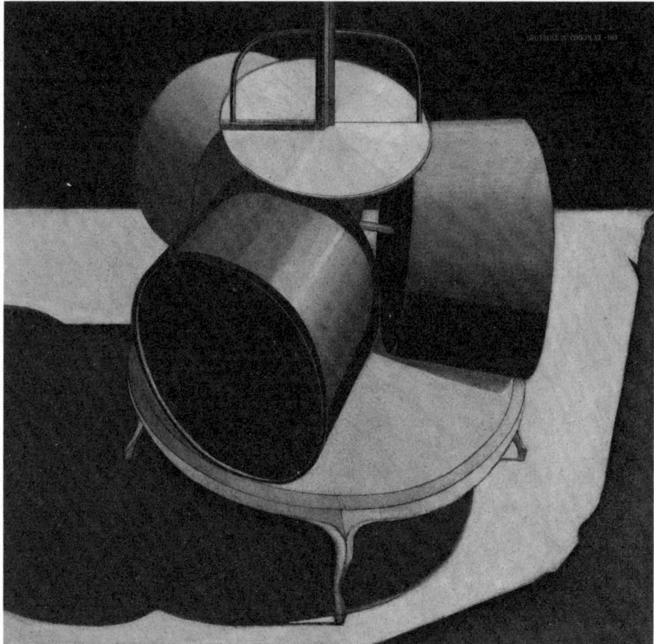

Marcel Duchamp
Chocolate Grinder No. 1, 1913
Oil on canvas, 61.9 × 64.5 cm
Collection Philadelphia Museum of Art, Philadelphia; bequest of Louise & Walter Arensberg, 1950

impersonal, precise style of mechanical drawings, Tinguely's *La Broyeuse de chocolat* emphasizes materiality and mass. Flipping the idealism and abstraction of Duchamp's images, *Le Cyclop* cocoa mill overtly displays its signs of weathering and prior use.[5]

Before arriving at *Le Cyclop*, *La Broyeuse de chocolat* had previously been on show in 1977 at the newly-opened Centre Pompidou, in the inaugural exhibition dedicated to Marcel Duchamp (*L'Œuvre de Marcel Duchamp* [*The Work of Marcel Duchamp*], February 2–May 2, 1977). The same year, the museum, under the leadership of its director Pontus Hultén, also hosted a vast interactive installation by Tinguely and his friends entitled *Le Crocrodrome de Zig et Puce* (The Crocrodrome of Zig and Puce, June 1, 1977–January 2, 1978). The latter included a giant dragon paw covered with edible chocolate available for children to sample.[6] While the Duchamp exhibition offered a retrospective of the work of the celebrated Dadaist, the *Crocrodrome* presented visitors with cutting-edge contemporary Neo-Dada art. Tinguely's subsequent incorporation of *La Broyeuse de chocolat* into *Le Cyclop* signaled its deep connection to this latter "Neo" phase of Dada. The readymade artwork—no longer a new, store-bought acquisition in the manner of Duchamp's *Porte-bouteilles* (*Bottle Rack*, 1914), but rather a mechanical object marked with physical traces of industrial use—now found itself repositioned in a secret fun-house setting with an edge. In a certain sense, Tinguely had trumped Duchamp, and over the coming years *Le Cyclop* would continue to process and reconceptualize Duchamp's lessons.

Tinguely remarked that one of the earliest Duchamp works he encountered was a photograph by Man Ray and Duchamp titled *Élevage de poussière* (*Dust Breeding*, 1920). When asked retrospectively about his knowledge of Duchamp in 1942 while still an art student, he explained that his impression of Duchamp at that time was "very inexact, very strange […] There were these incredible photos that he did together with Man Ray—the dust collecting on *The Large Glass*. That wasn't easy to understand."[7] Later, during the mid-1950s, his knowledge of Duchamp's work grew, encouraged by Hultén. In 1955 Tinguely helped persuade the Parisian Galerie Denise René

---

5   Pontus Hultén has elaborated on Tinguely's love of old, weathered machines: "Tinguely values the ornamentation on old machines, because it is an expression of human caring and love, which are often missing today. He loves the patina that results from continual use and handling, the traces of a long and busy life in the service of men. This feeling, and the awareness that man is the maker of the machine, spring more readily to mind with older forms of technology." In Pontus Hultén, *Jean Tinguely: Méta*, trans. Mary Whittall, New York Graphic Society, Boston 1975, p. 307–308.

6   The pseudonym "Zig et Puce" included the following group of artists: Seppi Imhof, Bernhard Luginbühl, Niki de Saint Phalle, Daniel Spoerri, Ruedi Tanner, Jean Tinguely, Rico Weber, and Paul Wiedmer. See https://www.centrepompidou.fr/en/program/calendar/event/ciyo9r (last accessed May 2025).

7   Jean Tinguely in "Often Neglected," p. 4–5.

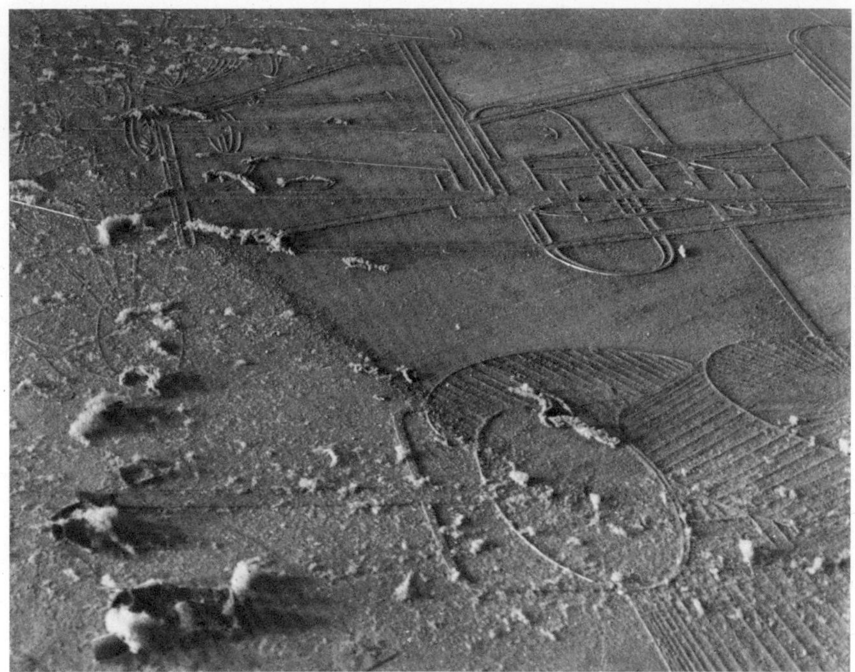

Marcel Duchamp and Man Ray
Dust Breeding, 1920
Silver print, 9.20 × 12 cm

[P. 102, 111]

to exhibit Duchamp's spinning *Rotoreliefs* in Paris, and five years later he completed one of several homages to Duchamp. *Homage to Marcel Duchamp* (1960) is a motorized, noisy salute to Duchamp's famous *Roue de bicyclette* (*Bicycle Wheel*) readymade of 1913, and consists of a shaking, agitated bicycle wheel positioned on a stone base, the latter taken from sculptor Constantin Brancusi's studio. Another unconventional tribute, *Frigo Duchamp* (Duchamp Fridge, 1960), consists of a refrigerator that once belonged to Duchamp, which Tinguely equipped with a bright red interior and a New York fire siren that goes off when the door is opened. As if blowing off the dust that had settled on the mechanical forms depicted in Duchamp and Ray's *Dust Breeding*, Tinguely boldly reanimated key elements of Duchamp's artistic vocabulary.

A transfigured section of *Dust Breeding*, moreover, indirectly reappears in Tinguely's *Hommage à Duchamp* in *Le Cyclop*. The forms of Duchamp's *Chocolate Grinder* are visible in the enigmatic 1920 photograph's lower right, which depicts part of Duchamp's celebrated "unfinished" work *The Large Glass* after it had accumulated "a year's worth of dust."[8] Duchamp described his *Chocolate Grinder* (1913) painting as a study, its motif "to be copied and transferred from this canvas to *The Large Glass*."[9] Rather than a stand-alone, it was thus conceived as part of a larger composition.

Duchamp's *The Large Glass* presents a strange mechanical world where seduction, sexual desire, and the physical shifts and movements that accompany such states are playfully evoked through images of implicitly anthropomorphic machines. Within the composition, a Bride half-floats, half-dangles above a group of Bachelors below, while a chocolate grinder positioned close to the Bachelors represents, according to Duchamp, the Bachelor-voyeurs' masturbatory actions. Duchamp equipped the chocolate mill with a mast-like mechanical rod protruding from its center, a detail that visually links the chocolate grinder with other mechanical parts of the Bachelors' domain. In Duchamp's imaginary scenario, however, the male and female protagonists never physically meet. For Duchamp, who outlined many of his interpretations of the work in a series of notes and sketches entitled *La Boîte verte* (*The Green Box*), *The Large Glass* is an allegory of frustrated love.

---

8   See www.metmuseum.org/art/collection/search/271420 (last accessed May 2025).

9   Marcel Duchamp, "À propos de moi-même (*Broyeuse de chocolat*, 1914)," in Michel Sanouillet and Paul Matisse (eds.), *Duchamp du Signe*, Flammarion, Paris 2013, p. 249.

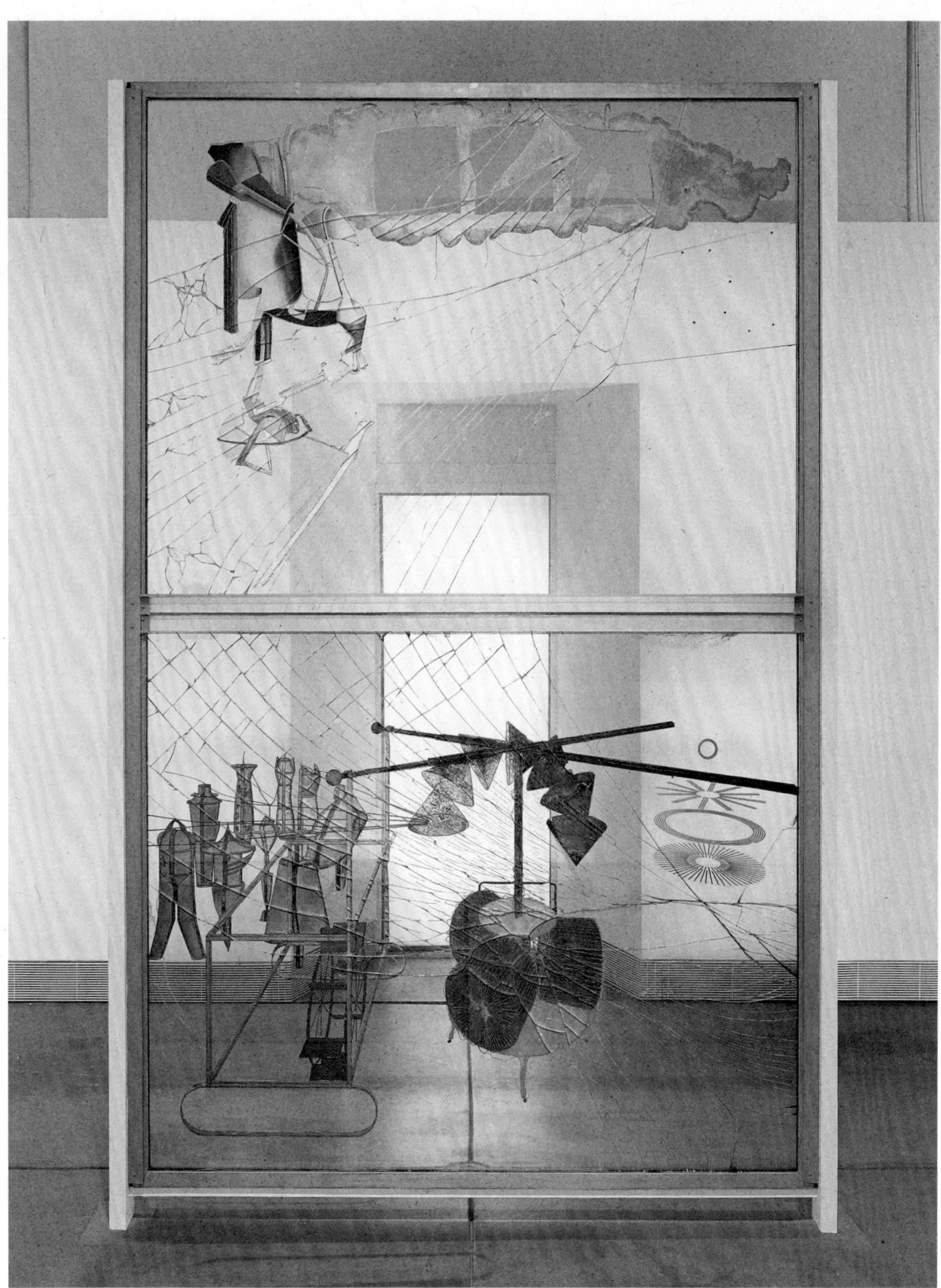

Marcel Duchamp
The Bride Stripped Bare by Her Bachelors, Even (The Large Glass), 1915–1923
Oil, varnish, lead foil, lead wire, and dust on two glass panels, 277.5 × 177.8 × 8.6 cm
Collection Philadelphia Museum of Art, Philadelphia; bequest of Katherine S. Dreier, 1952

In 1959 Tinguely met Duchamp personally for the first time, and in February 1960 they traveled together from New York to Philadelphia to visit the Philadelphia Museum of Art.[10] The latter holds an important collection of Duchamp's major works, including *The Large Glass* and both *Chocolate Grinder*. Tinguely recounted: "So Duchamp and I took the train to Philadelphia. It was wonderful! And he explained everything to me. For example, those sugar cubes in the cage—*Why Not Sneeze?*—were funny. I'll never forget how he talked my head off. Unfortunately, I didn't have a tape recorder with me. The irony, the breezy manner in which he touched on the past, on his own previous work—it was even more ironic than the pieces standing around."[11]

The two artists would continue to hold each other in mutual esteem. As Duchamp said of Tinguely: "He has this great thing, a sense of humor—something I have been preaching for artists all my life."[12]

From Grinding Bachelors to "Theater of Voyeurs"?

While *La Broyeuse de chocolat* stands as Tinguely's official homage to Duchamp in *Le Cyclop*, previously overlooked elements of it also allude to Duchampian themes. *Le Petit Théâtre* (The Little Theater), created by Tinguely and his collaborators between 1981 and 1994, is a case in point. Tinguely variously referred to it as the Mechanical Theater, the Automatic Theater, or the Theater of Voyeurs. Positioned on the third floor of the building, it consists of a room containing very odd seats, including a circular stool, a tractor seat, and a rocking chair. The seats face a small stage bordered by curtains. Once seated, visitors can wait for the performance to begin. When the giant machine at the heart of *Le Cyclop* is set in motion, noise fills the space, and the lights go down. Attention is focused on the spot-lit stage, where a gigantic hammer looms above a glowing dame-jeanne (demijohn) containing liquid. Meanwhile, the seats begin to quiver, throb, and in several cases, rise toward the ceiling. Others rock backward and forward.

Within *Le Petit Théâtre,* in front of a group of friends, Tinguely described the stage performance he envisaged for his mechanical play: "I wrote a piece called *L'Amour* (Love), which involves a hammer and a bottle that undergoes extraordinary luminous effects. A big bottle, transparent, with beautiful colors … Even Baudelaire would have enjoyed it.

10   Jean Tinguely: "Demain je vais à Philadelphie avec M. Duchamp," dated February 2, 1960. Postcard to Pontus Hultén, reproduced in *Museum Tinguely Basel. The Collection*, Museum Tinguely, Basel 2012, p. 395.

11   Jean Tinguely in "Often Neglected," p. 4.

12   Marcel Duchamp, quoted in Calvin Tomkins, *The Bride and the Bachelors: Five Masters of the Avant-Garde*, Penguin Books, Harmondsworth 1968/1976, p. 168.

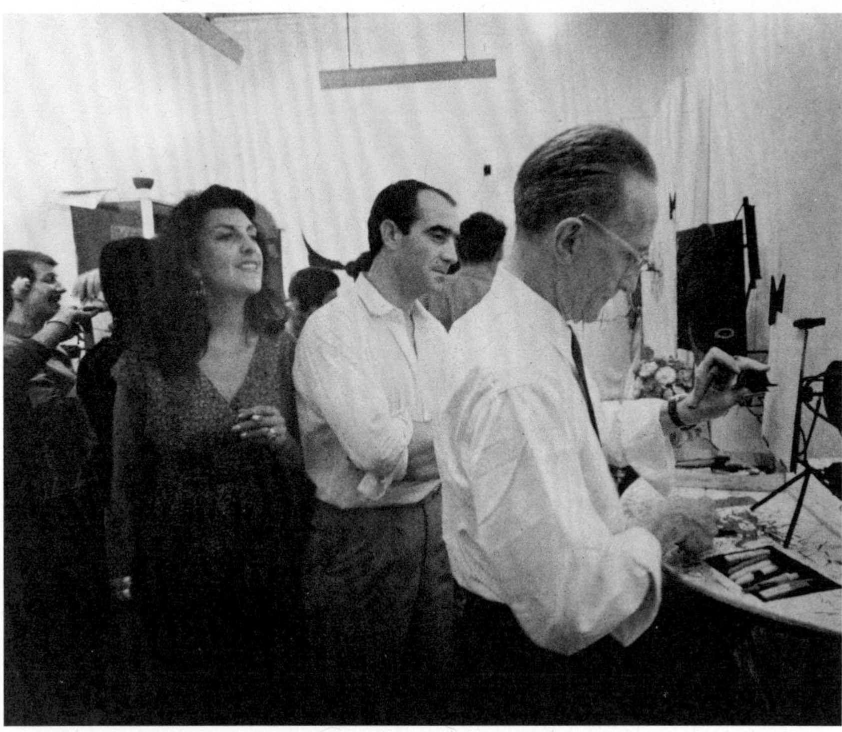

Iris Clert, Jean Tinguely, and Marcel Duchamp at the opening of the exhibition *Méta-Matics*, Galerie Iris Clert, Paris, July 1st, 1959

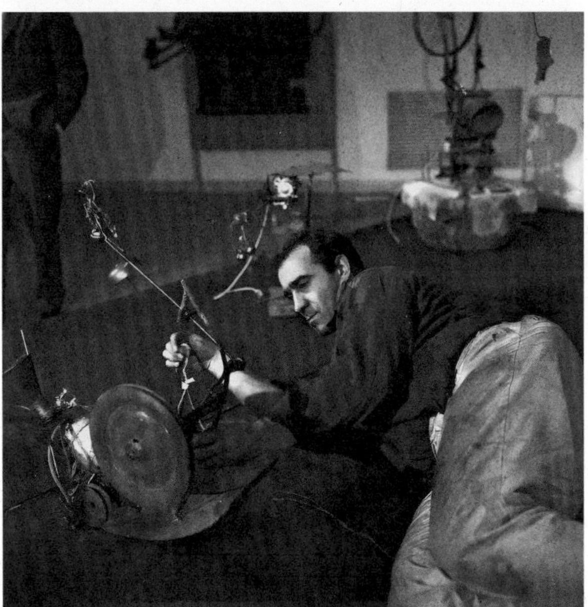

Jean Tinguely in front of *Hommage à Duchamp* (1960), unidentified location, 1961

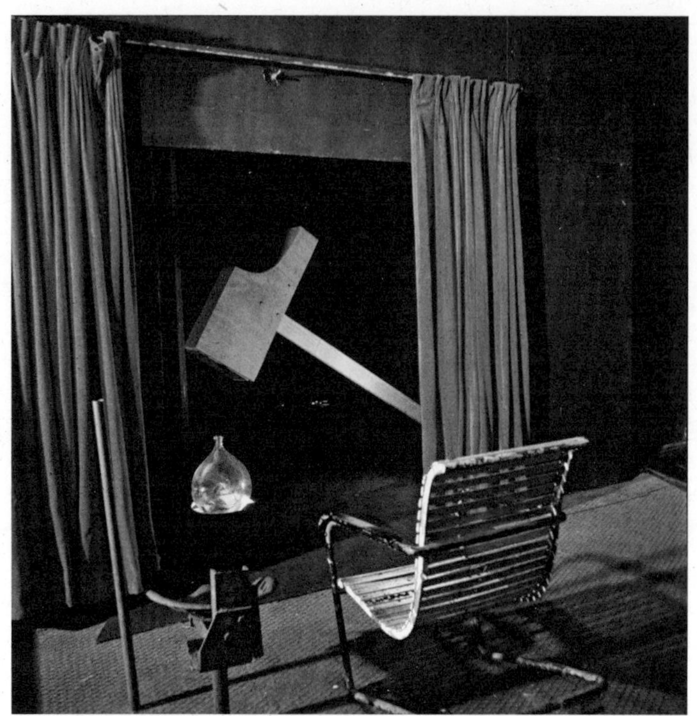

Jean Tinguely, *Le Petit Théâtre*, 1981/1994

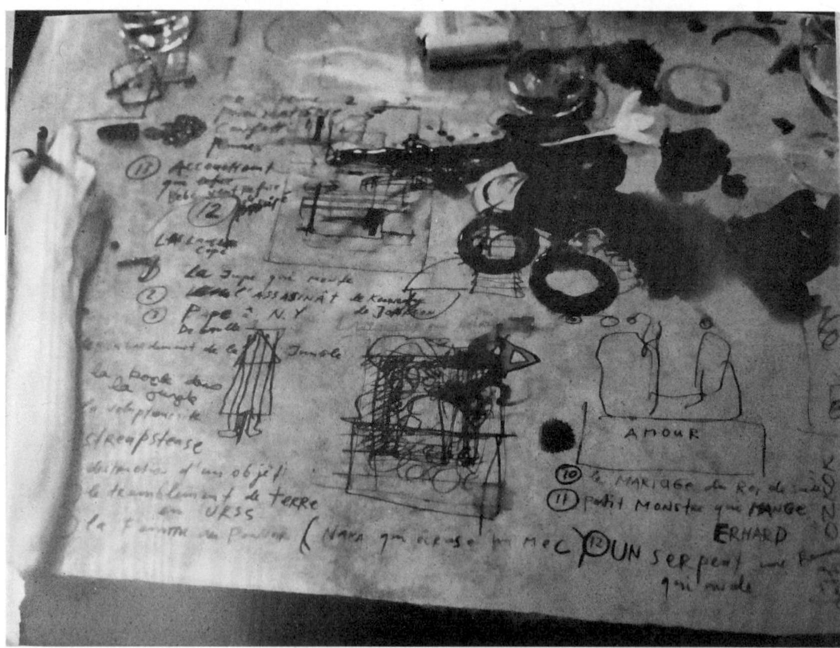

Drawing by Jean Tinguely, Niki de Saint Phalle, and Per Olof Ultvedt realized on a paper placemat, Stockholm, April 1966

And in this bottle […] one can feel the water vibrating. And there's
a hammer which, in a hammer-like voice, gently begins to declare its love,
more and more thunderous, for the bottle. And it rises […] it shifts into
a virile state, the hammer, bigger and bigger by its shadow […] And
the bottle vibrates, it feels the love coming over it. And the hammer rises,
the hammer rises … and, finally, it's really the declaration of total love,
and finally the hammer lets go, and breaks the bottle. And everyone's feet
get wet." As Tinguely noted mischievously, "You need a new bottle every
time, that's all!"[13]

Several ideas for Tinguely's mechanical play predate *Le Cyclop* and can
be seen on a tabletop sketch that Hultén photographed in April 1966.[14]
In 1994, artist and collaborator Philippe Bouveret transformed Tinguely's
ideas into a functioning artwork. Rather than have the bottle smash and
water splash, however, a new ending was created. As the hammer plunges
suddenly toward the glass vessel, the bottle disappears from sight, slipping
through a trapdoor beneath the stage floor just an instant before contact.
In this scenario, worthy of Duchamp, the Bride eludes her Bachelor.

For Tinguely, however, the main action in his *Petit Théâtre* occurs
"not on the stage," but rather among the spectators: "That's the Dada spirit,
but it has to be short and the intermission has to be important. The intermission being all those seats you're sitting on, which are animated from
below, by the relief underneath. They move you, they make you pass the
time in a hilarious way. You're in a ridiculous position, you move forward,
you almost fall out of your seats, and that's the main action […]
The action is not on stage, the action is in your heads, in your wet feet,
and in your situation as shaken spectators."[15]

In an early sketch for *Le Cyclop* from 1969–1973, Tinguely pictures
the *Petit Théâtre* seats as bicycle saddles that move "up and down"
repetitively on rods. (In its current configuration, eight eclectic seats are
attached to metal rods and levers, although nine were originally installed.[16])
Unsuspecting spectators, settling on the seats in order to passively watch
the stage-performance, instead find themselves hitched to Tinguely's
La Méta-Harmonie machine (1980–1981) and transformed into human
components of *Le Petit Théâtre*'s spectacle.

13 Excerpts from the film *Le Monstre de Tinguely* (1989, 52') directed by Jacques Huwiler (journalist) and Jaroslav Vizner (filmmaker) for the "VIVA" TV program broadcasted on TSR, the national French-language Swiss television.

14 The sketch was created by Tinguely, Niki de Saint Phalle, and Per Olof Ultvedt during a brain-storming session in Stockholm. It includes drawings and notes for a "kind of mechanical theater." One sketch is labeled "AMOUR" (Love), the same title as Tinguely's *Le Cyclop* play. Listed scenes for the project include "Streapstease," (sic) "The Rising Skirt," "The Marriage of the King of Sweden," and "Destruction of an Object." In Pontus Hultén, *Méta*, p. 289.

15 See *Le Monstre de Tinguely*, 1989.

16 One was dismantled for security reasons.

Le Petit Théâtre's seats suggest aspects of the Bachelors in Duchamp's *The Bride Stripped Bare by her Bachelors, Even.* According to Duchamp, the Bachelors are activated by the sight of the Bride stripping. Duchamp named his Bachelor figures "Malic Moulds"—"Moules Mâlic" in French—and represented them as nine vaguely mechanical suspended forms hovering in the lower left of *The Large Glass.* "Moules Mâlic" rhyme in French with "phallic," while in English "Malic Moulds" evoke "male-like" malleable forms. Duchamp compared the shapes of the Bachelors to male "uniforms or hollow liveries."[17] While the appearance of the eclectic seats in Tinguely's Theater of Voyeurs does not closely resemble that of *The Bride Stripped Bare*'s Bachelors, their masculine associations (metal tractor seat and rowing machine) and to-and-fro movement suggest a comparable parody of sexual activity.

Duchamp's *The Green Box* working notes supply further details on the components and operation of *The Large Glass.* The Malic Moulds, here described by Duchamp as eight in number, are attached to stretching, solidified "elemental rods." The Bride is described as a mechanical "desire motor" or "steam engine" equipped with "lubricious" gearwheels, cogs, and pistons. Her parts, Duchamp specifies, engage in "vibratory," jerking, or clockwork movement. Duchamp's notes also include descriptions of *The Large Glass* components that never made it into his famously "unfinished" work. One such element is a weighty bottle of Benedictine (a French liquor from Normandie) that first falls suddenly, then reappears in its initial position through the action of mechanical springs. A drawing by Duchamp depicts the bottle positioned above a clearly labeled trapdoor. Another imagined but unrealized element of the "definitively unfinished" *Large Glass,* as set out in *The Green Box,* is a prominent "Splash."

Ambulating Carts and Canon Shots

In addition to a chocolate grinder and nine Malic Moulds, the Bachelors' zone of *The Large Glass* features a sliding carriage-like construction titled the Chariot or Glider. Duchamp referred to it as a mechanical sleigh that slides backward and forward on runners while chanting "litanies" on themes such as "Onanism." Cannon shots are another feature of *The Large Glass* scenario. Fired by the Bachelors as they aim for the Bride, the shots land instead beside her (depicted in Duchamp's *The Green Box* notes at zone "A"). Duchamp recounts using a toy cannon to mark their landing points.

---

17   Here and following quotes: Michel Sanouillet and Elmer Peterson (eds.), *The Writings of Marcel Duchamp,* p. 39–63.

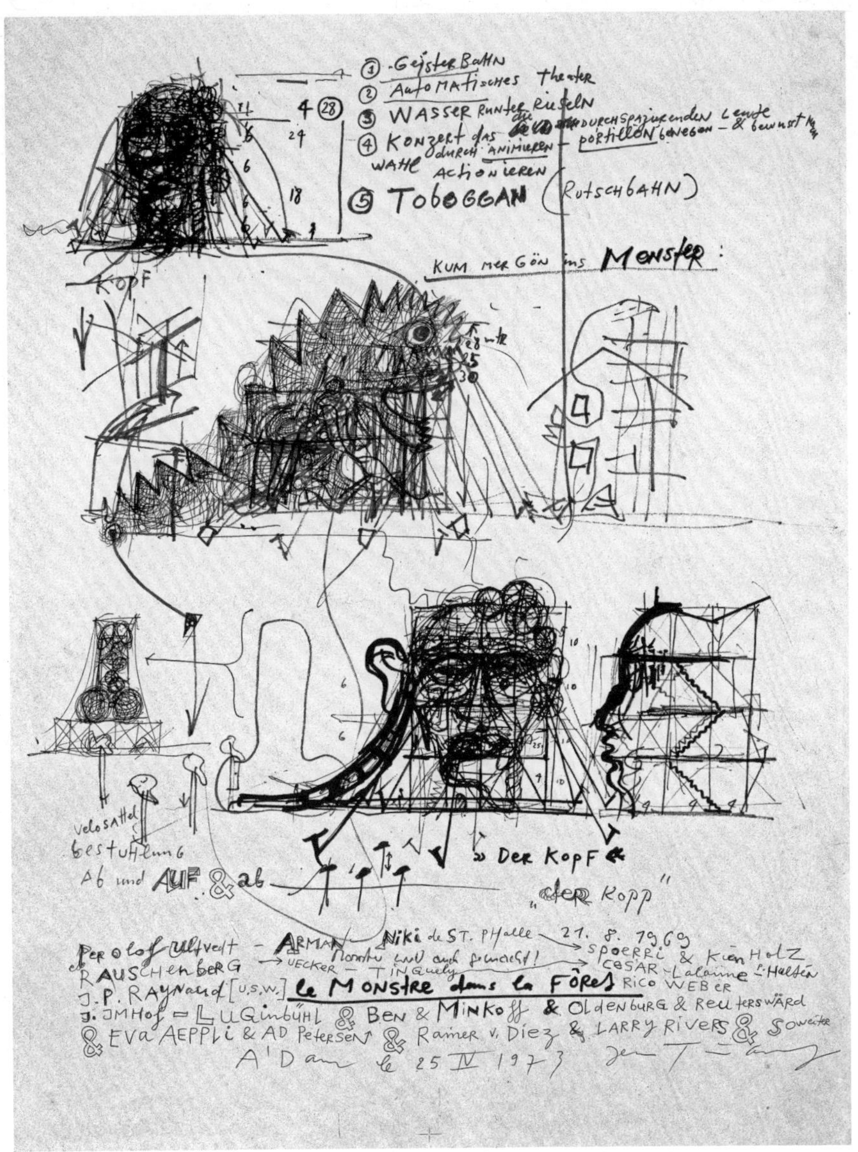

Jean Tinguely
Le Monstre dans la forêt, 1969–1973
Modified Xerox, 67.5 × 52 cm
Collection Museum Tinguely, Basel

Visitors to *Le Cyclop* may discover some analogies between these themes and Tinguely's work. One example can be found in the to-and-fro movement of a cart-like construction on runners that project from *Le Cyclop*'s external facade. Another example consists of giant moving steel balls that hurtle noisily along a metal cage-like structure that winds through both the interior and exterior of the building. The latter is pictured in a sketch by Tinguely of different components of *Le Cyclop* (where it is labeled as number 17). Titled *La Dégringolade* (The Helter-Skelter, 1975–1976), it springs into life when *La Méta-Harmonie* machine is activated.

The theme of Bachelors and their shots reappears in another work within *Le Cyclop* titled *Le Tellflipper: Hommage à Guillaume Tell* (The Tellpinball: Homage to William Tell; installed in 1978 in *Le Cyclop*) by Bernhard Luginbühl. It consists of a giant pinball machine in the shape of the Swiss folk hero's crossbow. As Virginie Canal notes, this one-ton behemoth requires "two muscly adults to work [its pistons], so powerful are the springs."[18] Luginbühl's work was initially on display at the Centre Pompidou in 1977, where it formed part of the *Crocrodrome* exhibition. In keeping with other aspects of the *Crocrodrome*, the work was interactive. When repositioned in *Le Cyclop,* it helped embody the latter's collaborative spirit. As in *Le Petit Théâtre*, spectators were again positioned in the role of Duchampian Bachelors, but unlike the Bachelors, their collaboration was required to launch the steel balls.

Cemeteries of Uniforms and Liveries

The Bachelors, as we have seen, were imagined by Duchamp as Malic Moulds linked to hardened rods. But they were also described by Duchamp as "castings" and a "cemetery of uniforms and liveries." Whether by chance or design, these too find parallels in *Le Cyclop*. Rico Weber's *Les Gisants* (Recumbent Statues) (1978) consist of several identical plaster casts of his body positioned on a ledge and exposed to the elements. Dressed in workmen's overalls and boots, Weber's figures lie in a relaxed horizontal position with hands behind their head and a smile on their face. The reclining figures evoke traditional recumbent statues adorning tomb sculptures found in European churches. Spectators encountering them at *Le Cyclop* may find the molded figures in different states and configurations, from whole (and freshly cast) to moss-covered disintegrating fragments.

---

18   Virginie Canal, *Jean Tinguely. Le Cyclop*, Centre
      National des Arts Plastiques/Isthme éditions, Paris
      2007, p. 168.

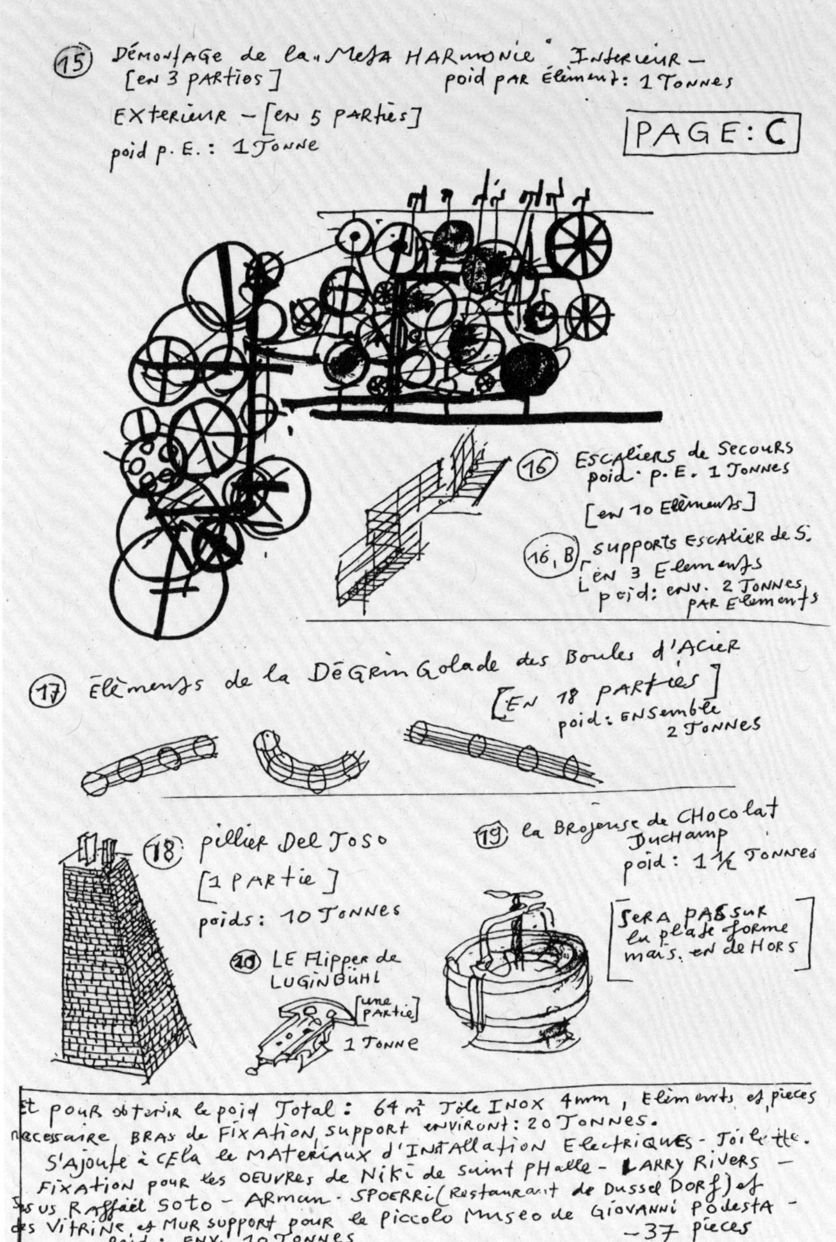

Jean Tinguely
Petite documentation pour le démontage-transport et reconstruction de Jean Tinguely, September 1985 (excerpt)
Xerox; Centre National des Arts Plastiques Archives, Paris

Arman's *L'Accumulation de gants* (The Accumulation of Gloves)
(1991, installed 1993) offers a different version of a "cemetery of liveries."
A black reliquary-like frame two by three meters in length encases hundreds
of densely packed welder's gloves used during the building of *Le Cyclop*.
As Arman noted, "Jean sent two large boxes of used gloves to my studio
[…] I took those greasy, heavy gloves and sandwiched them between two
sheets of plastic."[19] Like Weber's *Les Gisants*, Arman's *L'Accumulation de
gants* renders homage to the makers of *Le Cyclop*, that is to say Tinguely's
collaborators and friends such as Weber himself. Through their presentation
of working men's uniforms, the two works also stand as general (but clearly
gendered) memorials to physical labor. Each work foregrounds the action
of chance and the passage of time, while presenting a knowing nod to prior
artistic traditions.

Tinguely on Duchamp

How might we interpret those aspects of Tinguely's *Le Cyclop* that appear
to align with details of Duchamp's *The Large Glass* and notes? Tinguely's
comments on Duchamp offer some guidelines. Tinguely was questioned
by interviewer Dieter Daniels in 1987 about seeming parallels between
The Large Glass and two of his works from the 1970s: *La Vittoria* (1970)
and *Plateau agriculturel* (1978). Tinguely expressed some reservations.
In the process, however, he showed a sophisticated understanding of both
Duchamp's work, and differences between it and his own: "I don't think
that you can really compare the two. Everything that Duchamp created
seems to be incredibly deliberate and complicated and insidious and dissimu-
lated. You can look under it or on the back and still find something. That's
not true of my work—don't you agree? In mine, you can immediately
see what it's about."[20]

In addition to emphasizing the "coded" nature of Duchamp's art,
Tinguely reflected on their respective use of humor and irony. As he put it:
"The humor is different in every work. But in both cases the irony is there,
that would be one common element."[21]

Tinguely and Daniels' conversation variously turned to Duchamp's
and Tinguely's shared literary models (Max Stirner, Alfred Jarry, Raymond
Roussel) and to Tinguely's use of the readymade. Unlike Duchamp's varied
work, which can "explode in every direction," Tinguely noted, "My work
only seems to explode; in reality there is a perfectly functioning thread that

---

19   Quoted in Virginie Canal, *Jean Tinguely*, p. 157, and
     excerpted from the film *Le Cyclop de Jean Tinguely*
     (1996) directed by Arne Steckmest.

20   Jean Tinguely in "Often Neglected," p. 7.
21   Here and following quote: Jean Tinguely in ibid.,
     p. 8.

runs throughout my work. [For example] using the readymade principle once again I reanimated the debris of a burnt farmhouse, put new life into it, and created these terrifying ghosts. Ghosts of death, of sadness—but it's all basically the same. As I explained […] it's playful, there's still life in it that comes through, it's not exclusively sad, not only tragic. That's an example of the thread." Tinguely's combination of the "readymade principle" with a "reanimation" of "debris" clearly underpins much of *Le Cyclop*, including its official and unofficial homages to Duchamp. His fearless integration of more confrontational "ghosts of sadness," moreover, comes to the fore in some other sections of *Le Cyclop* such as Eva Aeppli's *Hommage aux déportés* (Homage to the Deportees, 1976/1993), and at times displaces the irony he championed.

"I've only ever made one Homage"

During his life, as we have seen, Tinguely created several homages to Duchamp as well as tributes to other artists. Early examples might include his *Méta* works such as *Méta-Malevich* (1954), *Méta-Herbin* (1955), and the *Méta-Kandinsky* (1955, 1956). His use of the prefix "méta," which as Mari Dumett points out signifies both "with" and "after," helps us appreciate these works as both imagined forms of collaboration, and homages to that which is past.[22] In 1988, however, Tinguely—ever one to embrace contradiction—adamantly declared: "I've only ever made one Homage, it's *Homage to New York*, but it was ironic."[23] "It was a simulation of catastrophe […] an ironic suicide, as Duchamp put it."[24] Tinguely here was referring to his famous self-destroying machine that sawed at its own components and set itself on fire in the courtyard of The Museum of Modern Art in New York in 1960.[25] As the many homages in *Le Cyclop* attest, however, while Tinguely's later tributes can be ironic, they are also powerful testaments to affection and respect.

Tinguely went so far as to attribute both his own capacity to appreciate and celebrate the work of other artists, as well as that of Hultén, to Duchamp. As Tinguely put it, "Marcel Duchamp could feel so much love for other artists! And it went a long way; the range of artists was quite large […] I think that Hultén learned a lot from him. And that was good for me too because I know how many artists I can love, young artists too

[P. 51]

22   Mari Dumett, "To Be an 'Exemplary' Machine: Tinguely's *Homage to New York*," in Serge Guilbaut and John O'Brian (eds.), *Breathless Days, 1959–1960*, Duke University Press, Durham, North Carolina 2017, p. 160.

23   "Jean Tinguely. Farces et attrapes. Interview par Catherine Francblin," *Art Press*, no. 131, December 1988, p. 22.

24   Ibid., p. 20.

25   See online the film by Robert Breer: vimeo.com/840436298 (last accessed May 2025).

[…] whose work I really enjoy."[26] Duchamp, Tinguely elaborated, "despite all the irony and maliciousness, the clarity of vision, the impudence that he had," was generous to fellow artists. In *Le Cyclop*, Tinguely's comparable generosity is eloquently demonstrated.

Pontus Hultén and *Le Cyclop*

Hultén's role in the creation of *Le Cyclop* calls for further investigation. He had a strong personal interest in Duchamp, and as an art historian, had contemplated writing a PhD on his art. As Tinguely noted, "I met [Hultén] one time with a case full of material on Duchamp. He wanted to write a doctoral thesis on him but then left it all to Ulf Linde."[27] Hultén's interest in and knowledge of Duchamp's *The Large Glass* and its notes was significant. Curator Ann Goldstein recounts that while sorting Hultén's books in his private library, she encountered "Marcel Duchamp's *The Green Box*, 1934, which Pontus told me the artist had left for him as a gift on his doorstep."[28] Hultén himself, as Pierre Ruault has shown, provided a glowing account of his first encounter with the contents of *The Green Box* in Paris in the late 1940s. Hultén wrote: "On one of my first visits to the Bibliothèque Doucet, I asked for everything available under the name of Marcel Duchamp. I could not believe my eyes when *The Green Box* was brought to my seat and I opened it. The incredible firework of ideas, the elegance of the presentation, the profound originality of the whole publication and the light it threw on the inaccessible, remote, and mysterious masterpiece that is the *Large Glass*. It was too much. The shock was so violent that I began to believe that I was dreaming, that it was a mirage. It was a strange and overwhelming feeling."[29]

Nearly 20 years later, Hultén's fascination with Duchamp's *The Large Glass* and *The Green Box* plans for the unfinished work remained strong. As he put it in the catalogue of his famous 1968–1969 exhibition *The Machine as Seen at the End of the Mechanical Age*, held at The Museum of Modern Art in New York, *The Large Glass* "is probably the largest single project in modern art and may also be the most important."[30]

---

26 Here and following quote: Jean Tinguely in "Often Neglected," p. 4.

27 Ibid., p. 10. Contrasting Hultén's deep knowledge of Duchamp to that of art critic Pierre Restany, Tinguely continued: "I don't think Restany had a natural relationship with Duchamp […] Duchamp's approach wasn't easily accessible to him, he had to ingest it in small doses at first and I helped him along too." Ibid.

28 Ann Goldstein, "Passages: Pontus Hultén," *Artforum*, no. 6, February 2007, available on www.artforum.com/print/200702/pontus-hulten-12381 (last accessed May 2025).

29 Pontus Hultén, in Pierre Ruault, *Le rôle de Pontus Hultén dans la promotion du Nouveau Réalisme (1954-1967)*, Université européenne de Bretagne, Rennes II, mémoire de master d'histoire de l'art contemporain, 2018–2020, p. 160.

30 Pontus Hultén, *The Machine as Seen at the End of the Mechanical Age*, exh. cat., The Museum of Modern Art, New York 1968, p. 80.

Hultén was a close friend of Tinguely, and according to the latter was responsible for reintroducing him to Duchamp's work some years after he had first encountered it at art school. In 1955–1956, for example, they had hunted together for Duchamp's *Anemic Cinema* film (1926).[31] Hultén, furthermore, was actively involved in the creation and completion of *Le Cyclop*. His name appears on drawings Tinguely sent him, as well as on sketches in which he is mentioned as a contributor.[32] As director of the Musée National d'Art Moderne, he was involved in the procurement of parts of *Le Cyclop* such as *La Broyeuse de chocolat*, *Le Tellflipper*, and a large spare air vent from the new museum building—which might itself fancifully evoke Duchamp's *The Green Box* plans for the inclusion of a "Ventilator" in *The Large Glass*.

The possibility that Hultén, with or without discussion with individual participating artists in *Le Cyclop*, engaged in a game of allusions to Duchamp's *The Large Glass* is not to be discounted. Tinguely himself had his own history of encounters with the work as we have seen, and also owned reproductions of *The Large Glass* in at least one book in his personal library (namely two copies of Hultén's exhibition catalogue *The Machine as Seen at the End of the Mechanical Age*).[33] *Le Cyclop*'s deep engagement with Duchamp's work is undoubtably shaped by the experience of both figures. In his role as a director of the Musée National d'Art Moderne and other key institutions, Hultén staged both Dada and Neo-Dada through exhibitions such as the Duchamp and the *Crocrodrome* shows, generating thoughtful dialogues and connections between the two. Tinguely, also involved in the *Crocrodrome* and other exhibitions of Duchamp's work, would create his own inspired and novel dialogues between old and new through *Le Cyclop*.

Comparisons and Transformations

Comparison of Duchamp's and Tinguely's works reveals not only common themes and motifs, but also ways in which Tinguely transformed Duchamp's artistic vocabulary. *Le Cyclop*, as we have seen, literalizes elements from Duchamp's *The Large Glass* such as *The Chocolate Grinder*, scales up the proportions of the readymade, and burlesques favorite Duchampian themes. Chance is wedded to movement in new ways as spectator-participants physically wander through and interact with the dynamic components

---

31 Jean Tinguely in "Often Neglected," p. 5.
32 See for example Jean Tinguely, *Dessin pour Maja Sacher*, 1973, in the collection of the Museum Tinguely, Basel, reproduced here on page 35.

33 Anja Seiler (Museum Tinguely, Basel), email correspondence with Jill Carrick, September 2022. The catalogue features images of both Duchamp's *The Large Glass* and Tinguely's *Homage to New York*.

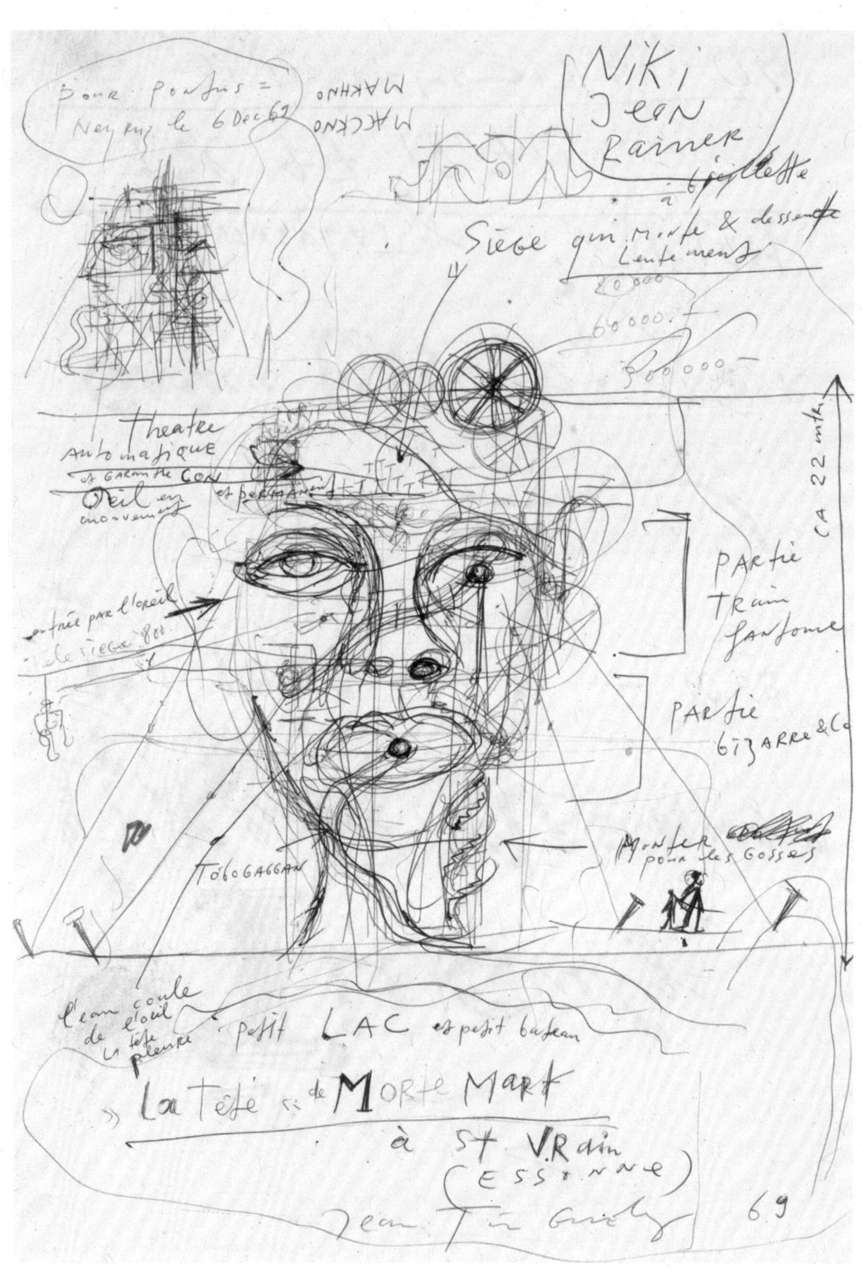

Jean Tinguely
Letter to Pontus Hultén describing *Le Cyclop*, 1969
Ballpoint and felt-tip on paper, 42.5 × 30.5 cm
Collection Museum Tinguely, Basel

of Tinguely's "Bachelors Machine." And humor fuses with social critique as *Le Cyclop* not only targets technology and efficiency, but deliberately evokes dirt, darkness, and a wide array of historical memories.

Le Cyclop and *The Large Glass*'s common cast of characters, as previously discussed, includes excited Bachelors and an alluring but elusive Bride. Tinguely's *Cyclop*, however, ultimately stands as a celebration of love and friendship rather than frustrated desire. On the one hand, Tinguely reshaped vocabularies from early 20th-century Dada into a distinctly 1960s, and eventually 1970s and 1980s, utopian project. On the other hand, he held on to the critical spirit of the old Dada, personified less by Duchamp (who Tinguely described as conservative) than by more politically radical figures such as Richard Huelsenbeck (1892–1974), Tristan Tzara (1896–1963), and Hugo Ball (1886–1927). In *Le Cyclop*, this spirit of contestation is visible in certain of its other homages to people or events such as Tinguely's *La Molécule RU 486: Hommage à Étienne-Émile Baulieu* (The RU 486 Molecule: Homage to Étienne-Émile Baulieu, 1991/1994), or Larry Rivers' *Hommage à Mai 68* (*Homage to May 68*, 1978–1979, installed 1994).

Beyond *The Chocolate Grinder*

Le Cyclop contains both official and unofficial homages to Dada that recast Dada in thought-provoking ways. Initiated in 1976, Tinguely's *Le Méta-Merzbau: Hommage à Kurt Schwitters* (The Meta-Merzbau: Homage to Kurt Schwitters), for example, pays tribute to Schwitters' extraordinary 1923–1933 construction built inside his home in Hannover. The *Méta-Merzbau* engages with the formal language of the earlier work while emulating Schwitters' aspiration to "construct a new world with the debris [of the old]."[34] As this essay has demonstrated, *Le Cyclop*'s unofficial homages include multiple components that together suggest an extended and ever-humorous tribute to Duchamp's *The Large Glass*.

Le Cyclop, moreover, harbors another unacknowledged reference to Dada that remains paradoxically dominant yet ignored. Both the finished *Cyclop*, and Tinguely's early sketches for it dating back to 1969, strikingly evoke aspects of the famous Dadaist sculpture *Mechanischer Kopf* (*Mechanical Head*, 1919) by Raoul Hausmann (1886–1971). Hausmann's sculpture consists of a wooden head embellished with mechanical fixtures

---

34   Kurt Schwitters, "Les merztableaux," in *Abstraction-création art non figuratif 1932*, Paris, 1932, p. 33. See https://monoskop.org/images/6/68/Abstraction-creation_1_1932.pdf (last accessed May 2025).

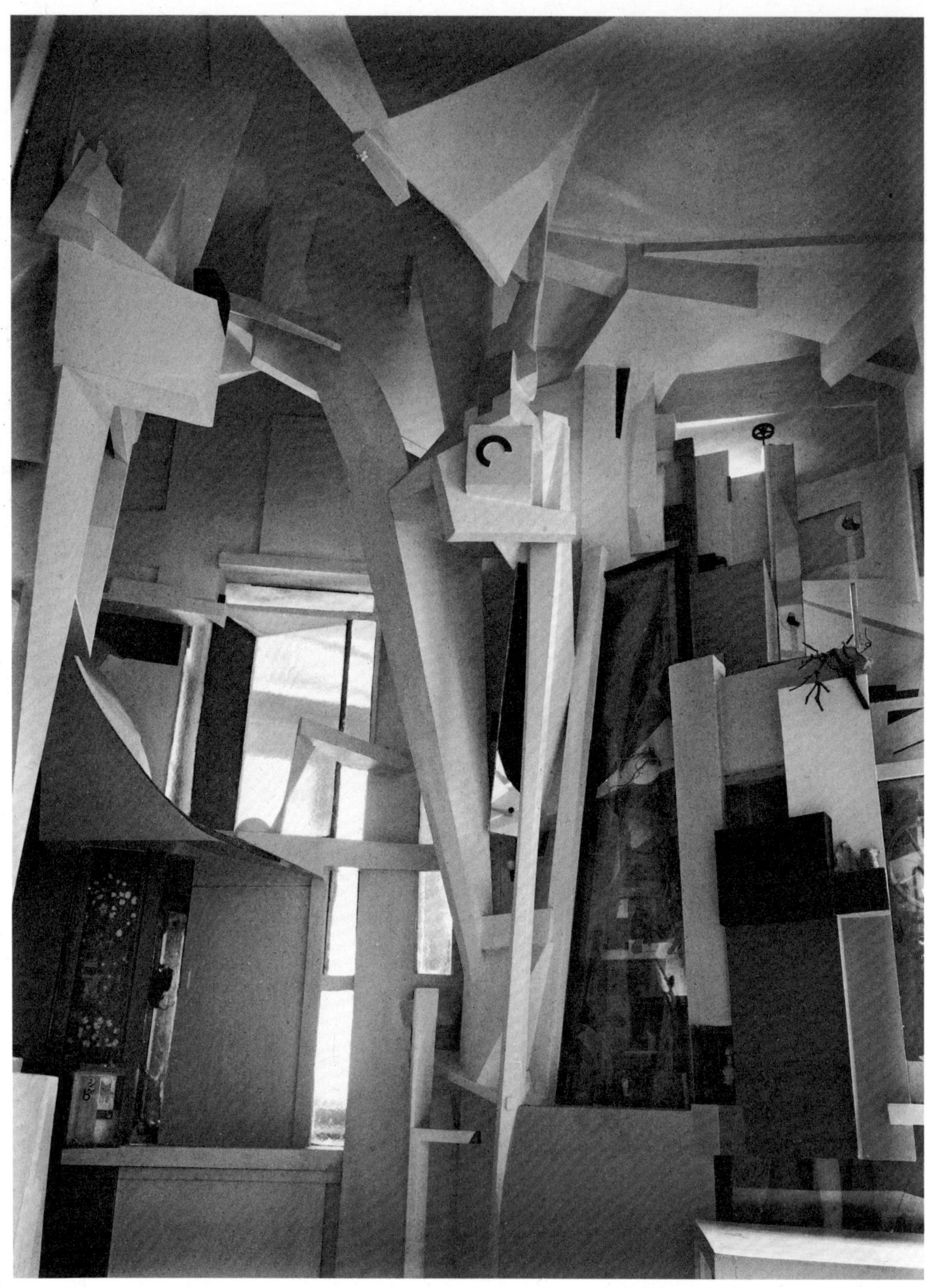

Wilhelm Redemann
Kurt Schwitters' Merzbau, Blue Window, 1933
Environment reconstructed in 1981–1983 at the Sprengel Museum, Hannover, by Peter Bissegger and Ernst Schwitters

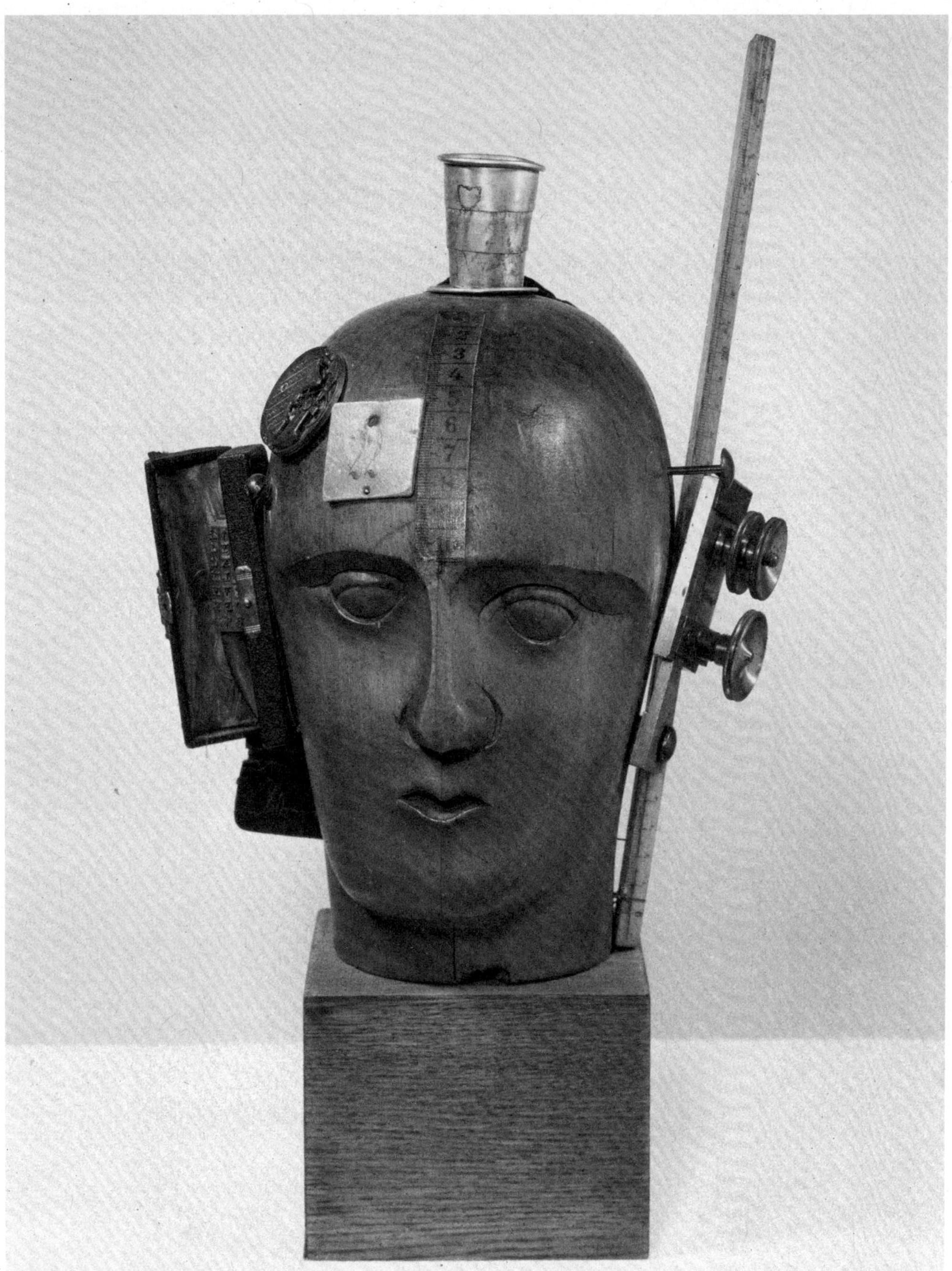

Raoul Hausmann
Mechanischer Kopf, 1919
Wooden mannequin head with various objects attached to it: telescopic beaker, leather case, pipe stem, white card bearing the number 22,
section of dressmaker's tape measure, wooden ruler, watch mechanism, metal cylinder with typeset letters, 32.5 × 21 × 20 cm
Collection MNAM/CCI, Centre Pompidou, Paris

such as wheels, cogs, and a ruler. *Le Cyclop* parallels many of its features, motif by motif, from the ruler on one side of the head, evoked by Jean Pierre Raynaud's *La Jauge* (The Gauge, 1975–1976/1990), to its single ear formed by a hinged case (Luginbühl's *L'Oreille* [The Ear, 1973]), to the watch-cog on its forehead that could be evoked by Tinguely's *La Méta-Harmonie* machine. A collapsible metal cup on the top of its head may even be evoked by Tinguely's *Hommage à Yves Klein* (Homage to Yves Klein, 1976–1979), a roof-top, pool-sized water container that reflects the sky. And where might one search for the numeral 22 so prominently positioned on the forehead of Hausmann's *Mechanischer Kopf? Le Cyclop*'s evocation is both direct and coyly discreet. After climbing to the highest point, visitors gain a clear view of the top of Raynaud's ruler. The water gage, which continues above the *Hommage à Yves Klein*, stops abruptly at the cut-off point of 22 meters.

In 1967, Hausmann retrospectively claimed he had intended his *Mechanischer Kopf* to evoke the limited, unimaginative, and programmed spirit of the early 20th-century German petit-bourgeoisie.[35] The complex contexts and shifting visions underpinning Hausmann and Tinguely's works are a promising topic for future analysis, and offer rich insights into relationships between Dada and Neo-Dada during the period of *Le Cyclop*'s construction. Like *La Broyeuse de chocolat*, Tinguely's amplified reworking of the *Mechanischer Kopf* suggests that his engagement with Dada's legacy is significantly deeper and more sustained than previously recognized.

---

35   Raoul Hausmann, quoted in Pontus Hultén,
     The Machine as Seen, p. 111.

General Views and Surroundings

Photographs taken in 2023–2024

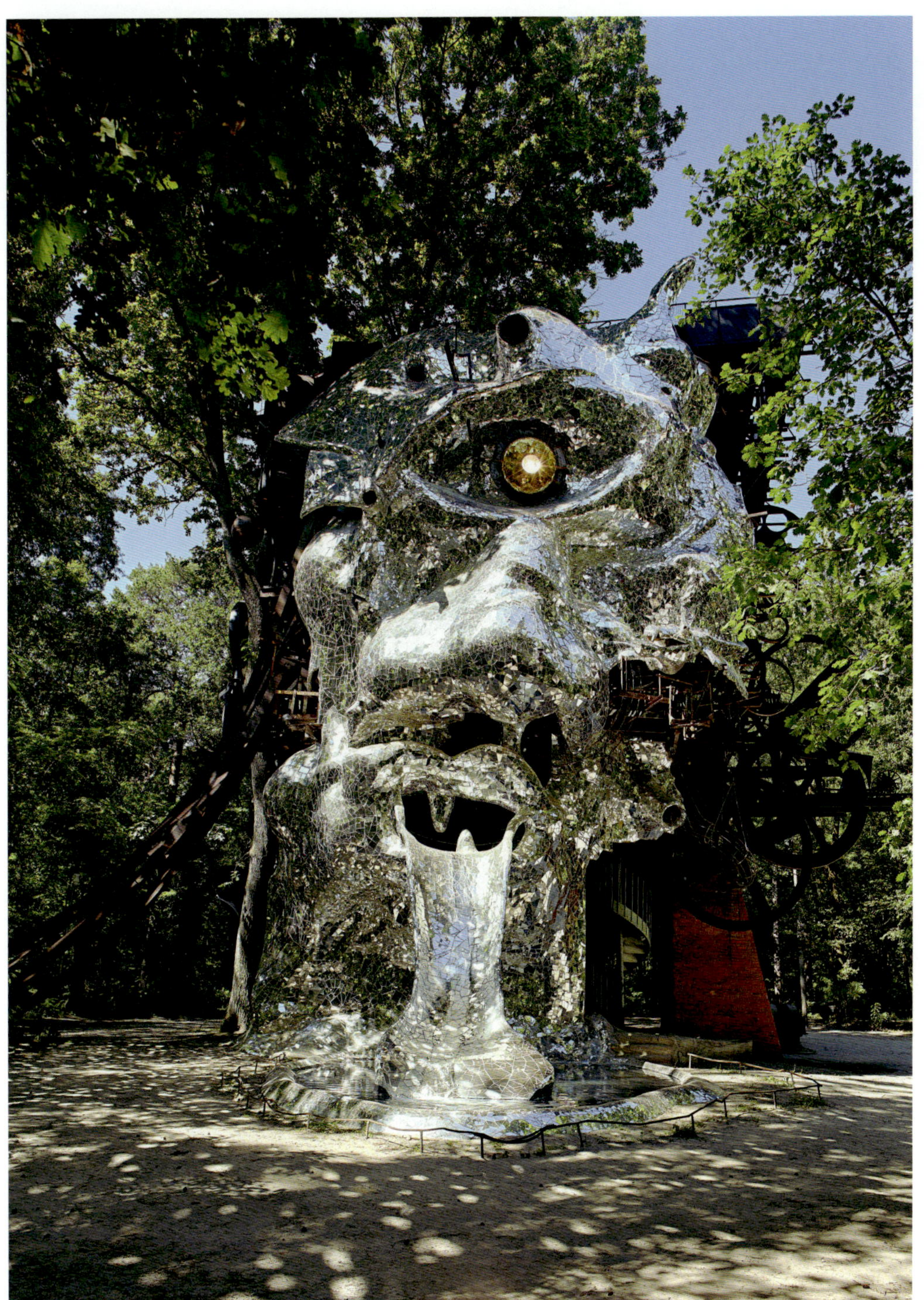

Niki de Saint Phalle, *La Face aux miroirs*, 1987–1991

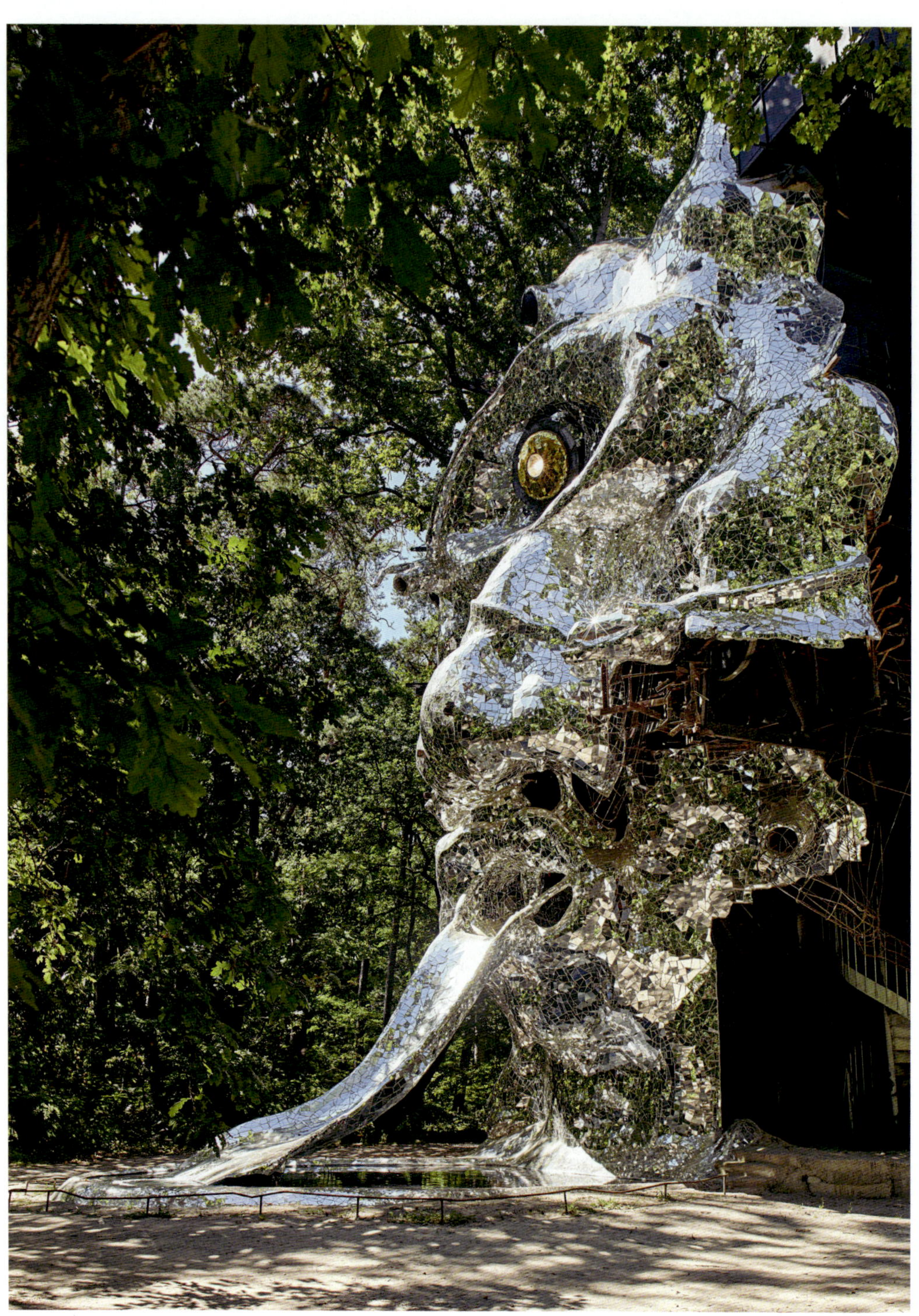

Niki de Saint Phalle, *La Face aux miroirs*, 1987–1991

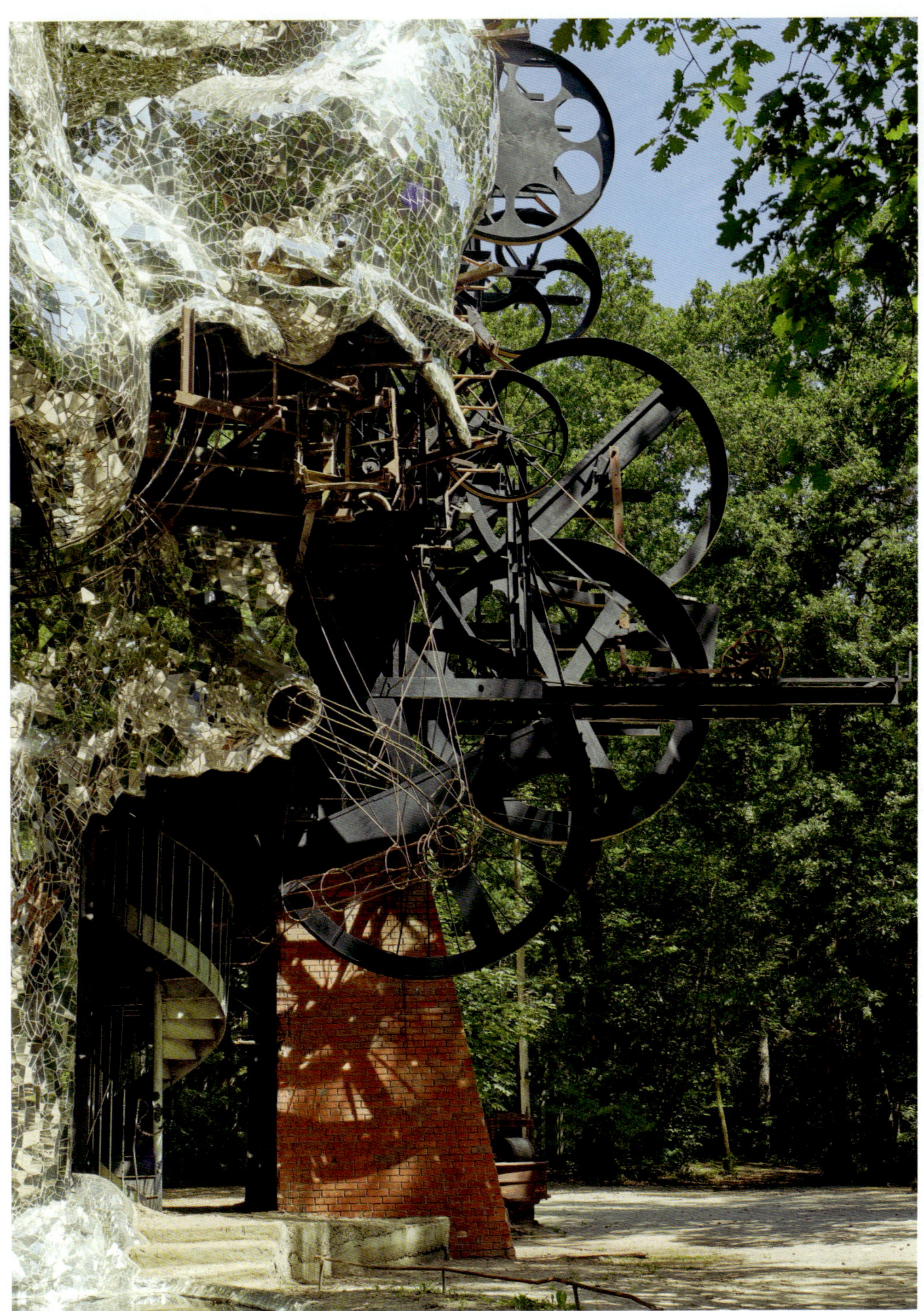

Niki de Saint Phalle, *La Face aux miroirs*, 1987–1991; Jean Tinguely, *La Méta-Maxi*, 1972–c. 1977

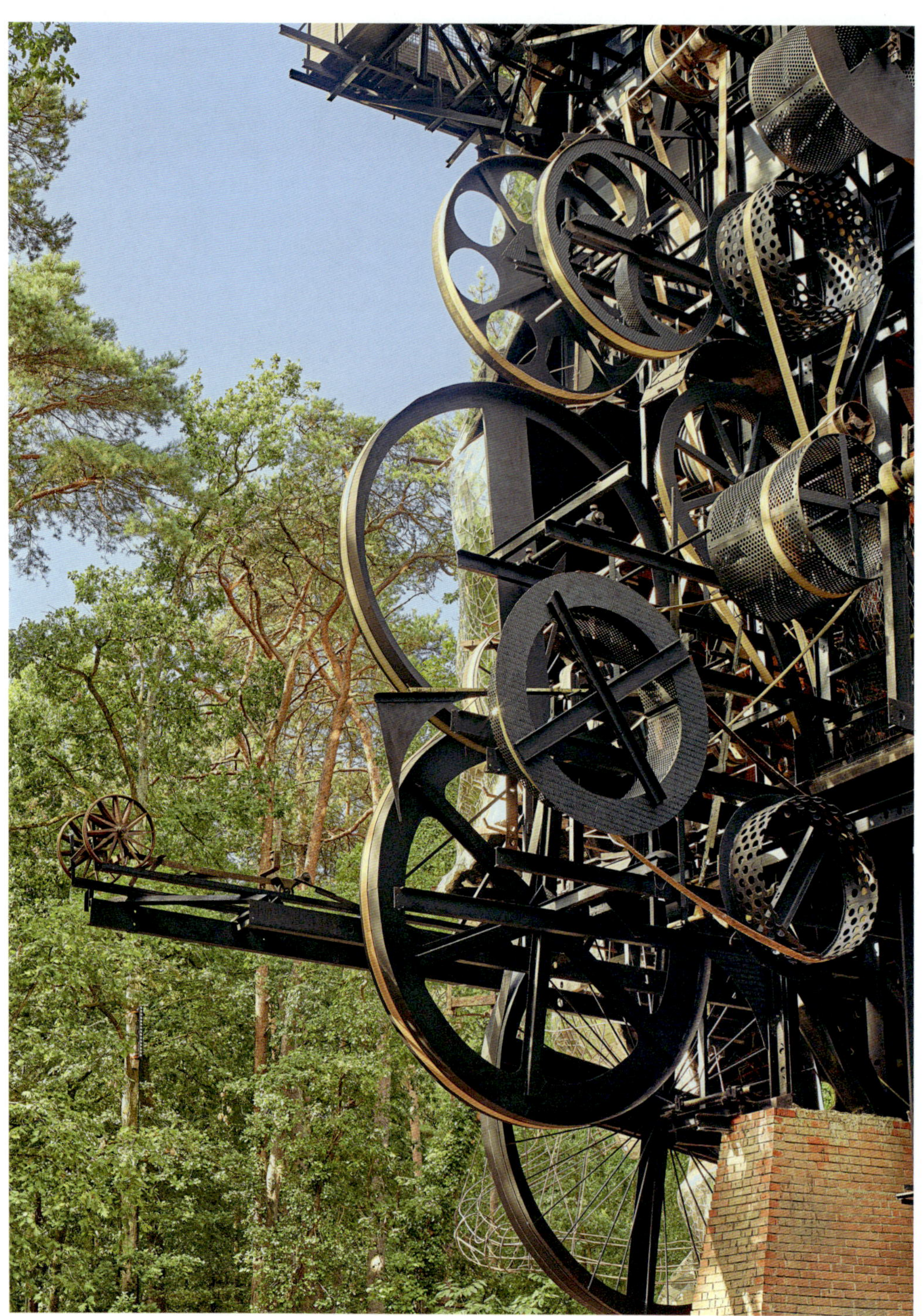

Jean Tinguely, *La Méta-Maxi*, 1972–c. 1977

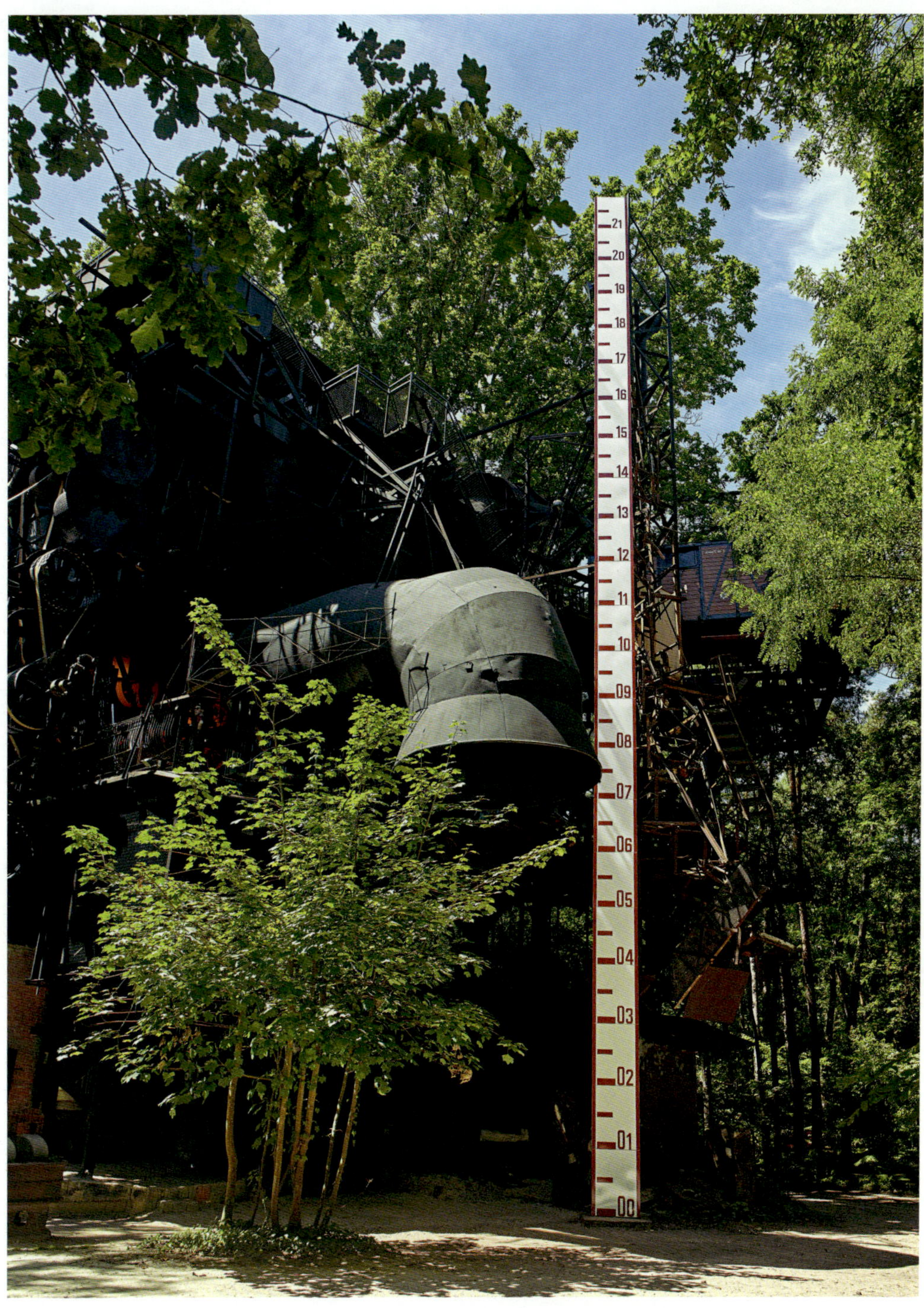

Jean Tinguely and Niki de Saint Phalle, *L'Incitation au suicide*, 1978/c. 1992; Jean Pierre Raynaud, *La Jauge*, 1975–1976/1990
→   Eva Aeppli, *Hommage aux déportés*, 1976/1993; Bernhard Luginbühl, *L'Oreille*, 1973

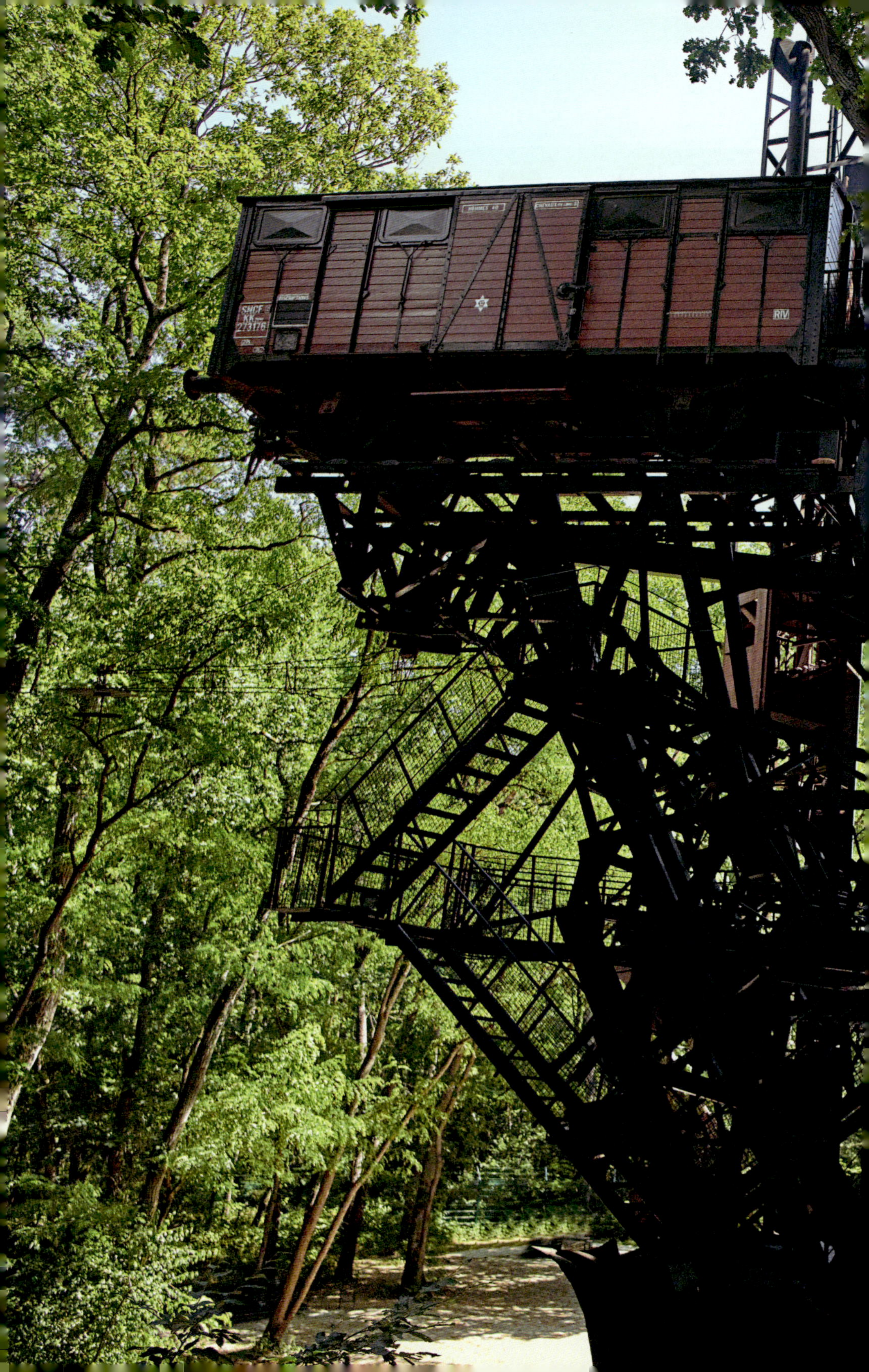
SNCF
KK
273176
HOMMES 40
CHEVAUX en long 8
RIV

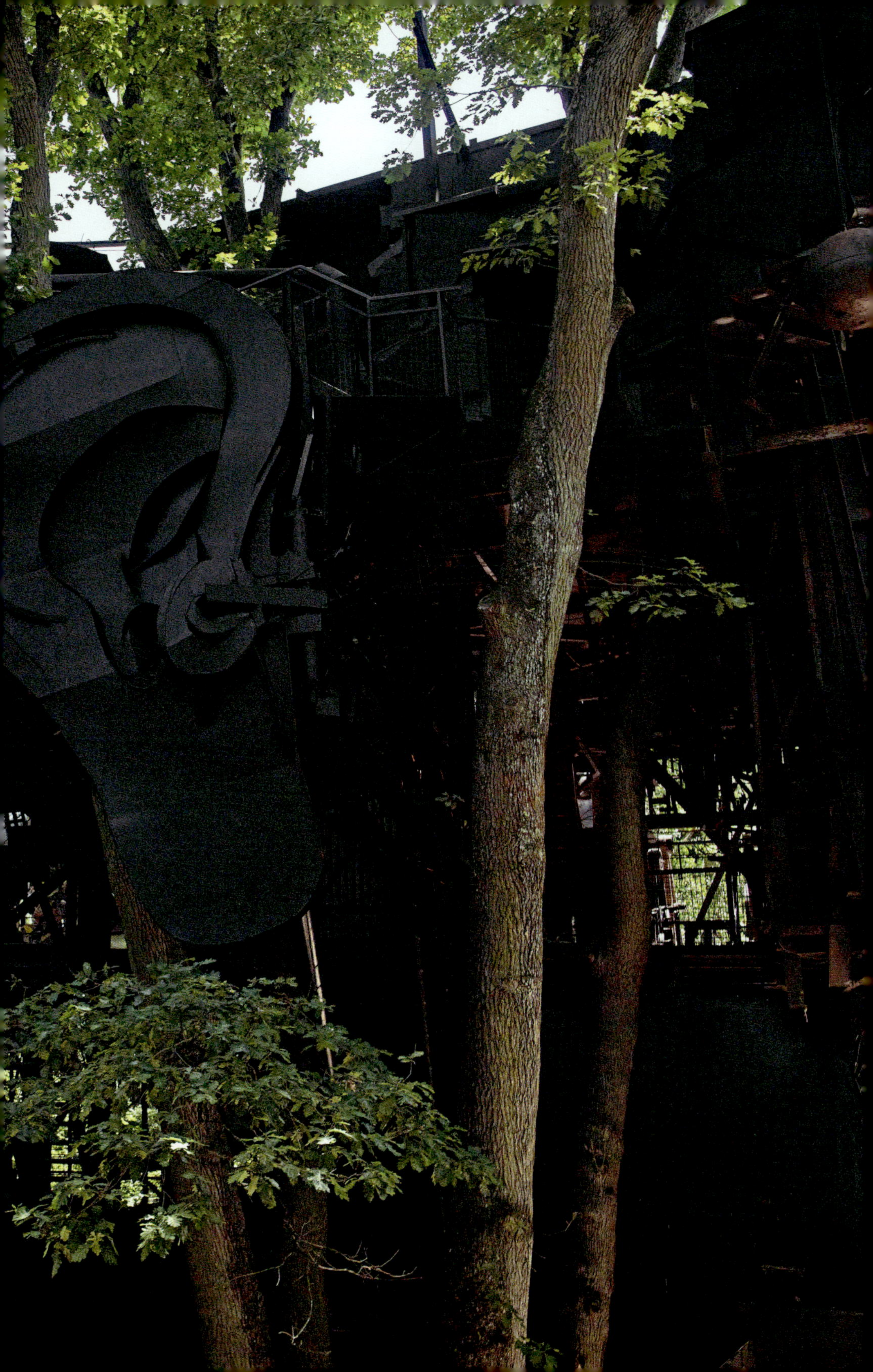

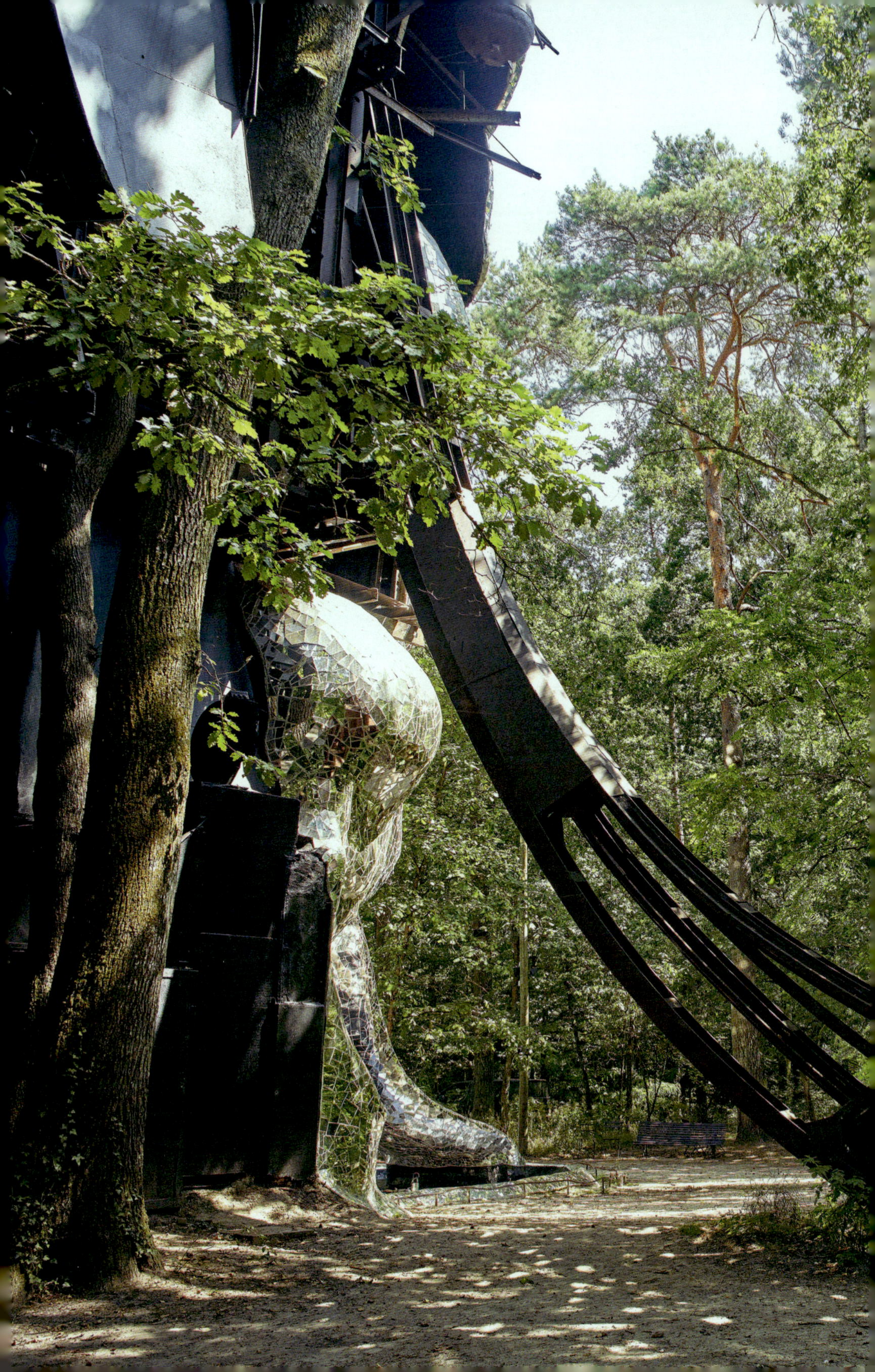

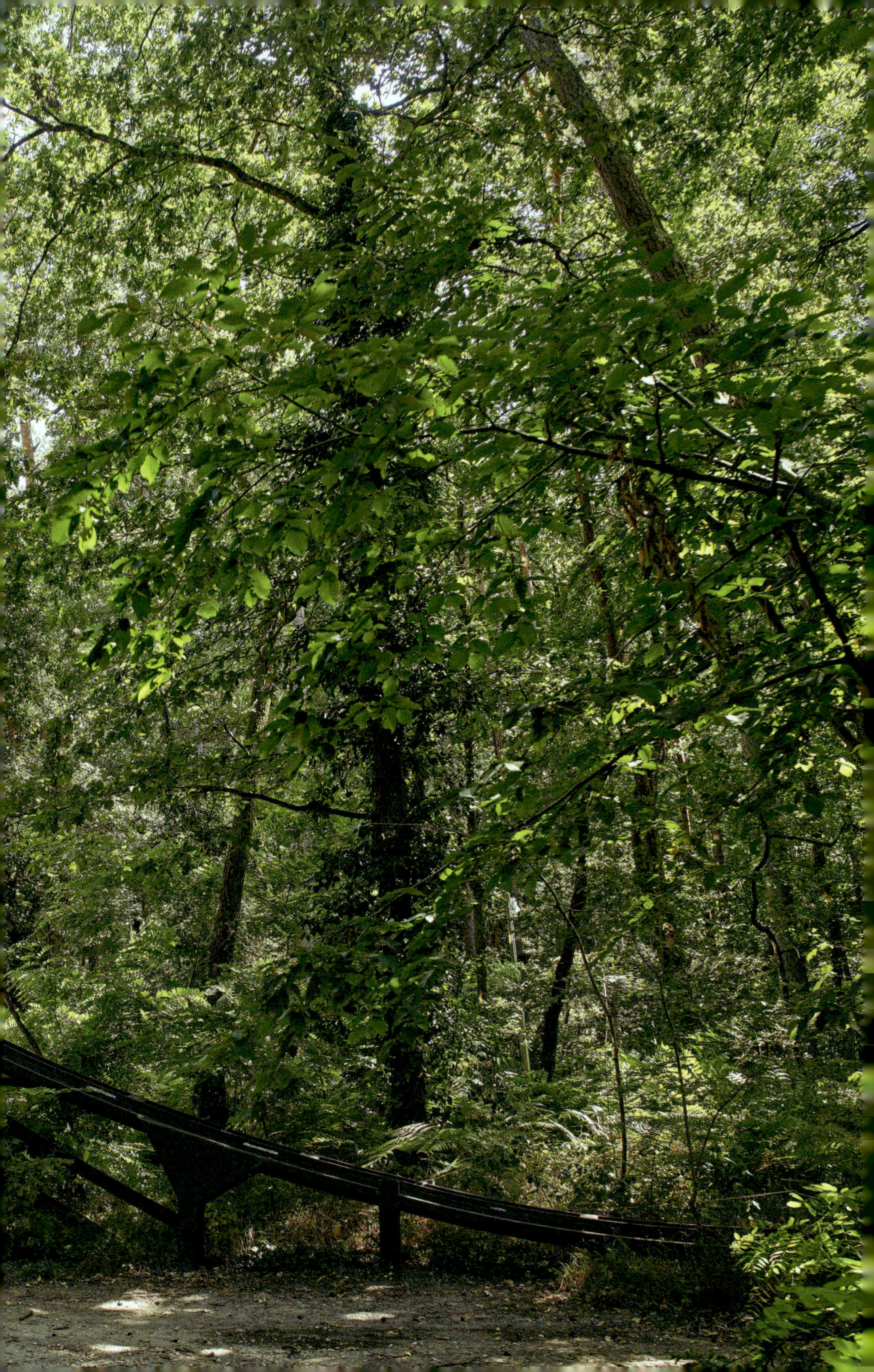

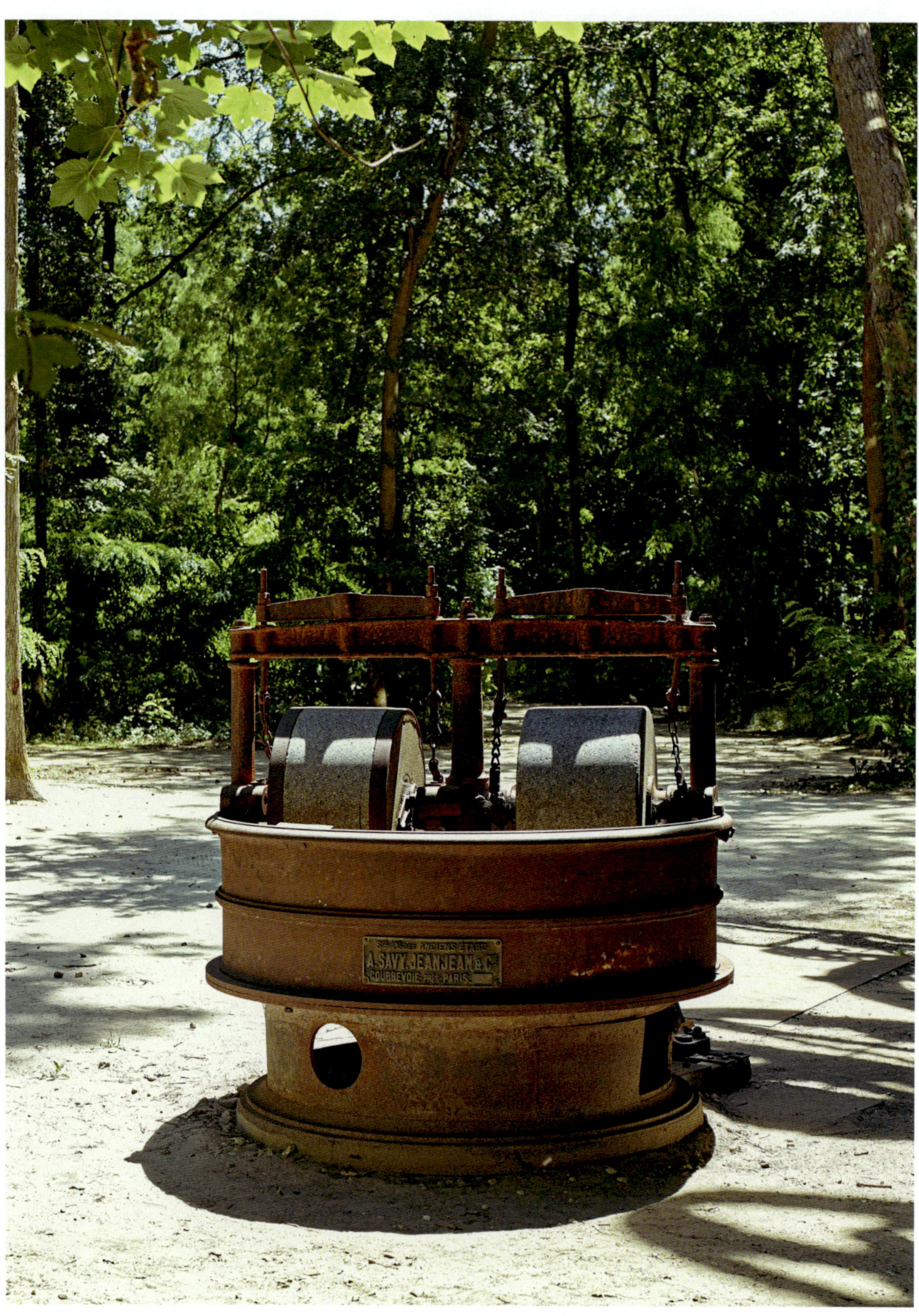

Jean Tinguely, *La Broyeuse de chocolat: Hommage à Marcel Duchamp*, 1977 (installed 1978)
←   Bernhard Luginbühl, *Hommage à Eiffel*, 1971

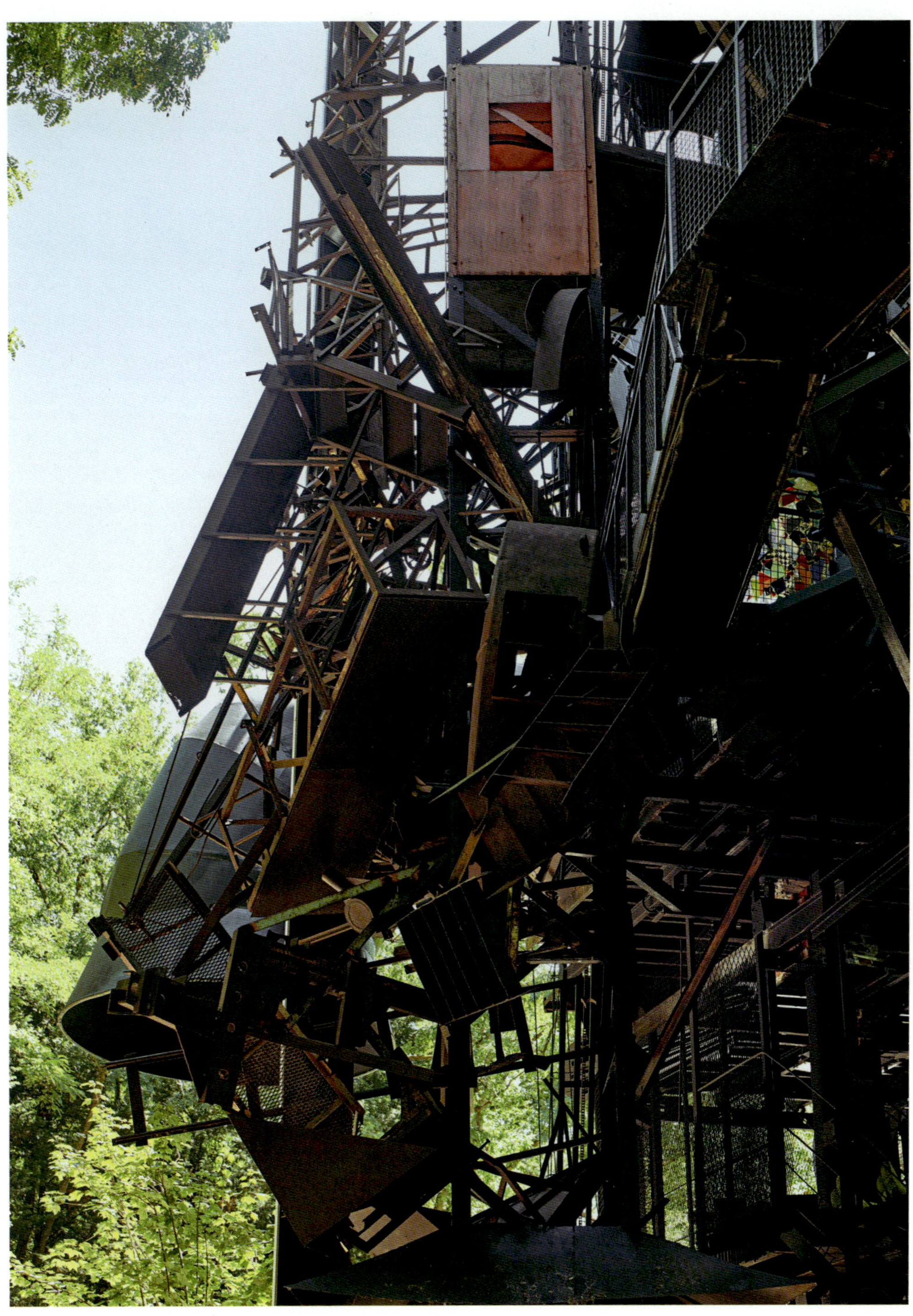

Jean Tinguely, *La Tour éphémère*, 1973–1989

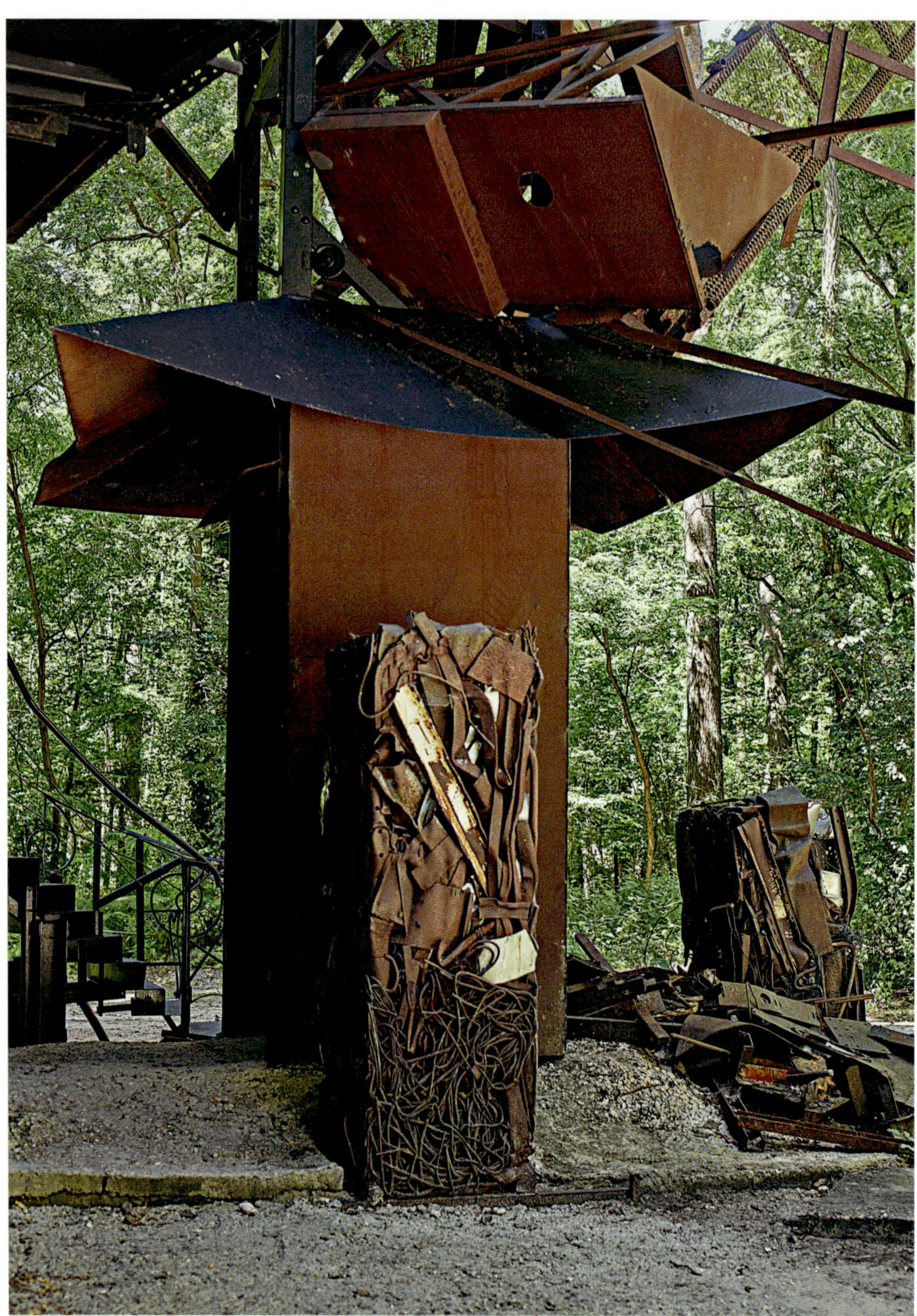

César, *La Grande Compression* and *La Petite Compression*, 1994

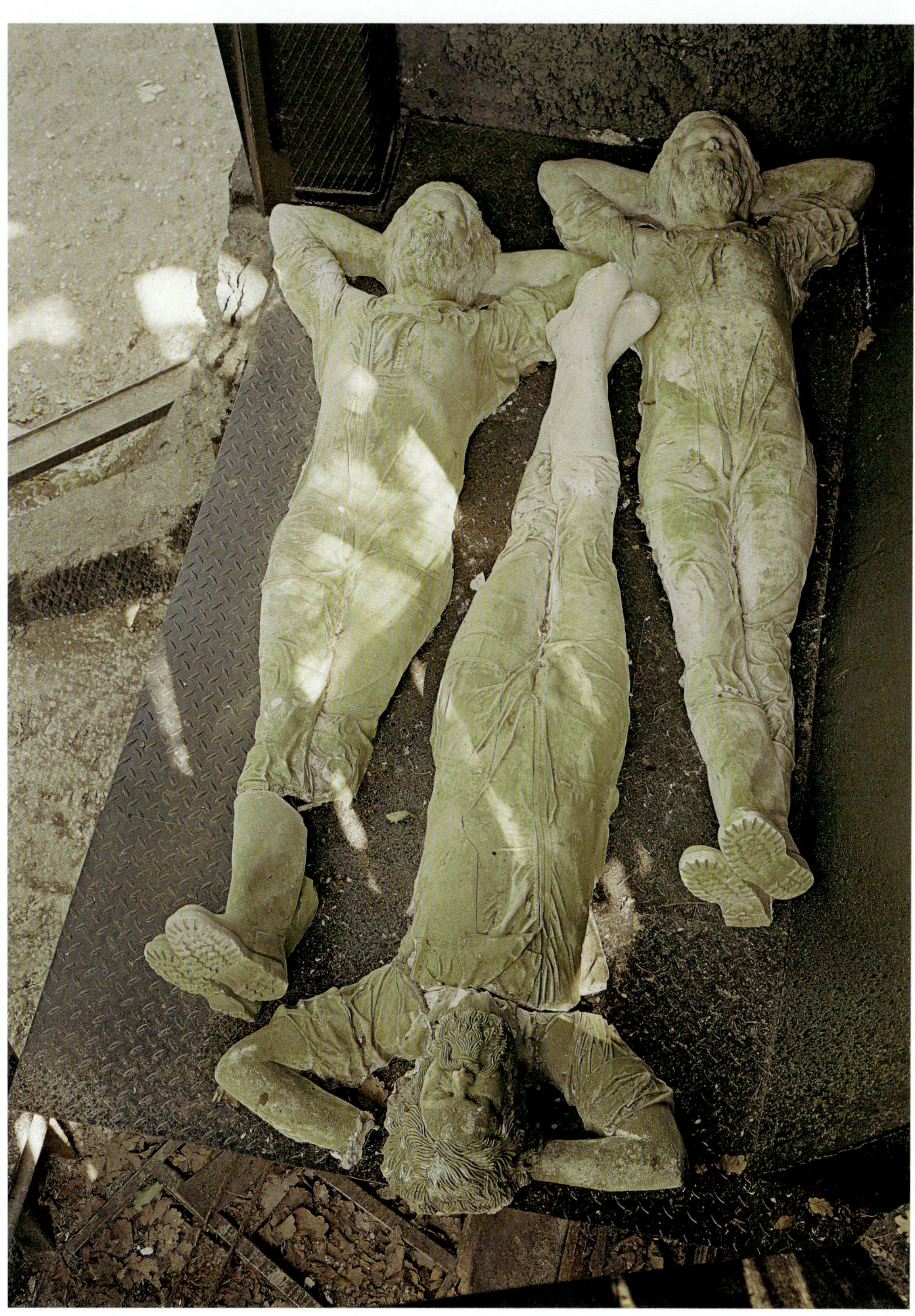

Rico Weber, *Les Gisants*, 1978 (installed 1994)

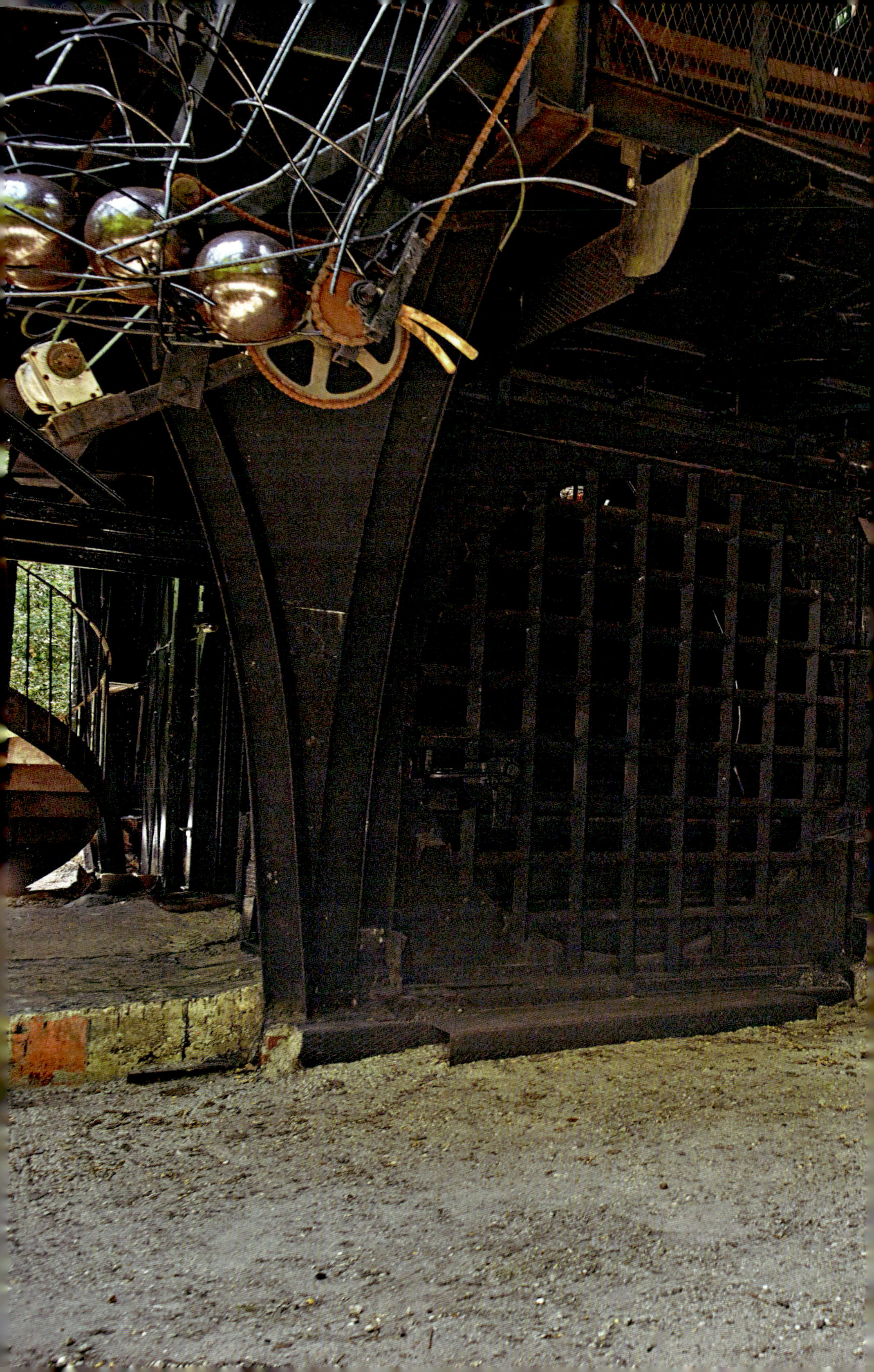

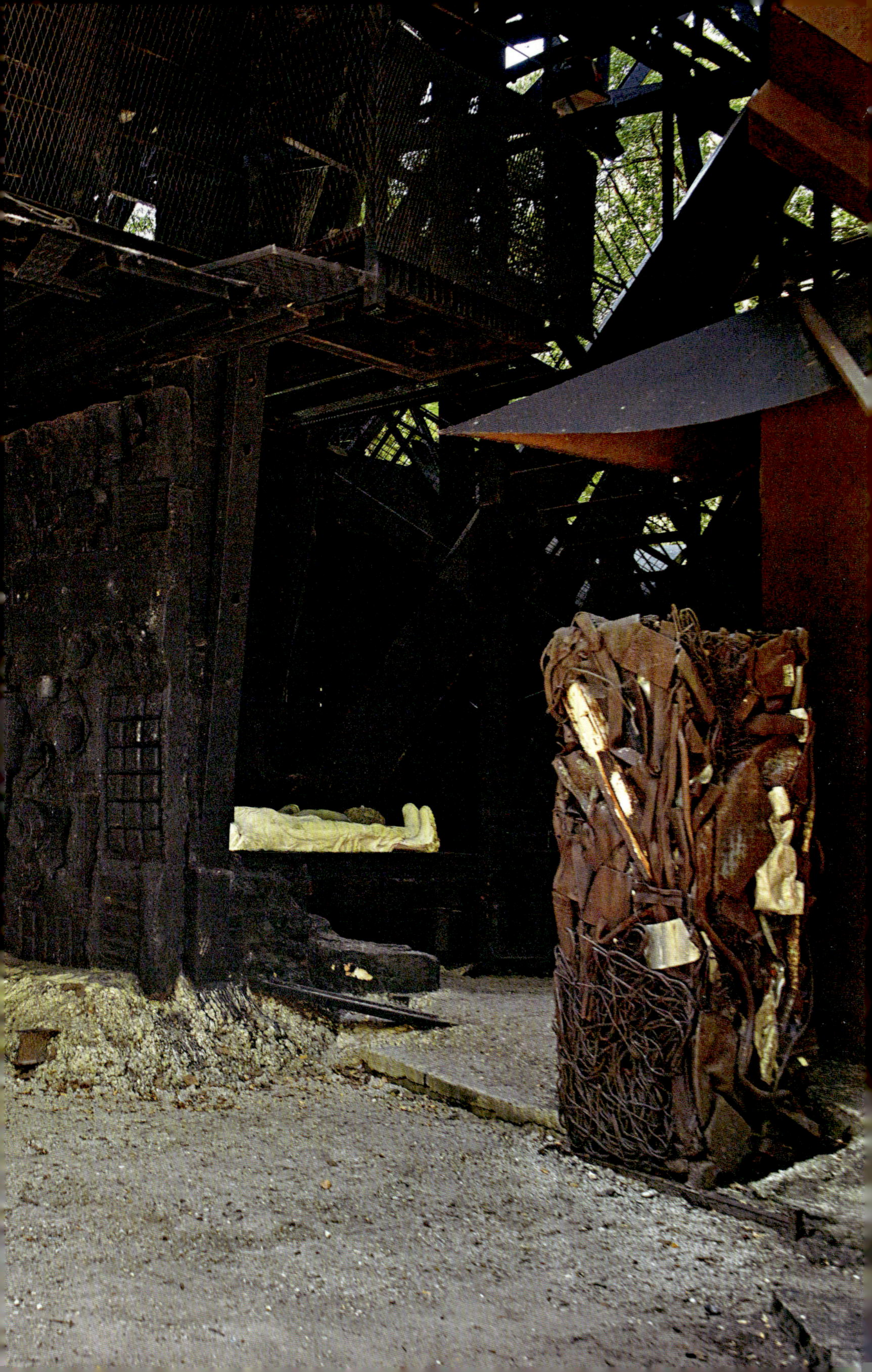

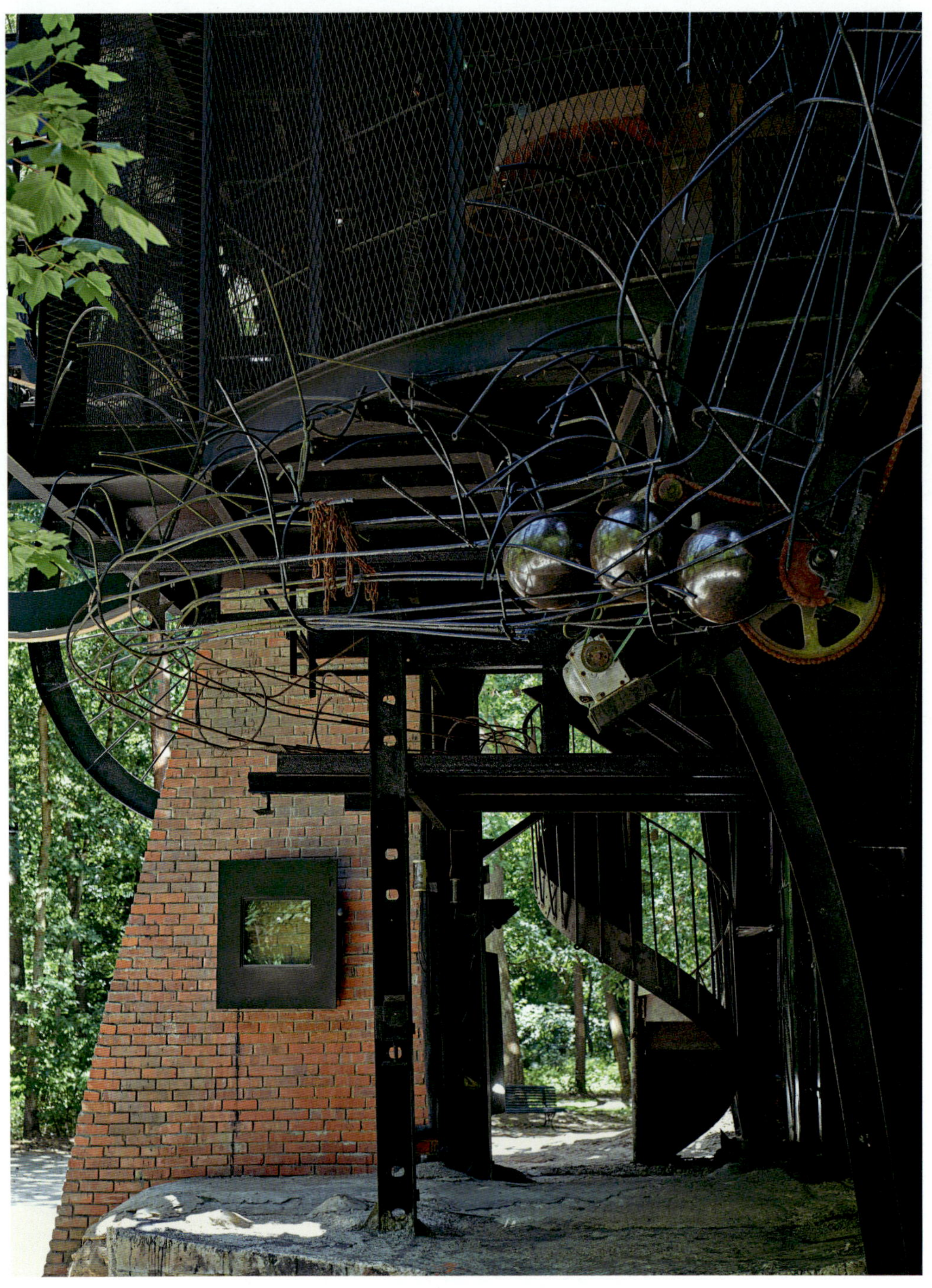

Philippe Bouveret, *Le Tableau générique*, 1994; Jean Tinguely, *La Dégringolade*, 1975–1976
← Jean Tinguely, *La Dégringolade*, 1975-1976; *La Porte-levis*, n. d.; Bernhard Luginbühl, *Boss Tor*, 1974–1975; *Hommage à Louise Nevelson*, 1978; Rico Weber, *Les Gisants*, 1978 (installed 1994); César, *La Grande Compression*, 1994

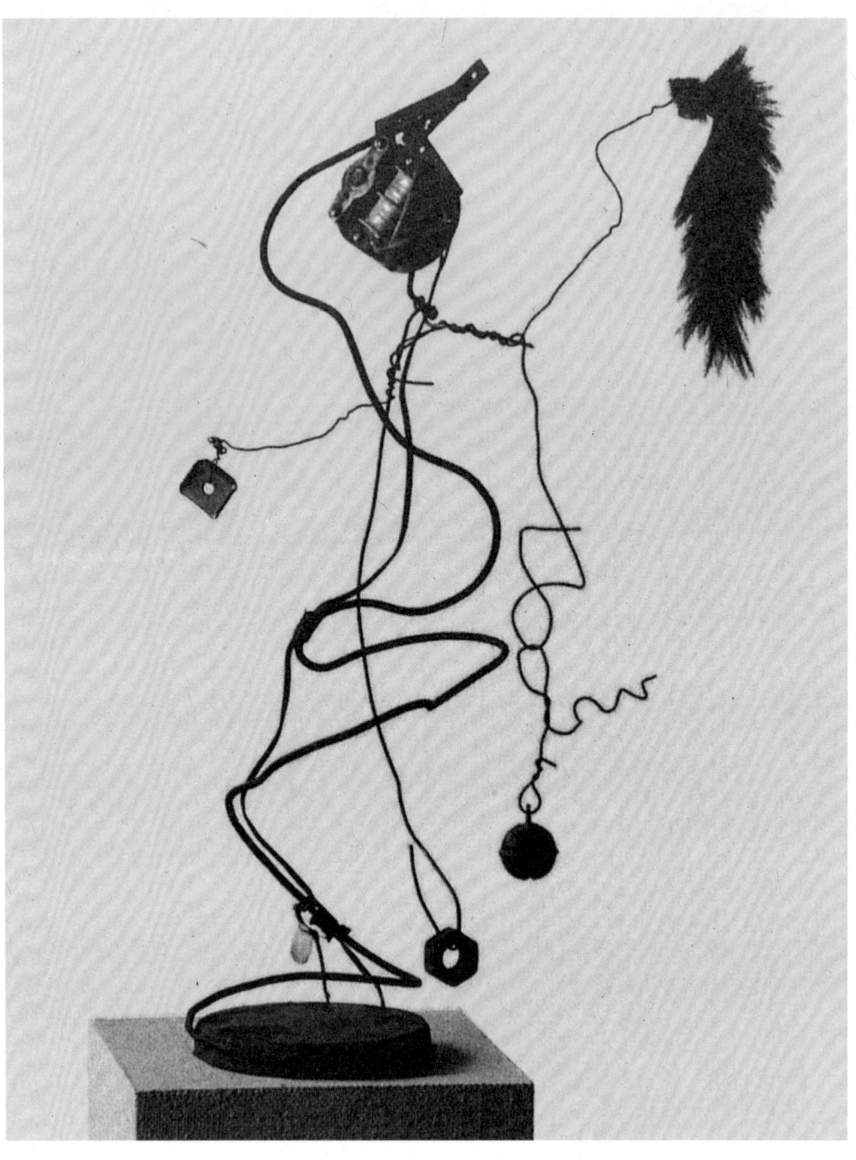

Jean Tinguely
La Folie, 1961
Iron base, wire and metal tubes, fur, nut, bell, electric motor, height: 115 cm

The Tinguely Folly or The Cyclopean Oscillation
Baptiste Brun

"What is it exactly? The materialization of the fantasies of a mental patient, the whims of a madman who can only be calmed by a straitjacket." This is how a journalist from the leading Soviet daily *Izvestia* described Jean Tinguely's oeuvre in early 1963. If, in the midst of the Cold War, the acerbic criticism of the work of "an abstractionist with an atomic bomb" clearly reflected the anti-American and anti-capitalist propaganda spirit of the column that hosted it ("The grimaces of bourgeois society"),[1] this criticism also manifested the permanence of a more than hostile feeling toward modern art shared from the shores of the Volga to those of the Atlantic, despite ideological divergences. Nearly 20 years after the end of the Second World War, it attested to the persistence of the belief in the degeneracy of the arts, forged at the turn of the 19th and 20th centuries by figures such as anthropologist and criminologist Cesare Lombroso (1835–1909) and physician and essayist Max Nordau (1849–1923), then brought to a climax by Nazism and Stalinism in the 1930s. The crude amalgam between modern art and madness was thus continuously reproduced by the most reactionary fringes of cultural criticism, year after year, decade after decade. And artists linked, more or less, to the avant-garde, paid the price, as did Jean Tinguely—Pontus Hultén describes the sense of violence

---

1   W. Silantjew[ski?], "абстракционист с атомной бомбой" ("An Abstractionist with an Atomic Bomb"), Известия *(Izvestia)*, January 3, 1963, reproduced and translated in Pontus Hultén, *Méta*, Pierre Horay Éditeur, Paris 1973, p. 246.

Tinguely felt upon reading this headline, reproduced in the Swedish art historian's first monograph dedicated to the Swiss artist, published in 1973. This was not the first attack Tinguely had suffered. His friend Daniel Spoerri confided after his death that the first artwork sent by the young Tinguely to a Christmas market (Weihnachtaustellung) in Bern had been thrown away, without any response from the organizing committee, who considered it inadmissible: the work of a madman.[2]

It is therefore understandable that, throughout his career, Tinguely would display a certain ambivalence toward this entangling of art and madness, oscillating in particular between a critical comprehension of the discourses in the field of Art Brut—commonly confused with an art of mental difference or illness—and a total fascination for the works annexed by this notion and their creators: Aloïse Corbaz (1886–1964), Ferdinand Cheval (1836–1924), Heinrich Anton Müller (1869–1930), Giovanni Battista Podestà (1895–1976), and Adolf Wölfli (1864–1930). For in this very entanglement lies the equivocal character of all things, the same character that Tinguely explored throughout his work. Even before the "Balubas" period of the 1960s, and right up to that reflected in his desire to honor the sculptures of Giovanni Battista Podestà at the very heart of the Cyclopean monster, and which Niki de Saint Phalle would follow through after his death, Tinguely looked, not without a particular fervor, at objects that eluded art circuits by walking hand in hand with madness and a certain sense of excess.

The "Period of the Madmen"

In 1961, following on from the "Méta-Matics" (Meta-Matics), Tinguely created a machine from welded metal rods, to which he attached a nut here and a bell there. It is crowned by a fur toupee. The electric motor that propelled the entire object generated many jolts to the structure, an arrhythmia accentuated by its cobbled together aspect, a cacophony. The artist called the work *La Folie* (Madness). The bell referred directly to the title. The European iconographic tradition has never stopped identifying this instrument with mental otherness and madness.[3] More generally, the bell is a sign of ambivalence. Although, at least since the Middle Ages,

[P. 146]

---

2   Daniel Spoerri in Michel Beretti and Hervé Nisic, *La Beauté crue*, film, Atopic et Louise Productions, Lausanne 2008, 65'.

3   See for example Gabriel Huquier, *Iconologies où sont représentés les vertus, les vices, les sciences, les arts et les divinités de la Fable, en deux cent seize estampes*, Chez Huquier, Paris, pl. E6. The bell is associated with madness, along with the following variations: bell, tambourine, rosary of shells—percussion instruments to which masks and marottes are added. On the appearance of this motif in the 14th century, see Maurice Lever, *Le Sceptre et la marotte, histoire des fous de cours*, Fayard, Paris 1983, p. 37.

it has been ringing the hours and marking Christian time, a symbol of
the Voice of God and the ordering of the cosmos, it can just as easily,
in its agitation, signify the irruption of a discordance in the course of things.
The mark of a "passage between two worlds or two eras,"[4] it constitutes
a liminal object that underlines the established order while disrupting it.
It is hardly surprising, then, that this essential carnival ornament—a moment
of celebration of life and death, laughter and fear, the profane and the
sacred—should make Tinguely's "machins" (gizmos) jingle.[5]

La Folie of 1961 heralded the series of "Balubas," and seemed to
inaugurate what the artist would later call the "period of the madmen."
During this period, he asserted a "wild" dimension that literally inhabited
the machine—embodied it, as it were—and made it the oscillating sign
of the society that celebrated it: "I feel fairly well rooted in our society,
which I love. I know perfectly well: what I make corresponds to something
that's in the air, that's been in the air; whether it's wild or not, useless or
not, not wild or *baluba*. Total absurdity, the crazy, self-destructive, repetitive
side, the playful, Sisyphian side of machines stuck in their to-and-fro: I feel
that I'm a pretty valid part of this society. Let's put it this way: my work
is a salty, satirical commentary, in which a lot of equivocation enters."[6]
The equivocation of the bell, and that, also, of fur: the latter refers to the fox
celebrated for its cunning as much as it is hated for the passionate relationship it has with the henhouse, the fruit of human labor! Its punishment:
to end up as a trophy around the neck of a lady of rank, a patron of art
galleries. In many "Balubas," it is this same fur—the kind you turn inside
out like a glove—that Tinguely resurrects and makes dance, at the end
of a spike, to the din of a hullabaloo, a parable of a society founded on the
primacy of a crazed and terrifying machine, a distorted image of progress
and its double, the obsolescence of humankind.

The interweaving of madness and the carnival at work in Tinguely's
oeuvre during this period is hardly surprising, an acerbic and droll
commentary on the triumph of productivism, celebrated and undermined in
the same gesture. His contribution in 1966, in the company of Saint Phalle

---

4   Fabienne Pomel, "Pour une approche littéraire des
cloches et des horloges médiévales: réflexions
méthodologiques et essai de synthèse," in Pomel
(ed.), *Cloches et horloges dans les textes médiévaux*,
Presses universitaires de Rennes, Rennes 2012,
p. 19. See also in this collection Karin Ueltschi,
"Clochettes, sonnestes et campanelles: la parure
de Carnaval," p. 127–141.

5   On the distinction and intertwining of "machins"
and "machines," see Déborah Laks, *Des déchets
pour mémoire: l'utilisation de matériaux de
récupération par les Nouveaux Réalistes (1955–1975)*,
Les presses du réel, Dijon 2017, p. 121–168.

6   "Parole d'artiste. Extraits d'une interview de
Jean Tinguely recueillie par Charles Georg et Rainer
Michael Mason, juin 1976," reproduced in *Tinguely*,
exh. cat., Musée National d'Art Moderne, Centre
Pompidou, Paris, December 8, 1988–March 27,
1989, Centre Pompidou, Paris 1988, p. 361.
La Folie is registered under number 213 of the Jean
Tinguely catalogue raisonné: *Catalogue raisonné.
Sculptures and Reliefs*, compiled by Christina
Bischofberger, Galerie Bruno Bischofberger, Zurich
1982, 1990, 2005, 3 volumes.

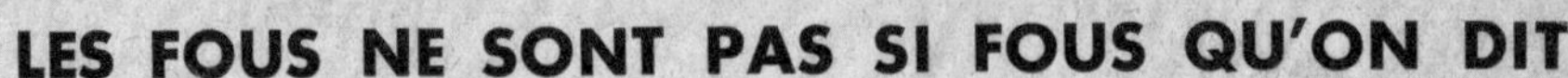

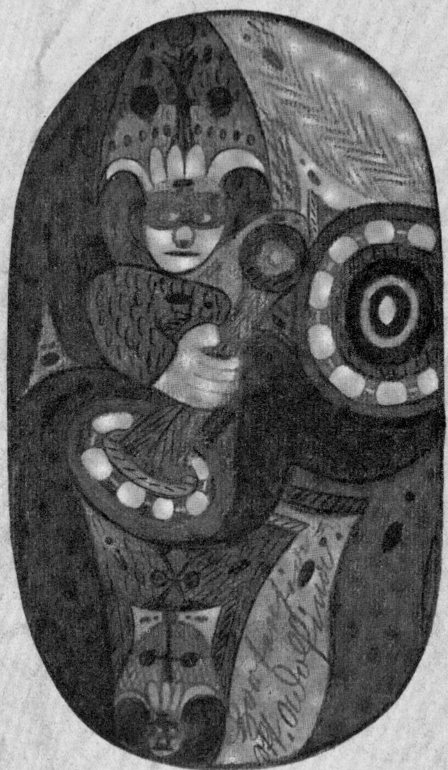

Back cover of Jean Dubuffet, *Les Barbus Müller et autres pièces de la statuaire provinciale*, booklet no. 1 of his review *L'Art Brut*, Gallimard, Paris 1947
Archives de la Collection de l'Art Brut, Lausanne

and Martial Raysse, to the set and staging of choreographer Roland Petit's *L'Éloge de la folie* (In Praise of Folly) clarifies this point. Presented at the Théâtre des Champs-Élysées, the ballet took its title from the work by Erasmus of Rotterdam, published in 1511. It brought humanist satire up-to-date. Silhouettes taken from the *Vitruvian Man* by Leonardo da Vinci stood out against the stage backdrop, where Tinguely mounted a monumental machine propelled by a dancer converted into a cyclist who activated, by pedaling, the mechanisms of a mad world. This ambivalent world is one of oscillating signs, where notions of progress and reason, calculation and profit, measurement and objectivity are implicitly questioned, foreshadowing a critique of value, or even its reversal. In praise of madness, subjectivity, modesty, indigence? Here we hear the distant echo of an assertion made by artist Jean Dubuffet (1901–1985) on the back cover of the first and only issue of the magazine *L'Art Brut*, which he founded and published in 1947: "The mad aren't as mad as we say, nor the sane as sane."[7] This sentence framed the announcement of the publication of a second issue dedicated to Adolf Wölfli, a Swiss artist interned at the Waldau asylum in Bern.[8]

Tributes to Heinrich Anton Müller

One of the most imposing "Balubas" was created for the *Dylaby* installation put in place at Amsterdam's Stedelijk Museum in August 1962. In this "dynamic labyrinth," created in collaboration with Robert Rauschenberg, Martial Raysse, Niki de Saint Phalle, Daniel Spoerri, and Per Olof Ultvedt, Tinguely assembled his favorite materials for the "Balubas" in the center of the fifth room. Dismantled at the end of the exhibition, this machine referred to a figure who was little-known at the time: Heinrich Anton Müller.[9] Following on from those dedicated to Wassily Kandinsky, Kazimir Malevich, Marcel Duchamp, and Salvador Dalí—some of the most famous artists, or those whose influence was to grow after the war—this was the Swiss artist's first tribute to one of the art world's most obscure figures, known only to a small circle of amateurs, artists, and psychiatrists, in the early 1960s. In 1922, art historian and psychiatrist Hans Prinzhorn

[P. 67]

---

7   Jean Dubuffet, *L'Art Brut. Les Barbus Müller et autres pièces de la statuaire provinciale*, Gallimard, Paris 1947.

8   Following the editorial failure in 1947 due to Gallimard's withdrawal, Jean Dubuffet successfully resumed his publication project 15 years later. Published in 1964, the second booklet of the second series was devoted to Adolf Wölfli, with a partial translation of the study by Swiss psychiatrist Walter Morgenthaler originally published in 1921. See *L'Art Brut*, booklet no. 2, Compagnie de l'Art Brut, Paris 1964.

9   On the reception of Heinrich Anton Müller's work, see Roman Kurzmeyer, "Hinweis auf einige Freunde seiner Maschinen," in Kurzmeyer (ed.), *Heinrich Anton Müller (1869–1930): Katalog der Maschinen, Zeichnungen und Schriften*, Stroemfeld Verlag, Basel and Frankfurt 1994, p. 190–198.

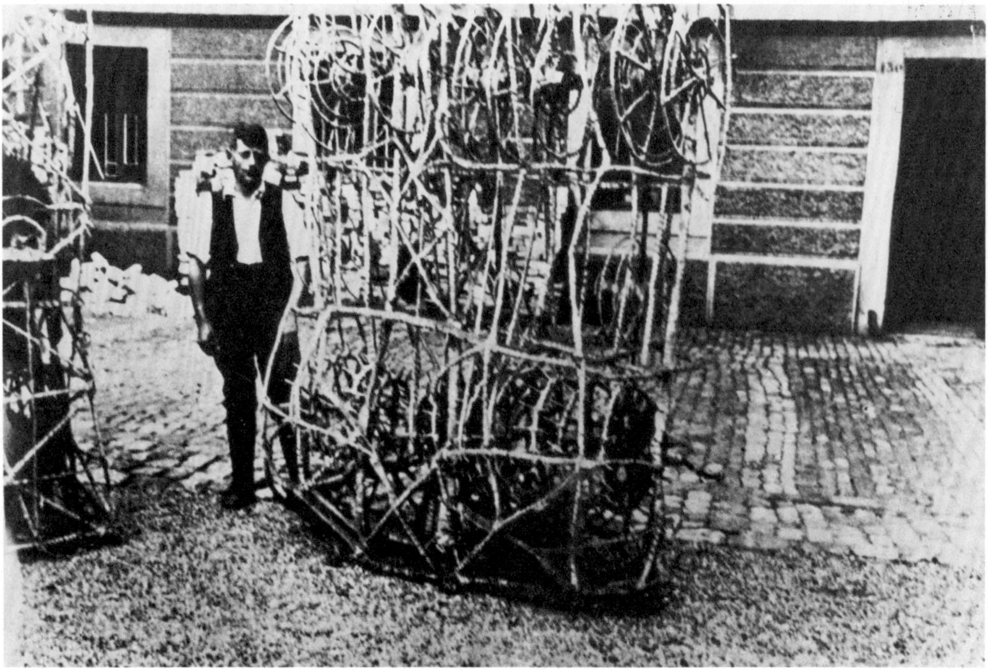

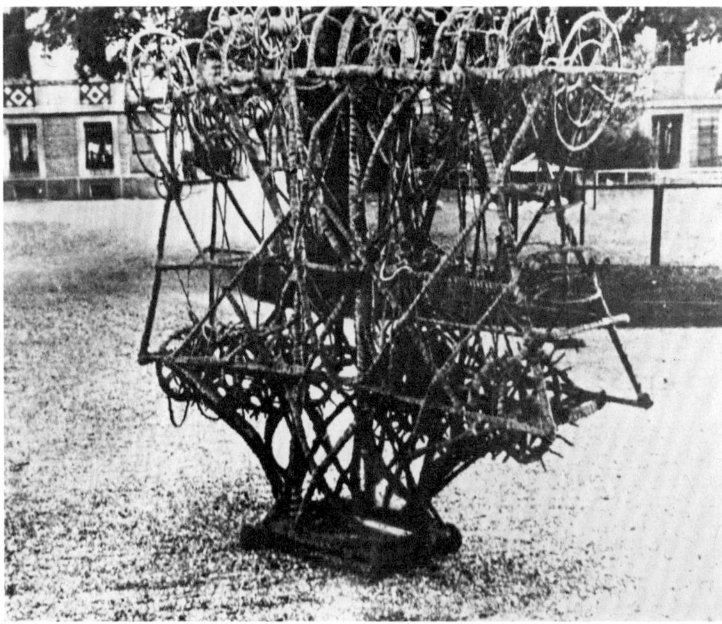

Heinrich Anton Müller next to one of his Machines, n. d.
Archives de la Collection de l'Art Brut, Lausanne

Heinrich Anton Müller, Untitled (Machine), n. d.
Archives de la Collection de l'Art Brut, Lausanne

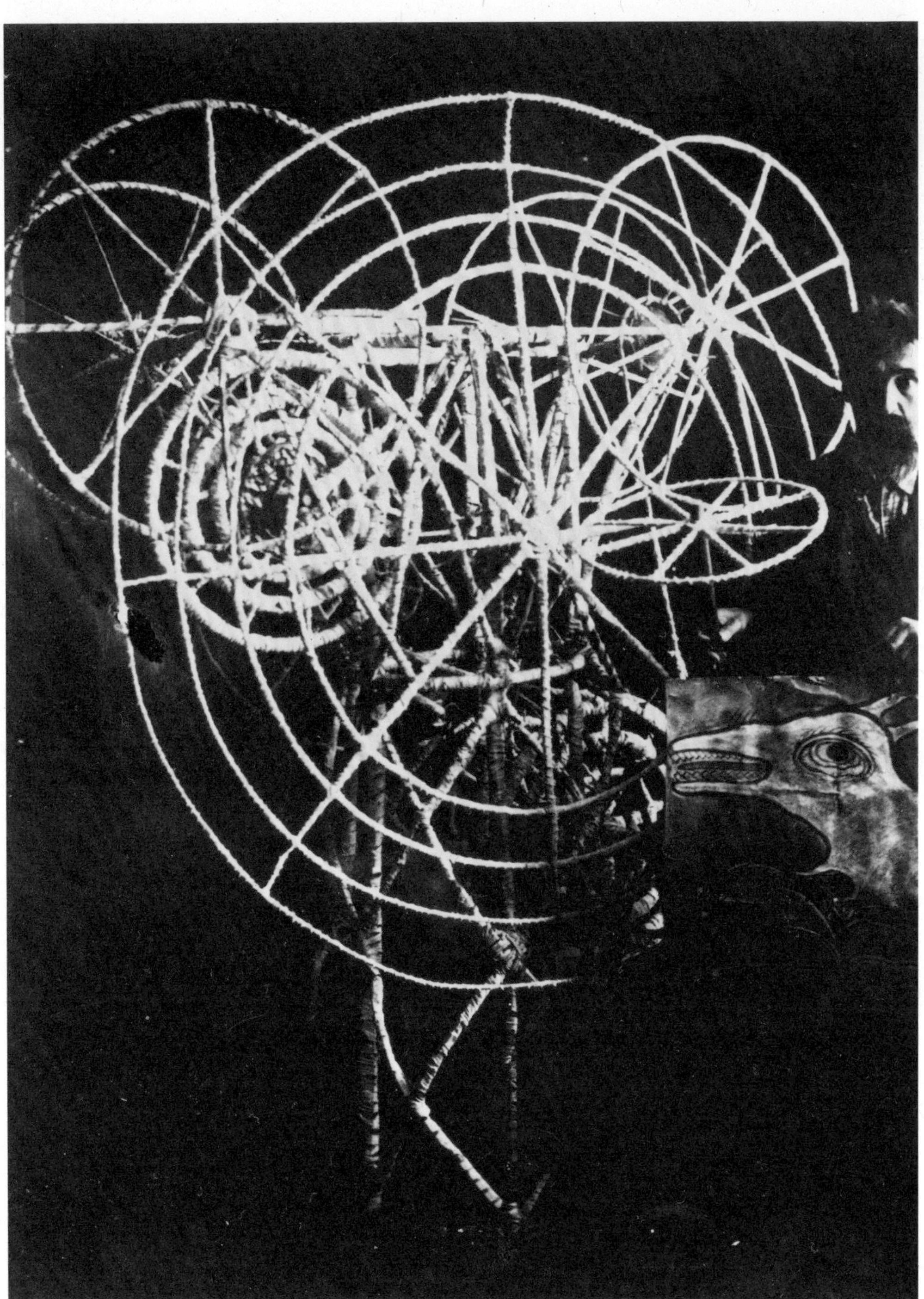

Heinrich Anton Müller next to one of his Machines, n. d.
Archives de la Collection de l'Art Brut, Lausanne

(1886–1933) was the first to reproduce drawings by this winegrower from Vaud, who died in the psychiatric hospital of Münsigen, Switzerland, after 24 years of internment.[10] Later, in 1949, Dubuffet organized the first monographic exhibition of his works, until then considered mainly as documents of madness. A booklet accompanied this modest event, presented at the Foyer de l'Art Brut at the pavillon Gallimard in Paris, headquarters of the Compagnie de l'Art Brut.[11] The painter had asked a psychiatrist, Professor Jakob Wyrsch (1892–1980), who had access to the archives and certain testimonies, to publish a short note on Müller, outlining his biography, and mentioning in a lapidary fashion his "hallucinations and delusions of grandeur" and his "paintings and inventions."[12]

It is highly plausible that Tinguely heard about Müller and his creations as early as 1954. Living in Basel at the time with fellow artist Spoerri, the two would visit the latter's cousin Theodor Spoerri (1924–1973), a psychiatrist at the Waldau. Famous among artists, not least because it had sheltered Adolf Wölfli, the Waldau hospital was a repository for extremely heterogeneous artifacts. Theodor and his wife, Elka (1924–2002), were very interested in these objects, which they never failed to show to their visitors. In a film by Michel Beretti and Hervé Nisic, Bernhard Luginbühl testifies after the fact to this period: "In the museum [at the Waldau], we devoured all these things. Tinguely, Spoerri, and later other famous artists, we used to meet on Sundays in this little museum."[13] This is probably how Tinguely became aware of the drawings and machines created by Müller, whose photographs—according to Spoerri in the same documentary—were copied by hand by the artist.

According to psychiatrists, these machines betrayed Müller's obsession with perpetual motion (*perpetuum mobile*), a mania often described by the medical profession since the 19th century (to each his own obsessions …). Human-sized or slightly larger, they were a priori composed of wheels, hubs, belts, and frames made of branches and other organic elements, partly glued together with his bodily secretions, notably his excrement. The mechanism was operated by a crank that Müller, the designer and

---

10 Hans Prinzhorn, *Bildnerei der Geisteskranken: ein Beitrag zur Psychologie und Psychopathologie der Gestaltung*, Julius Springer Verlag, Berlin 1922.

11 Concerning this story, see Baptiste Brun, *Jean Dubuffet et la besogne de l'Art Brut. Critique du primitivisme*, Les presses du réel, Dijon 2019.

12 The mimeographed booklet distributed at the Foyer de l'Art Brut in 1949 was based on the text written by Jakob Wyrsch for the *Almanach de l'Art Brut*, a project that remained unpublished during Jean Dubuffet's lifetime. See Jakob Wyrsch, "Heinrich Anton M.," in Jean Dubuffet (ed.), *Almanach de l'Art Brut*, edition established and presented by Sara Lombardi and Baptiste Brun with Vincent Monod, Collection de l'Art Brut/5 Continents, Lausanne/Milan 2016.

13 Michel Berreti and Hervé Nisic, *La Beauté crue*. Bernhard Luginbühl added in an interview: "Ah, for Wölfli! Yes, but Wölfli … We've been wölflying and wölflying all our lives! One day we should have finished wölflying, shouldn't we? I've spent almost half my life with Wölfli. He always came first, Wölfli. Of course, I thought he was the best artist who ever lived, this Wölfli."

user, seemed to activate at the approach of people crossing the hospital courtyard where he set them up. In the literature devoted to him by Dubuffet, mention is also made of a "disproportionate telescope through which he gazes, day after day and for hours on end, at a singular large-scale object made by himself from stones and all manner of materials." "Mental castles,"[14] said the inventor of Art Brut, cryptograms; the power of fascination that they provoked in artists in search of new avenues of creation is easy to imagine.

In the documentary by Beretti and Nisic, artist Armin Heusser asserted after Tinguely's death—he had been Tinguely's assistant—that the "Moulins à prières" (Prayer Windmills) are a direct echo of Müller's machines. He argued that Number 1, dated 1954 and now in The Museum of Modern Art in New York, is "a copy in structure, in function, not in material or size, but it is a direct translation."[15] However, if we explore Tinguely's bibliography, and in particular the most important books devoted to him during his lifetime, this early discovery and supposed direct influence is never really advanced, either by the artist himself or by his main exegetes, led by Hultén. A double hypothesis can be devised to explain the shunting aside, if not outright omission of Müller. On the one hand, the dominant discourses—in particular that of Dubuffet—on art considered by some to be "brut" ("raw") suggested a disconnect between these productions and the society that excluded them. Tinguely resolutely opposed this idea. Taking a stand against the idea of autistic art, produced independently of all social interaction, he asserted that "art must be in society and not outside it."[16] On the other hand, and above all, it is highly likely that the artist—already suspected, as we have seen, of deception or even outright alienation—had to face the discomfort of defending, as the sources of his work, forms and artifacts fashioned by people deemed insane.

The fact remains, however, that Tinguely's admiration for Müller continued unabated in the 1960s and beyond. The three rolling machines from the late 1970s are a reminder of this: *Klamauk*, *Radau*, and *Krawall* (only the first two were made between 1979 and 1980) were conceived as both "Super-Balubas" and tributes to Müller. Rare drawings attest to this. Tinguely's relationship with Saint Phalle undoubtedly enabled him to take on this crazy side within his work, to face it head-on and explore it further.

---

14 Jean Dubuffet, "Heinrich Anton M.," *L'Art Brut*, booklet no. 1, 1964, p. 137.

15 Armin Heusser added in the film: "I think Jean was living Heinrich Anton Müller's impossible dream. And I am personally of the opinion that Heinrich Anton Müller and his oeuvre were the main source of Jean Tinguely's constructive force."

16 Niki de Saint Phalle wrote about this in "Lettre à Jean," *Niki de Saint Phalle*, exh. cat., Musée d'Art Moderne de la Ville de Paris, Paris Musées, Paris 1992, p. 153.

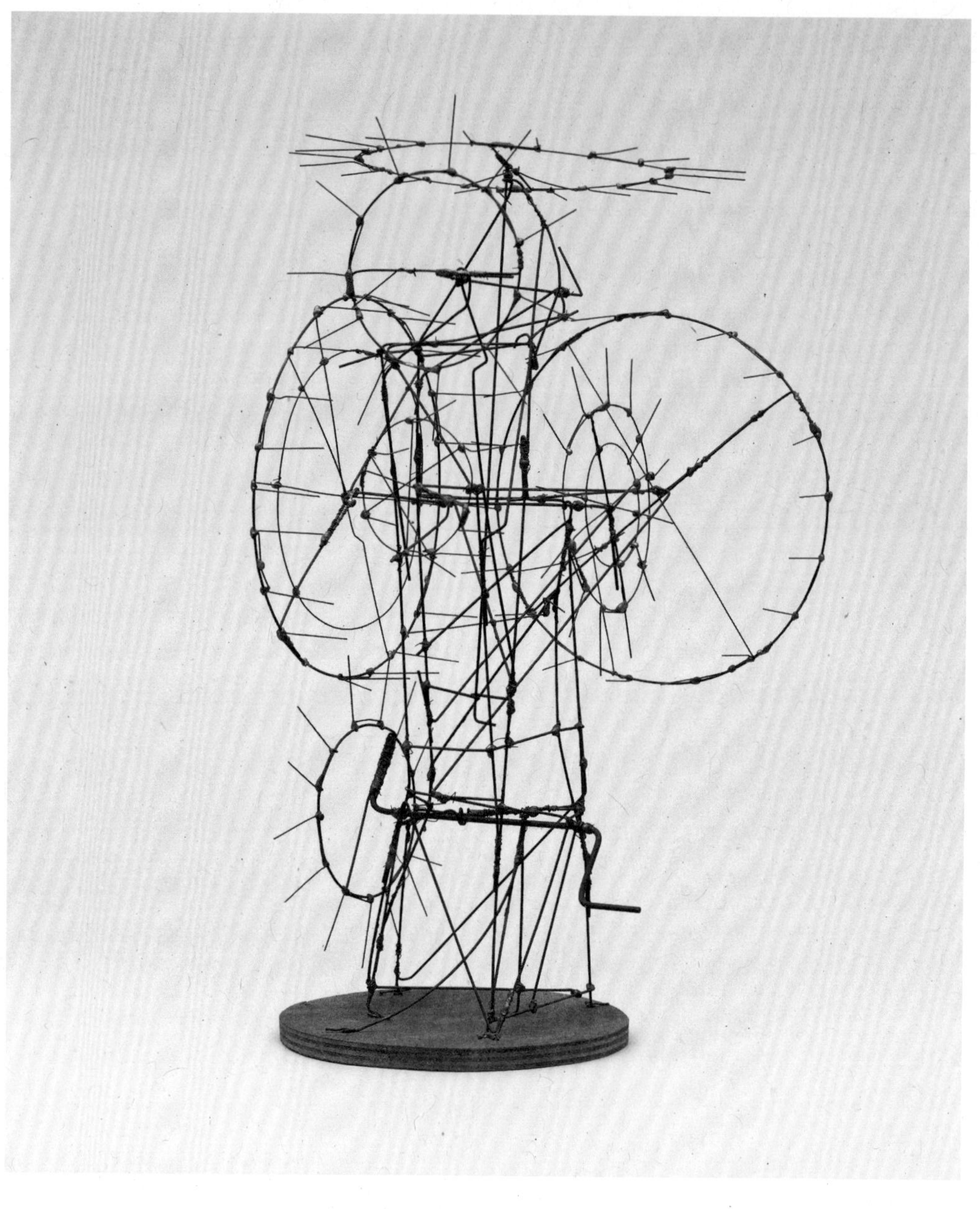

Jean Tinguely
Moulin à prière I (Prayer Windmill I), "Méta-Mécaniques" series, 1954
Wire, metal, and winch handle, 61 × 39 × 29.8 cm
Collection The Museum of Modern Art, New York; The Riklis Collection of McCrory Corporation

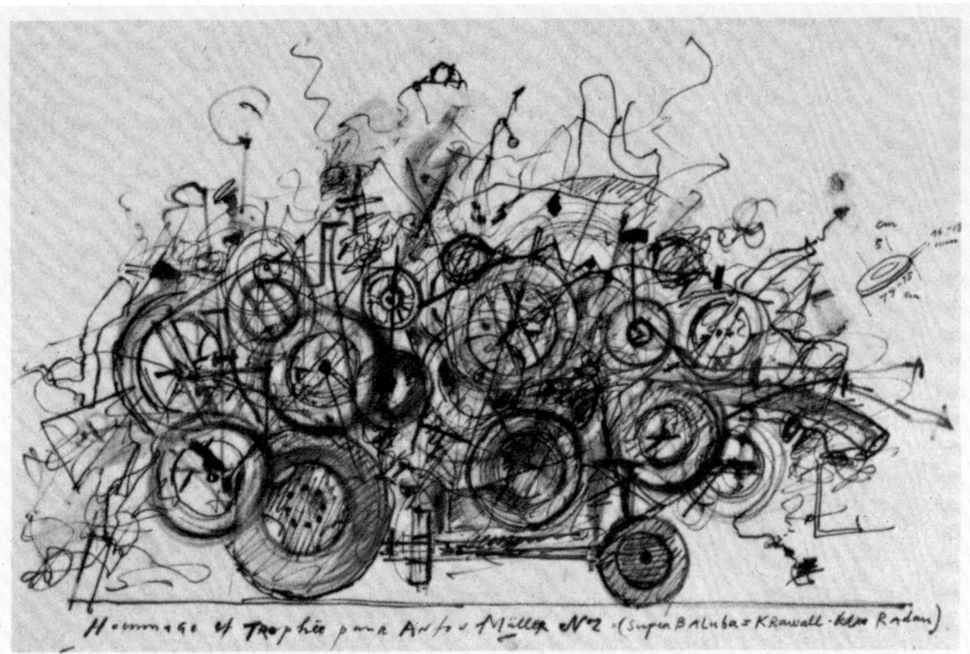

Projet pour la sculpture
Hommage et trophée pour Anton Müller II = Super Balouba = Kravall = Radou, 1978

crayon, plume, stylo-feutre et pastel sur carte

Drawing reproduced in Pontus Hultén, *Jean Tinguely*, Éditions du Centre Pompidou, Paris 1992, p. 282

The Monster and Art Brut

Taking as her starting point a portrait made by photographer Ed van der Elsken for the *Dylaby* exhibition, Saint Phalle created an unusual graphic montage. In place of the torn upper right-hand corner of the photograph, she drew a clock face in pen flanked by a heart, a question mark, and the handwritten words "No" and "Yes." Is it a mischievous love ultimatum? Uncertainty and impatience emerge. Saint Phalle's frontal, insistent gaze, coupled with this graphic appropriation, transforms the damaged image into a self-portrait that emphatically manifests a psychic fragility paired with a steely determination often asserted by the artist as the very driving force behind her artistic identity. Here we find the oscillation of signs that Tinguely and Saint Phalle liked to provoke in their art. Their meeting in 1955, then their love affair, which extended into their creative collaboration, crystallized in a shared taste for the "irréguliers de l'art"[17] ("art unconventionals"), the non-professionals and the insane, the madmen and the amateurs whose work fascinated many professional artists throughout the 20th century.

Following Saint Phalle's obsession with fantastical architecture and outsider artists, with her Tinguely visited the *Watts Towers* built by the mason Simon Rodia (1879–1965) in Los Angeles in February 1962. Saint Phalle had visited the Facteur Cheval's *Palais idéal* (Ideal Palace) in France a few years earlier, in the late 1950s.[18] When she took her partner there in the early 1960s, it was a shock. In a letter dated 1990, into which Saint Phalle recalls their relationship, which was included in the catalogue of her touring monographic exhibition in 1992–1993, she writes: "[The] discovery of this marginal creator gave you immense satisfaction. 'You're right. He's a greater sculptor than I am.' You were seduced by the poetry and fanaticism of this little postman who had realized his immense and crazy dream."[19] The convergence of views is obvious, the fantasy heady. Saint Phalle and Tinguely, along with others, nurtured the possibility of producing a total work of art, a fantastic architecture to rival the *Palais idéal* in Hauterives. Already in the wake of the Amsterdam *Dylaby* and in connection with the unfinished project for a *Dylaby II*, also known as *Liberty Hall*, Saint Phalle wrote to Pontus Hultén: "I've probably

17   The term is scattered through Jean Dubuffet's writings on Art Brut from the late 1940s. It spread to art criticism in the 1960s and beyond.

18   *Niki de Saint Phalle. Monographie. Peintures, tirs, assemblages, reliefs, 1949–2000*, Acatos, Lausanne 2001, p. 494. As for Saint Phalle's obsession with outsider artists and everything to do with Art Brut, see her letter to Barbara Freeman, July 19, 1991, cited in Carol S. Eliel and Barbara Freeman, "Contemporary Artists and Outsider Art," in Maurice Tuchman and Carol S. Eliel (eds.), *Parallel Visions. Modern Artists and Outsider Art*, exh. cat., Los Angeles County Museum of Art, Los Angeles, October 18, 1992–January 3, 1993, Princeton University Press, Princeton 1992, p. 205.

19   "Lettre à Jean," *Niki de Saint Phalle*, p. 153.

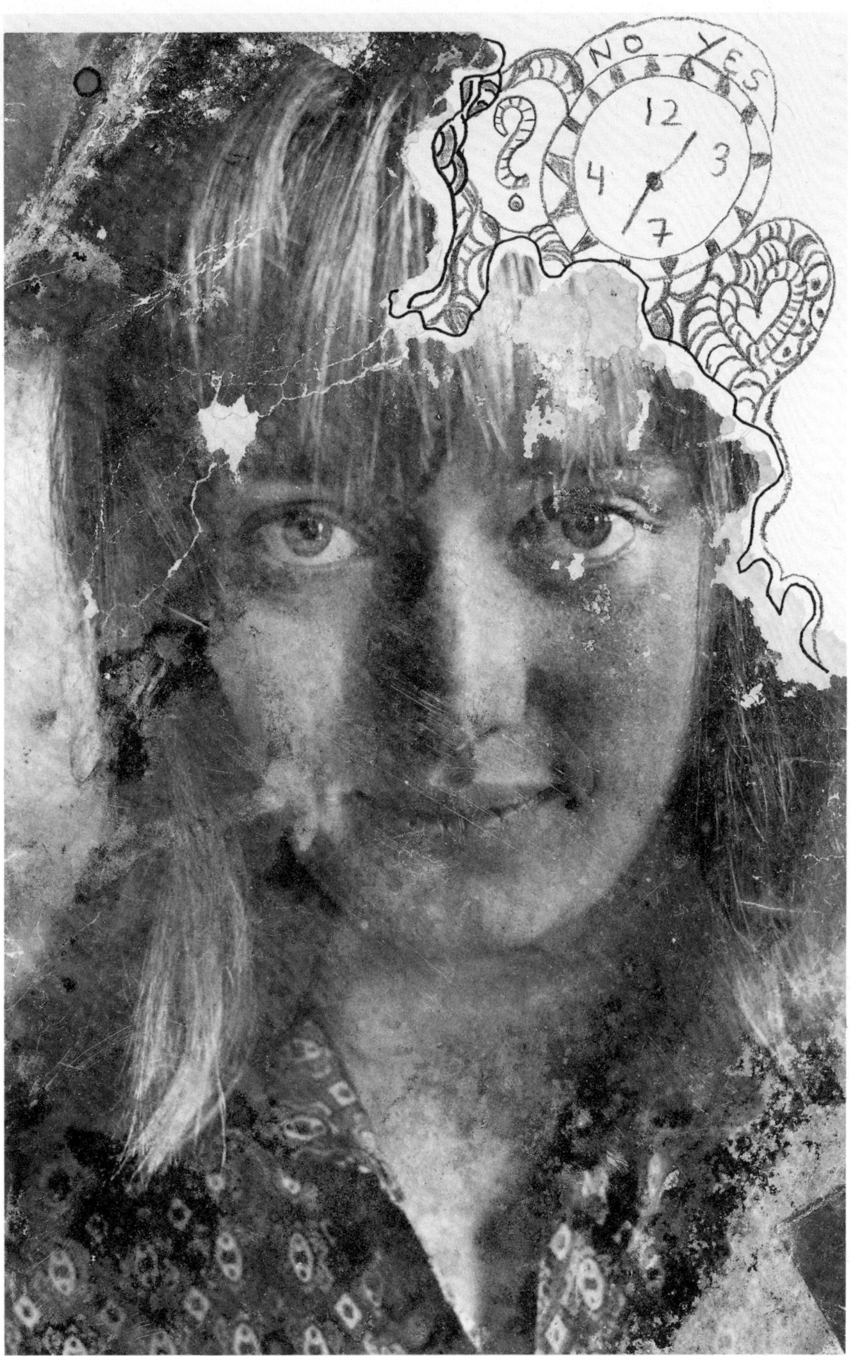

Niki de Saint Phalle
Untitled (Autoportrait à l'horloge), n. d.
Drawing on a damaged photograph taken by Ed van der Elsken during the exhibition *Dylaby*, Stedelijk Museum,
Amsterdam, 1962

already told you that for years I've had the project of making a castle that beats the Facteur Cheval and the *Watts Towers*."[20] *Hon* in 1966 at Stockholm's Moderna Museet and *Le Crocrodrome de Zig et Puce* (The Crocrodrome of Zig and Puce) in 1977 at the Centre Pompidou in Paris echoed this desire, and were solid, if temporary, milestones on the road to the *Jardin des Tarots* (Tarot Garden) (1979–1993), located in Garavicchio, Italy. In parallel with these projects, the Monster was gradually poking its head out of the humus of the Fontainebleau forest, responding eye for eye to the "poetry" and "fanaticism" that Tinguely celebrated in connection with the *Palais idéal*.

Although he did not speak of it much, the sculptor seemed more than a little preoccupied with his illustrious predecessor, his work marked by the stamp of the empire of Facteur Cheval. In the mid-1980s, when the Milly-la-Forêt construction was well advanced, Tinguely revisited a motorized sculpture created in 1984 in one of the imposing macabre installations produced at the time—*Die Hexen oder Schneewittchen und die sieben Zwerge* (The Witches or Snow White and the Seven Dwarfs, 1985). Conceived as a 60-centimeter-high bust, placed on what looks like a traditional sculptor's saddle, it was made from a horse skull. Its name was *Ferdinand*. Amid the many witty and ironic allusions the sculptor made to great men, artists and philosophers in particular, throughout his oeuvre, this was a new type of tribute to an art "irregular," complementing those made in Müller's memory.

The last that was addressed to this fringe of artistic creation, Art Brut and the like, would be carried out by Saint Phalle after the death of Tinguely, who had imagined it at the heart of *Le Cyclop* (The Cyclops). In fact, inside the head of the Monster, as you climb the steps leading to the theater, unusual elements are revealed in the form of polychrome sculptures from the *Piccolo Museo* (Small Museum) by Italian artist Giovanni Battista Podestà. In a surprising staging for the site—niches were carved into the walls, closed off by a vitrine and lit by carefully-placed spotlights—one of the most renowned figures in the world of Art Brut, a field that was still little known at the turn of the 1990s, is honored at the very heart of the dystopian, joyous palace designed by Tinguely. By planning a museum-like display of Podestà's sculptures, the Swiss sculptor clearly demonstrated his desire to call into question the values associated with artistic creation,

---

20   *Hon - en historia (katedral):* "hon," "she," "elle," "sie," "lei," "zij," Moderna Museet, Stockholm 1966, p. 31.

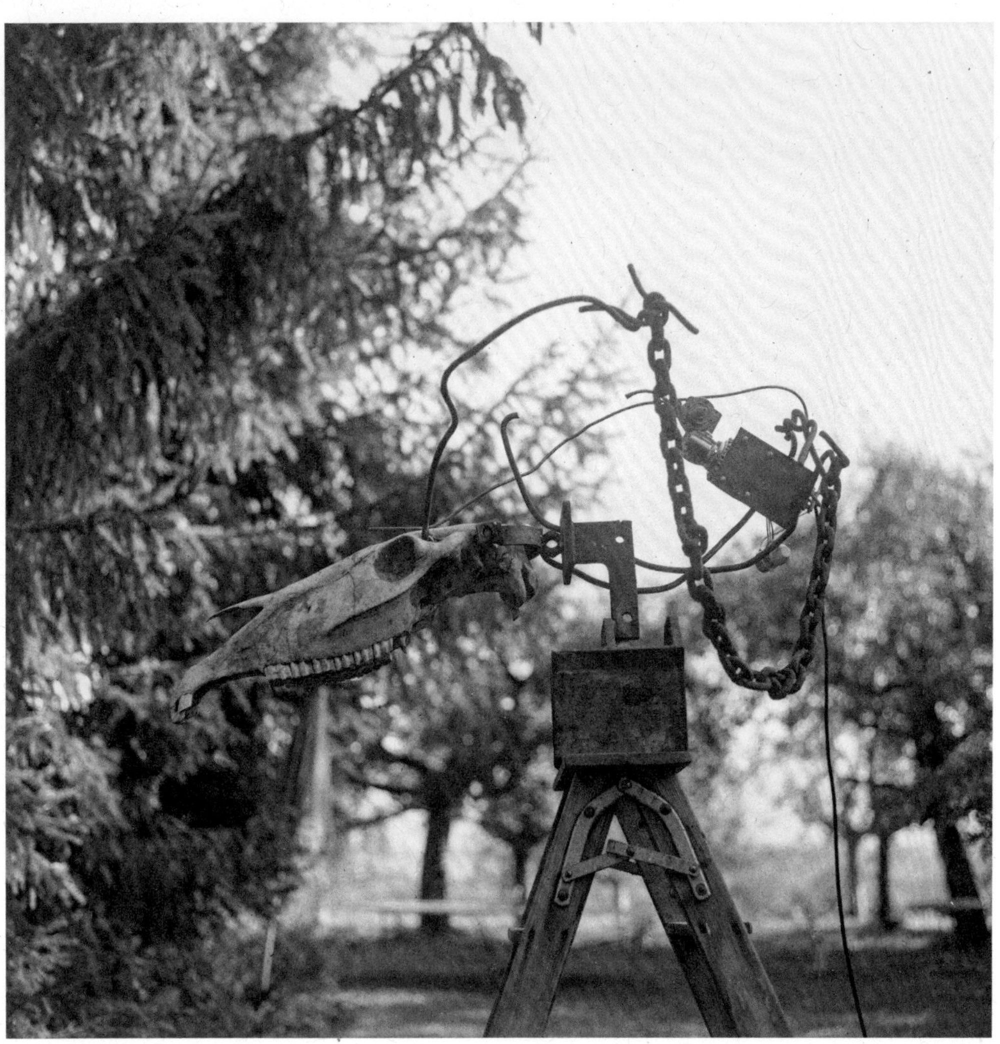

Jean Tinguely
Ferdinand, 1984
Metal, motor, horse skull, height: 65 cm

its conservation and commodification.[21] Echoing the monster's cloaca grafted onto the back of its head—a ventilation chimney from the Musée National d'Art Moderne turned 90 degrees, a tube of dejection mischievously placed at the service of Cyclopean criticism by Pontus Hultén, who was the director of the Musée National d'Art Moderne between 1973 and 1981—the *Piccolo Museo* translates into action the celebration of "art unconventionals" dear to Tinguely, Saint Phalle, Spoerri, and Luginbühl, all *Cyclop* artisans and aficionados of works akin to Art Brut. Podestà's little things nestled in the core of the Monster contributed to the pitched battle waged by Tinguely and his followers against the values market orchestrated jointly by museum and trade institutions.

Tinguely first became aware of Podestà's work through the Basel-based artist Marischa Burckhardt (1927–2018). She had discovered the Italian's production during a trip to the peninsula. She was subsequently instrumental in gaining recognition for Podestà's artworks. Through her, Tinguely acquired numerous pieces, including those now part of *Le Cyclop*, and others now in the collections of the Espace Jean Tinguely–Niki de Saint Phalle in Fribourg. Fascinated, Tinguely was an ardent promoter, financing with his own money a monograph entirely devoted to Podestà by art historian Lucienne Peiry, which appeared in the 15th issue of the magazine *L'Art Brut*.[22]

In this respect, the *Grand Buste* écaillé *aux deux langues* (Large Scaly Bust with Two Tongues) acquired by Tinguely and displayed on the staircase is analogous to *Le Cyclop* in many ways. The content responds to the container, the interior to the exterior and vice versa. Like the reliquary heads of Catholic ritual, this bust focuses the viewer's gaze on its face with its frontal demeanor and wide, staring eyes. But the presence of metallized paper sheets all over the surface, painted with myriad scales enhanced at their center by dots of silver or gold paint, lends the figure's hieratic stance a shimmer that enlivens it. The oversized ears reinforce the sculpture's truculent, baroque dimension, which is amplified by the presence of small beings dotting its surface, agitated angels and demons. The death's head overhanging the occiput recalls human fragility and vanity, echoing the tragic freight car in which Aeppli's dying bodies are piled at the back of

---

21 Hultén mentions the presence of Podestà in Tinguely's overall design for la Tête (the Head) in 1987, in Pontus Hultén, *Tinguely. Une magie plus forte que la mort*, Le Chemin vert, Paris 1987, p. 207. On the Piccolo Museum as an anti-museum manifesto within *Le Cyclop*, see Baptiste Brun, "Au Cyclop dessillant. L'antimusée de Jean Tinguely au regard du *Piccolo Museo Podestà*," in François Taillade (ed.) *La Forêt réenchantée. Une saison au* Cyclop *de Jean Tinguely*, Association Le Cyclop/ Centre National des Arts Plastiques, Milly-la-Forêt/ Paris 2015, p. 49–52.

22 Lucienne Peiry, *Giovanni Battista Podestà. L'Art Brut*, no. 15, 1987. The booklet reproduces 27 works by Podestà that belonged to Tinguely at the time. They include six of those subsequently installed in *Le Cyclop*.

Le Cylop's monumental head. The duality of good and evil is emphasized by the fervent Podestà, who chromatically splits the head in two, blue on the right, red on the left. At the back, this partition is reinforced by a crime scene surmounted by the inscription "Violenza," contrasted with a scene of mutual aid surmounted by the inscription "Conscienza." The bifurcated tongue insists on the ambivalence inherent in all things, which is made explicit by the sentence written by the artist on a phylactery on the top of the bust: "La lingua. La più grande fedele serva [del] volere del'istinto di ogni singolo cervello per pronunciare col volere della propia coscienza = verità e falsita." Not without awkwardness, since orality prevails in Podestà's work, this sentence could be translated as follows: "Language. The greatest and most faithful servant of what the instinct of each individual brain wants, to pronounce truths and falsehoods with the will of its conscience." The ambivalence inherent in *Le Cyclop* is found here as a mise en abyme, characteristic of the work of Tinguely, who liked to blow hot and cold together in his ironic celebration of humankind's obsolescence in the face of the machine.

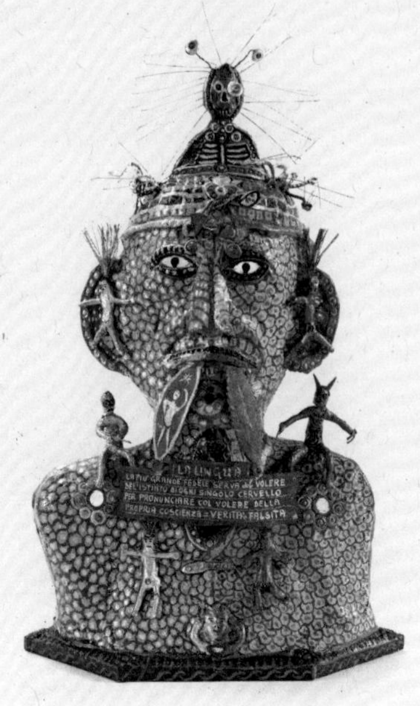

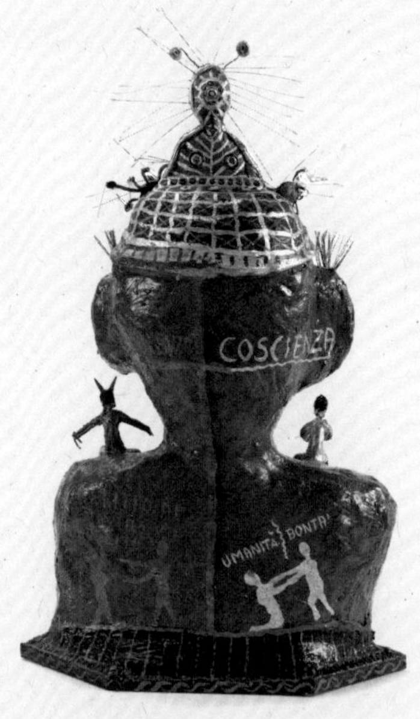

Giovanni Battista Podestà
Grand Buste écaillé aux deux langues, n. d.
Part of the *Piccolo Museo* installed in *Le Cyclop* in 1993

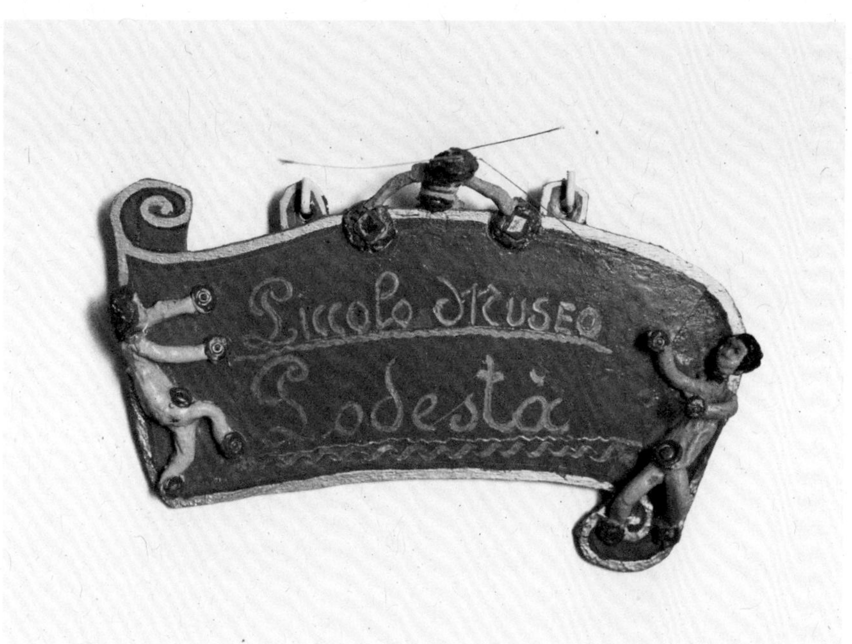

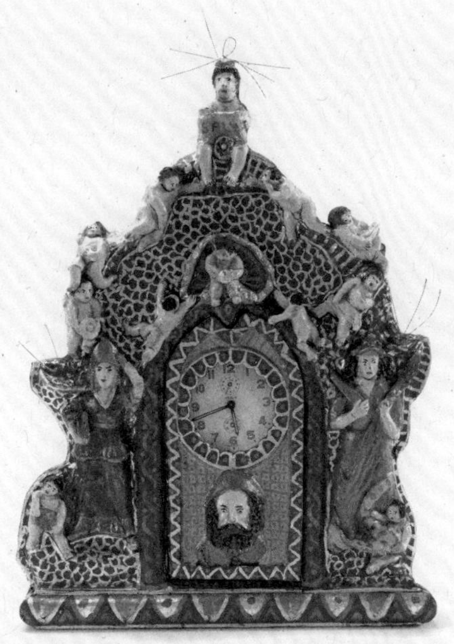

Giovanni Battista Podestà
L'Écriteau and *Pendule aux enfants*, n. d.
Parts of the *Piccolo Museo* installed in *Le Cyclop* in 1993

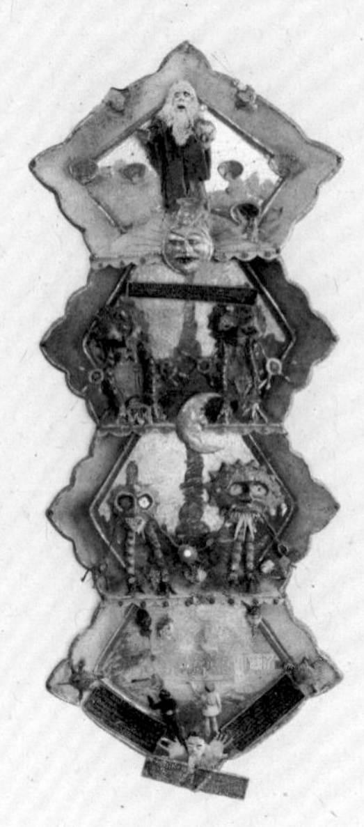

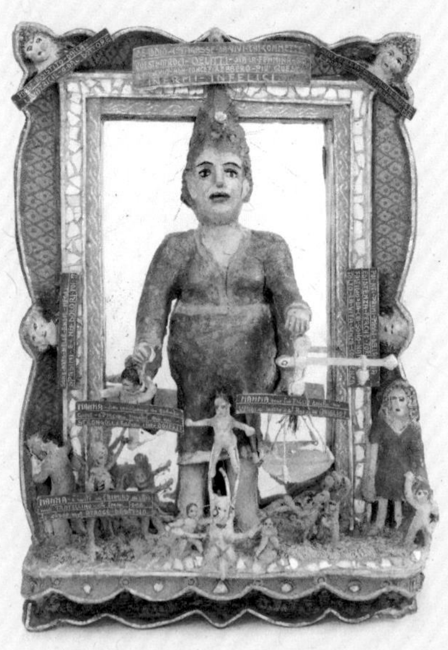

Giovanni Battista Podestà
Le Bien et le Mal and *La Terre, l'Espace et Dieu*, n. d.
Parts of the *Piccolo Museo* installed in *Le Cyclop* in 1993

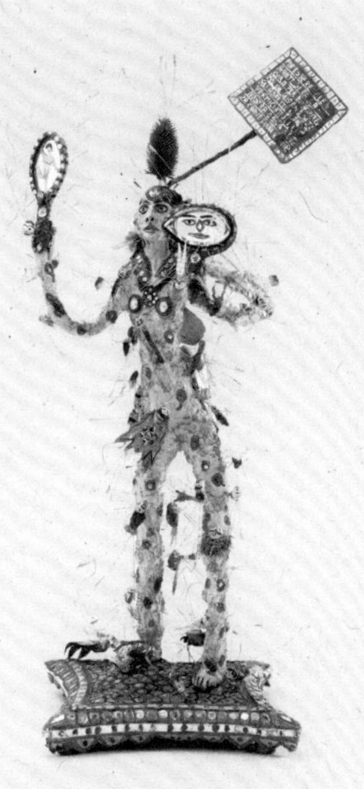

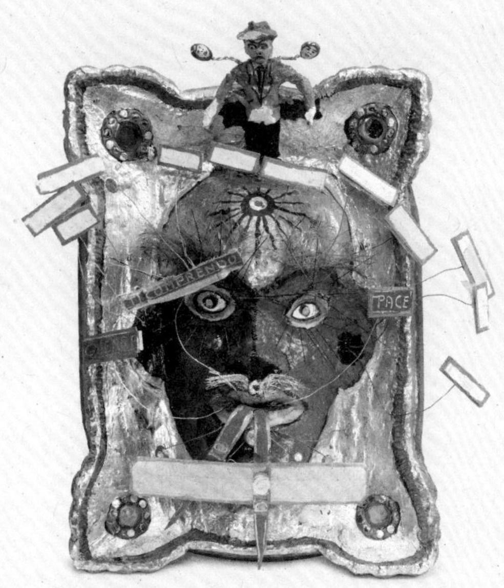

Giovanni Battista Podestà
La Cure d'amaigrissement and *La Procréation*, n. d.
Parts of the *Piccolo Museo* installed in *Le Cyclop* in 1993

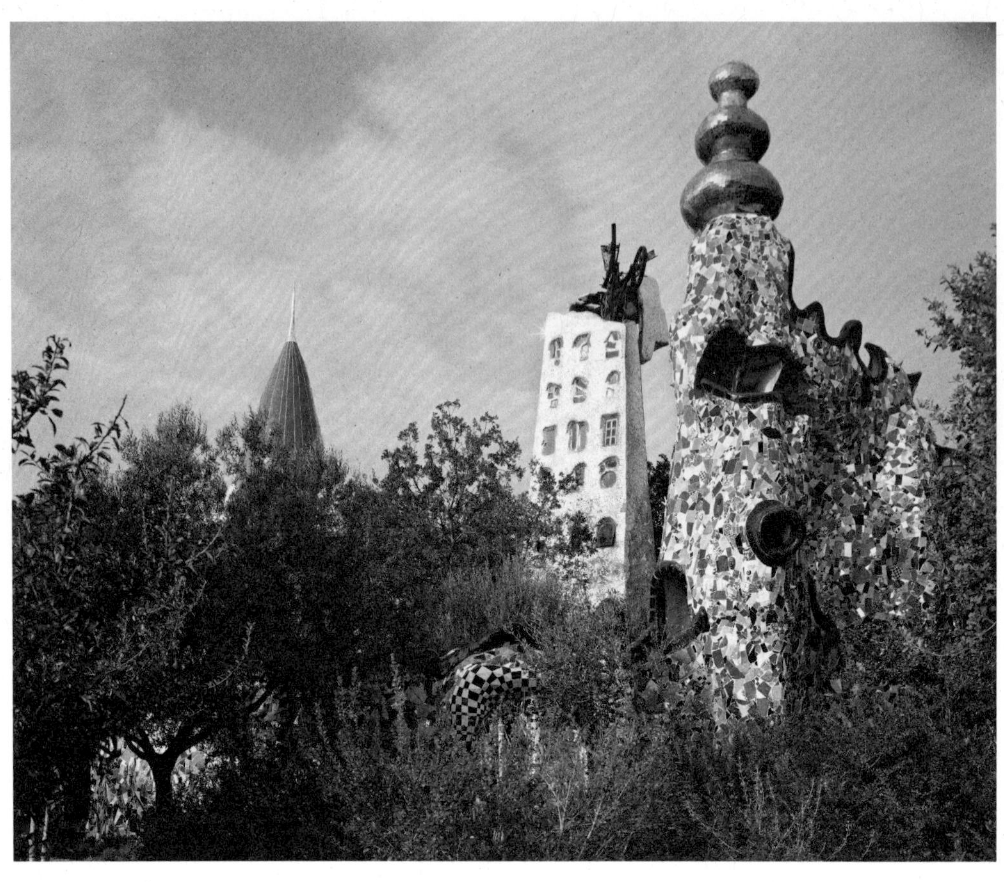

Niki de Saint Phalle
Le Jardin des Tarots, Garavicchio (Pescia Fiorentina), 1979–1993

Long Live/Down with Free Monuments!
About Non-Commissioned Monuments

Denys Riout

In its first edition, the *Dictionnaire de l'Académie française* (1694) gives a definition of the monument linked to time and memory: "A public mark left to posterity to preserve the memory of some illustrious person, or of some famous deed." It wasn't until the sixth edition (1835) of this constantly updated dictionary that an important clarification appeared—"Work of architecture or sculpture, made to transmit memory to posterity [...]"— and a broadening of the scope of this word, which is masculine in French: "Said also of certain public or private buildings, which impose by their grandeur or by their antiquity." The current version of this reference work adds yet another clarification, opening up to aesthetic criteria: "A public or private building remarkable for its grandeur, age, or beauty." Hence, in addition to a commemorative function, public character, grandeur, and beauty can all play a part, to varying degrees, in our idea of what a monument is. But these definitions do not say, or not clearly enough, what everyone understands when the word is used. Always more or less official, monuments are often considered to be associated with "power." Moreover, placed in the public space, or at least accessible to the eyes of all, they impose their memorial charge and compel everyone to yield to their aesthetic.

Monuments—whether sculpture, architecture, or a combination of the two, sometimes with the addition of painting or, at least, color—were created for a wide variety of purposes. Some were designed and built to defy time, while others, linked to temporary events—festivals, *entrées solennelles* (triumphal processions of great pomposity for which structures were erected)—assumed their ephemeral nature. These artifacts were always commissioned before artistic activities were gradually liberated from all supervision. This movement, which began in the modern period, came into its own in the 19th century. Since then, we have seen the coexistence of works created in the context of a public or private commission, and those created freely by artists hoping to meet with the approval of a public, and arouse the desire of buyers, collectors, or private individuals. Today, as in the past, there are specialists in public commissions, most abundantly in France.[1] But there are also artists working independently who respond to a call for tenders, or accept a direct request. However, to the sociological category under whose banner artists of all specialties and aesthetics can take their place, we must add, since the beginning of the 20th century, creators gathered within a nebula that has yet to find a name capable of achieving unanimity. These "singuliers de l'art"[2] ("singular artists") practice activities that are not fundamentally different from those of established artists, especially given the continuous expansion of the artistic field. The interest shown in them by eminent personalities bears witness to this. Yet these "singuliers" usually work without being commissioned to do so. Driven solely—but imperiously—by their desire to create, they always work without a patron when they undertake a monumental project. Admittedly, their creations differ greatly from those of others in many respects, not least in terms of what becomes of the works. But are these differences in fate between commissioned and non-commissioned works as considerable as they first appear? Or, on the contrary, does a certain porosity between the two worlds augur an imminent rapprochement?

While the number of statements in favor of "singular" works of art are indeed increasingly common, few of these works have achieved real fame. Rare, too, are the artists who, like Niki de Saint Phalle, truly abolish borders. In a public letter to Jean Tinguely, written long after their first

---

1   For example, since the 1950s, the "obligation to decorate public buildings," commonly known in France as the "1% artistique" (the equivalent of the percent for art policy, whereby a percentage of federal building costs has to be applied toward art and decoration), which is imposed on the French state, its public establishments, and local authorities, has led to the creation of over 12,000 projects by some 4,000 artists, according to the French Ministry of Culture website. Some of these artists have gone on to become "1% artistique" specialists.

2   This term was used in a memorable exhibition held at the ARC; see the exhibition catalogue, *Les Singuliers de l'art. Des inspirés aux habitants paysagistes*, ARC 2, Musée d'Art Moderne de la Ville de Paris, Paris 1978. "Art of the insane" obviously does not fit the bill, nor does "Naïve Art," and "Art Brut," often used, and rightly so, does not meet with unanimous approval. Bruno Montpied, who has little use for the terms "inhabitant-landscapers" or "roadside visionaries," speaks of "spontaneous vernacular environments," while Rémy Ricordeau refers to "tinkerers of Paradise." See Bruno Montpied, *Éloge des jardins anarchiques*, accompanied by a film by Rémy Ricordeau, *Bricoleurs de Paradis*, L'Insomniaque, Montreuil, 2011.

encounter, she recalls one of their momentary differences, when they had only known each other for a short time in the late 1950s: "I was talking to you about Gaudí and the Facteur Cheval, who I had just discovered and who I had made my heroes: they represented the beauty of man, alone in his madness, with no intermediaries, no museums, no galleries. You were against this idea, you thought that art must be in society and not outside it. So I provoked you by telling you that the Facteur Cheval was a far greater sculptor than you. 'I've never heard of that idiot,' you said. 'Let's go and see him right away.' You insisted. So we did, and the discovery of this marginal creator brought you immense satisfaction."[3] As we know, not only the Facteur Cheval's *Palais idéal*, but also Simon Rodia's *Watts Towers*, and the various versions of Kurt Schwitters' *Merzbau* had an impact on the development of Tinguely's oeuvre, and in particular on his decision to undertake *Le Cyclop* (The Cyclops) in complete freedom, without any commission. These relationships, and even influences, merit further study, and in particular they deserve to be observed from both shores, for while it is certain that marginal works, once they become known, do not leave many artists indifferent, we know less about whether there is sometimes a certain reciprocity.

The Case of Land Art

Few creators recognized as "artists" by society have taken the risk of creating a monumental work that was not commissioned. Apart from Tinguely and Saint Phalle, those we immediately think of belong to the Land art movement. Their most spectacular creations were often installed in desert areas. But even in these vast, desolate spaces, the question of property rights arises. Gilles A. Tiberghien, one of the world's leading specialists on the subject, rightly reminds us: "American deserts do not belong to just anyone. The soil, however arid, is the property of the state or of private individuals."[4] This is why, for example, when James Turrell (*1943) chose the volcano in and with which he was to create his master-piece, he bought it, with the help of the Dia Foundation. Since the purchase of Roden Crater (Arizona) in 1977, the project's development has continued calmly. Of course, such works still need to be financed. Artists with a certain reputation can call on foundations, patrons, gallery owners, or use their own funds, notably acquired through the sale of works, to realize

3   Niki de Saint Phalle, "Letter to Jean," spring 1990,
      published in *Niki de Saint Phalle*, exh. cat., Bonn,
      Glasgow, and Paris, 1992–1993, and reproduced in
      Niki de Saint Phalle. La Donation, exh. cat.,

MAMAC – Musée d'Art Moderne et d'Art
Contemporain, Nice 2002, p. 280 and 281.
4   Gilles A. Tiberghien, *Land Art*, Éditions Carré, Paris
      1993, p. 115.

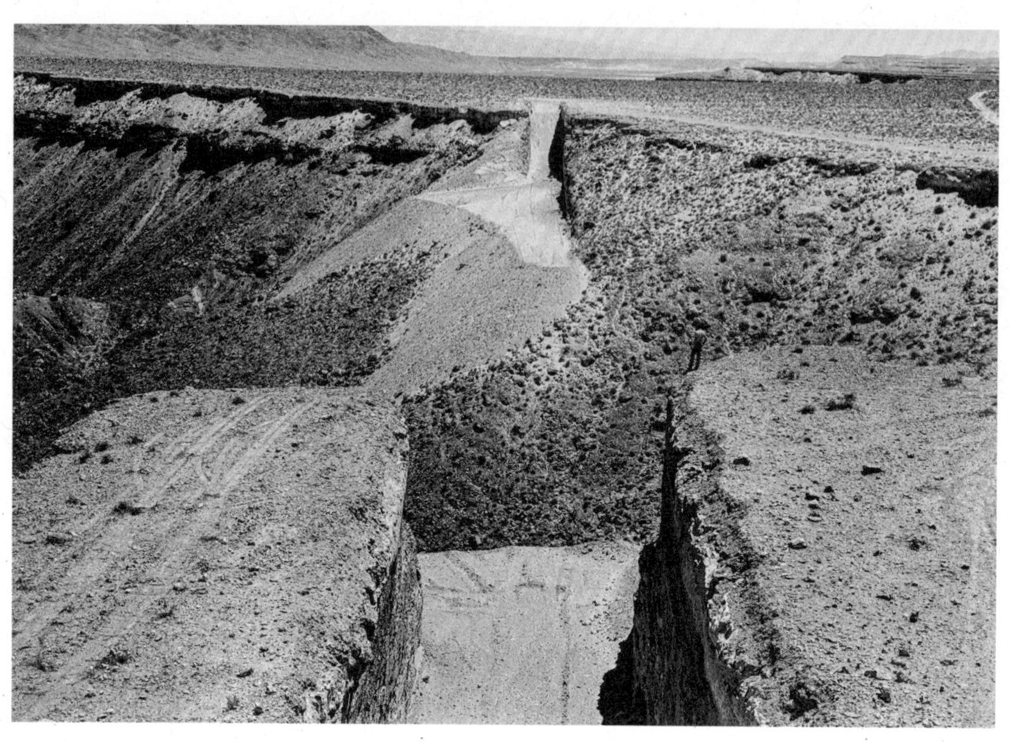

Michael Heizer
Double Negative, Mormon Mesa (Nevada), 1969–1970
Width: 13 meters, depth: 15 meters, length: 457 meters

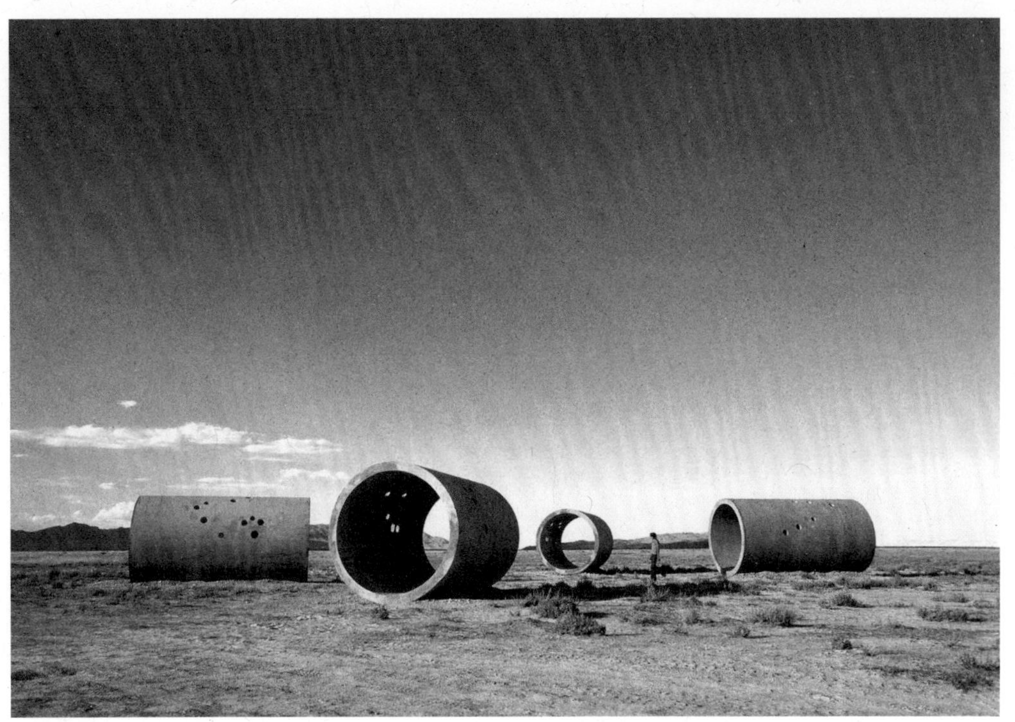

Nancy Holt
Sun Tunnels, Lucin (Utah), 1973–1976
Concrete, four parts, length: 5.4 meters, diameter: 2.75 meters (each)

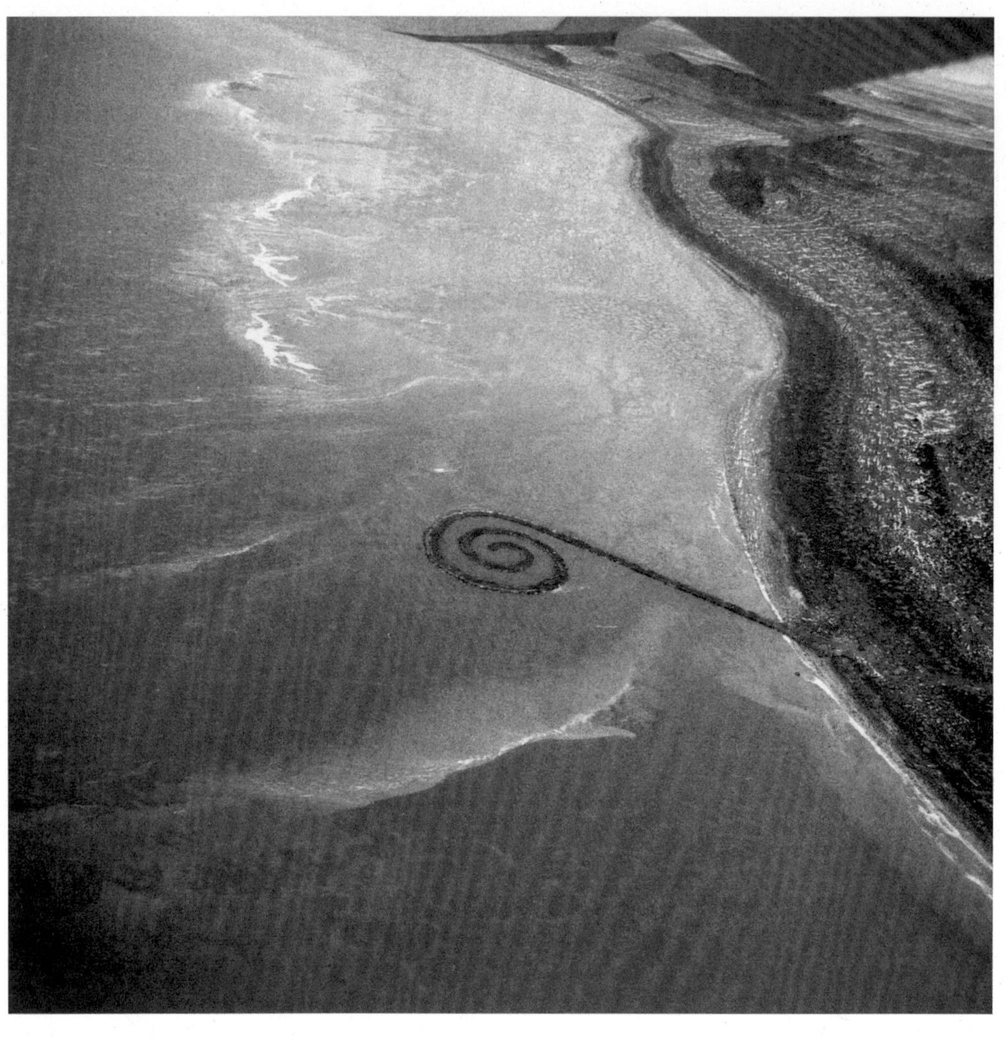

Robert Smithson
Spiral Jetty, Great Salt Lake (Utah), Utah, April 1970
Length: 457 meters, width: 4.5 meters

their most audacious projects, which are always costly when the dimensions
are monumental. This is moreover true of all monuments, and the pedestals
of many of the statues erected in our towns, villages, and sometimes even
the countryside, indicate the how they were financed—public subscription,
donations, or subsidies granted by various local authorities.

Ownership of the site in no way guarantees the artwork's longevity.
Spiral Jetty (1970), one of the best-known works of Land art, was completed
after around two weeks' labor under the direction of its creator, Robert
Smithson (1938–1973). The artist had leased the site from the State of Utah,
which owned the land, and obtained the necessary permits to move some
6,500 tons of rocks and earth, extracted from a nearby hill, into the
shallow waters of the Great Salt Lake. The material was laid out in the
shape of a spiral. This jetty, a coil winding in a counterclockwise direction,
barely protruded above the lake's surface. As the water rose, the construction disappeared. Engulfed by the lake, it remained visible through the
transparent water from the sky. After several decades, the water level
dropped and the spiral reappeared. A change in color was then observed,
due to the salt crystals that had settled on the rocks. What all outdoor
works have in common is that they change over time. Subjected to the
vagaries of the weather and the effects of disruptive agents in circulation,
they are constantly changing, forming a patina, or deteriorating. Another,
more insidious cause of change is the relationship a monument has with its
environment. Once again, this type of indirect transformation can be
observed in all outdoor installations. In the case of *Spiral Jetty*, a certain
amount of anxiety gripped art connoisseurs the world over in 2008.
The announcement of a preliminary drilling project for oil development
some six kilometers from the work sparked a strong rallying movement.
Thousands of messages were sent to the Utah Department of Natural
Resources urging them not to grant permission for this project. Drilling
was not undertaken. An important element in this fortunate outcome was
the fact that the artist's widow, Nancy Holt (1938–2014), had donated
Spiral Jetty to the Dia Foundation in 1999. Protecting the intact state of
artworks is always easier when they are placed under the auspices of a
recognized and powerful institution. However, success itself brings new
risks. Recently, increased visitor numbers have necessitated the construction
of a parking lot, and the Dia Foundation, concerned with the preservation
of the site, asks visitors to leave no trace of their passage. The page dedicated to *Spiral Jetty* on the Dia Foundation website states in part: "Do not
take existing rocks from the artwork nor trample vegetation." "Making fire
pits near the artwork or on the parking lot is strictly prohibited and will
result in significant fines." This list of injunctions finishes with the order:

"Carry out any waste with you." In short, this is nothing out of the ordinary, but it shows the extent to which a site's visitor numbers, proof of success and often used as an argument to perpetuate its protection, are also a potential source of degradation.

It should be noted that the non-commissioned monumental Land art works are not exempt from the general rules governing the creation, dissemination, and conservation of artworks.[5] Built in full legality, they have generally been financed by institutions or personalities from the art world. Virginia Dwan, an important American gallerist in the 1960s and 1970s, notably supported Smithson, Michael Heizer (*1944), and Holt. Last but not least, one of these artworks' special features—the relative protection from human harm afforded by their remoteness—is undermined when success and ease of travel increases the number of visitors tenfold.

Welcome Everyone!

Far from the art world, but nonetheless at the heart of creation, "tinkerers of Paradise"[6] toil for years, decades, to construct an artwork destined to enchant themselves and enthrall their loved ones. The public comes later, or not. Neighbors may take offense, others may support them, but most of their creations remain under threat. These occasional creators show a rare obstinacy. Unlike artists, who always diversify their output, they concentrate their energy on a single project, however proliferous. Most of them are simple folk with no artistic education, but there are exceptions—such as Roger Chomeaux (1907–1999), known as Chomo, creator of the *Village d'art préludien* (Village of Preludian Art) in the Forêt de Fontainebleau (early 1960s to 1999). What they all have in common is that they work as they please, at their own expense, and, above all, on their own initiative. Never commissioned, their creations rarely correspond to an initial overall project. Made haphazardly, they become monumental over time, through sedimentation, growth, and accumulation, without any preconceived overall plan or planning. Scattered all over the land, they rarely stray far from a dwelling. Their preferred locations are small gardens, farmyards,

---

5   It should be noted that many Land art works are installations, ephemeral by nature, and that many of the monuments designed for a site are commissioned, generally by institutions, more rarely by collectors. Spectacular, non-commissioned monuments remain the exception, and all owe their survival to the protection of art institutions, notably foundations. The Dia Foundation, for example, owns and manages *Spiral Jetty*, as well as *Sun Tunnels* (1973–1976) by Nancy Holt, and *The Lightning Field* (1977) by Walter De Maria. As for the Museum of Contemporary Art in Los Angeles, it houses *Double Negative* (1969–1970) by Michael Heizer, a work about which Virginia Dwan said it has "always been for sale" (Virginia Dwan interview with Charles Stuckey, 1984, quoted by Anne-Françoise Penders, *En chemin, le Land Art*, vol. 2: *Revenir*, La Lettre volée, Brussels 1999, p. 72).

6   This name, coined by Rémy Ricordeau, seems to me to sum up the essential aspirations of these indefatigable people who are determined to (re)enchant their world.

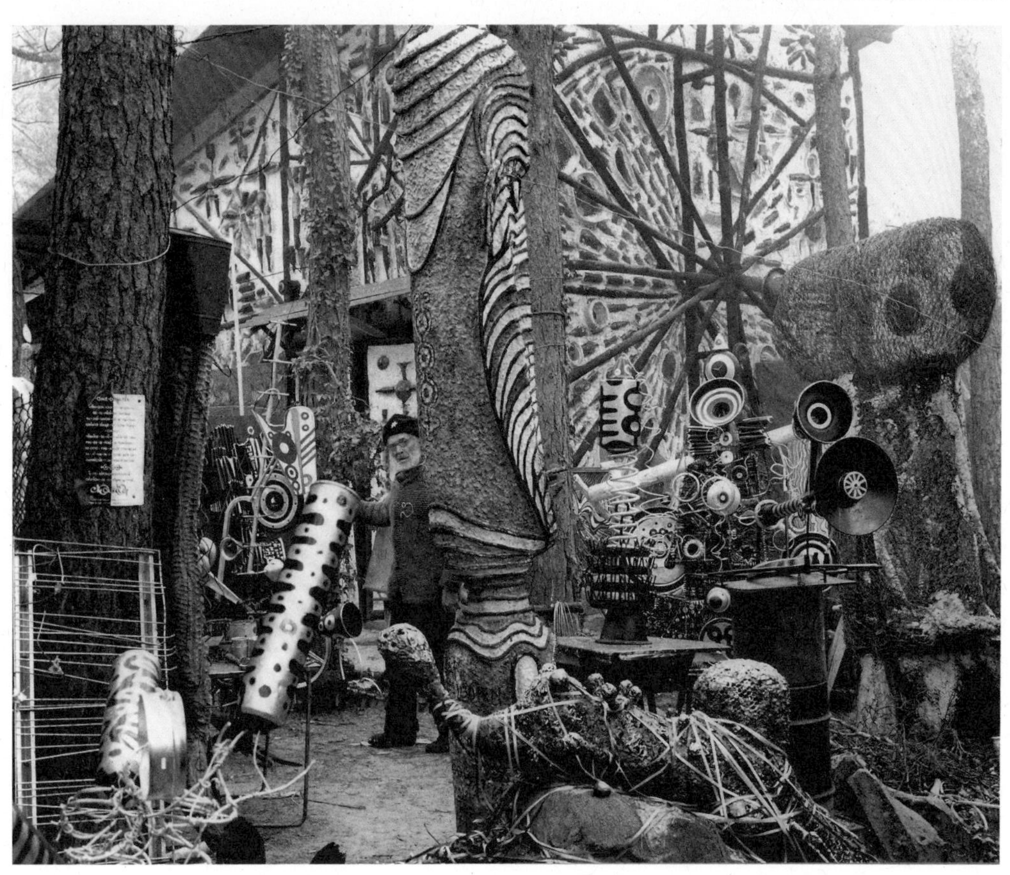

Roger Chomeaux, known as Chomo
Village d'art préludien, Achères-la-Forêt (Seine-et-Marne), 1960–1999

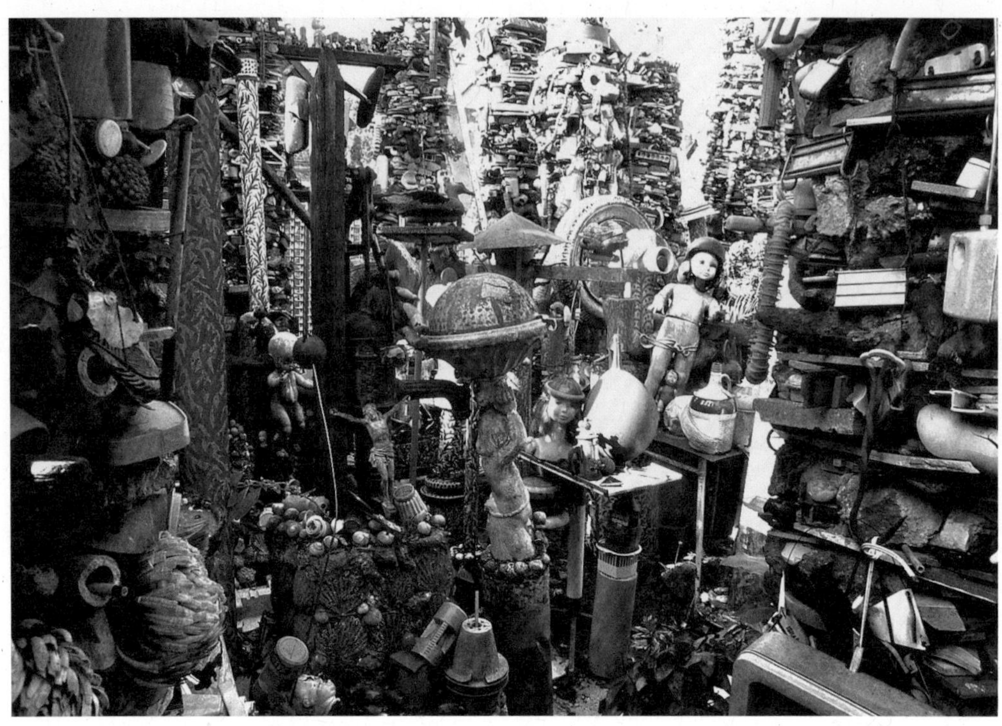

Bodhan Litnianski
Le Jardin des merveilles, Viry-Noureuil (Aisne), 1975–2005

and modest detached houses. That is why they are more likely to be found on the outskirts of towns and small cities than in the chic neighborhoods of metropolises, where the stricter application of town-planning regulations would no doubt have quickly got the better of their fantasy.

These inspired people, these inhabitant-landscapers[7] work from home. Often working alone, they use ordinary tools that are easy to handle and inexpensive—the kind that every DIY enthusiast and gardener has. Although they have to buy the paint or cement they use, the plaster, glue, and so on, they collect most of the materials they put to use close to home, often from public rubbish dumps brimming with colorful bric-a-brac. Bodhan Litnianski (1913–2005) was one of the gleaners in Agnès Varda's film *Les Glaneurs et la glaneuse* (*The Gleaners and I*, 2000). In her preface to a small book devoted to this "mason-artist," Varda notes: "Just as others work in their vegetable garden in a space between the road and their house, growing their leeks and salads, Bodhan Litnianski has created himself an artistic garden where he grows cement vegetables, totem poles made of seashells, garlands in plastic and bouquets of leftovers. The Facteur (postman) Cheval brought his stones home in his wheelbarrow to construct his *ideal palace* (*Palais idéal*) […] As for Litnianski, he brought his treasures home in a trailer behind his moped to construct his *ideal garden*, which his neighbors referred to as the *seashell garden*. This site is already famous."[8]

Fame, though relative, offers little protection, and therefore no guarantee of preservation. Litnianski died in 2005, as did his wife. Not all the neighbors seemed to appreciate the exterior decoration of the walls of the couple's small property, nor the constructions that had gradually transformed the garden into a monument. Several councilors also felt that this colorful jumble, located at one of the entrances to Viry-Noureuil (c. 1,800 inhabitants, Aisne), did not enhance the image of their commune. Bruno Montpied reports in his *Éloge des jardins anarchiques* (In Praise of Anarchic Gardens) that, during a visit in 2008, he observed that "the vegetation had swallowed from within, like a voracious vampire jungle, the pillars made of agglomerated discarded objects, the footbridges connecting them with their numerous plastic foosball figurines."[9]

---

7   I am obviously referring to two terms used in the *Les Singuliers de l'art* exhibition catalogue.

8   Agnès Varda, "Préface," *Le Jardin des merveilles de Bodan Litnianski*, text Denys Riout, photographs Benjamin Teissèdre, Éditions Vivement Dimanche, Amiens 2004, p. 3. I have corrected the spelling of the first name, Bodhan, in the quotation and in my text, which is spelled with an h, contrary to what we believed 20 years ago.

9   Bruno Montpied, *Éloge des jardins anarchiques*, p. 141–142. Today, in 2022, I cannot say what the situation is, but a few years ago, at the end of the 2010s, the damage was already considerable. Ed. note: although published in 2025, this text was written in 2022.

This fate is by no means reserved for "unauthorized" creations, for contrary to what common sense might suggest, nothing is more fragile than a monument. Even when they have been commissioned, authorized, protected by law, crafted from resistant materials, and built according to the rules of the art, all remain vulnerable. This vulnerability is due, first and foremost, to their location in space. Exposed to the elements, they are also potential targets for the most banal forms of ordinary, carefree vandalism. But they can also arouse quite deliberate fury. Whatever the causes of this destructive iconoclasm, whether ideological, political, religious, racial, or other, the result remains the same. How many statues have been knocked from their pedestals, overturned, how many monuments recently smashed, desecrated, or soon will be? For the destructive rage that transmutes a form, always innocent in itself, into a reviled symbol is by no means a phenomenon of the past. A recent example in France? This took place in Amboise, in front of the royal château. The idea of erecting a monument here had been advocated by the report on "questions of memory concerning colonization and the Algerian War," submitted to French President Emmanuel Macron by historian Benjamin Stora. Erected in honor of Emir Abdelkader (1808–1883), and commissioned from sculptor Michel Audiard (*1951), it depicted this hero of Algerian resistance to the French conquest, who was placed under house arrest at the Château d'Amboise from 1848 to 1852. On the eve of the official inauguration scheduled for February 5, 2022, in the presence of elected representatives, government officials, and the Algerian ambassador to France, the monument was vandalized. The reasons for this ransacking, more political-ideological than aesthetic, had nothing to do with the greed of scrap merchants who had salvaged a bit of metal, as was reported—an attempt at humor?—on social networks.

Sometimes, however, predators covet a material or hanker after its monetary value. In France, our cities still bear many traces of this. Here and there, passers-by may come across a stone pedestal deprived of the statue that rested upon it, confiscated during the Occupation because it was made of bronze—the metals of this alloy, then in short supply, were used, in particular, in the arms industry. More recently, a relative shortage of copper led to higher prices. This economic situation inspired criminals to steal on December 15, 2005, a monumental sculpture by Henry Moore (1898–1986) from a park near London, and more than 20 other statues were stolen at the same time in the United Kingdom for similar reasons.

A site for debate, public spaces host or receive monuments of all kinds. The embodiment of memory, all of them are potentially endangered. That said, not all benefit from identical protection, as their status may differ. The vast majority of them reside in the public space in complete

legality, with the most unquestionable legal authorizations, because they
have been commissioned by, or in partnership with, the public authorities.
When they give rise to controversy, militant rejection, or determined,
violent hostility, the state owes them protection. Vandalism is punishable
by law. The perpetrators of damage are sought out, tried when identified,
and, where appropriate, punished. What is more, these monuments are
considered to be works of the mind, and are subject to copyright, even when
they are the result of collaboration between several artists. This in no way
prevents malicious acts, of which there are many examples, nor simple
negligence, such as lack of maintenance, since sometimes, once the inauguration is over, monuments are of little interest to either their sponsors
or passers-by. Only art lovers and heritage conservationists raise the alarm
when artists or their beneficiaries fail to do so themselves.

Non-commissioned works by non-artists are clearly more fragile
than others. When Tinguely, Saint Phalle, and their friends set about creating
a work of art, without authorization, on land they owned, the result of
their efforts was protected by their reputation. At least up to a point.
The state, for example, never considered calling for the destruction of this
construction, erected without any legal basis. But Tinguely's renown did
not prevent thefts from the site surrounding the artwork, and acts of
vandalism by those he called "penetrators." Faced with varying degrees of
damage, he even considered relocating *Le Cyclop*, believing it would be
better protected in the Saint-Cloud national estate. Donated to and accepted
by the French state in 1987—although the latter does not systematically
accept all works it is offered, far from it—and inaugurated in 1994 by the
then French President, François Mitterrand, *Le Cyclop* is now open to
the public and enjoys the protection due to all public heritage monuments.
This is a serious guarantee, but by no means absolute, nor eternal, as tastes
change, and a relative lack of interest in a particular artistic production
generally does not augur well for the preservation of its material integrity.

The artworks devised by the humble, the little people, the common
creators who work independently and freely in a space they own, are rarely
the object of active vandalism. Hatred between neighbors, or disapproval
from elected officials, generally does not result in destruction. Rather,
the dangers arise with the creator's death, after which the house, garden,
or field may remain abandoned for some time. Then, whatever happens,
it changes hands. And the new owners, even if they are family members,
do not always want to live in the clutter conceived by their forebears, let
alone restore objects, sculptures, and imposing structures for which they
have little admiration, if not abhorrence. These differences in taste and usage
must be acknowledged. You can admire the *Mona Lisa* without wanting

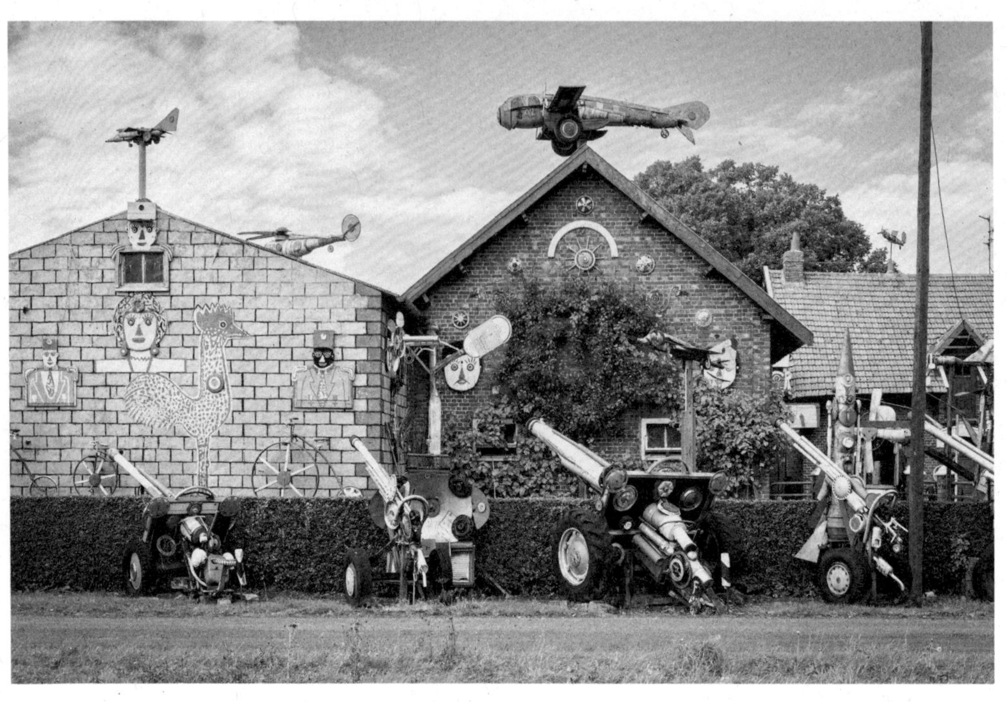

Arthur Vanabelle
La Ferme aux avions, Steenwerck, 1960–2014

to live under her gaze. Hence, what can we say about these overcrowded spaces that inhabitant-landscapers, however inspired the former may be, are so fond of? Paradise remains a personal matter. Double-faced, it can become for others a prefiguration of Hell. That is why the occasional visitor may retain a fond memory of a visit to a place that someone else would have considered truly unlivable.

This potential discrepancy between the feelings of a visitor who has come there on purpose, full of hope, and one who is unwillingly subjected to a situation, must be taken into account in order to understand the complexity of the relationships maintained, and the diversity of reactions aroused by the presence of non-commissioned monuments. In a documentary filmed for France 3 in 2015, the mayor of Steenwerck (Nord), a municipality of 3,500 inhabitants, offers a well-balanced account. Aware of the importance of the "Ferme aux avions" (Airplane Farm) created over the decades by Arthur Vanabelle (1922–2014), he sheltered some of its elements that were in danger of being stolen or destroyed after their creator's death. A connoisseur of Bruegel and Rubens rather than Art Brut, he shared his personal feelings in this report. A neighbor of the farm that became famous in the region and beyond in the 1990s, he confided to his interviewer: "You know, it's never very interesting to be next to a property where someone puts up any old thing, things that catch the eye, that attract the curious, in short, you can't say that it's beautiful […] People prefer to have a property with a nice draft horse or a nice saddle horse or a nice herd of cows. In the countryside, that's what people want to see.[10]

A completely personal work of art, created without authorization, at home, can generate mixed reactions, even a certain hostility, but only when it is visible from the public space. Commissioned works are no exception to this rule. Reactions, whether favorable or unfavorable, always have an impact on the preservation of human productions. In the case of works undertaken "at the creator's expense," only the significant mobilization of a determined public can guarantee, if not perpetuity, at least a reprieve. This is undoubtedly one of the reasons why we know of no pre-19th-century examples of non-commissioned monuments, whereas the oldest preserved monuments—the megaliths of Europe or the pyramids of Egypt, for example—were built well before the beginning of the Christian era. It is true that the private construction of large-scale works requires social conditions that were rarely met before the industrial revolution—having

---

10   Transcript of remarks made in the report directed by
     Hélène Desplanques, *Pourquoi chercher plus loin.*
     Les chemins de l'art brut, a program produced by
     France 3 Nord Est, 2015.

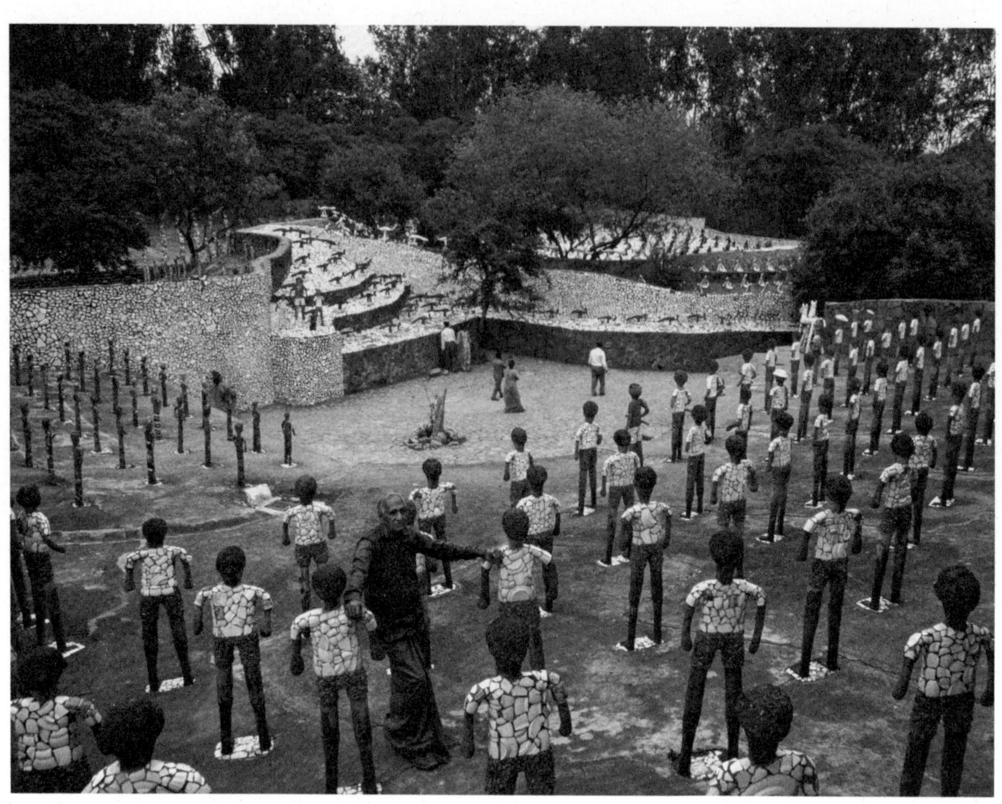

Nek Chand
Rock Garden, Chandigarh, 1957–2015

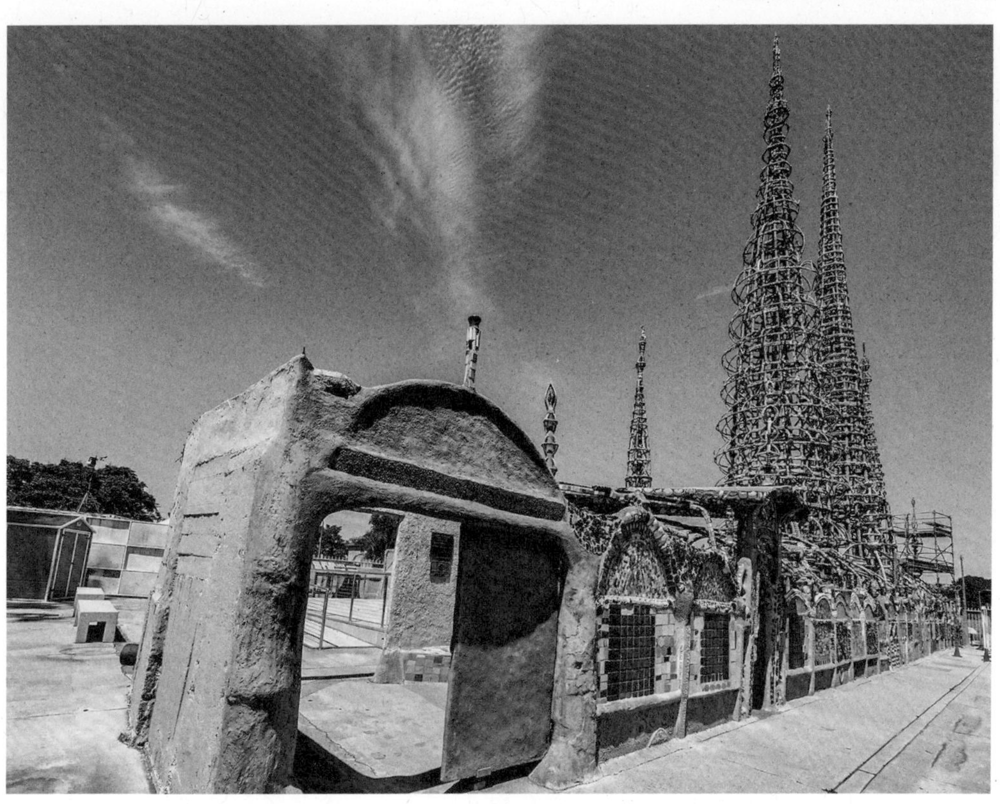

Simon Rodia
Watts Towers, Los Angeles, 1921–1954

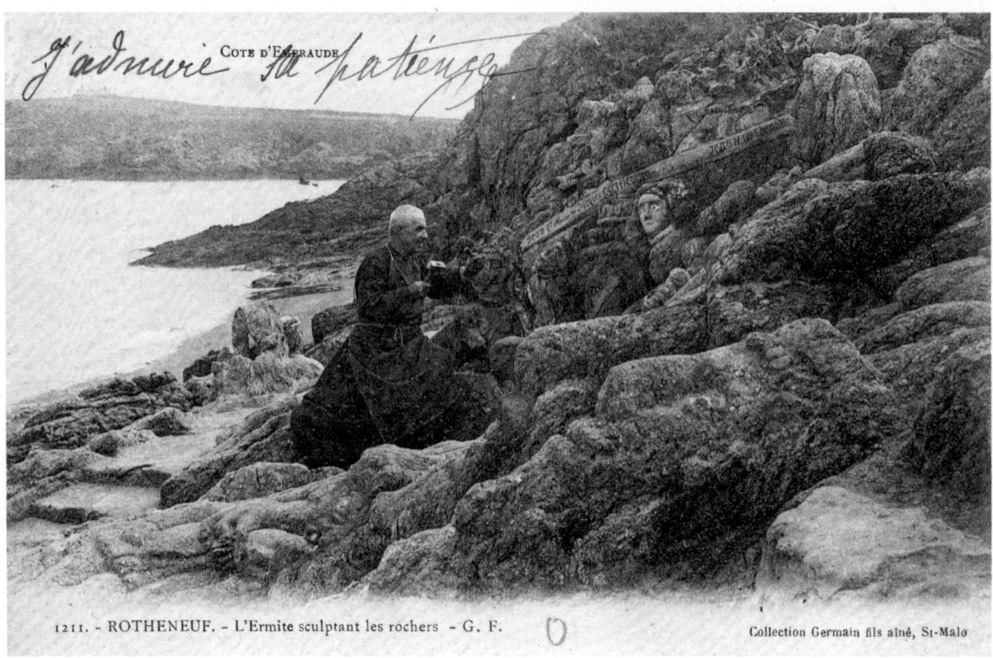

Adolphe Julien Fouéré, known as Abbé Fouré
Sculpted rocks, Rothéneuf, 1894–1907
Postcard, 18 × 13 cm

free time, owning at least one house, a plot of land. But this in no way explains why the Art Brut creations we know of rarely predate the second half of the 19th century, when it would have been entirely possible to preserve any drawings, paintings, or small sculptures with more eccentric ambitions than those of the more consensual, long-accepted objects of folk art. Only graffiti related to the monuments and buildings on which it was engraved has survived the centuries.

Another question that has received little attention to date is that of the location of these unusual monuments or "environments." According to Colin Rhodes, a specialist in outsider art, they are most common in France and the USA.[11] Rightly cautious—the somewhat informed reader immediately thinks of one of the most grandiose sites of this kind, *Rock Garden*, in Chandigarh, India, initiated in 1957—Rhodes' assertion raises other questions. If it is true that more individually-initiated monuments were built in France and the USA, what cultural and artistic soil, what social tolerance, what collective benevolence would have encouraged their appearance? Moreover, it is also not impossible that curiosity and interest, more keenly felt here than elsewhere, have contributed to their preservation, and consequently to the increase in their numbers.

Preserve, Conserve, Enhance Heritage

Begun in 1879 and completed in 1912, the *Palais idéal* by Ferdinand Cheval (1836–1924) was classified as a historic monument in 1969, thanks to the tenacity of André Malraux. Famous since the late 19th century, the building was visited, commented on, and reproduced on postcards long before the famous mailman died. Today, a similar procedure protects the *Watts Towers* built between 1921 and 1954 in Los Angeles by Simon Rodia (1879–1965). Some monuments have been saved from accelerated decay. Others remain under threat, such as the group of sculptures carved directly into the granite rocks of the seaside at Rothéneuf, near Saint-Malo. Abbé Fouré (1839–1910) committed himself to this task for 15 years, from 1894 to 1907. Subject to erosion, they are difficult to preserve.[12] Periodically, however, articles are published expressing alarm. They reflect the growing interest of art lovers, institutions, and public authorities alike. Denigration has given way to celebration, all the more so as these rebellious, or at least independent, monuments attract the public and contribute to the growth

---

11   See Colin Rhodes, *Outsider Art. Art Brut and its Affinities*, Thames & Hudson, London 2022.

12   Created in 2010, the nonprofit organization Les Amis de l'Œuvre de l'Abbé Fouré works to protect the site. It also carries out a range of activities designed to raise the awareness and understanding of Abbé Fouré and his works, https://rochersrotheneufart-brut.com/ (last accessed May 2025).

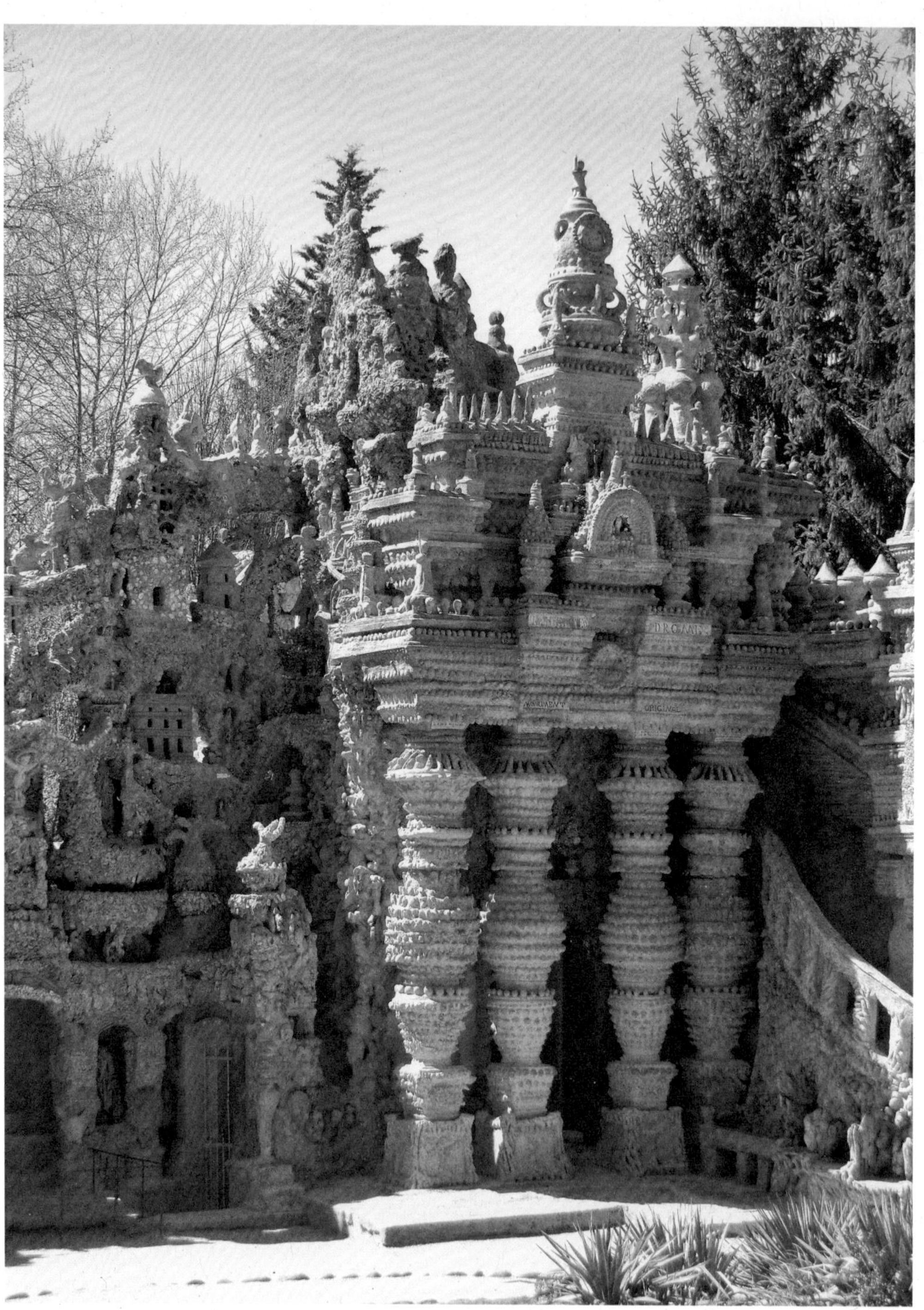

Le Facteur Cheval
Palais idéal, Hauterives, 1879–1912

of tourism. In other words, there is an emerging trend toward heritage preservation. It is attracting an ever-growing public. The regional and national press echo this trend. They denounce the threats hanging over such works,[13] or, sometimes, announce the hope of classification or safeguarding.

This movement really began after the end of the Second World War with the creation of the Foyer de l'Art Brut at the Galerie René Drouin, followed by the Compagnie de l'Art Brut. Jean Dubuffet brought together writers, poets, critics, and artists. Since 1976, his collection has been on display at the Musée de l'Art Brut (Lausanne), created to house it. Initiatives have since proliferated. The LaM (Lille Métropole Musée d'Art Moderne, d'Art Contemporain et d'Art Brut, Villeneuve d'Ascq) has been home to the Aracine Collection since 1999, and presents this ensemble devoted to Art Brut on the same site as its modern and contemporary art collections. La Maison Rouge, founded by Antoine de Galbert in 2004 and closed in 2018, was one of the focal points for the dissemination and recognition of works from this movement, hung on the same walls as those of artists better integrated into the art world. The boundary between outsider art and art recognized as such is becoming blurred, or, even better, tending to vanish. A recent donation by Bruno Decharme to the Musée National d'Art Moderne – Centre Pompidou opened the door to works that had hitherto been confined to the margins of art, if not kept well away from it. In a presentation of this donation published on the museum's website, the collector explains one of his motivations: "It was essential for me to create a body of work bringing together the major pieces in the collection […] To make them inalienable, to protect them from the risks of dispersal linked to the vagaries of time and family inheritance." The desire to make the collection part of general cultural heritage is clearly expressed here. The works received by the museum, now protected, will be preserved, restored, if necessary, catalogued, studied, and exhibited for public enjoyment—just like the other masterpieces brought together in the museum. These works, long relegated to the register of psychiatric curiosities or the minor fantasy section, now have a completely different status. If they are to be protected, the rights of their creators must also be protected.

A symposium entitled "Art Brut. Identity and Artists' Rights" was held on October 15, 2019. Organized by the #ArtSansExclusion (#ArtWithoutExclusion) endowment fund and the nonprofit EgArt – Pour un accès égal à l'art (For an Equal Access to Art), it was sponsored by

---

13   Among many others, particularly in the regional press, I will mention an article by Patrick Martinat in *Le Monde* on January 6, 2012, "Art Brut Masterpieces Seek Saviors." Its subtitle remains relevant today: "Most sites are disappearing, along with the death of their creators with their teeming minds. Enthusiasts are sounding the alarm."

the French Ministry of Culture and hosted by the ADAGP, the society of artists and authors in the graphic and visual arts, which manages the copyright of its members. Marie-Hélène Vigne, a lawyer specializing in intellectual property law, reminded participants that it is not necessary for a work to be considered a work of art in order to be protected by law. All "works of the mind" are works of art, without discrimination, if they are "original," emanate from their author, or, to put it in more legal terms, bear "the imprint of his or her personality." As such, no one should be able to destroy or even damage them. But someone has to assert this right before it is too late.

The question of heritage preservation is essential, but remains complex. If we want to preserve everything, we run the risk of immobilizing the world, and, as a result, drying up the living sources of creation. Memory goes hand in hand with forgetting. But what should be preserved, what can be neglected? The answer to this question does not lie in the sphere of pure ideas. Fluctuating and differing from one era and culture to another, it is now, more than ever, the subject of debate. Once ignored, non-commissioned monuments are increasingly attracting attention. Many of us are delighted by this.

Photographs taken in 2023–2024

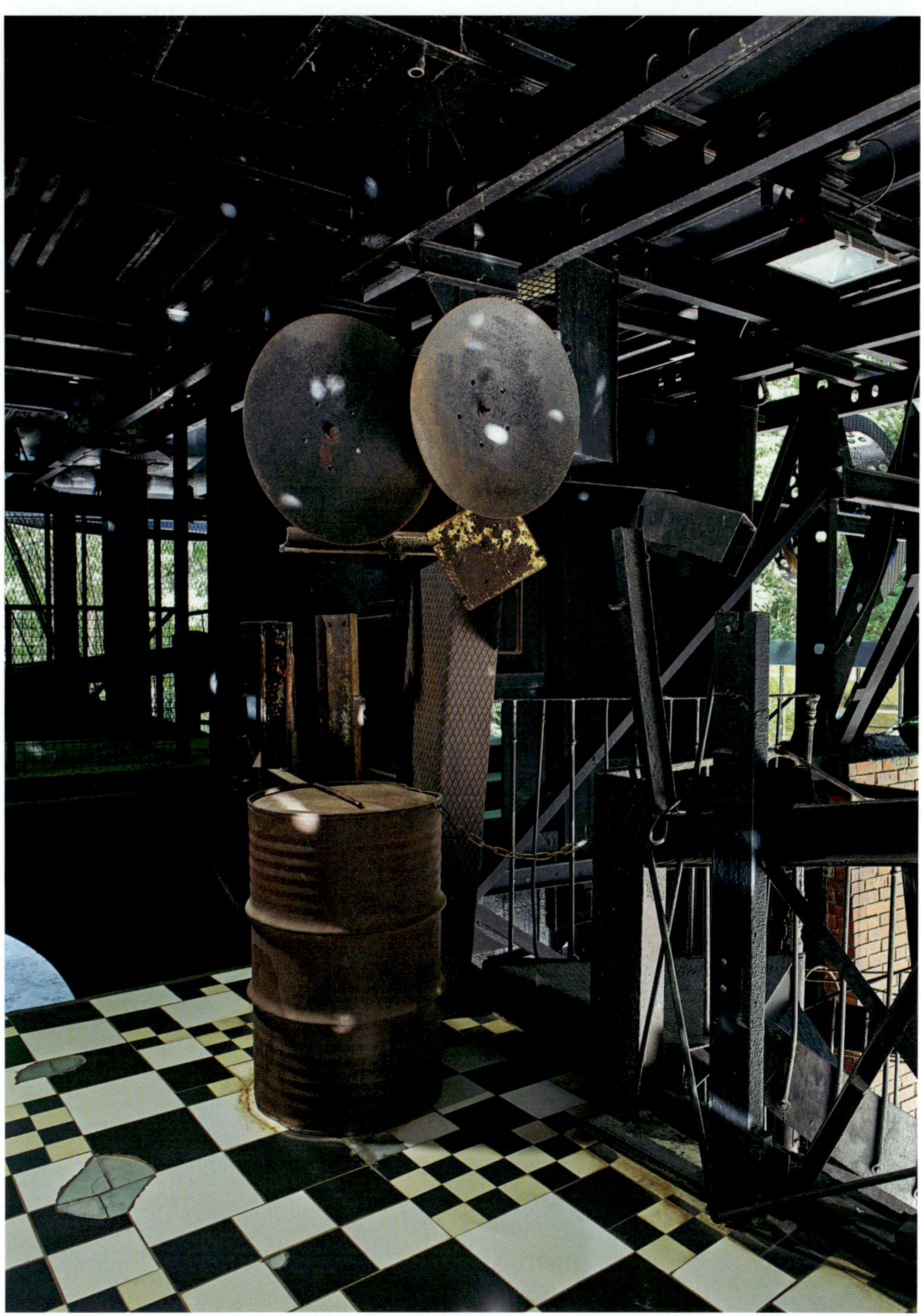

Jean Tinguely, *La Batterie*, c. 1976

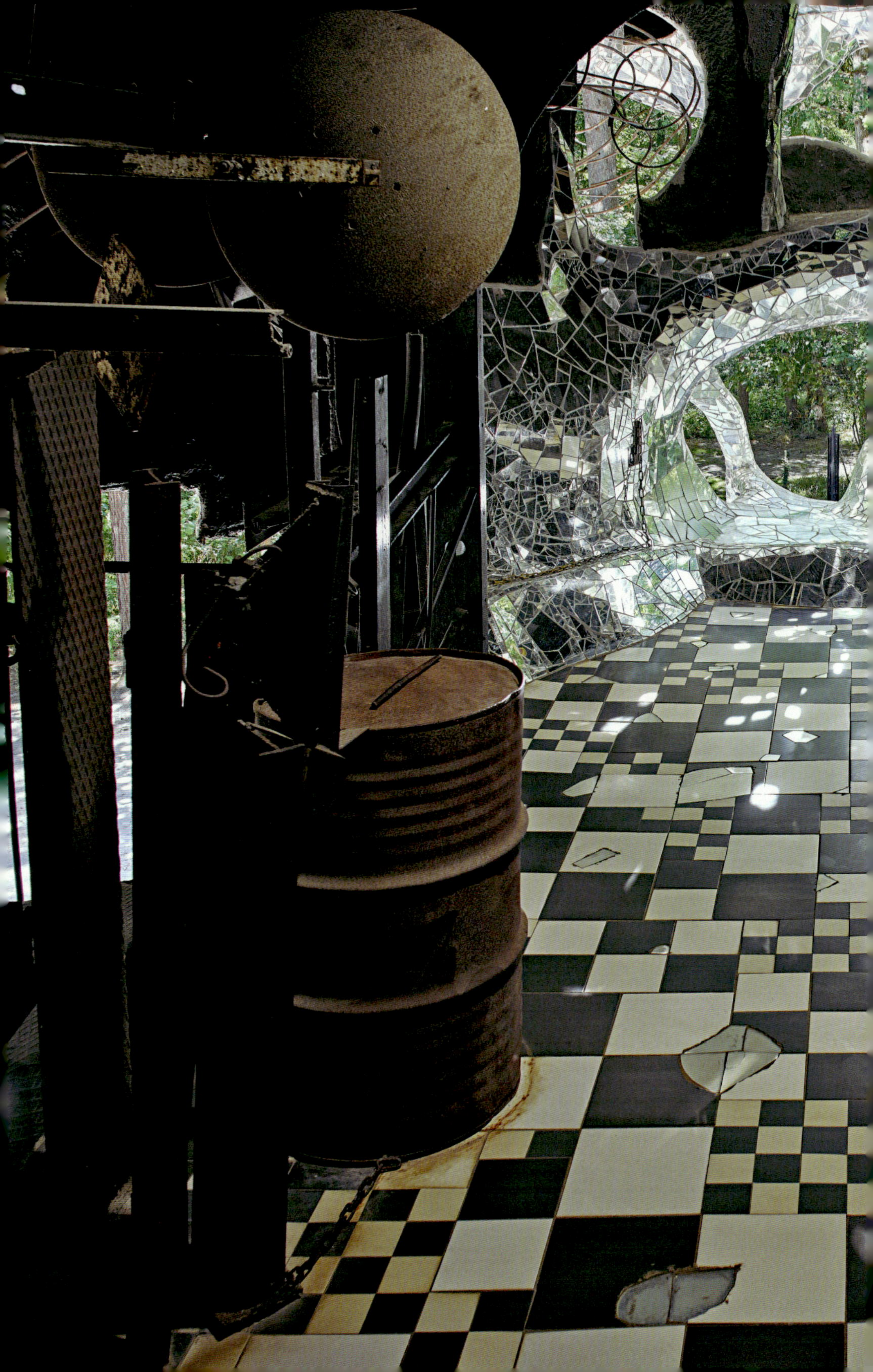

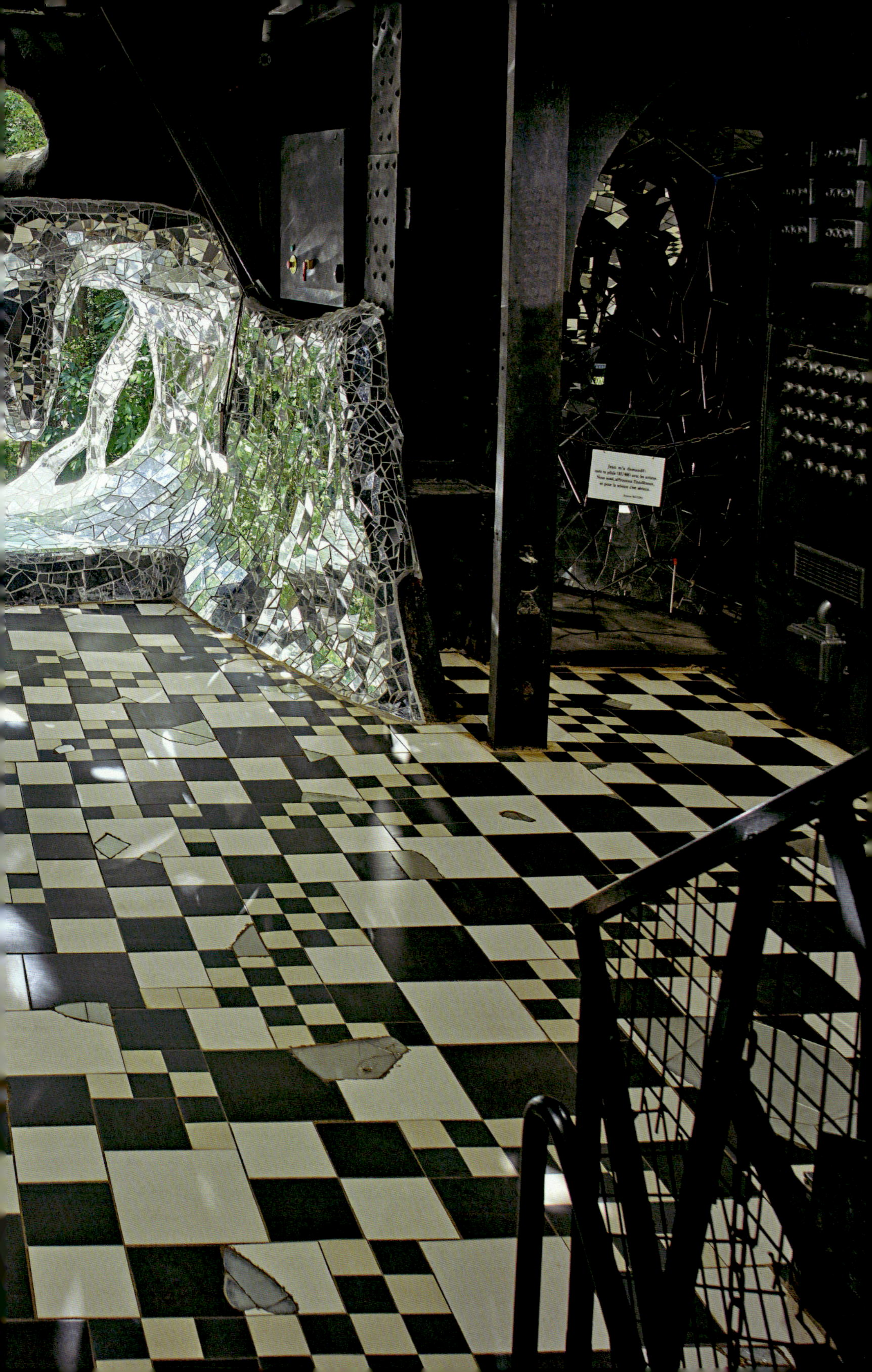

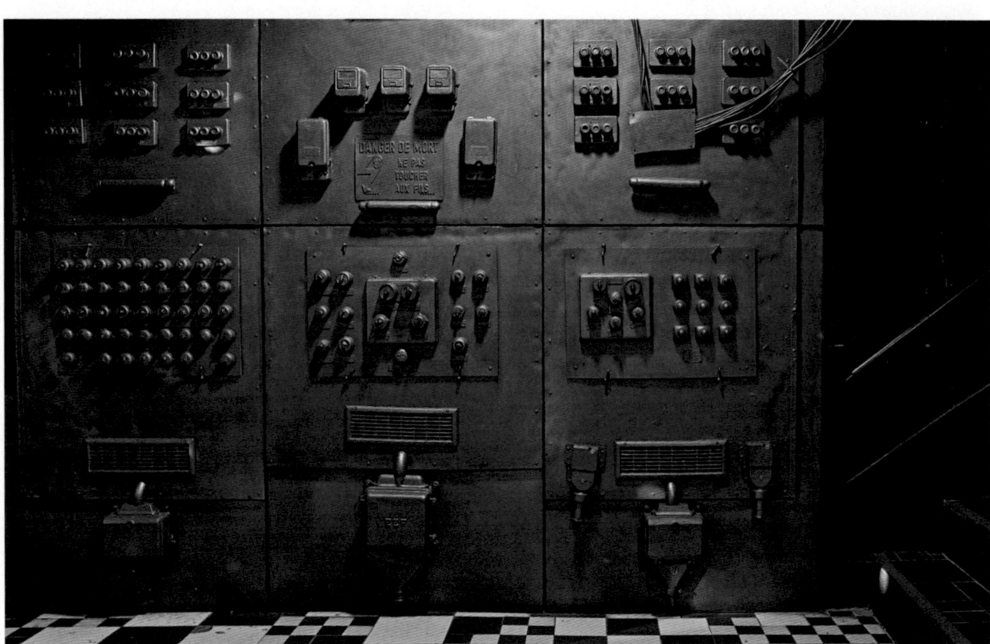

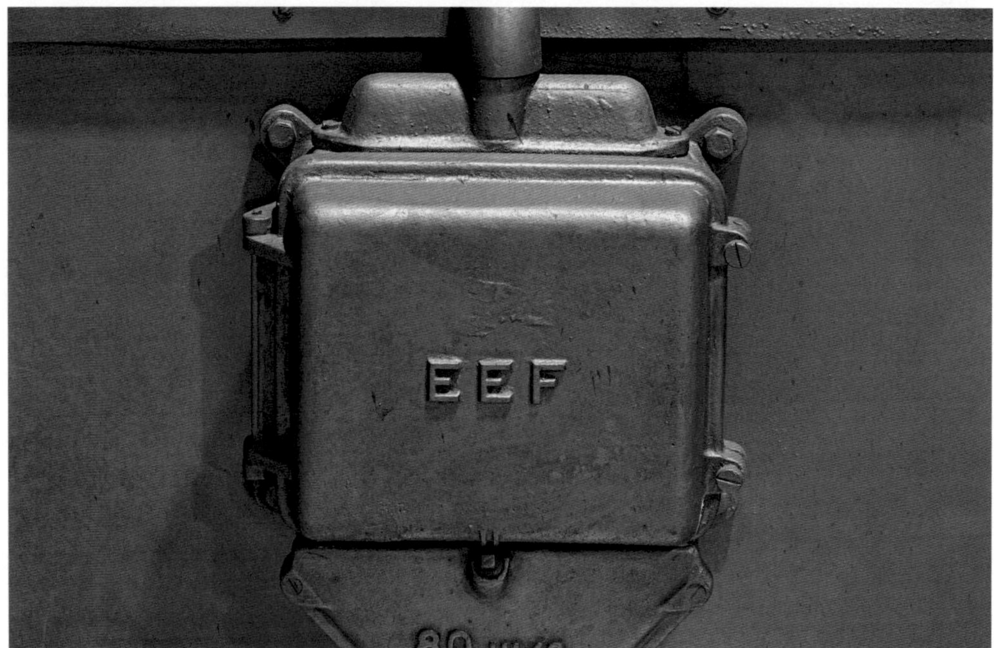

Rico Weber, *Le Tableau électrique*, 1994

←   Jean Tinguely, *La Batterie*, c. 1976; Niki de Saint Phalle, *Le Carrelage au damier: Hommage à la course automobile*, 1992–1993, *La Face aux miroirs*, 1987–1991; Jean Tinguely, *La Molécule RU 486: Hommage à Étienne-Émile Baulieu*, 1991/1994; Rico Weber, *Le Tableau électrique*, 1994

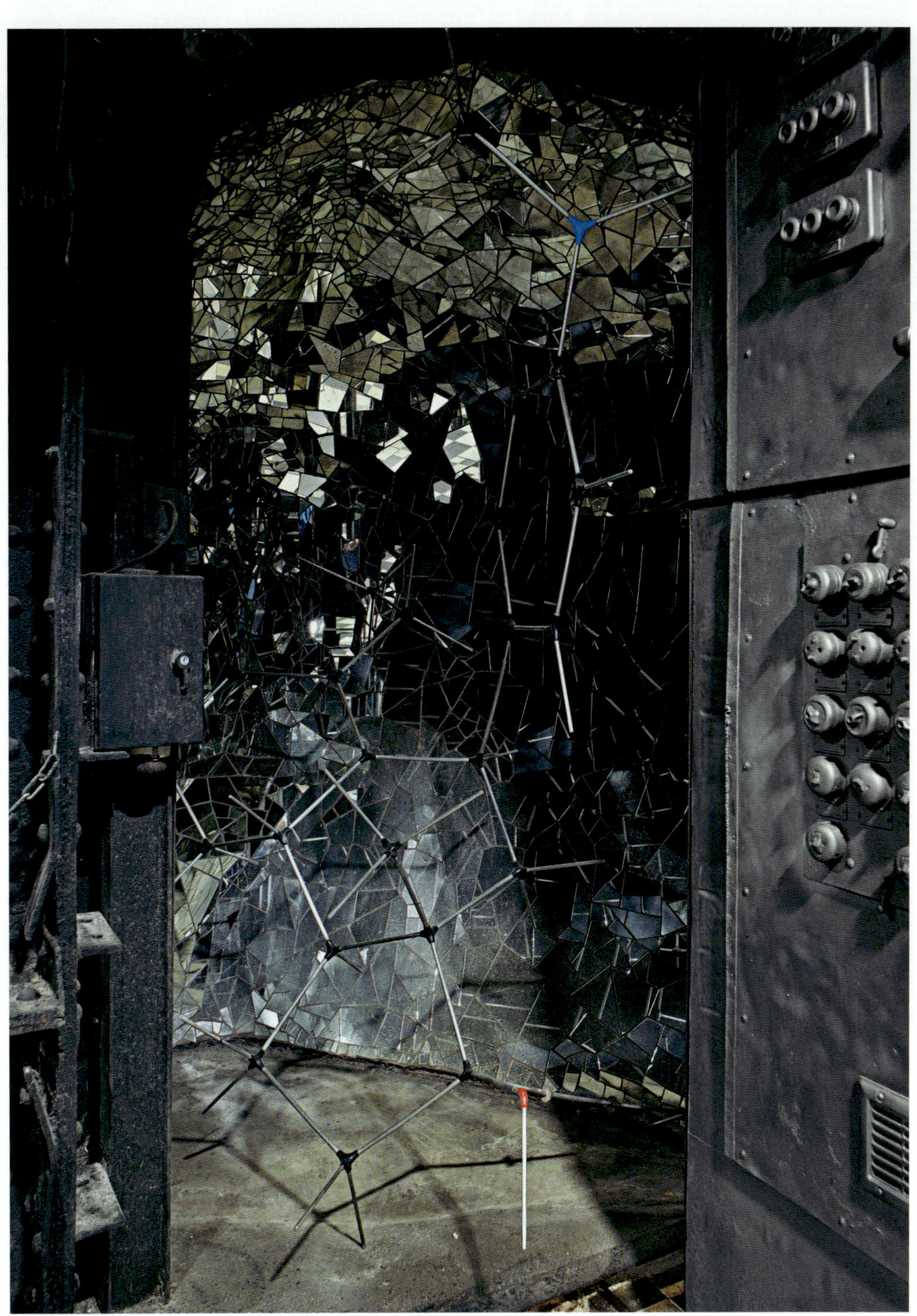

Jean Tinguely, *La Molécule RU 486: Hommage à Étienne-Émile Baulieu*, 1991/1994

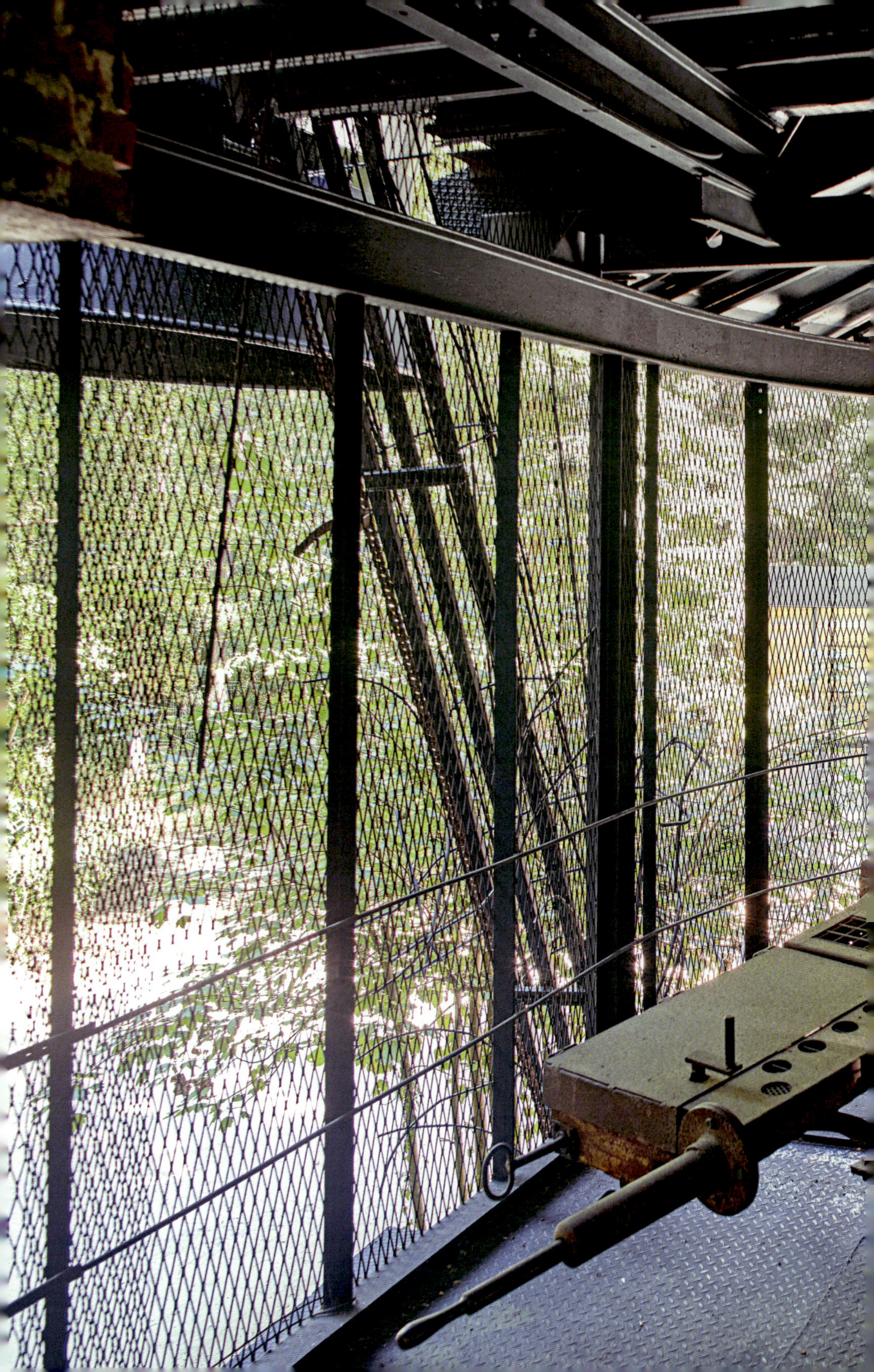

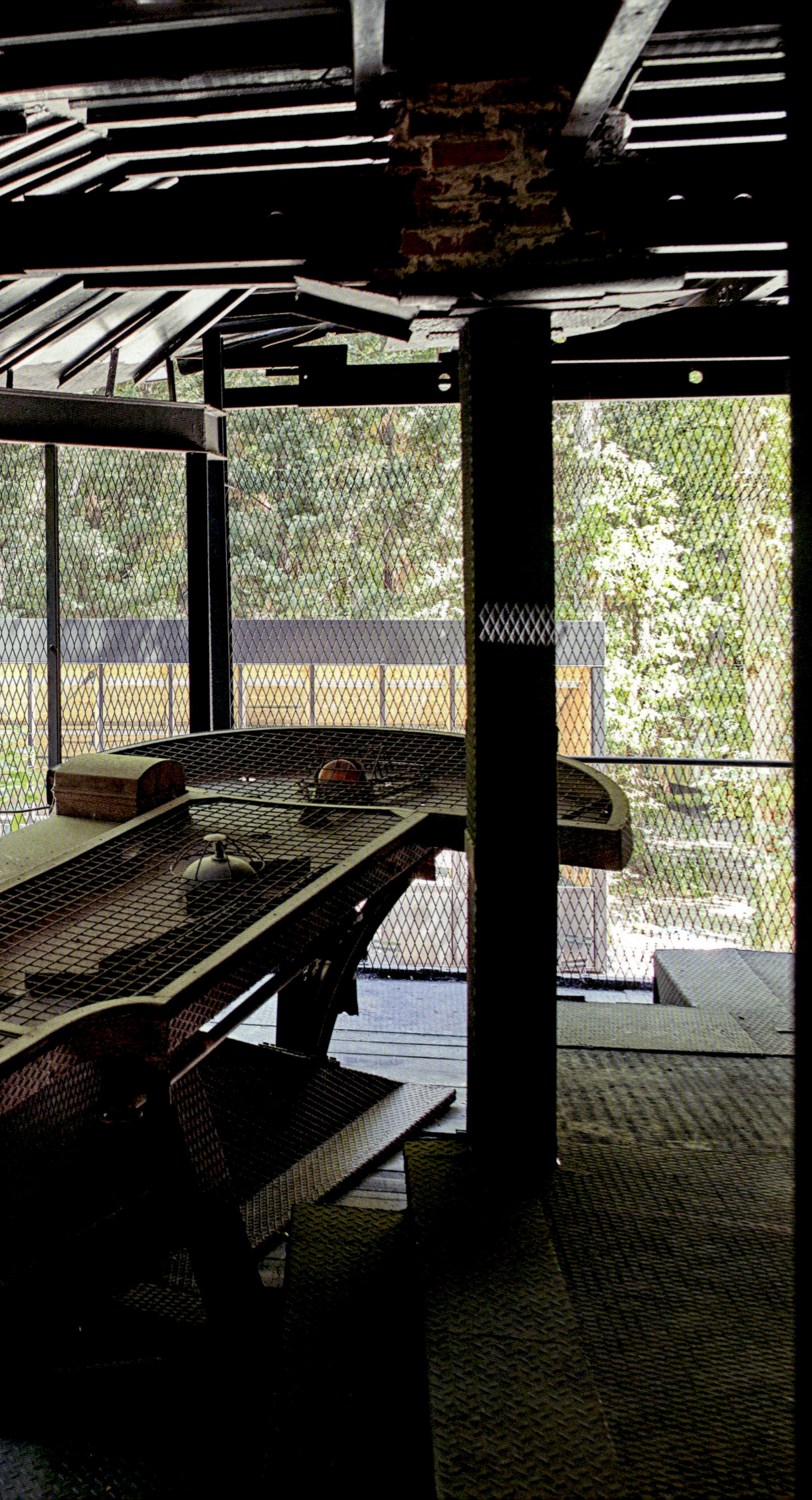

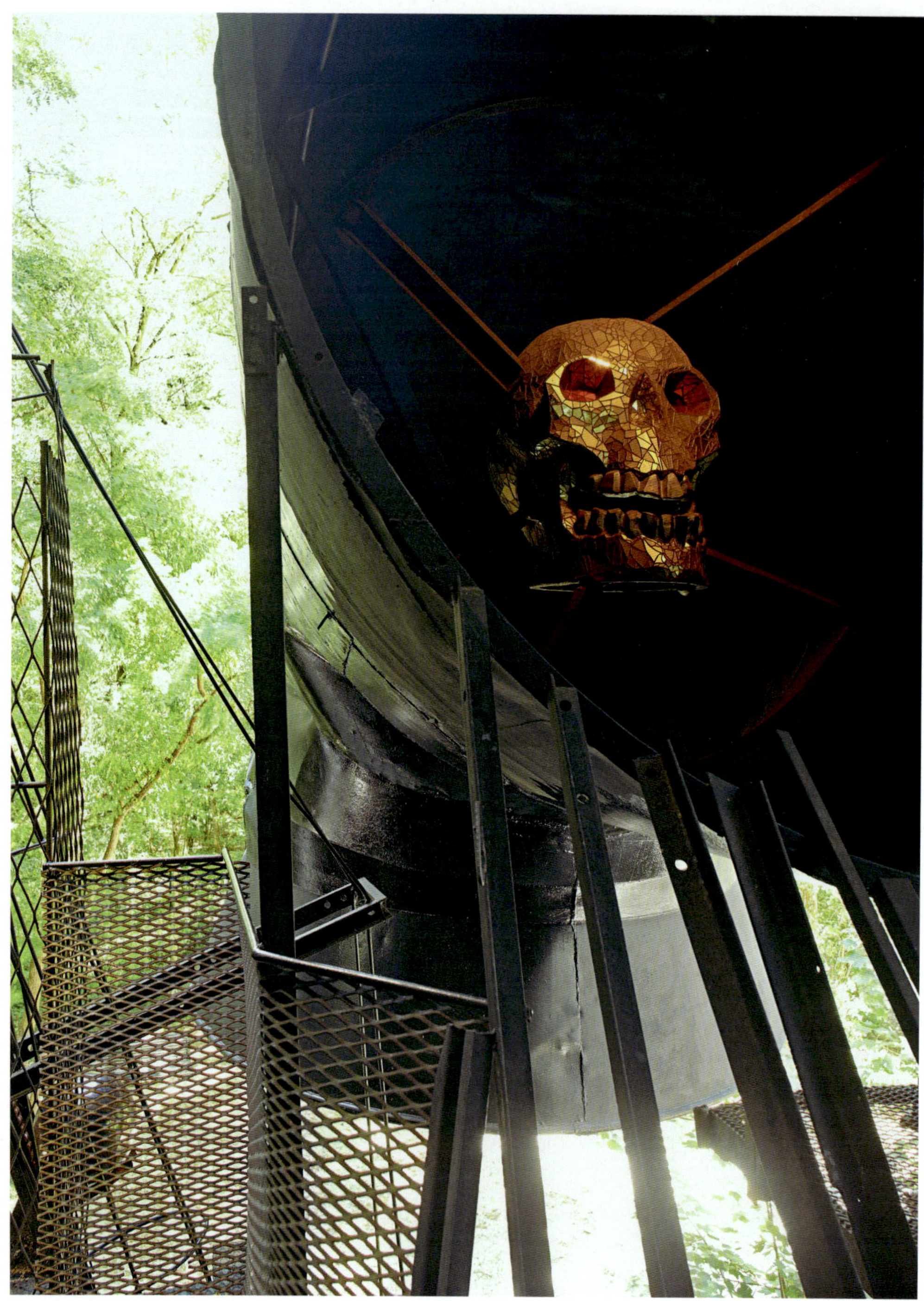

Jean Tinguely and Niki de Saint Phalle, *L'Incitation au suicide*, 1978/c. 1992
← Bernhard Luginbühl, *Le Tellflipper: Hommage à Guillaume Tell*, before 1973 (installed 1978)

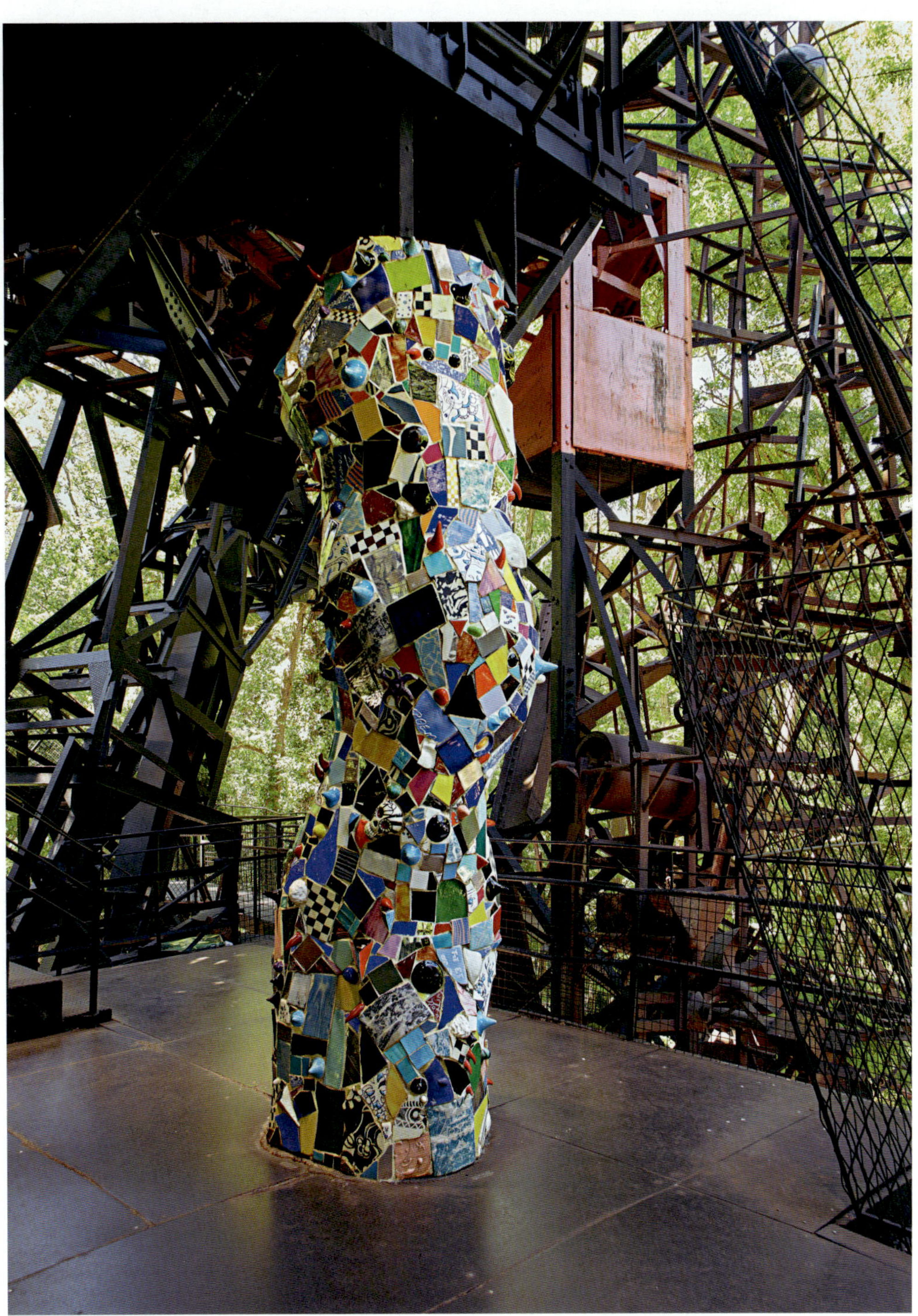

Niki de Saint Phalle, *La Colonne*, 1993

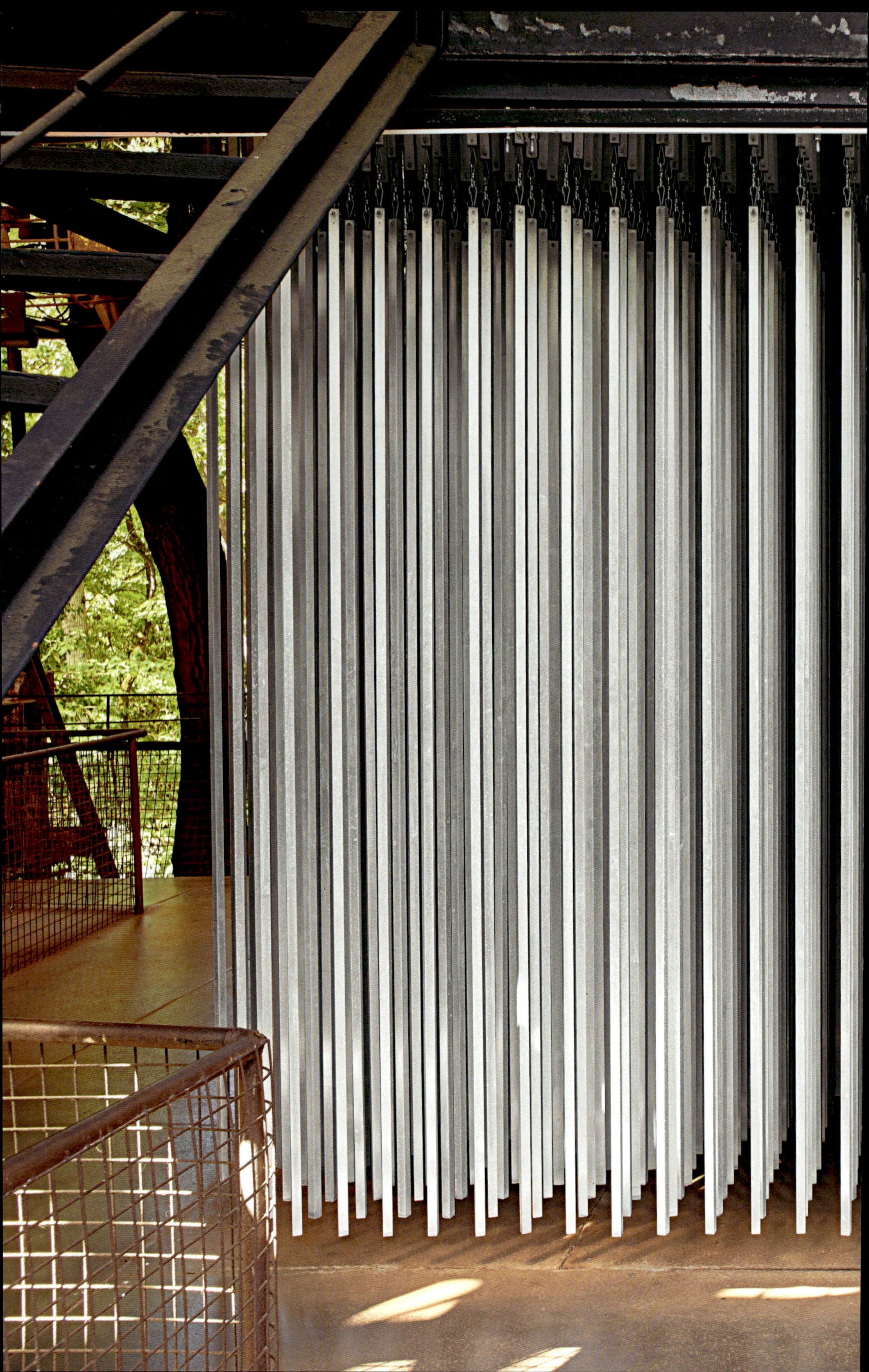

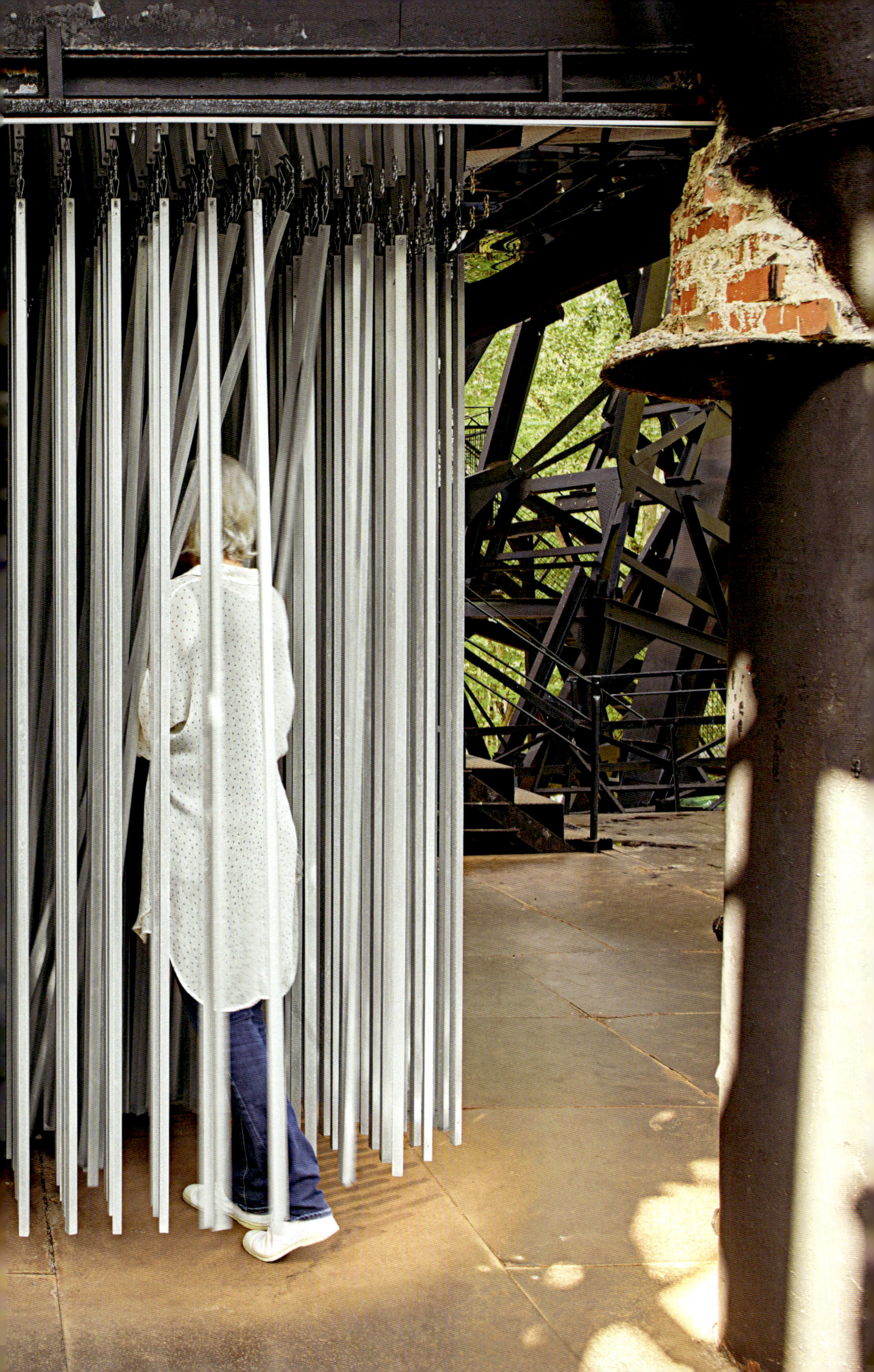

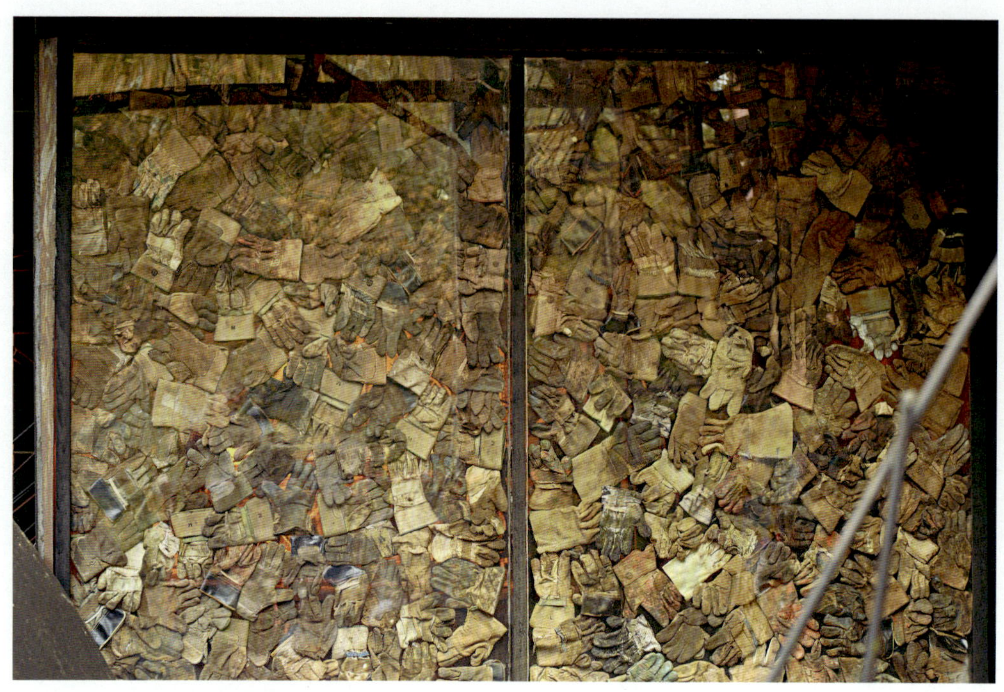

Arman, *L'Accumulation de gants*, 1991 (installed 1993)
←   Jesús Rafael Soto, *Le Pénétrable sonore*, 1972 (installed 1993)

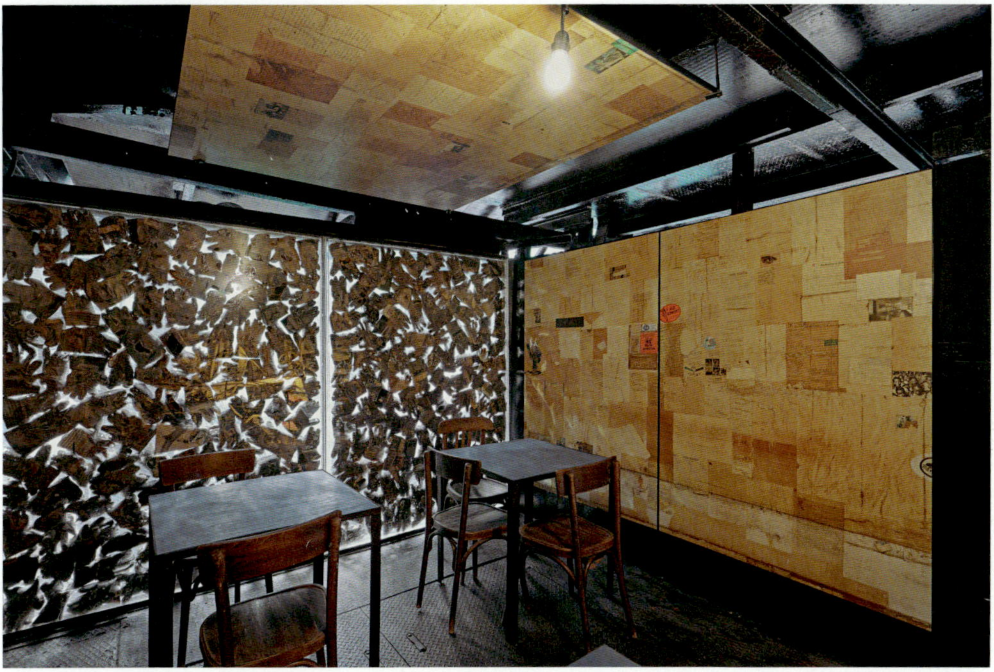

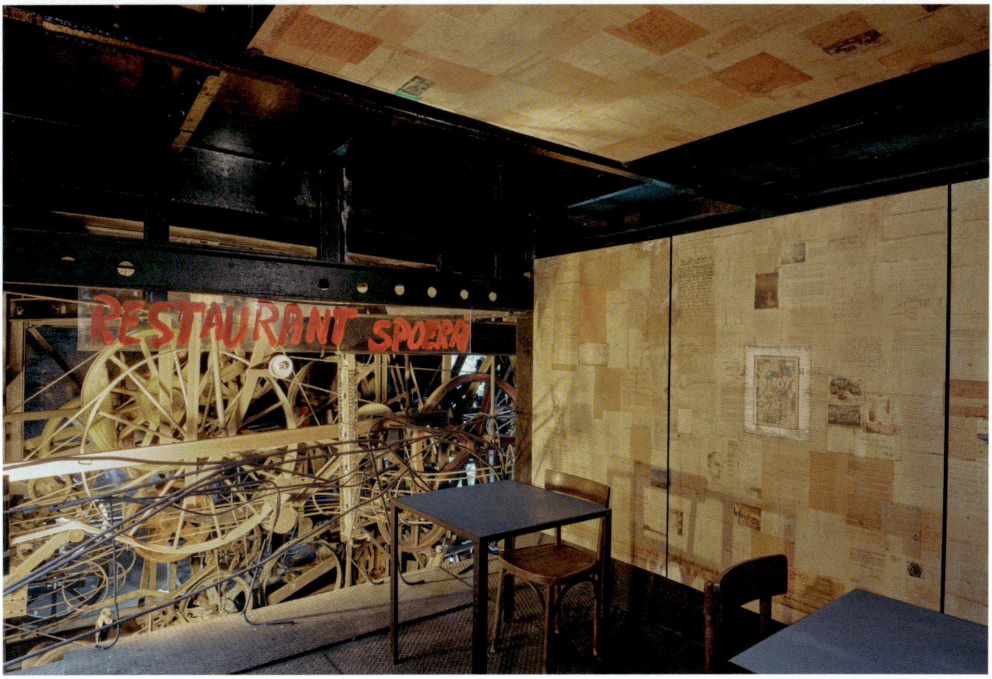

Daniel Spoerri, *Restaurant Spoerri*, 1994

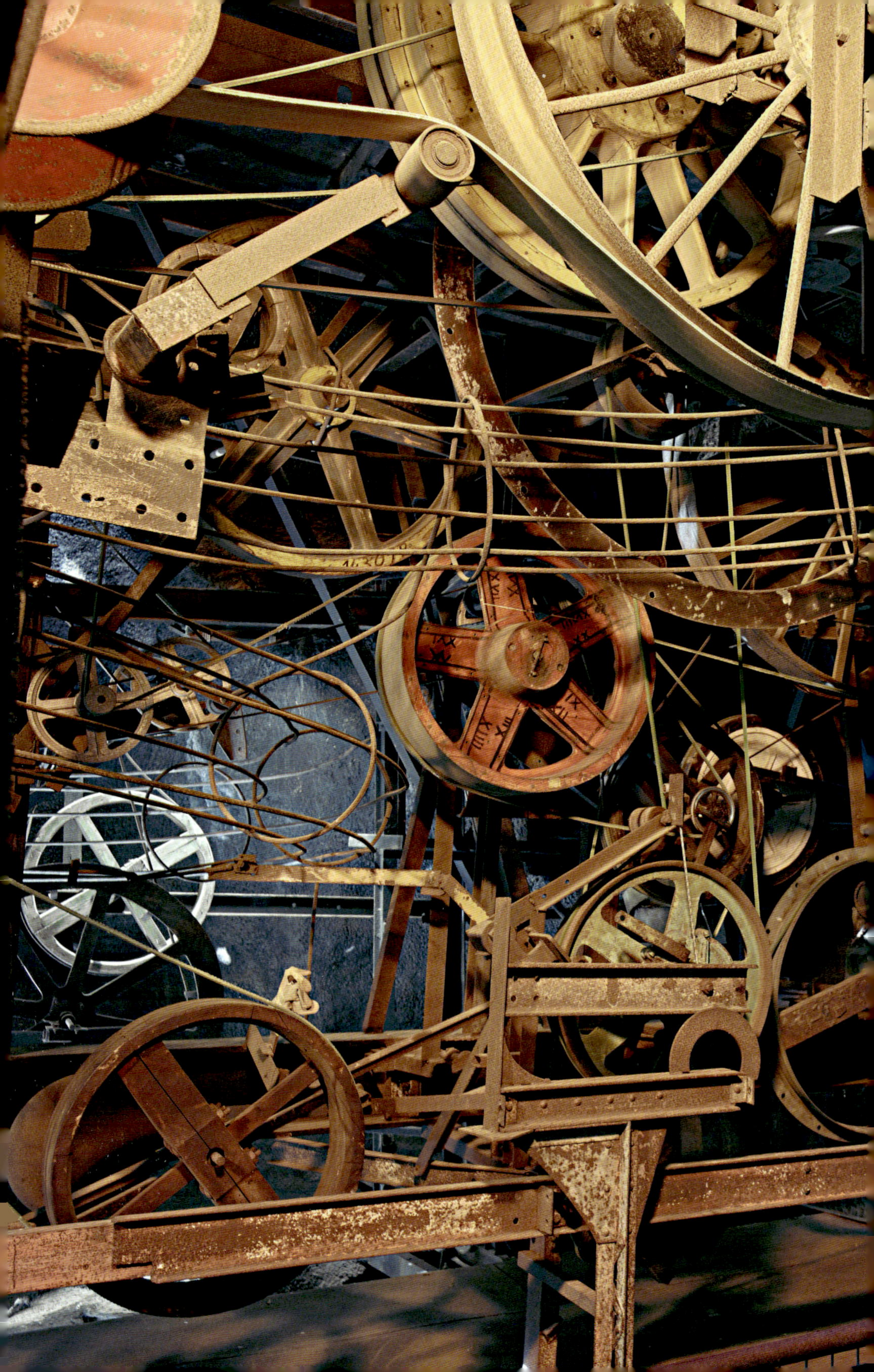

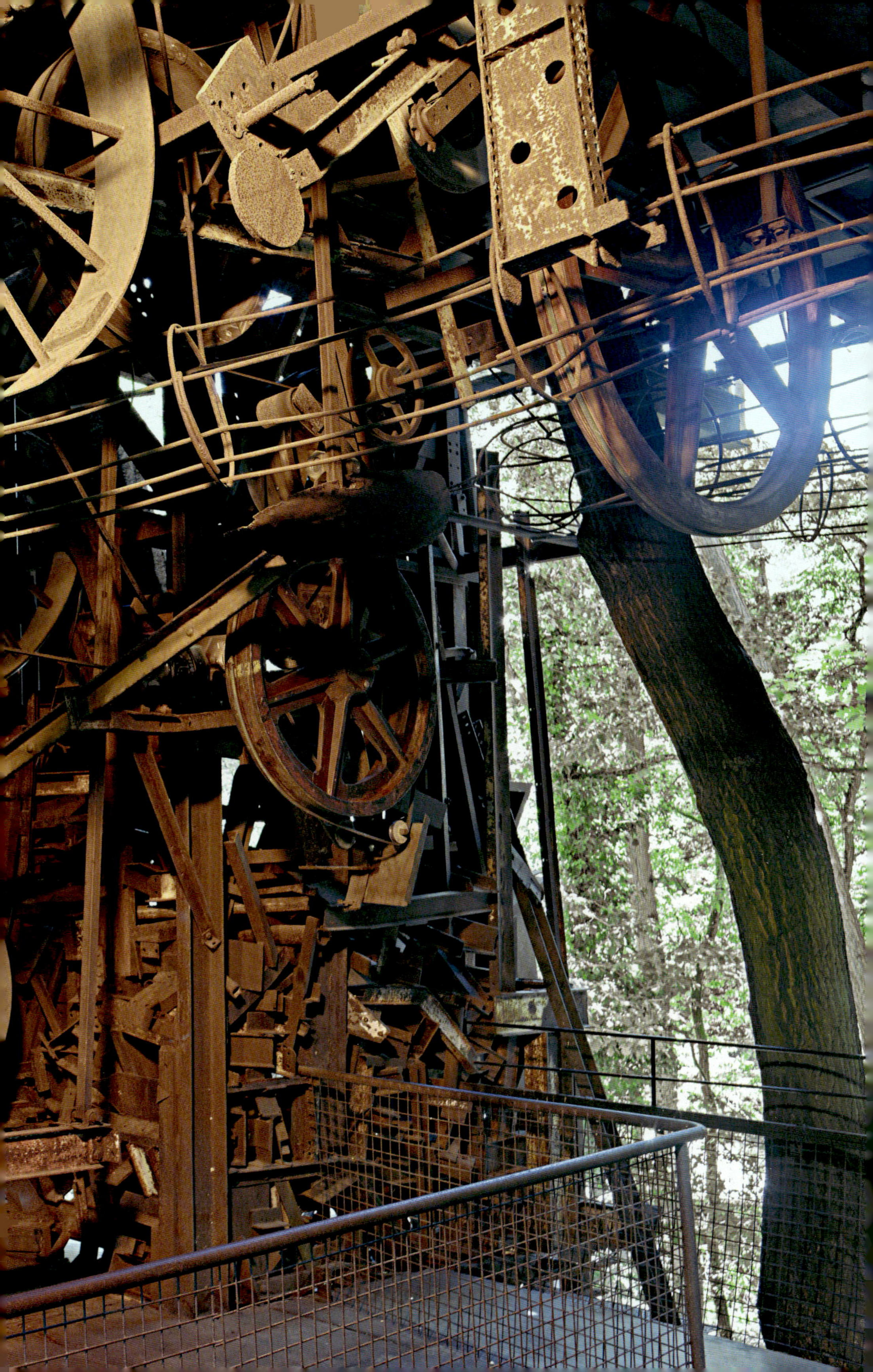

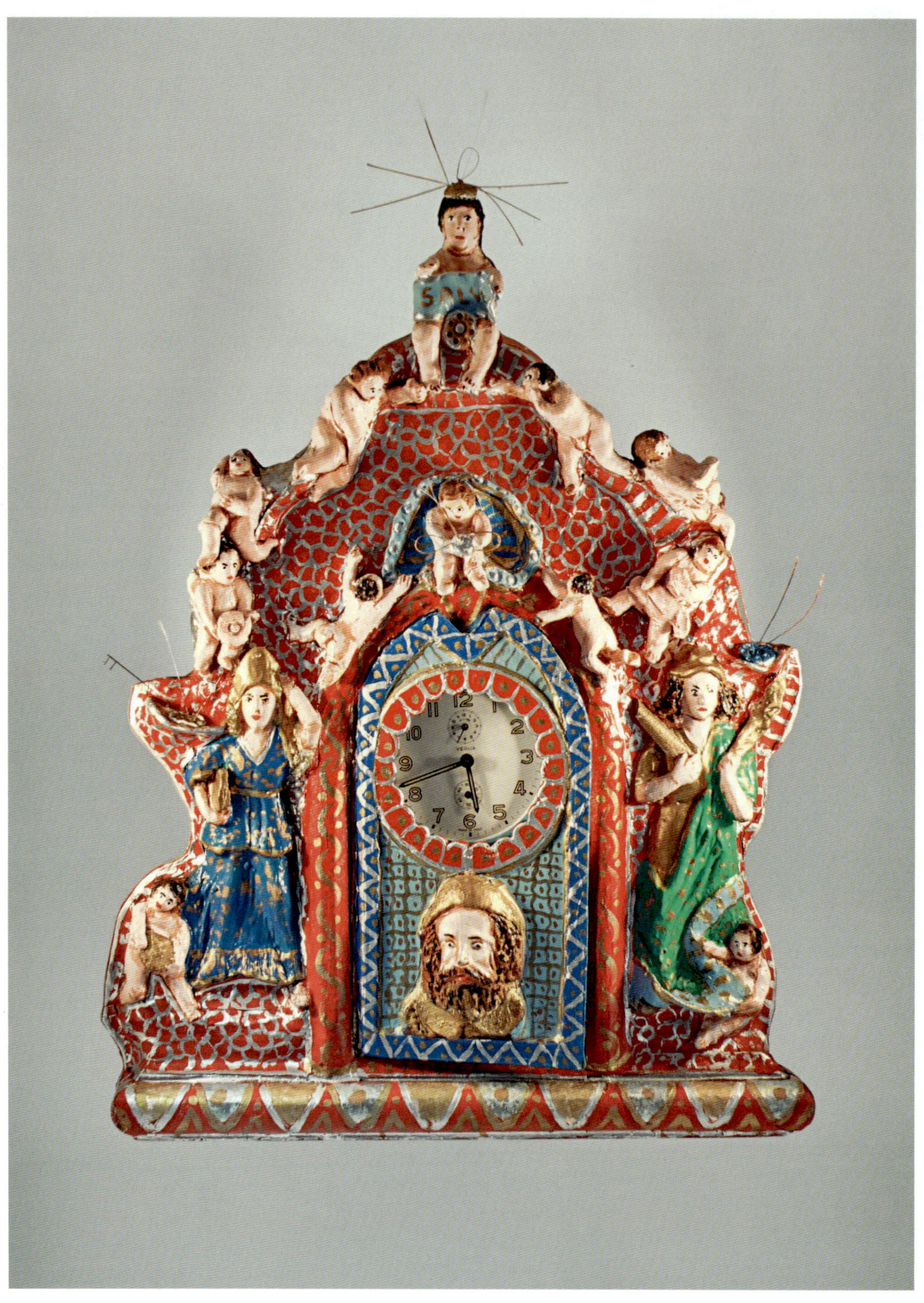

Giovanni Battista Podestà, *Pendule aux enfants*, n. d., part of the *Piccolo Museo* (installed 1993)
← Jean Tinguely, *La Méta-Harmonie*, 1980–1981; Seppi Imhof, *La Tour Imhof*, 1972

4

Chronology

A History of *Le Cyclop* by the People Who Made It

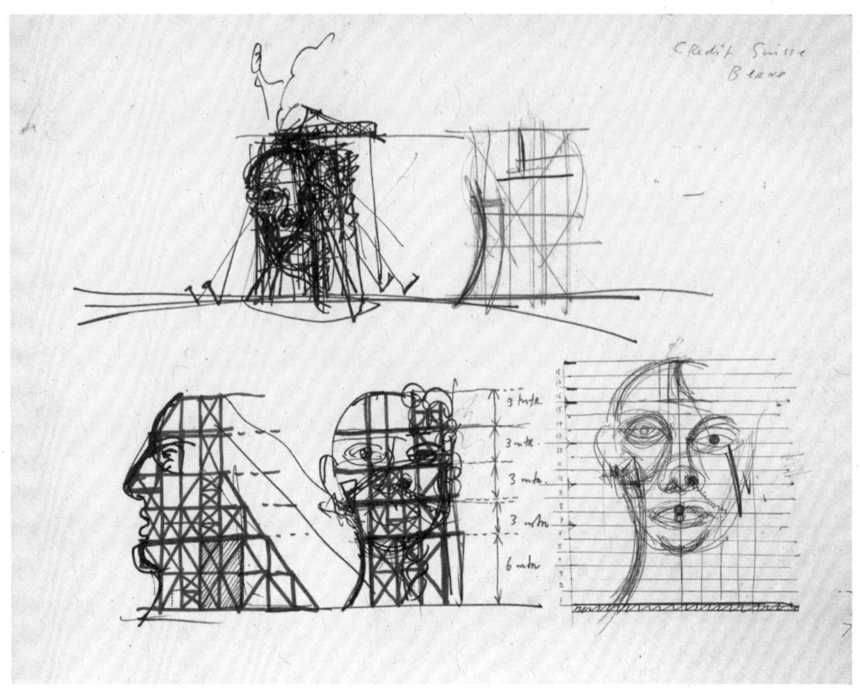

Jean Tinguely
Le Monstre dans la Forêt – Cyclop – Kopf ("Crédit Suisse Berne"), 1969
Pencil, ballpoint, and felt-pin on paper, 50 × 65 cm
Collection Museum Tinguely, Basel

"One day, Tinguely announced he wanted to build an immense head. Niki de Saint Phalle had convinced him to do something monumental, for instance a monster sunk into the ground, with only its head showing."

Bernhard Luginbühl, in *Le Monstre dans la forêt*, 7'53"

"I can't really tell the difference between imagination and reality. It's normal for me, my imagination is as normal as that of a man who sells fabric by the meter, or the head of marketing for a department store. I can't tell the difference. It makes perfect sense to me, you do it, you do it well, you do it fully. It's really well done. You take care, you enjoy the process, you get stuck in! And you want it to be logical and you want the absurdity to be well planned!"

Jean Tinguely, in *Le Monstre de Tinguely*, 46'11"

"There were sketches that gave an idea of the work and explained the thinking behind it. But his presence and explanations were extraordinary. There was a lot of passion and charisma. [Tinguely's] way of defending, explaining, and planning his ideas was fascinating. To this day, no-one has been able to do anything similar. For him, what was most important was to take concrete action very fast. When he wanted to do something, it had to be done right away. Whatever he had in mind had to be done right away. And then it was over. Speed was what interested him. I never had enough time, he never left me a minute to finish up properly. He wasn't interested in the finishing touches, those could always come later! And his body of work was produced at speed. It was magnificent that he could react so fast and do whatever he wanted."

Seppi Imhof, in *Le Monstre dans la forêt*, 23'05"

"Working in the forest, we dream of utopia and unlimited action (which is illusory, I know) and we adopt an attitude of Research into Gratuitous and Useless Acts. And we are perfectly happy this way, provided that no one prevents us from working (like mad—it goes without saying)."

Jean Tinguely, in *Jean Tinguely. Le Cyclop*, p. 16

This chronology was compiled in December 2024.
The chronology on the website of the Archives Cyclop
(https://archivescyclop.fr) is updated and expanded
on an ongoing basis.

1970–1980
A Monster in the Forest

1970   **Construction begins.**

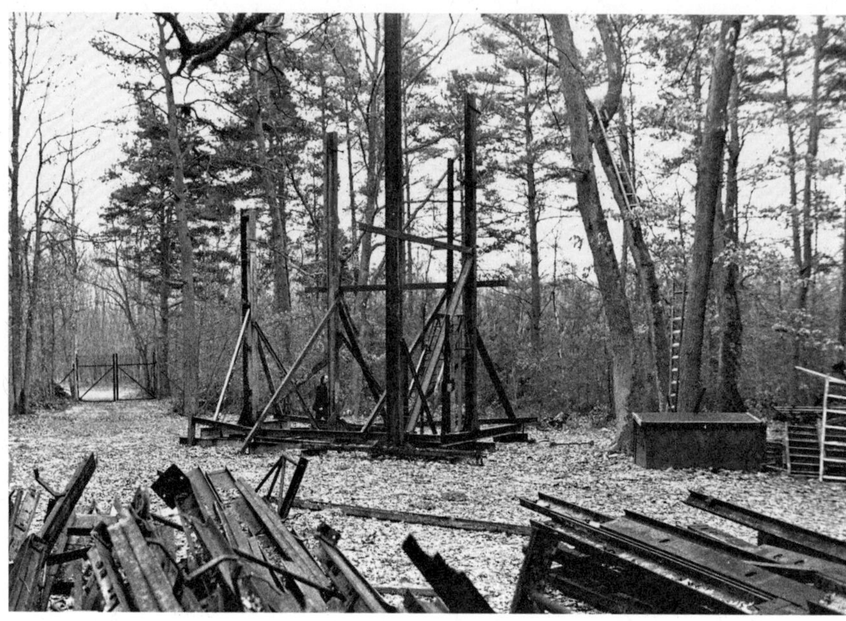

"It was just the two of us when we set to work. We started the structure on the ground in a small clearing. We arranged metal girders in a square on the dead leaves, which represented the plan of the thing. Ad Petersen photographed the first girders that rose up after three days in the forest."

Bernhard Luginbühl, "Letter to Margrit Hahnloser," in *Pandémonium – Jean Tinguely*, p. 317

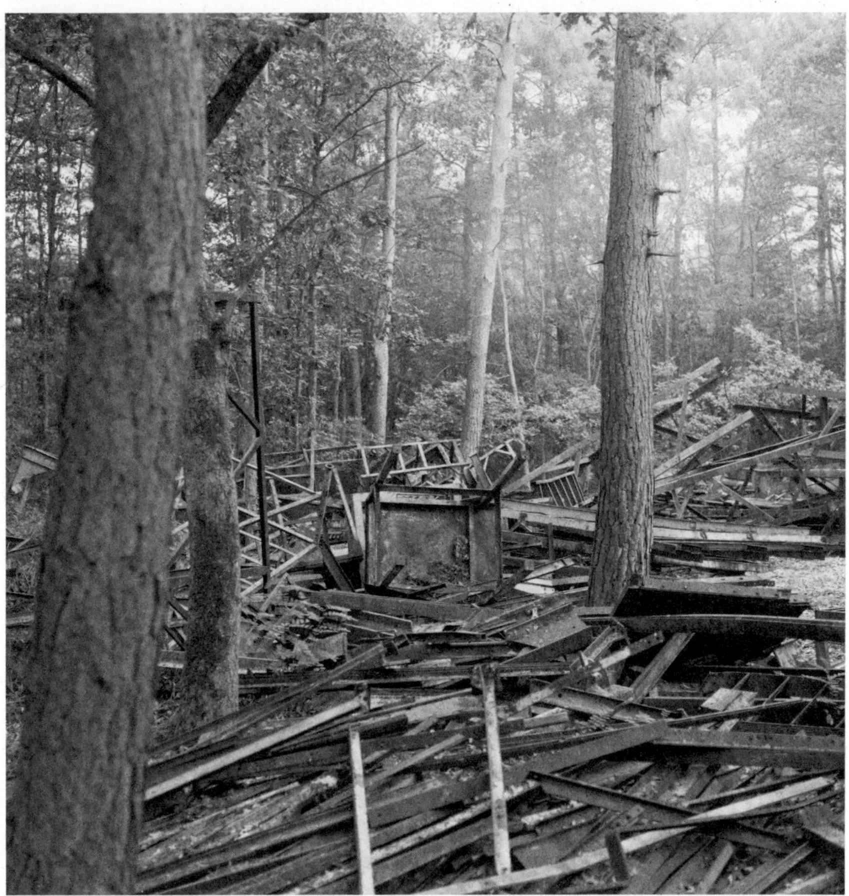

"That was the start of long years of work. Tinguely brought heaps of scrap
metal, some of it good quality, building materials, and the like. Most of it
came from the local scrap-metal dealer, Duperche. The good-quality scrap,
farm machinery, and iron made in France, often ended up as skeletons for
Tinguely's sculptures, but we also used some for the Head. We piled tonnes
of heavy scrap up in heaps. The stairs and flooring were in new iron,
not scrap."

Bernhard Luginbühl, "Letter to Margrit Hahnloser," p. 317

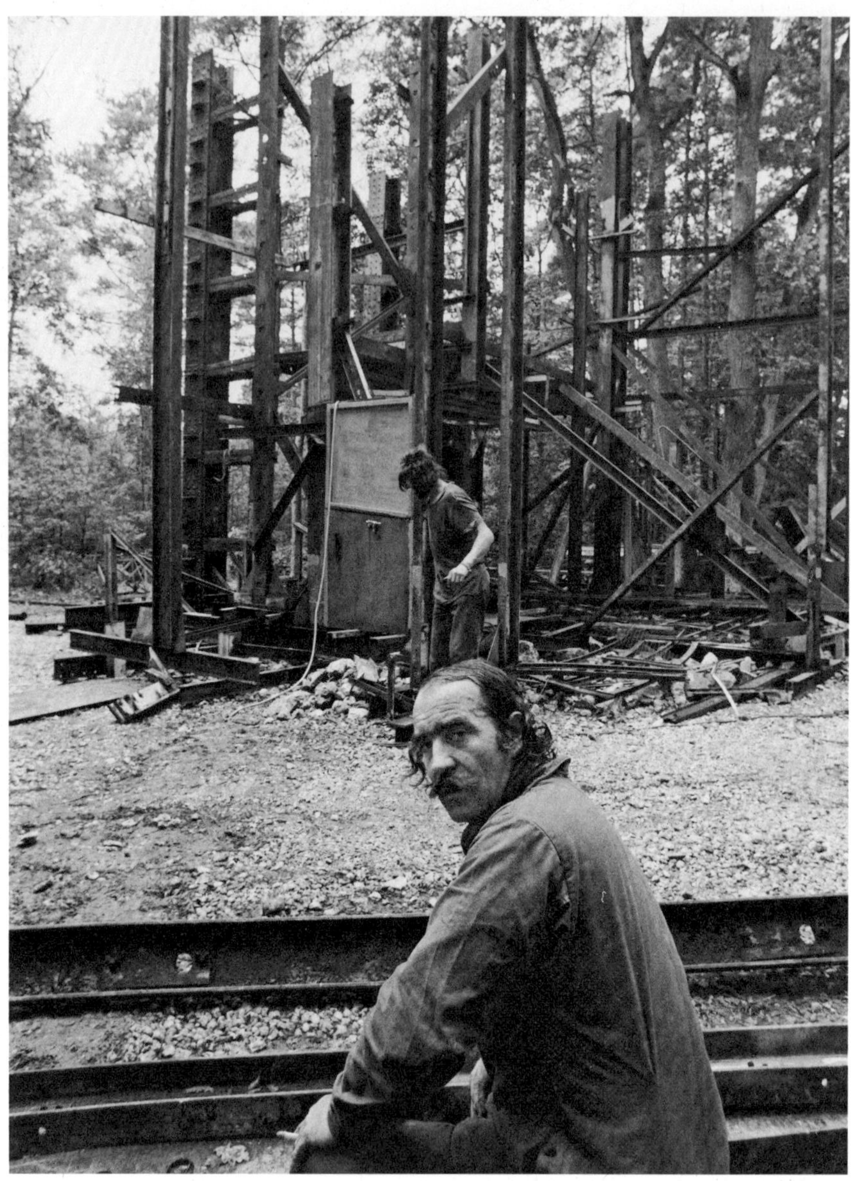

"There's scrap metal galore. Our industrial society produces so much scrap we have tonnes of it."

Jean Tinguely, in *Le Monstre de Tinguely*, 34'39"

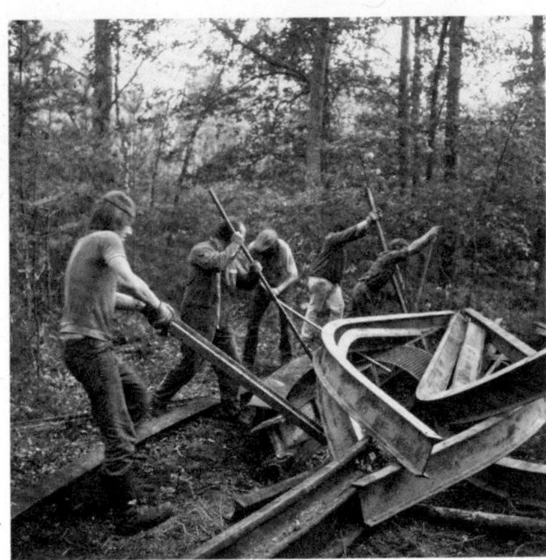

"A head filled Tinguely's head and the head had to get out of his head fast.
No room in Tinguely's head for anything but the head, we had all caught
the HEAD bug. All our associates were called on to help."

Bernhard Luginbühl, "Letter to Margrit Hahnloser," p. 317

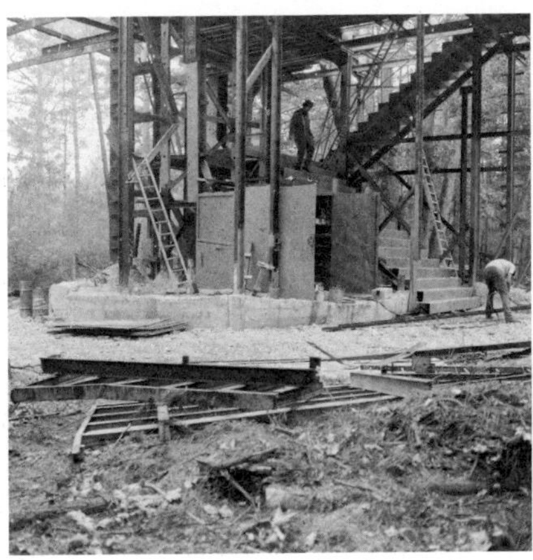

"We ordered a vast quantity of concrete to dump on site. I told Tinguely
he was crazy, it would never work, we had to pour foundations. But as
it turned out, dumping the concrete on the ground was the only solution
for building a head, because the terrain was sandy. The concrete seeped
into the ground and set a firm base to build on. Then we stuffed the
concrete full of iron to be able to keep building."

Bernhard Luginbühl, in *Le Monstre dans la forêt*, 16'50

1970   **Seppi Imhof arrives to join the team working on *Le Cyclop*.**

Jean Tinguely
Neyruz 1751

den 22 VII 1970

Lieber Herr Imhof

Leider muss ich
Ihnen mitteilen dass
das ganze Projekt auf
nächstes Jahr verschoben
ist (Aufgehoben ist es nicht!)
& ich bitte Sie nun ume
auf nächstes Jahr Ihre
Bereitschaft (mitzumachen) auf zu bewahren.

Mit freundlichen Grüssen
Jean Tinguely

Letters from Jean Tinguely to Seppi Imhof about the terms of his employment, July 1970 and March 1971
Collection Museum Tinguely, Basel

Jean Tinguely
Soisy sur Ecole
(Dep. ESSONNE)   den 20 MÄRZ 71

Lieber HERR Josep
IMHof =

ICH bestätige Ihnen,
dass Sie AB ERSTE Mai
1971 (von mir bezahlt)
bei mir Arbeiten werden
LOHN 1200.— S. FR.
LOGie & Speise & Reise—
spesen zu meinen Lasten
Kündigungs FRist
2 WOCHEN.
Mit FreundliCHEN Grüssen
und in ERWARtung Ihrer
schriftlichen Bestätigung:
Jean Tinguely

"Quite by chance, I saw a job ad in the *Berner Zeitung*. Someone was looking for a welder. As well as welding, applicants needed to be able to drive, play Swiss belote, and know how to weld. So I thought, why not go and work in Paris for six months? I saw it as a challenge. I sent in a postcard, and I was fortunate enough to work for Tinguely. In the end the six months passed in a flash and that was the start of 20 years of work."

Seppi Imhof, in *Le Monstre dans la forêt*, 15'30"

1971 The first two levels of *Le Cyclop* are in place.

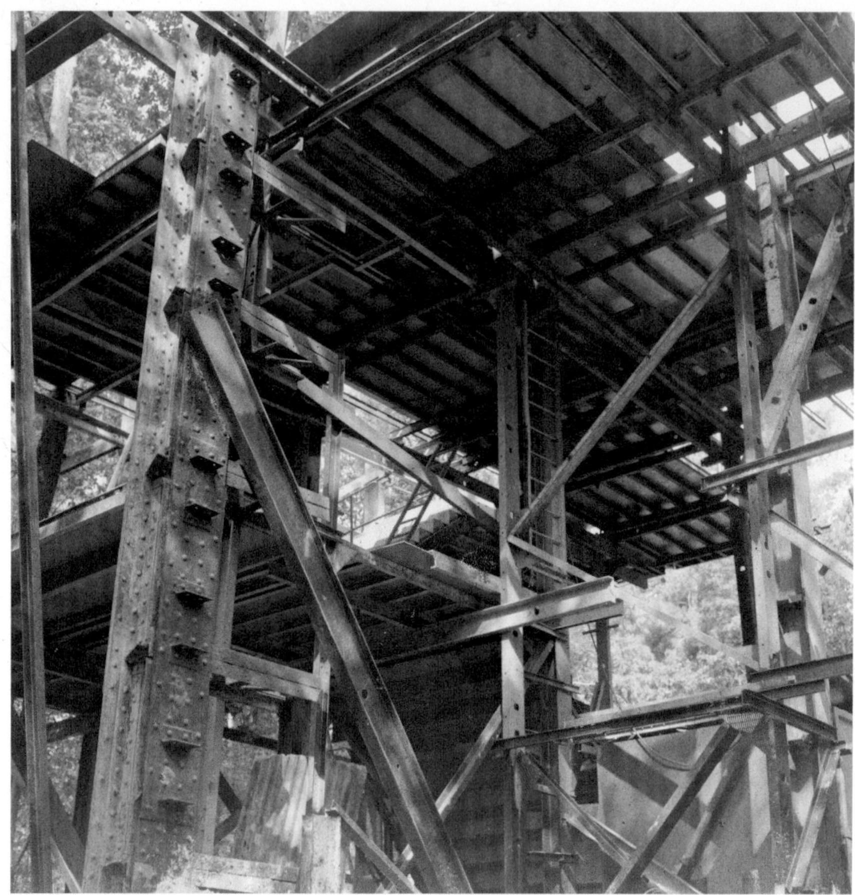

"In the early days, it wasn't as comfortable. We got hold of some old staircases and they were OK to reach three meters. The next sets of stairs took us from three to seven meters. Then there was the first platform. Getting the stairs upright and in place was very acrobatic. We needed [to install] the platform first because you can't have stairs opening onto nothing—a gap between staircases is nerve-wracking."

Seppi Imhof, in *Le Monstre dans la forêt*, 18'02"

Bernhard Luginbühl creates his *Hommage à Eiffel*.

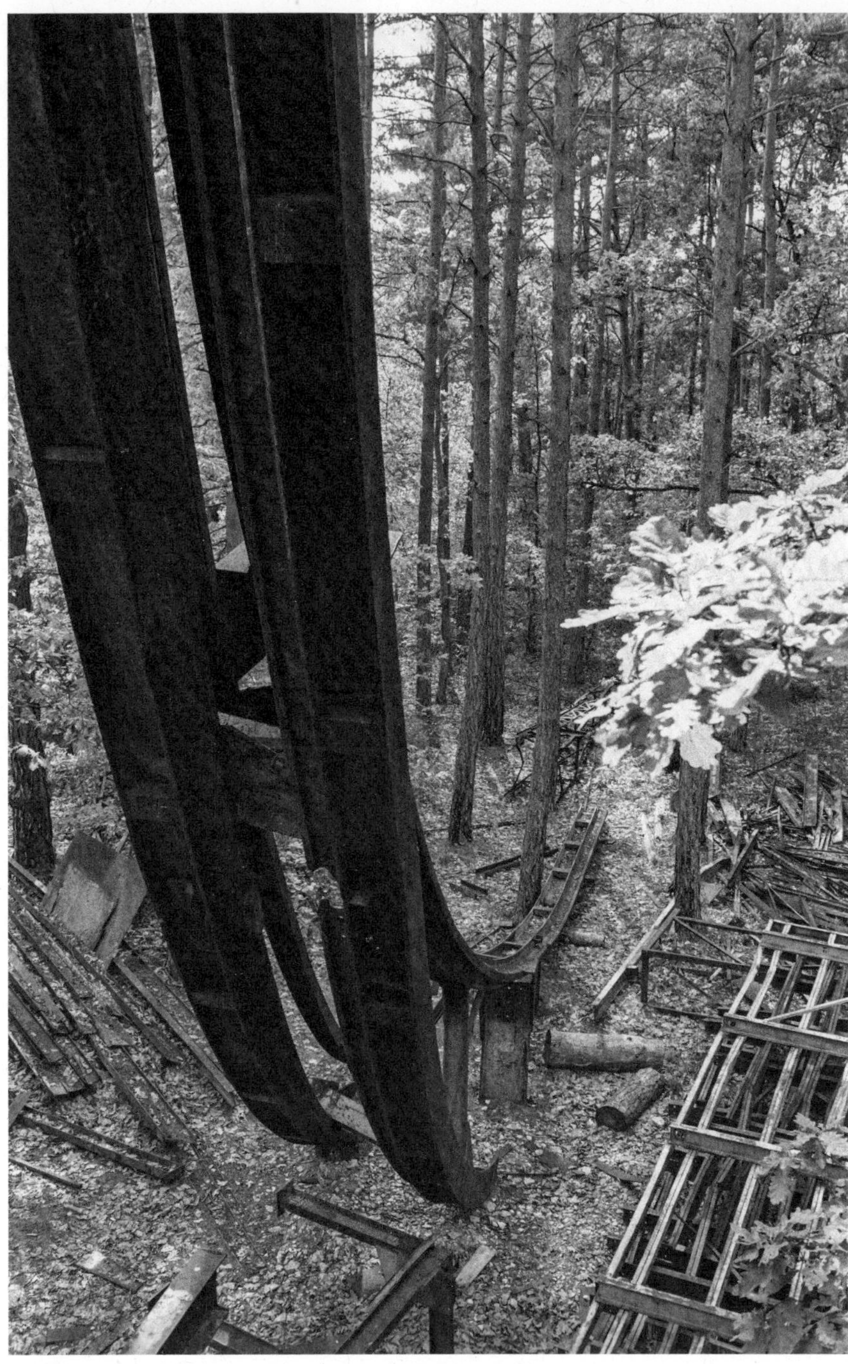

1972   Seppi Imhof creates his *Tour Imhof.*

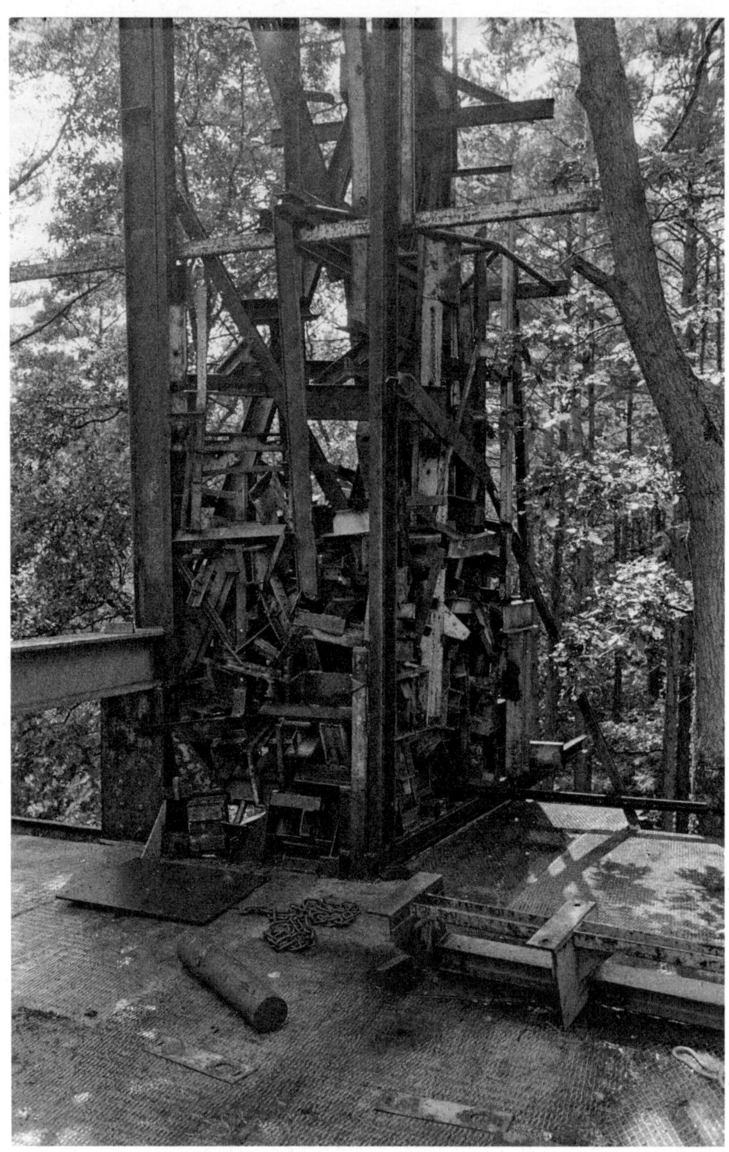

"He is a builder, assistant, tradesman, and he is also an artist, as the builder of a completely mad accumulation known as the *Tour Imhof*. It is a mass of scrap metal piled in colossal quantities to give nocturnal birds a place to nest—which they do."

Jean Tinguely, in *Le Monstre de Tinguely*, 33'43"

Work begins on Jean Tinguely's *La Méta-Maxi.*

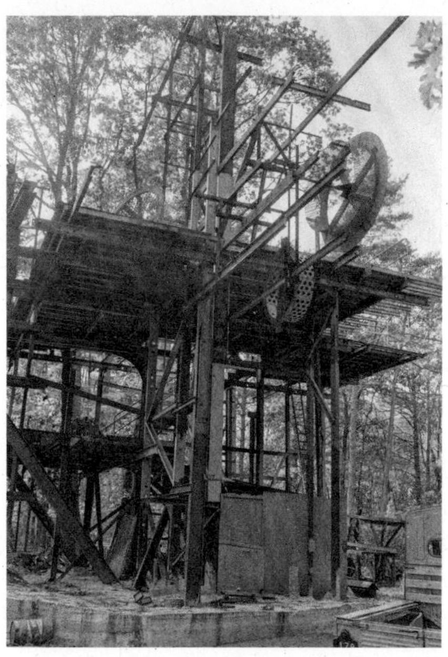

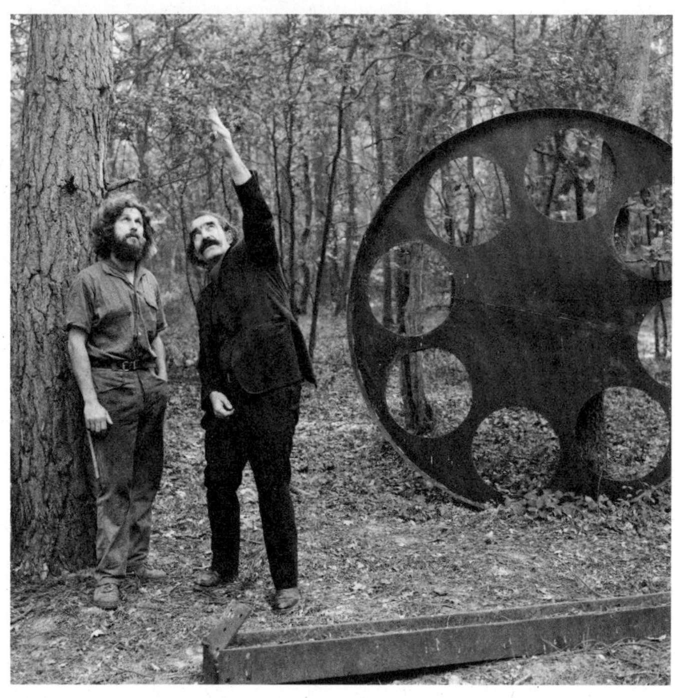

1972 The face of *Le Cyclop* takes shape.

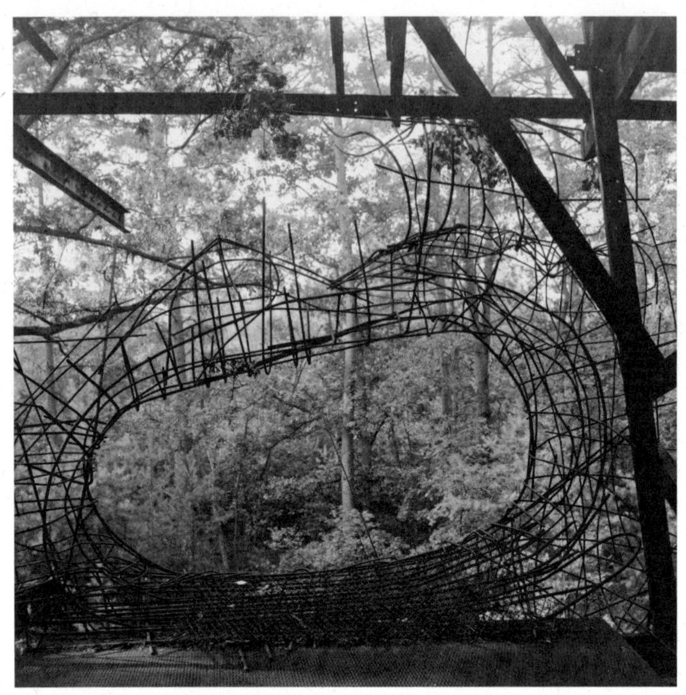

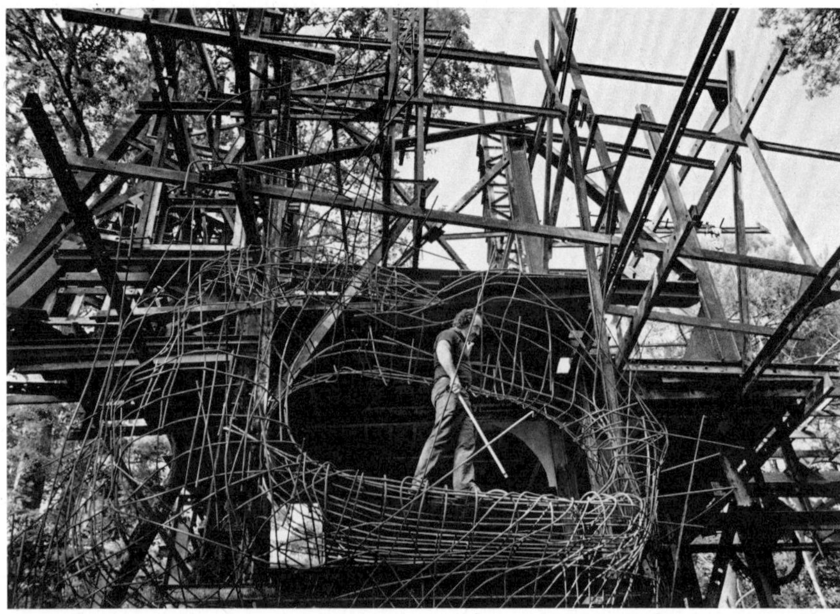

1973   Work begins on Jean Tinguely's *La Tour éphémère*.

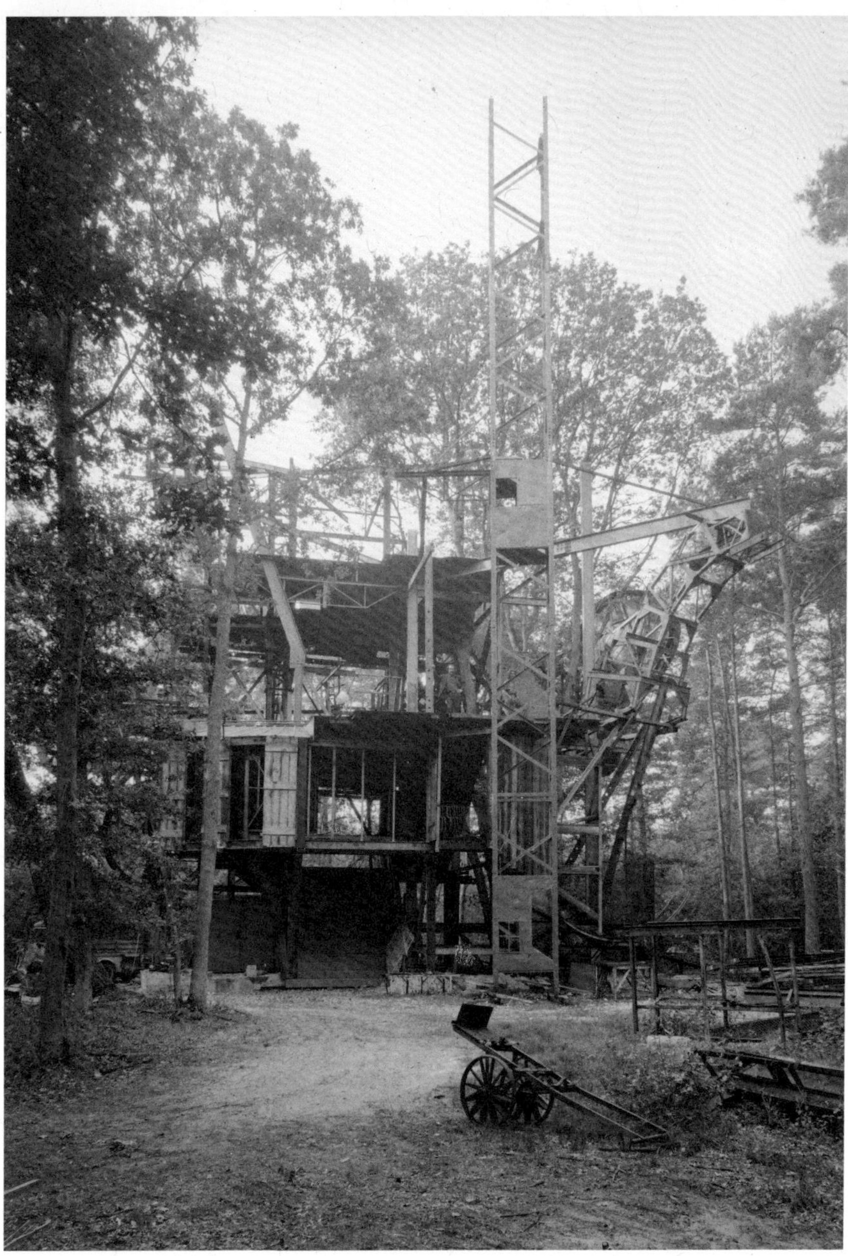

Work begins on Jean Tinguely's *La Tour éphémère*.

1973   Per Olof Ultvedt builds the pavilion.

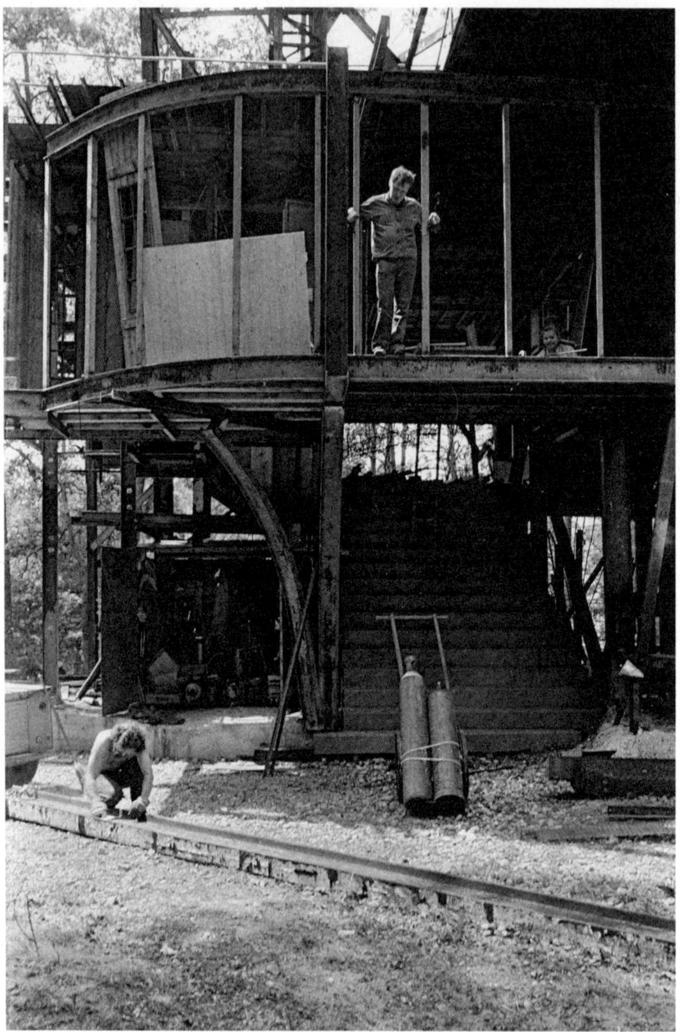

"This zone was originally intended for the Swedish artist Per Olof Ultvedt. He had come up with a pastiche of suburban house design, a kind of detached house topped with a fan-shaped glass roof. Not much is left of Ultvedt's work, because Tinguely probably came to consider in the mid-1970s that his task with other artists would be to present them with a monumental backdrop for their own personal works, and that a cooperation around architecture itself would be too complicated."

Pontus Hultén, in *Jean Tinguely*, p. 204–205

Bernhard Luginbühl creates *L'Oreille*.

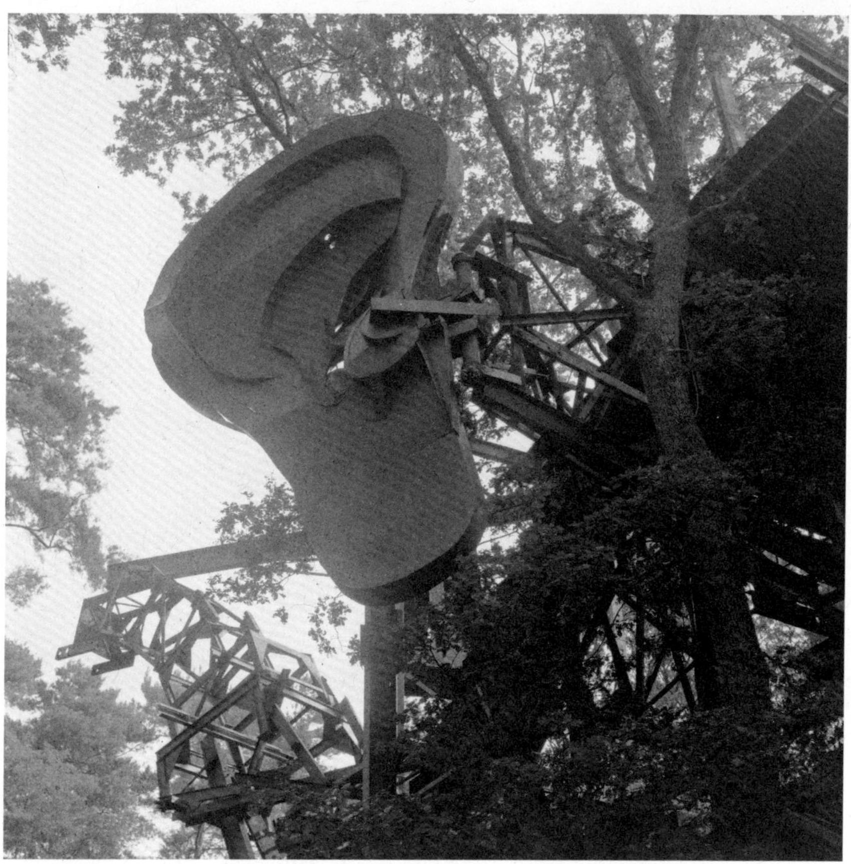

"I made the ear in a day. We were young, we worked fast."

Bernhard Luginbühl, in *Le Monstre de Tinguely*, 48'07"

1973   The support structure for the train carriage in Eva Aeppli's *Hommage aux déportés* is put into place.

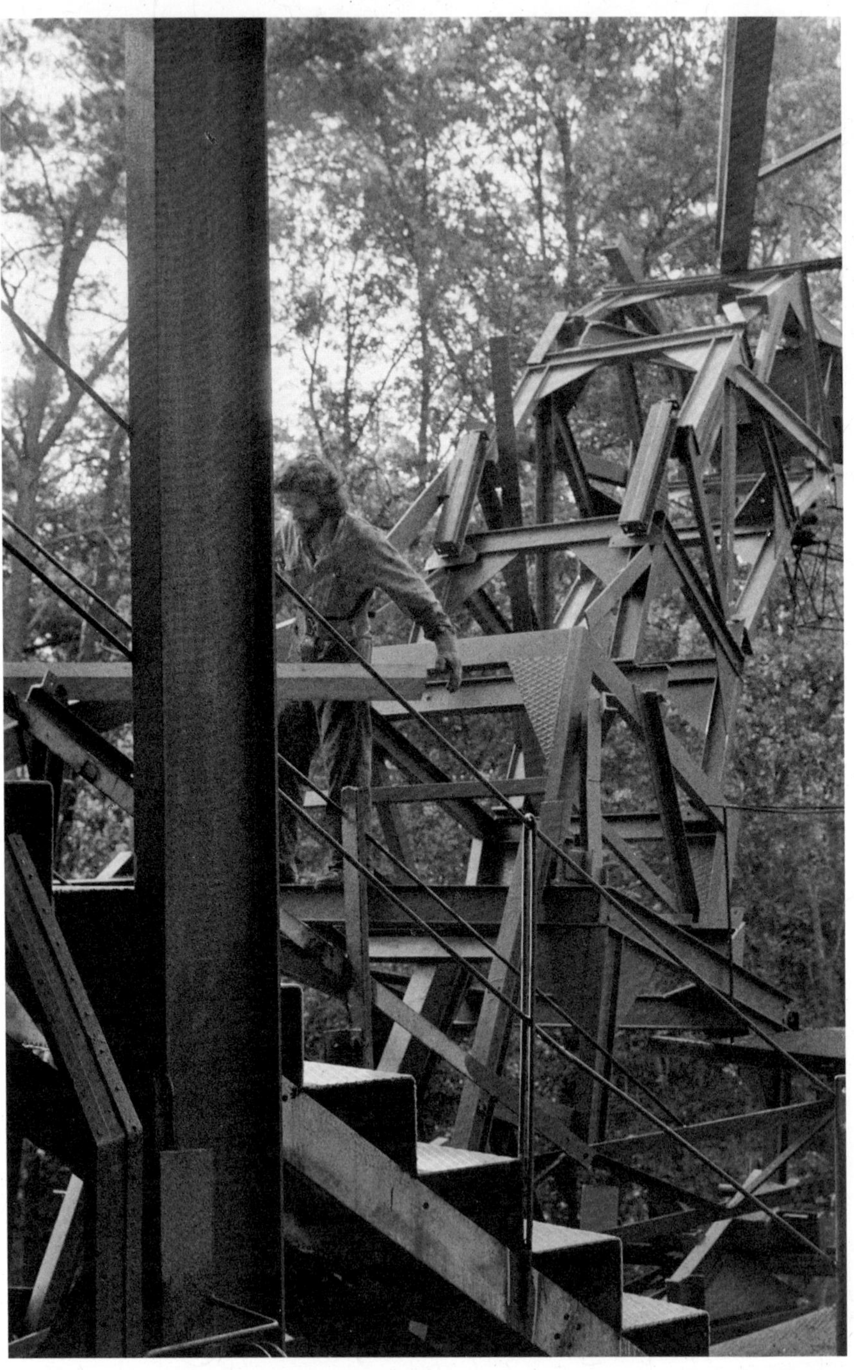

1974   Construction of the top two levels.

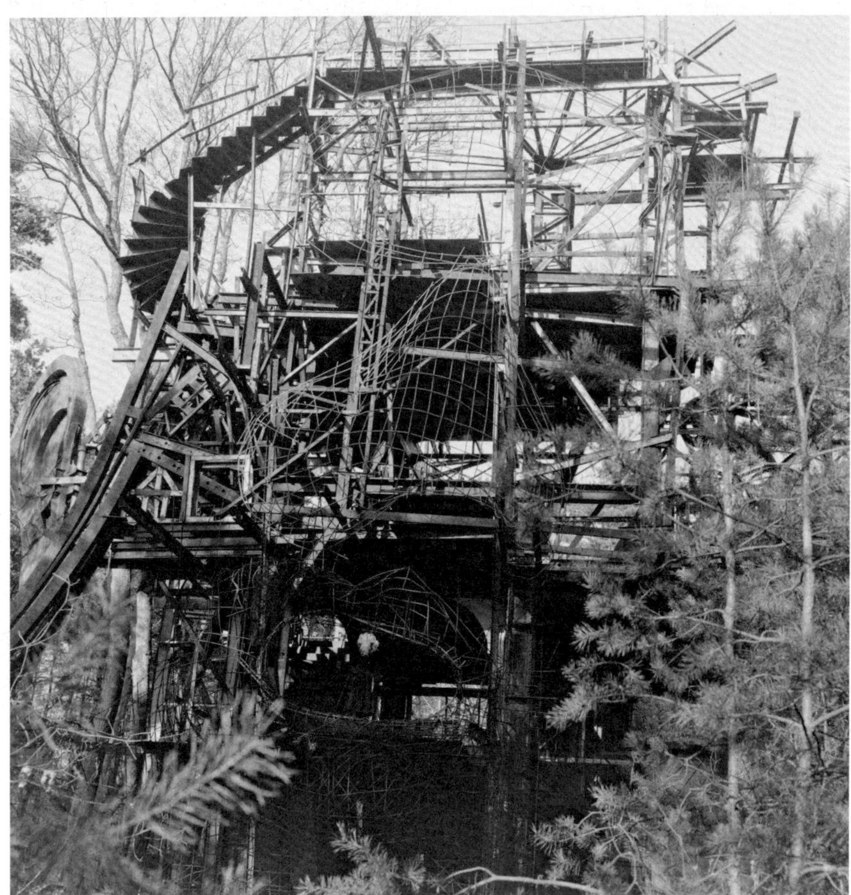

1974   **The del Toso pillar is made.**

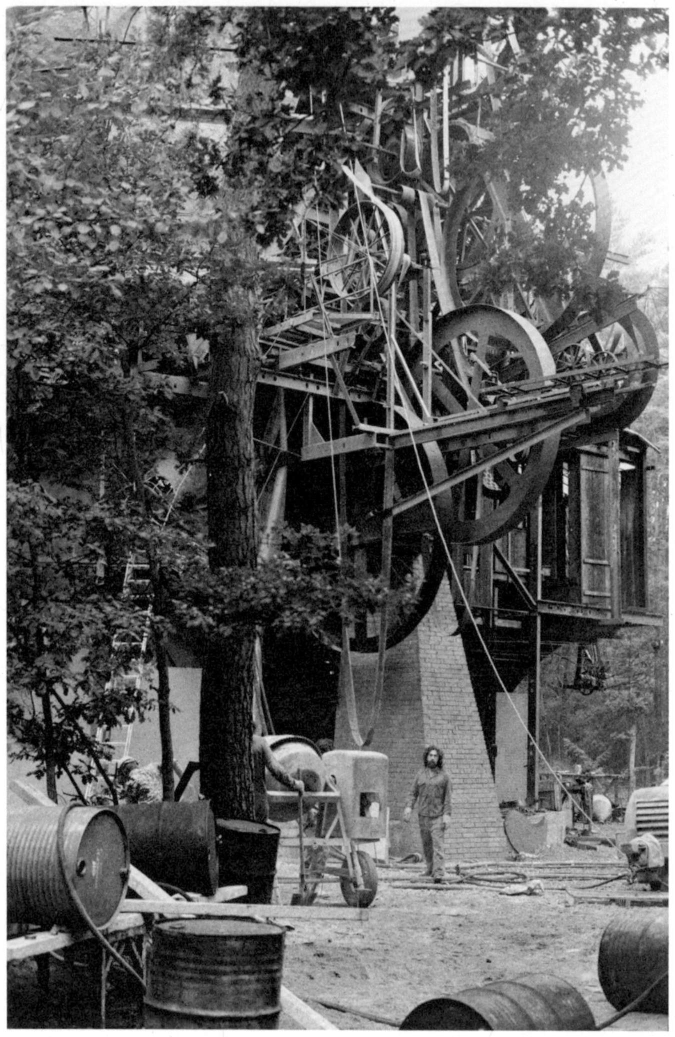

"November 6, 1974, Milly: Tinguely built a fine brick plinth around the monster's neck. We hired the best mason."

Bernhard Luginbühl, "Letter to Margrit Hahnloser," p. 317

"I'm leaving it as a reminder of man's constructiveness, and so that people feel, 'but you know, that's what we had at home, my grandmother had that at home.'"

Jean Tinguely, in *Le Monstre de Tinguely*, 19'47"

1974–1975   Bernhard Luginbühl creates *Boss Tor*.

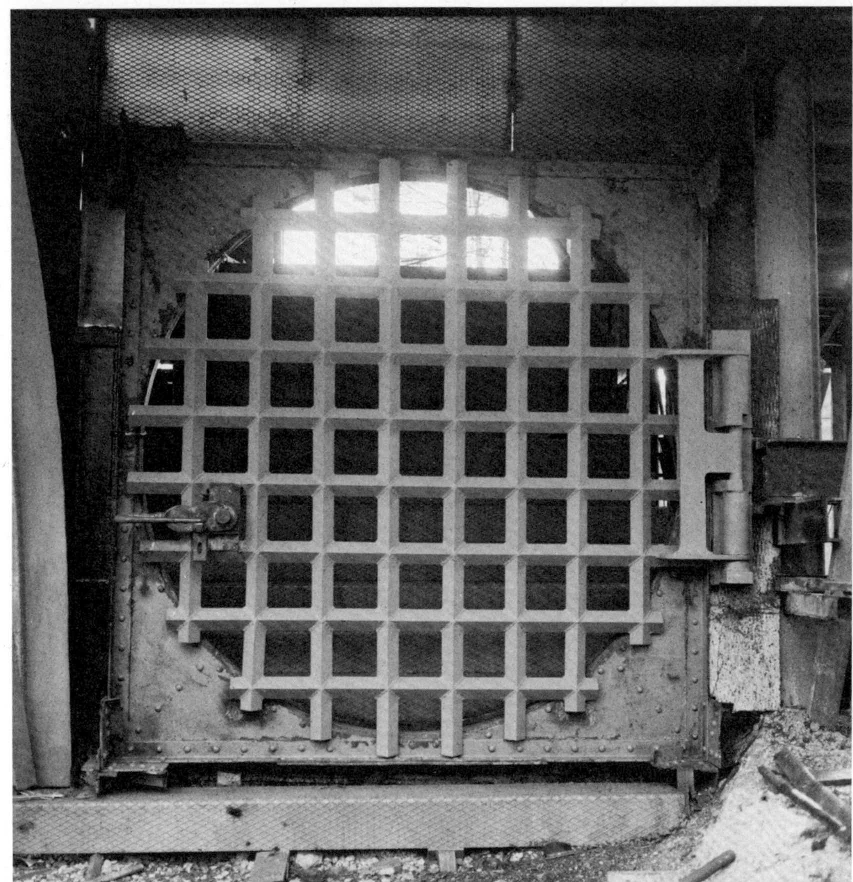

"There are several entrances, real and fake, but the main entrance is
at the back of the Head. Luginbühl made two doors for the opening.
The grand inner door is steel, round, with a pattern of squares, a nod
to the entrance to the safe room in a prosperous bank."

Pontus Hultén, in *Jean Tinguely*, p. 203

1975 **Work begins on Jean Tinguely's *La Dégringolade*.**

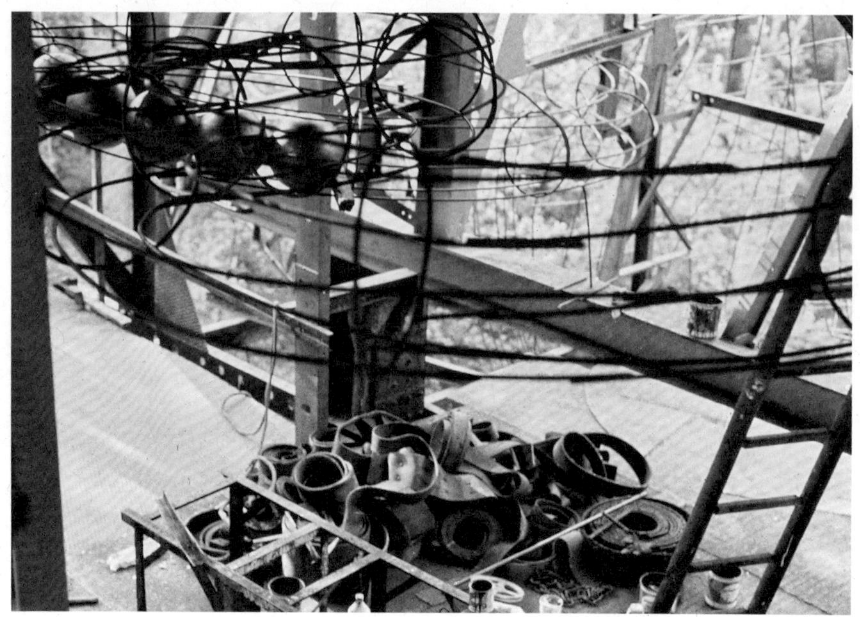

"The rolling balls hark back to the age of total machinism."

Jean Tinguely, *Le Monstre de Tinguely*, 47'16"

1975–1976 Jean Pierre Raynaud creates *La Jauge*.

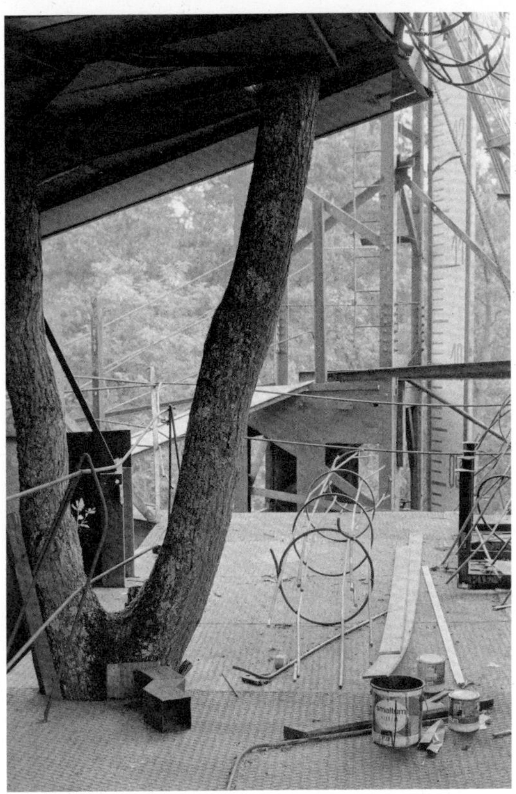

"When Jean said to me, 'We're going to do something together, we're going to join forces on a grand project,' I remember telling him, 'Listen, Jean, I can carry out a project on my own, but group projects are not my strong point.' But I couldn't refuse. In my case he 'violated' me in this way, as it were. I soon realized that I could very well sit tight in my corner, and they would just keep moving all around me. That's life, when it comes down to it. And now, *La Jauge*, the gauge, created in those very early years, is present, but at one remove, because it takes the measure—in the true sense of the word—of what Jean and Niki did, their energy, their madness, and so I am there, present and yet absent, like a sort of marker through the red that I had got just right back then. Then there's the sort of centimeter-by-centimeter calibration that says, 'You see, Tinguely's machine stands, let's say, at 23.52 meters in height.' I am there, we are there together. Separate, but together."

Jean Pierre Raynaud, in *Le Cyclop de Jean Tinguely*, 17'05"

1976 Daniel Spoerri creates *La Chambre renversée de l'hôtel de l'Étoile.*

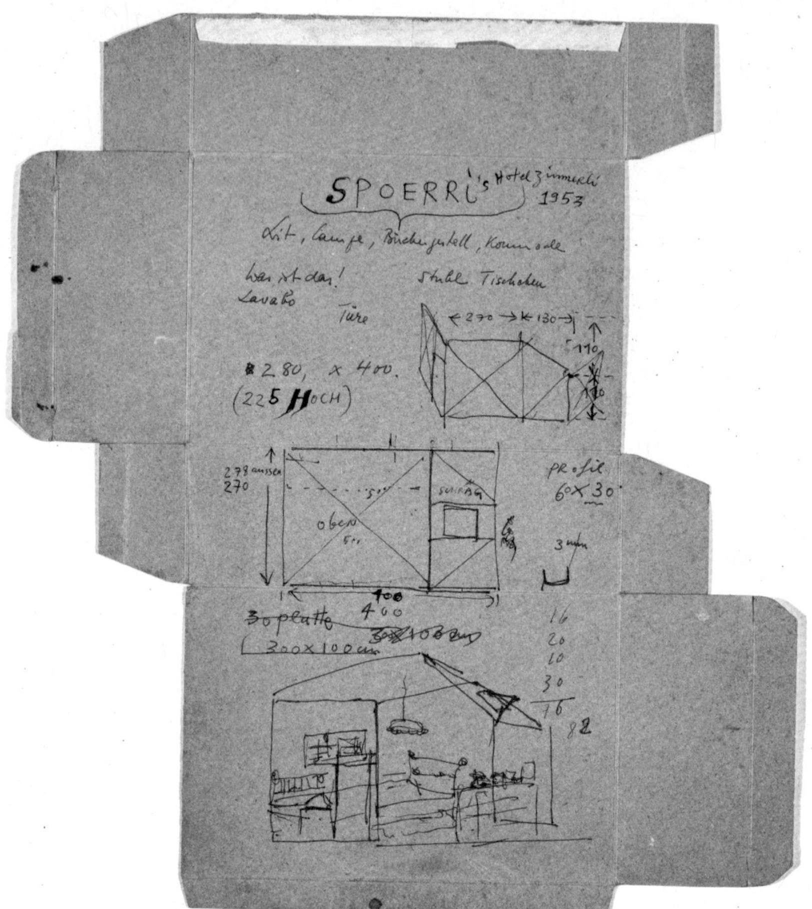

Jean Tinguely and Daniel Spoerri
Sketch for *La Chambre renversée de l'hôtel de l'Étoile*, n. d.
Felt-tip and ballpoint pen on cardboard, 21 × 29.7 cm
Collection Museum Tinguely, Basel

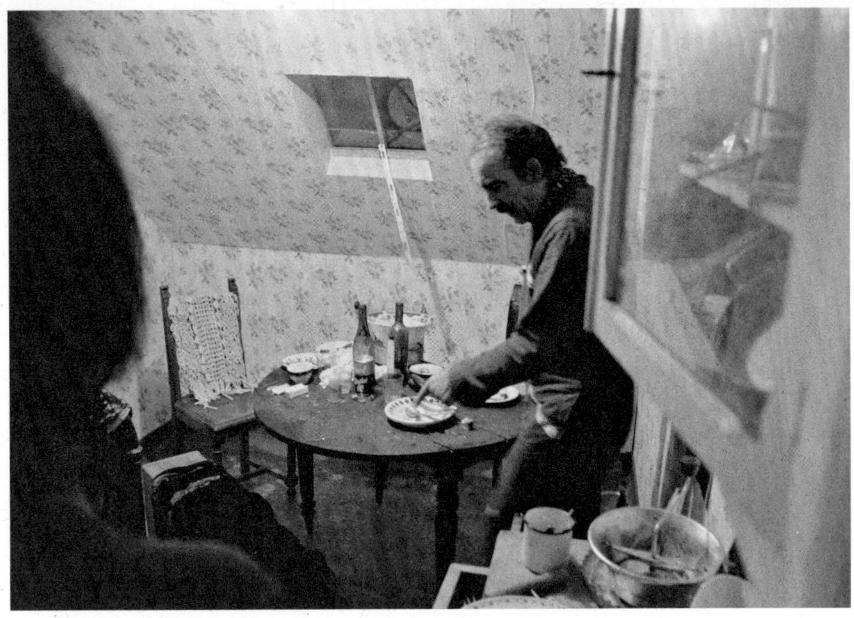

"It was his first hotel room in Paris when he [i.e. Daniel Spoerri] was
a dancer. He was the only one with any money—Eva and I were penniless.
This room was [his] room, our refuge that allowed us to survive in Paris
in that super difficult time. And there is also one of my very first attempts
at art in France, hanging over his bed."

Jean Tinguely, in *Le Monstre de Tinguely*, 38'50"

"On the third floor [of *Le Cyclop*], Daniel Spoerri's Paris hotel room
comfortably wallpapered, that would later be turned upside down,
with its old hotel iron bedstead. Jeano told us, 'If you're tired, go to bed,
you can lock yourselves in.' Daniel's room was put to use. In the wall
cupboard we kept sugar and tea bags, and on the nightstand, a kettle
and two ersatz cognacs, a cheap Spanish one and a Dresden MARTELL
(Luginbühl's favorite)."

Bernhard Luginbühl, diary, August 5, 1976, n.p.

1976   *Le Cyclop* face is encased in concrete.

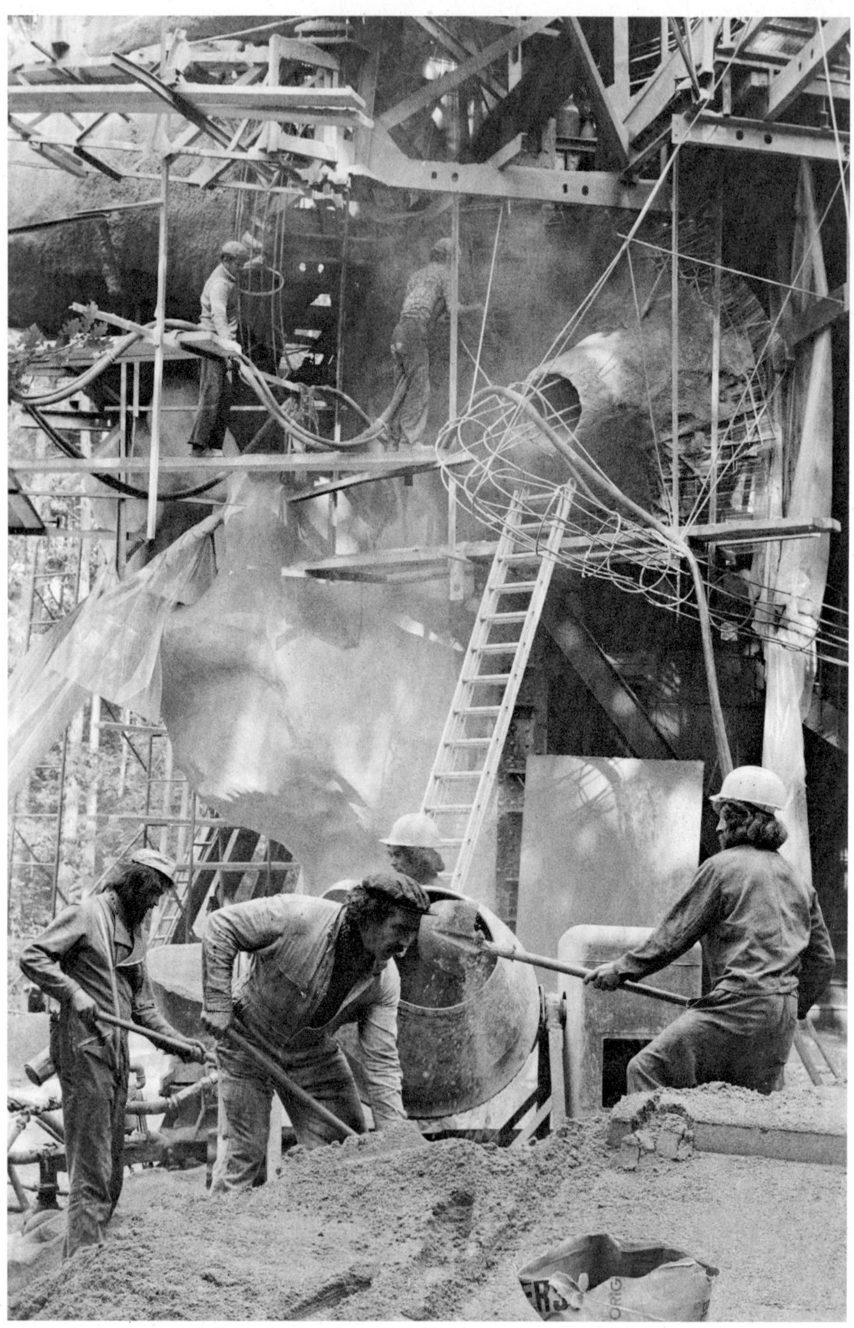

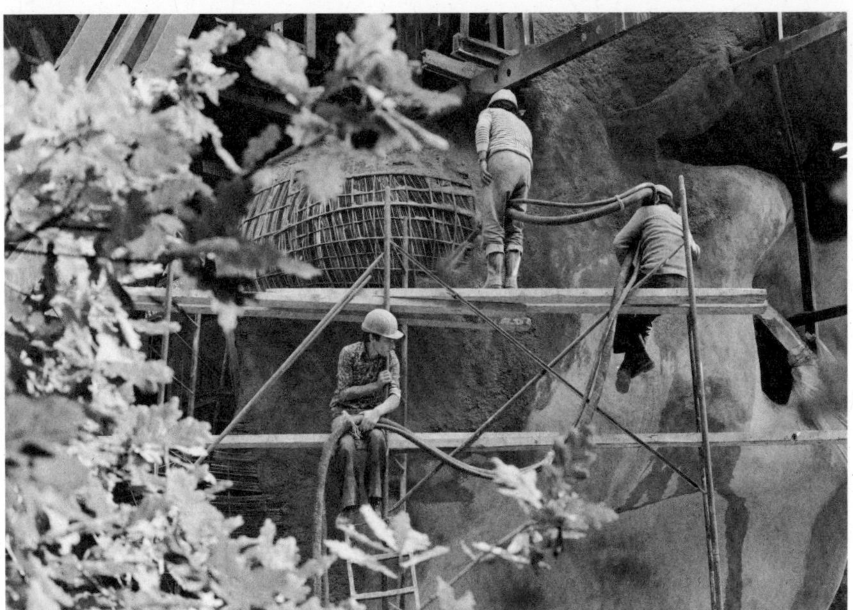

"120 tonnes of concrete was poured and the cement mix was shoveled
by hand into the small mixer. The sludge was then piped up in twin pipes
that doubled as a mixer, and spewed out onto the mesh, like runny
shit at high pressure. So weird was this little man with the hose between
his legs attached to the scaffolding like he was taking a great, gray piss.
In five days, hard on all of us, the facade was sprayed on and the ghost left."

Bernhard Luginbühl, diary, August 15, 1976, n.p.

1976   Eva Aeppli's *Hommage aux déportés* is completed.

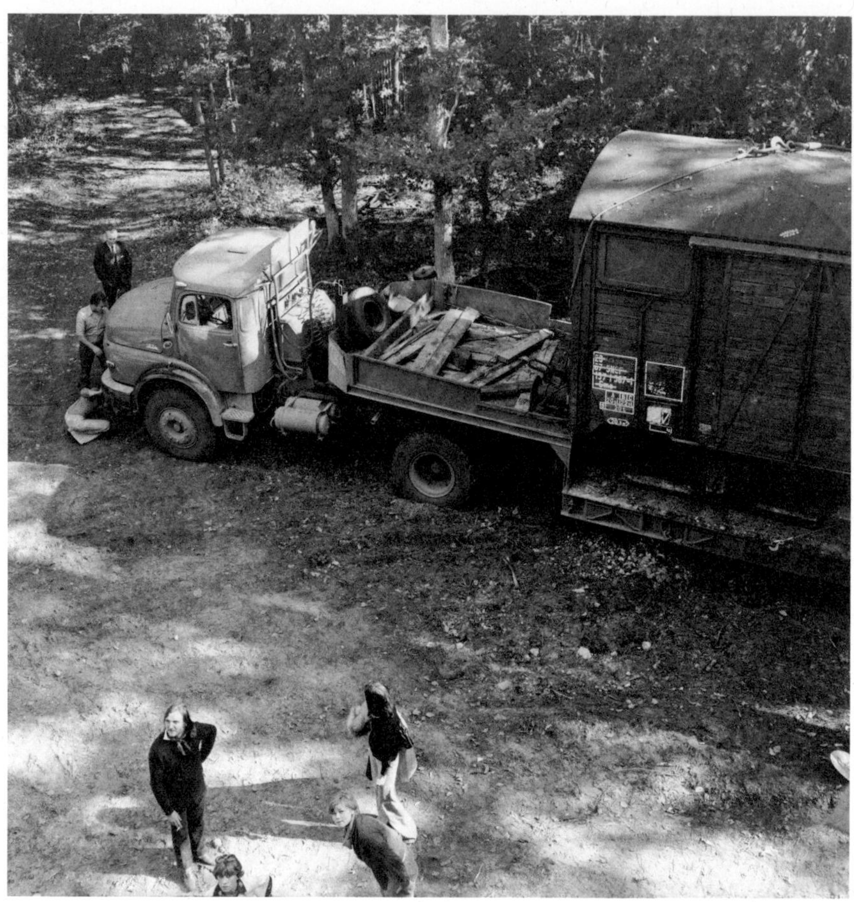

"It's still a miracle to me that we were able to transport the carriage on the sandy forest paths with the huge crane bringing up the rear."
Bernhard Luginbühl, "Letter to Margrit Hahnloser," p. 320

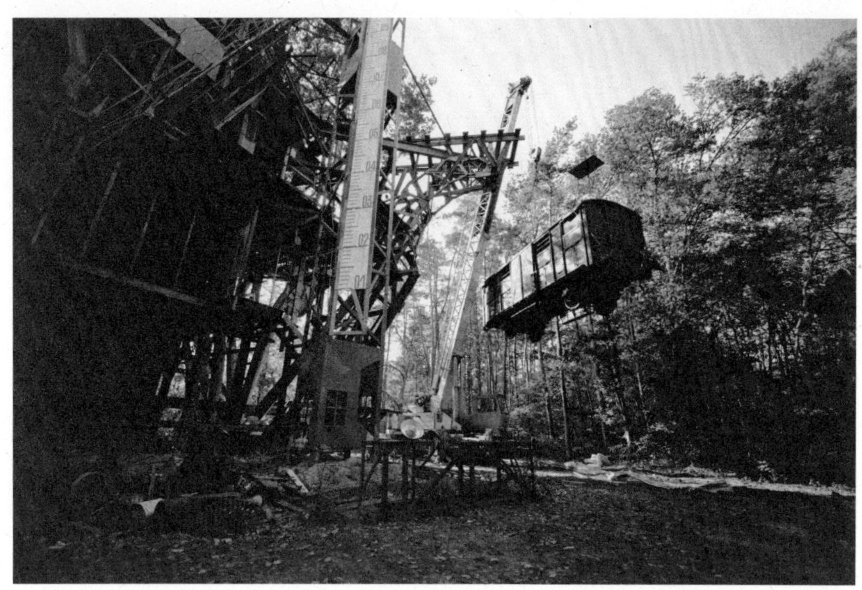

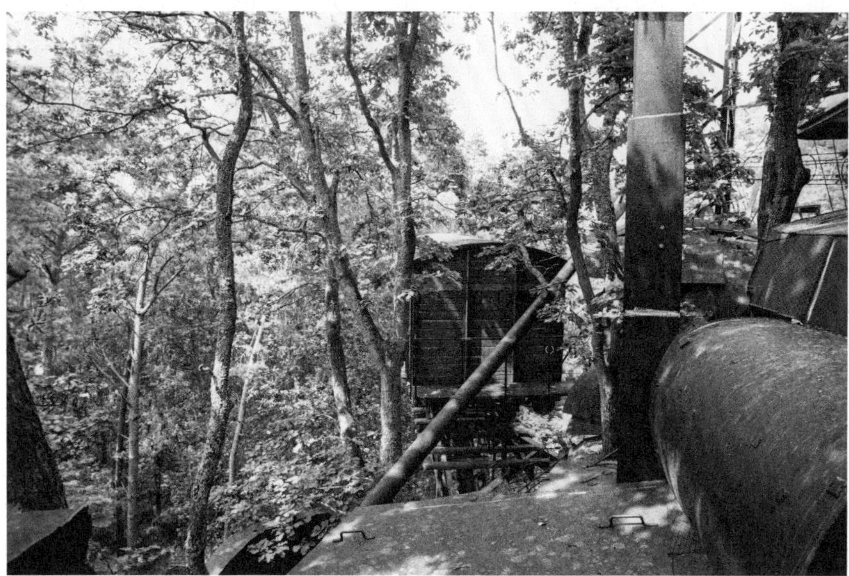

1976 Work begins on Jean Tinguely's *Le Méta-Merzbau.*

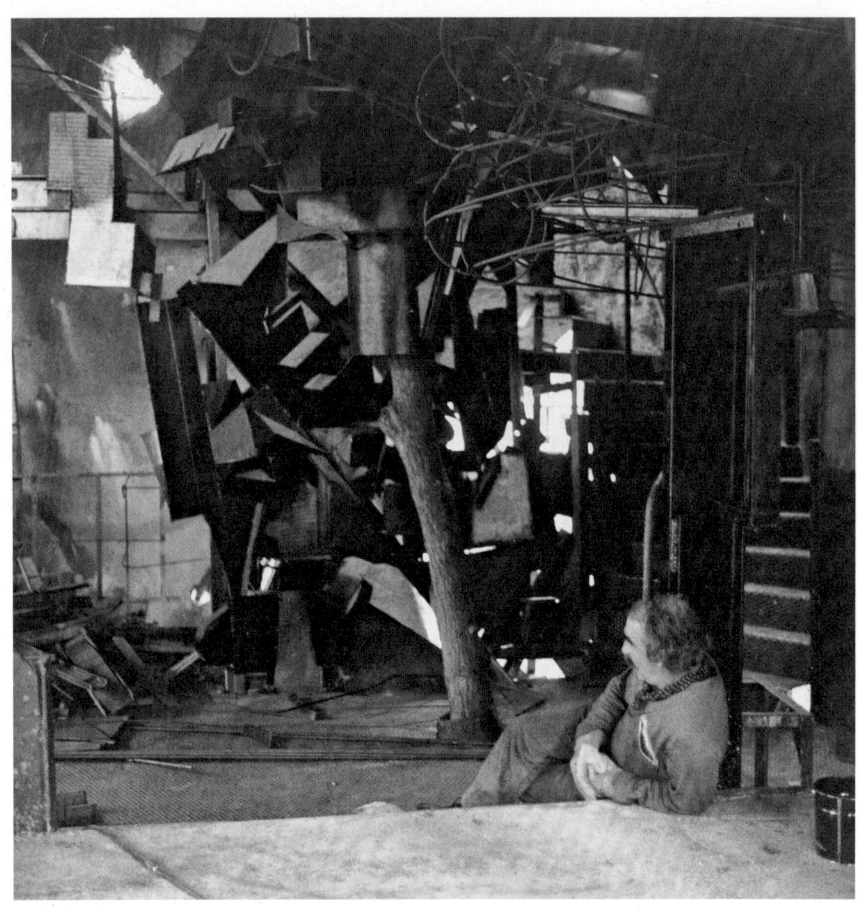

"I made it in metal, in other words in anti-Schwitters,
in counter-Schwitters."

Jean Tinguely, in *Le Monstre de Tinguely*, 23'54"

Work begins on Jean Tinguely's *Hommage à Yves Klein.*

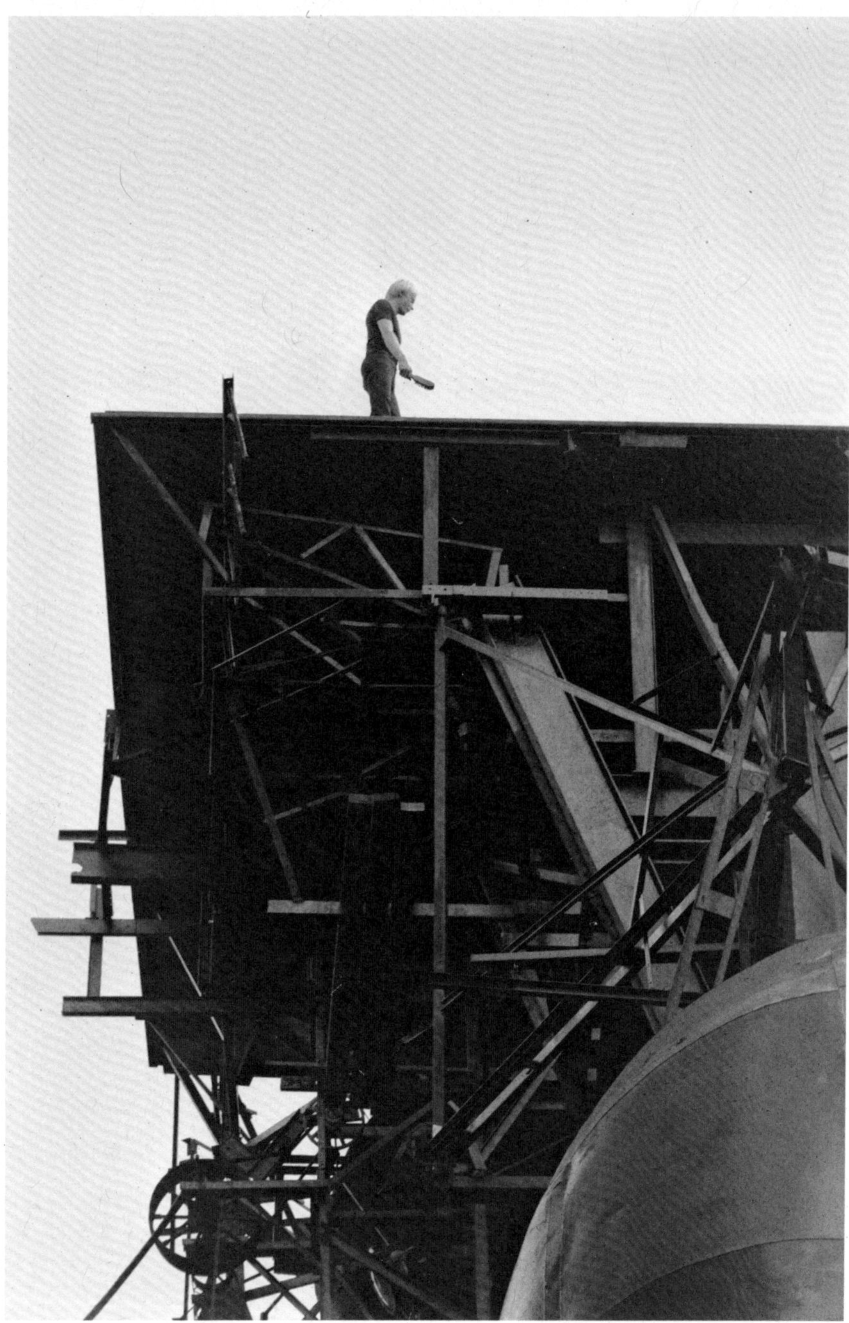

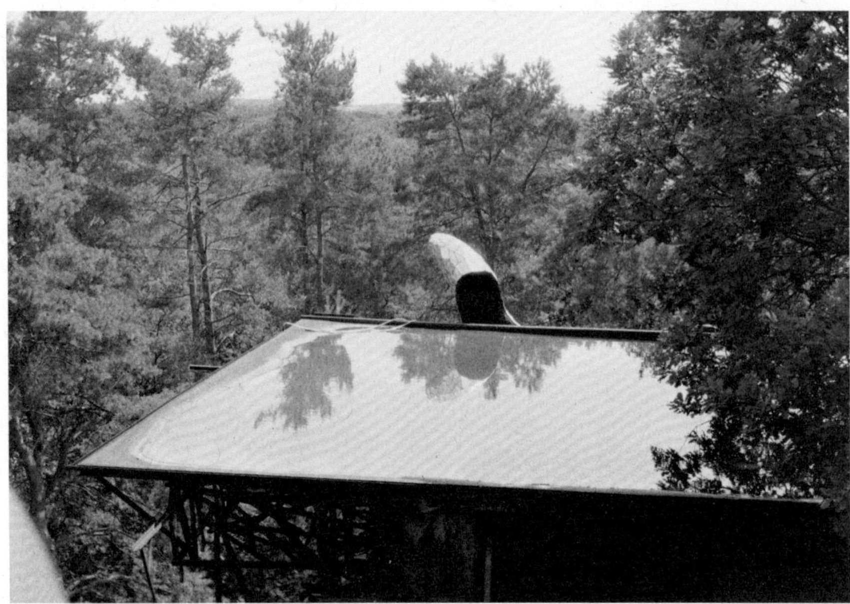

"At the very top is the water, right up to the brim. It ends with water so you can see the sky, and the water is flat and square, and what the water means is a homage to Yves Klein, who died in 1962, my great friend, my great love, marvellous, extraordinary, and absurd battler of monochrome, space, and the void. Yves Klein is dead and I have paid homage."

Jean Tinguely, in *Le Monstre de Tinguely*, 36'06"

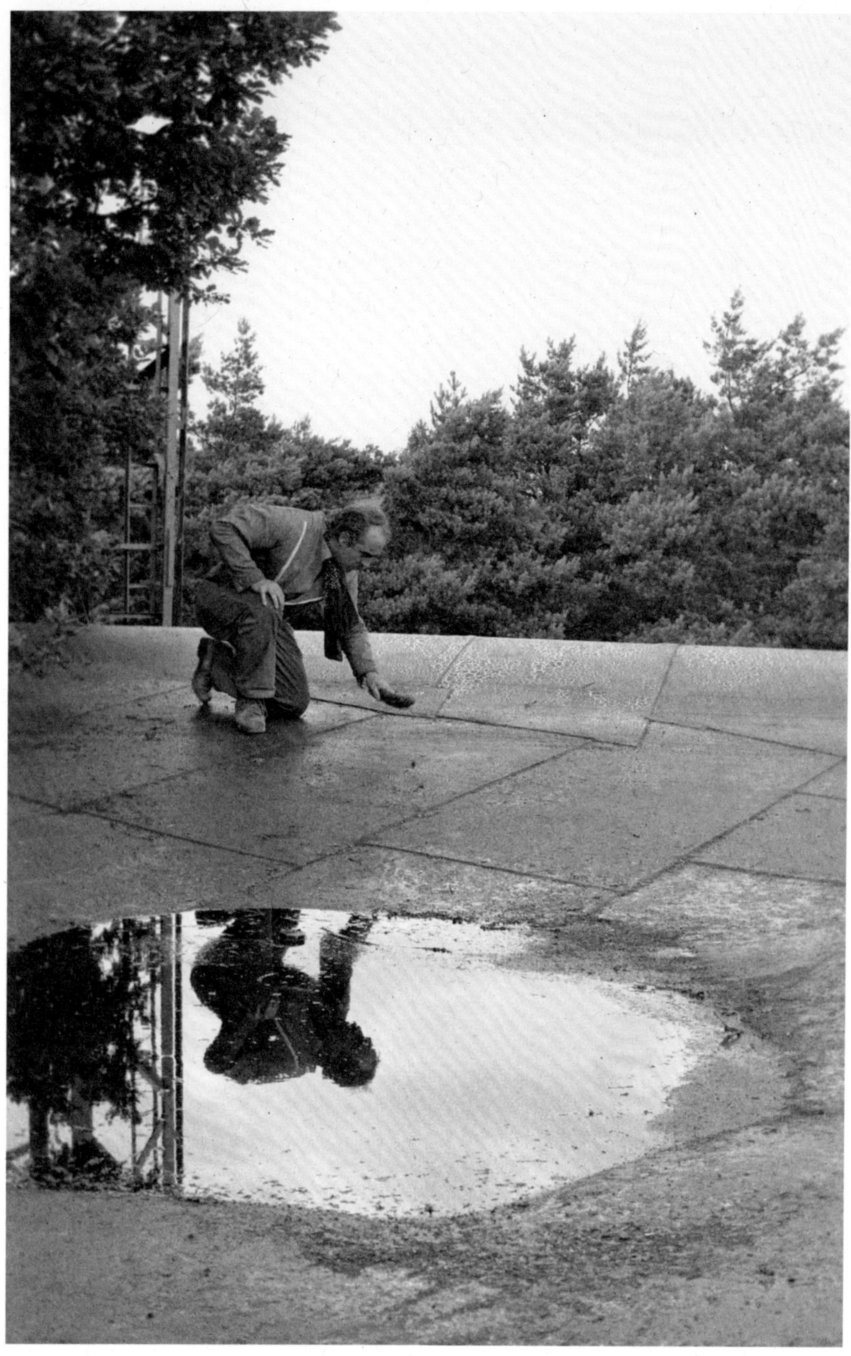

1976 Jean Tinguely's *La Batterie* is installed.

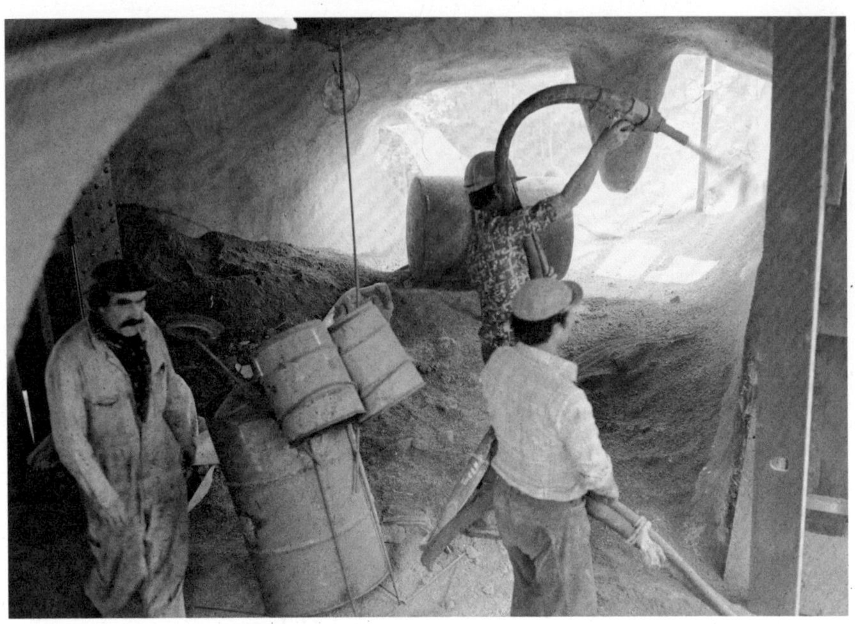

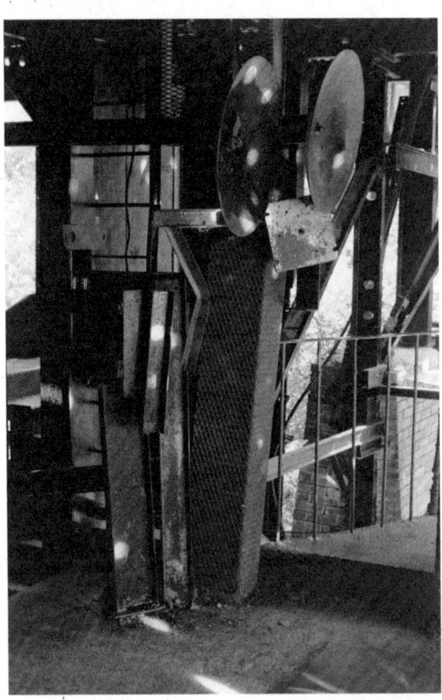

1978 The levels are reinforced with concrete.

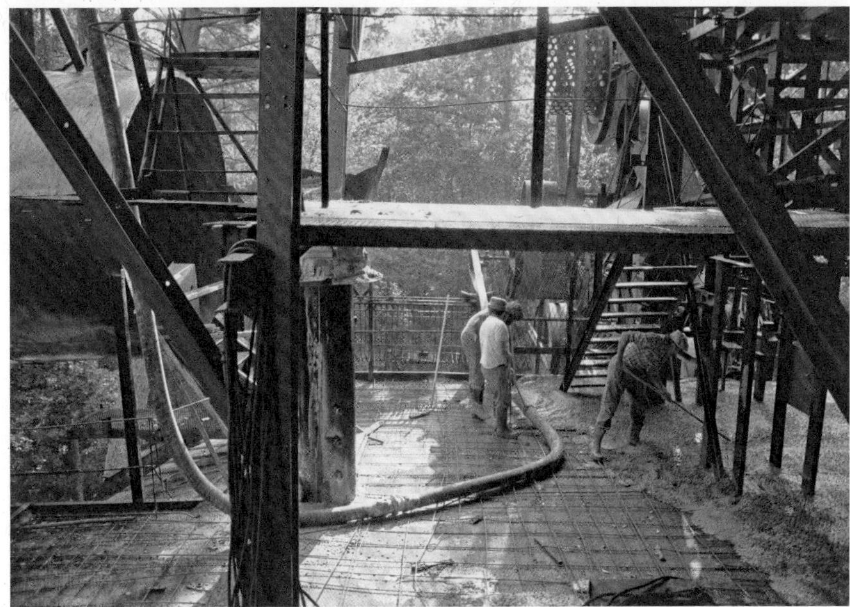

"Tinguely wanted to pour concrete floors to reinforce the Head. Concrete became more and more important. To begin with, iron took pride of place, then it became caught up in a vast mass of concrete. It was like a concrete cake with enormous scrap-iron knitting needles sticking out of it."

Bernhard Luginbühl, "Letter to Margrit Hahnloser," p. 317

1978

Work begins on *L'Incitation au suicide* by Niki de Saint Phalle and Jean Tinguely.

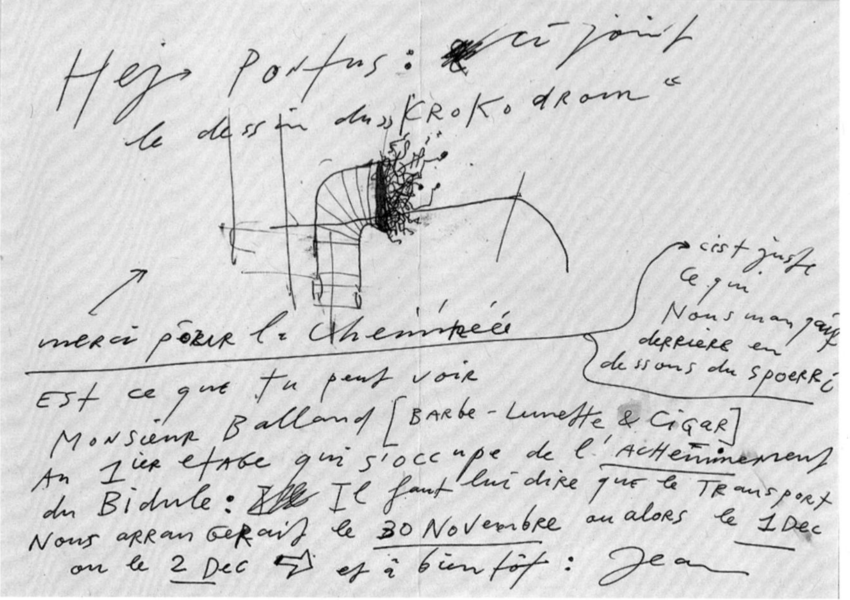

Jean Tinguely
Letter to Pontus Hultén, 1978
Felt-tip and ballpoint pen on paper, 21 × 29.7 cm
Collection Museum Tinguely, Basel

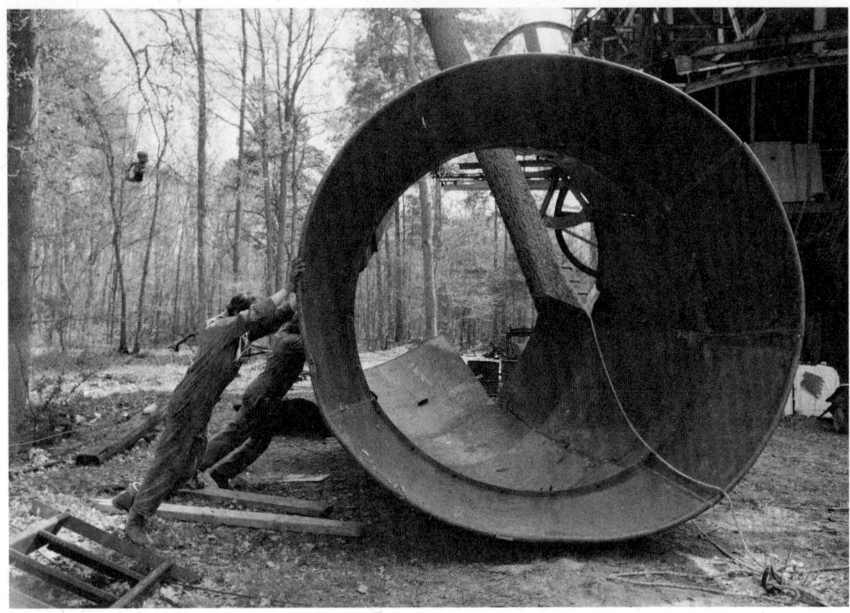

"Met Jeano in the forest of the head and then Daniel that evening at Beaubourg where we discovered a spare conduit for the Milly monster, and the Aunts and Uncles Museum which is in fact cheap for hanging up wet washing or very useful as a flower vase or wine rack or multi-purpose gallows or as a beehive with propellors or a monument for an oil slick or as a gym for gorillas or as … "

Bernhard Luginbühl, diary, November 17, 1976, n.p.

1978 Bernhard Luginbühl's relief *Hommage à Louise Nevelson* is created.

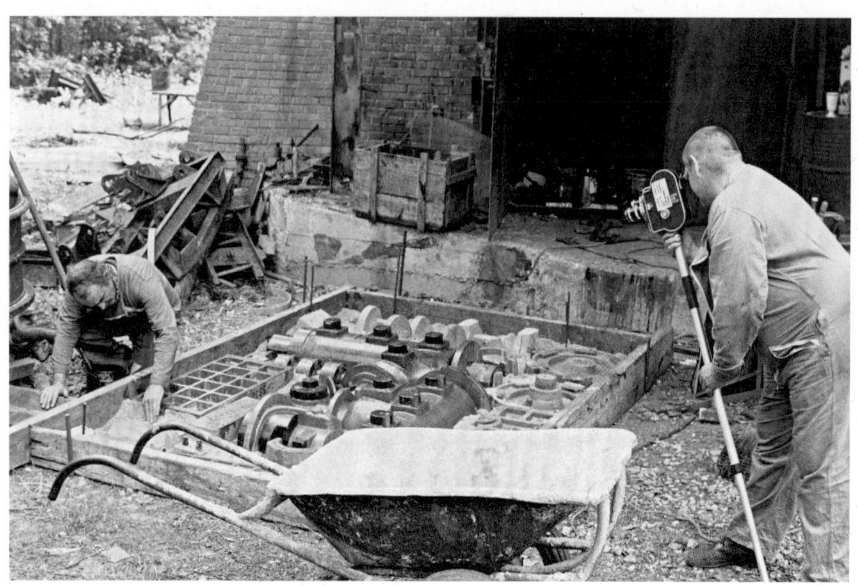

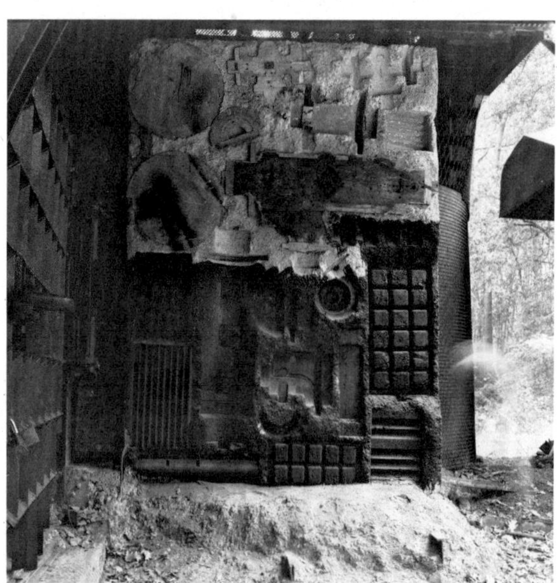

"We got to work fast on the relief, making a wooden frame and putting the wooden models in place so that the orgy of concrete can begin tomorrow,"

Bernhard Luginbühl, diary, August 24, 1978, n.p.

Jean Tinguely's *La Broyeuse de chocolat: Hommage à Marcel Duchamp*
is installed.

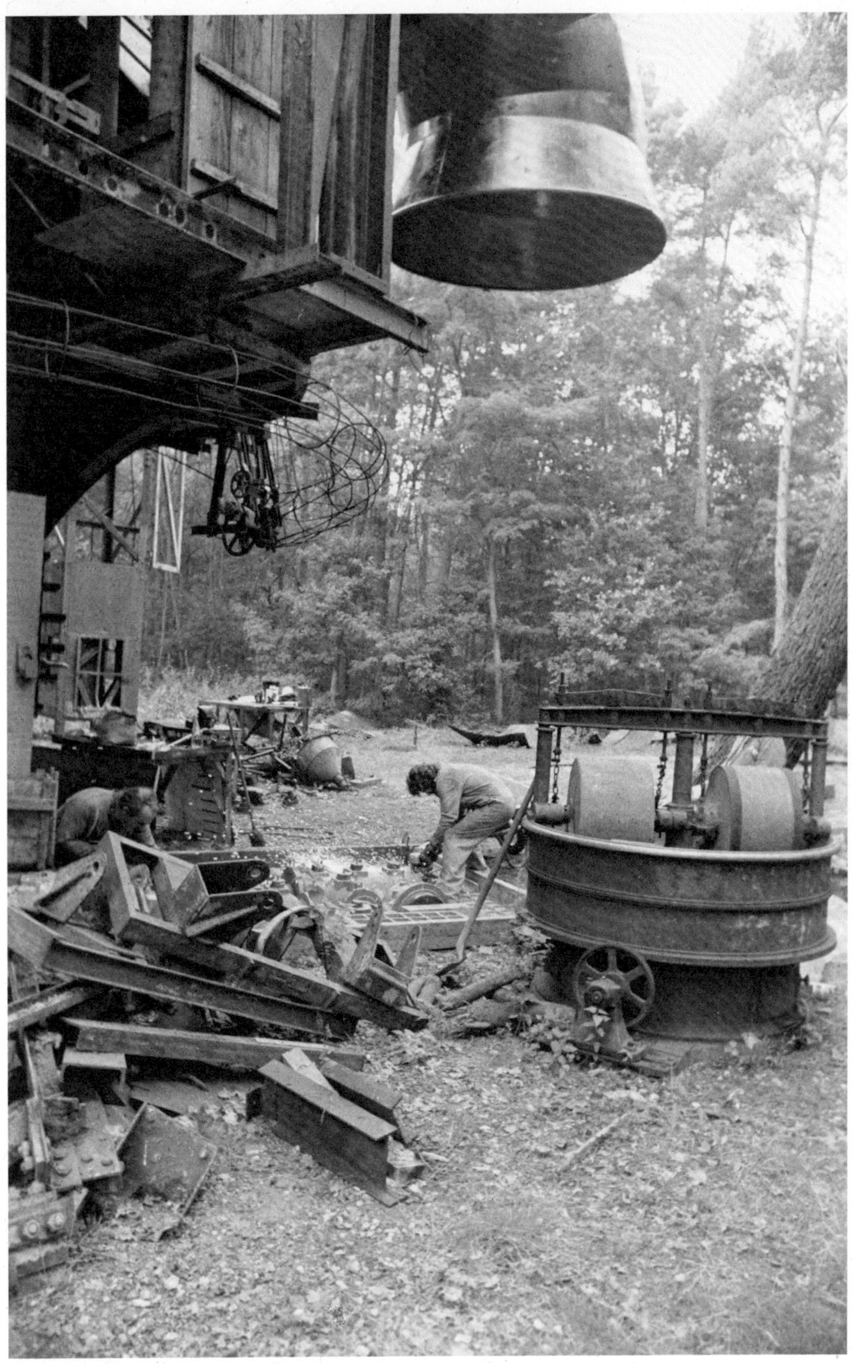

1978   Seppi Imhof welds the cubist west roof.

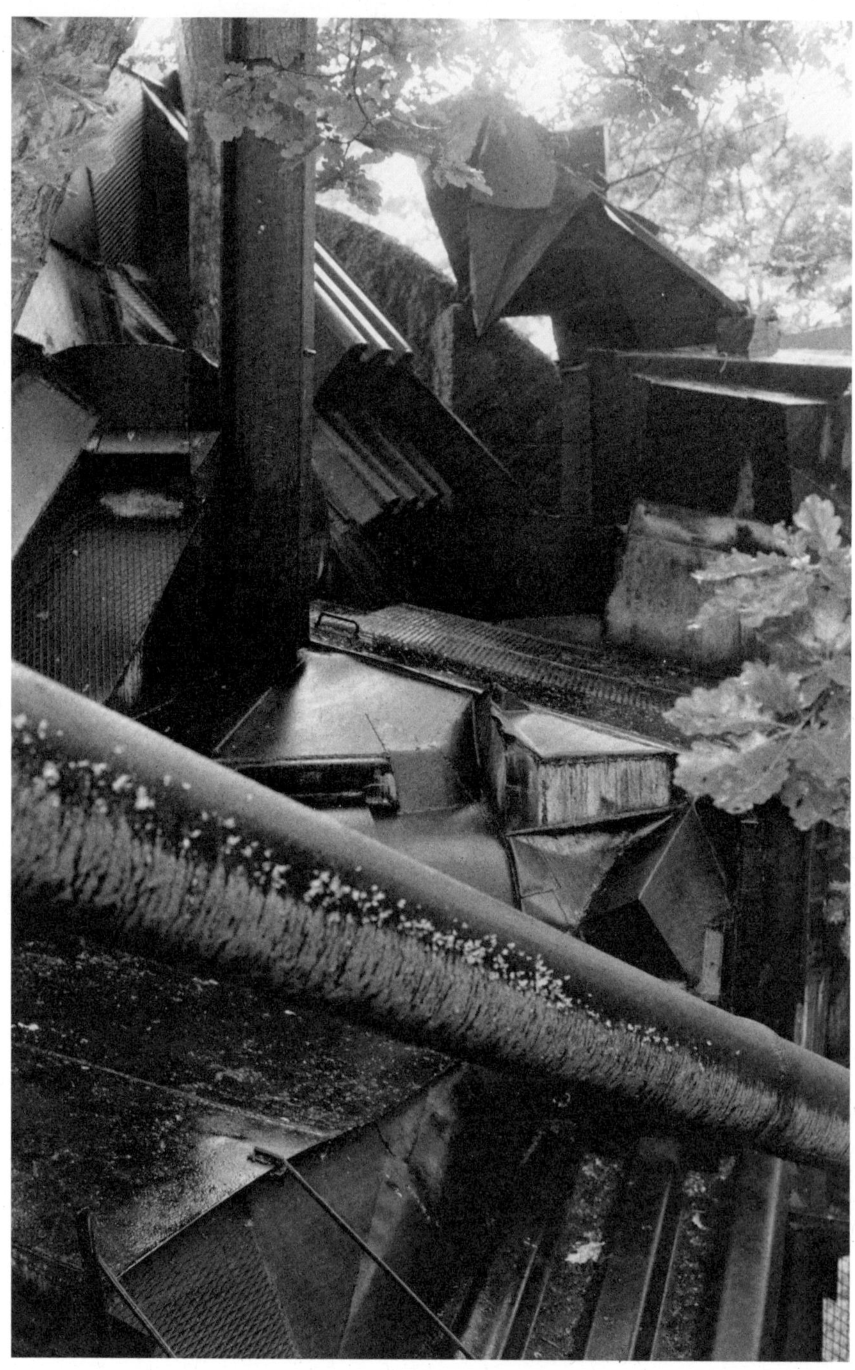

Bernhard Luginbühl's *Le Tellflipper: Hommage à Guillaume Tell*
is installed.

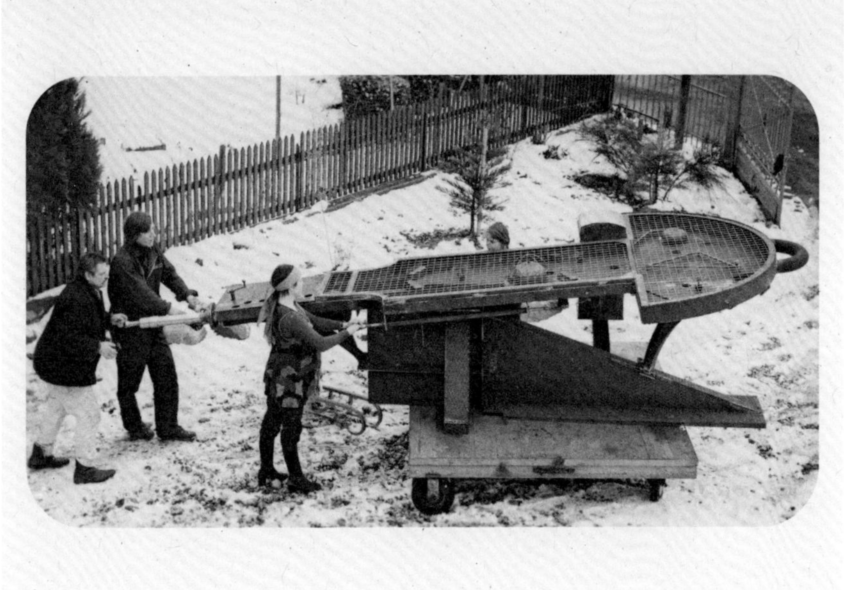

Bernhard Luginbühl
Le Tellflipper, before 1973
Front of a postcard given, at the beginning of the game, to players in exchange for a coin dropped into a box attached
to the side of the work
Centre National des Arts Plastiques Archives, Paris

1980   Work begins on Jean Tinguely's *La Méta-Harmonie*.

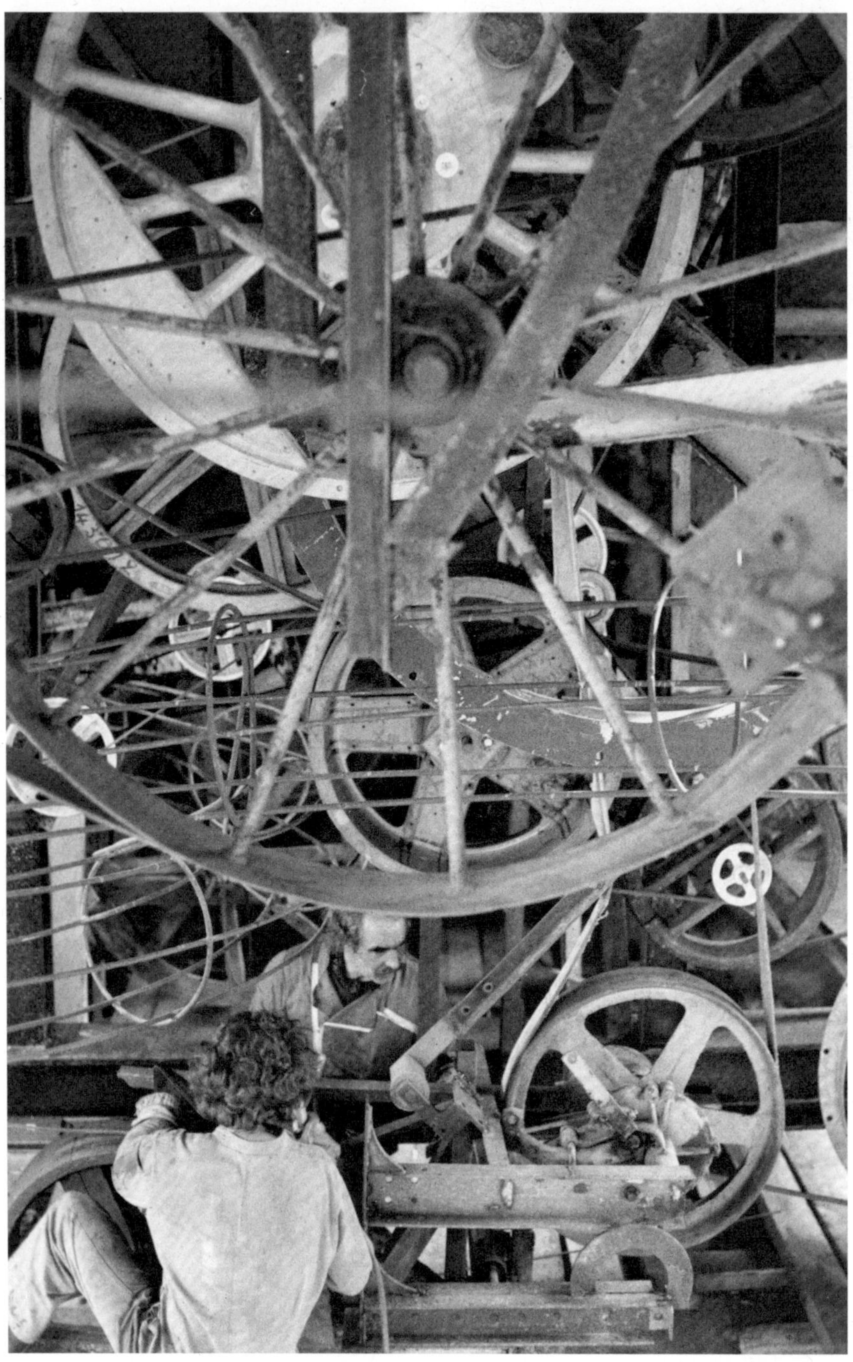

Jean Tinguely's *Les Sièges du Petit Théâtre* are created.

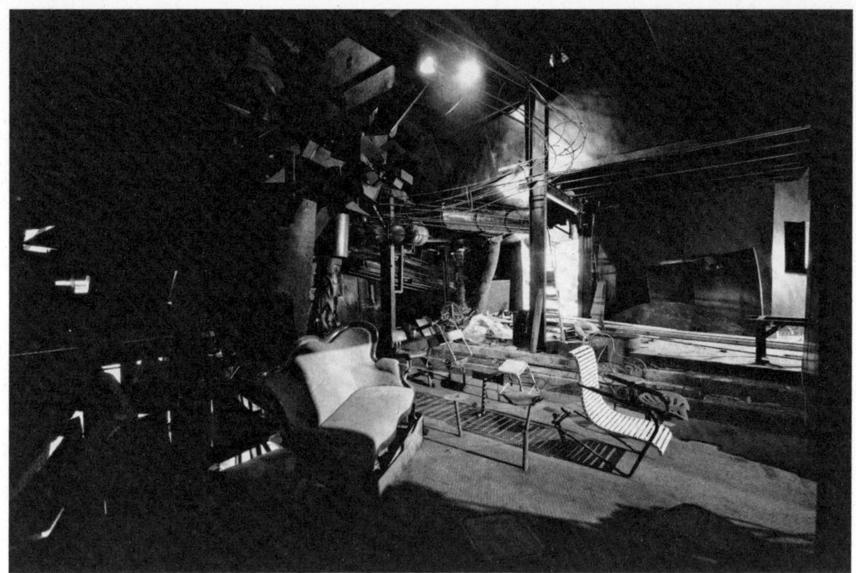

1980 · Work is completed on the apartment.

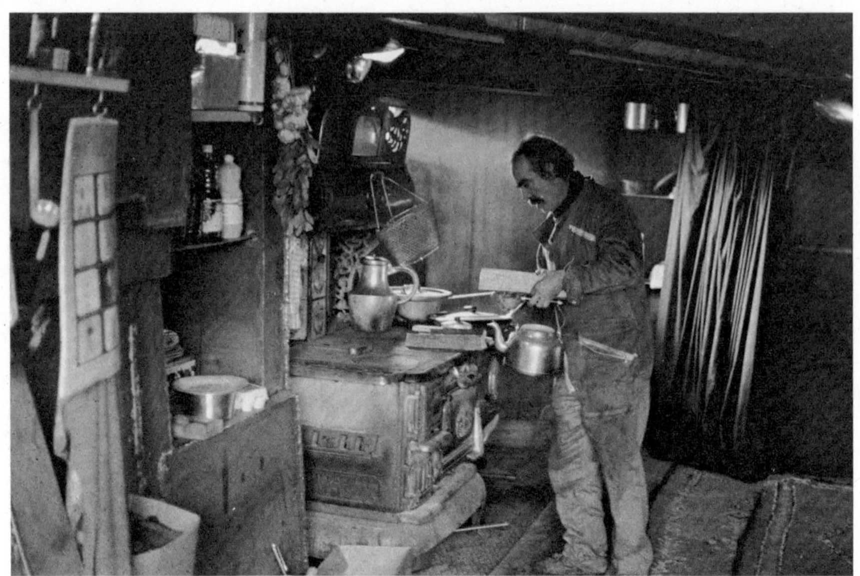

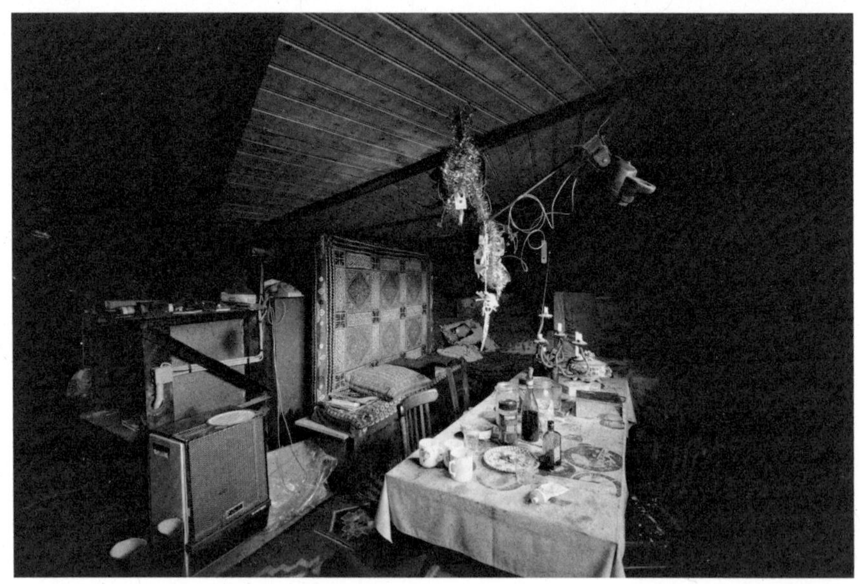

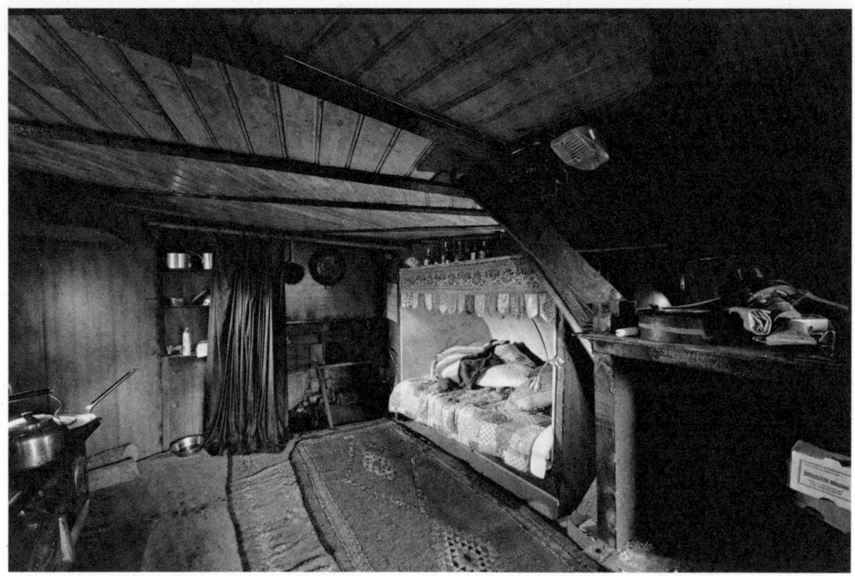

"Jean sent Sepp into the forest to see the head; there was constantly something going on. The central point becomes the acts of vandalism that keep on happening. Jeano wants to set up an apartment in the head as fast as possible and have a man living in it with a big stick and a dog. Chickens and ducks must live in the head too, ducks swimming on the pond at the top … Jeano also wants to go into the forest to keep an eye on the head himself and talk to the mayor in Milly etc."

Bernhard Luginbühl, diary, April 16, 1980

"Sepp Imhof then appeared in the afternoon, in the passage to the south side of the head: the apartment is ready. For the first time, Jeano shows a lack of interest in working on the monster's head. A two-page article has been printed in a local French paper and people are coming to see the THING, more disturbers, gypsies, hippies, rockers, and Frenchies who want to steal something. In spite of everything, the apartment will be covered in wood, and insulated, as Seppi promises me. Seppi finds the idea of making the head inhabitable ridiculous. Who would want to climb to the third floor all the time? He thinks it would be better to put a caravan in front of the head."

Bernhard Luginbühl, diary, August 3, 1980

1981–1990
A Decade in Suspense, and a Happy Ending

1981–1985 Work stops on *Le Cyclop*.

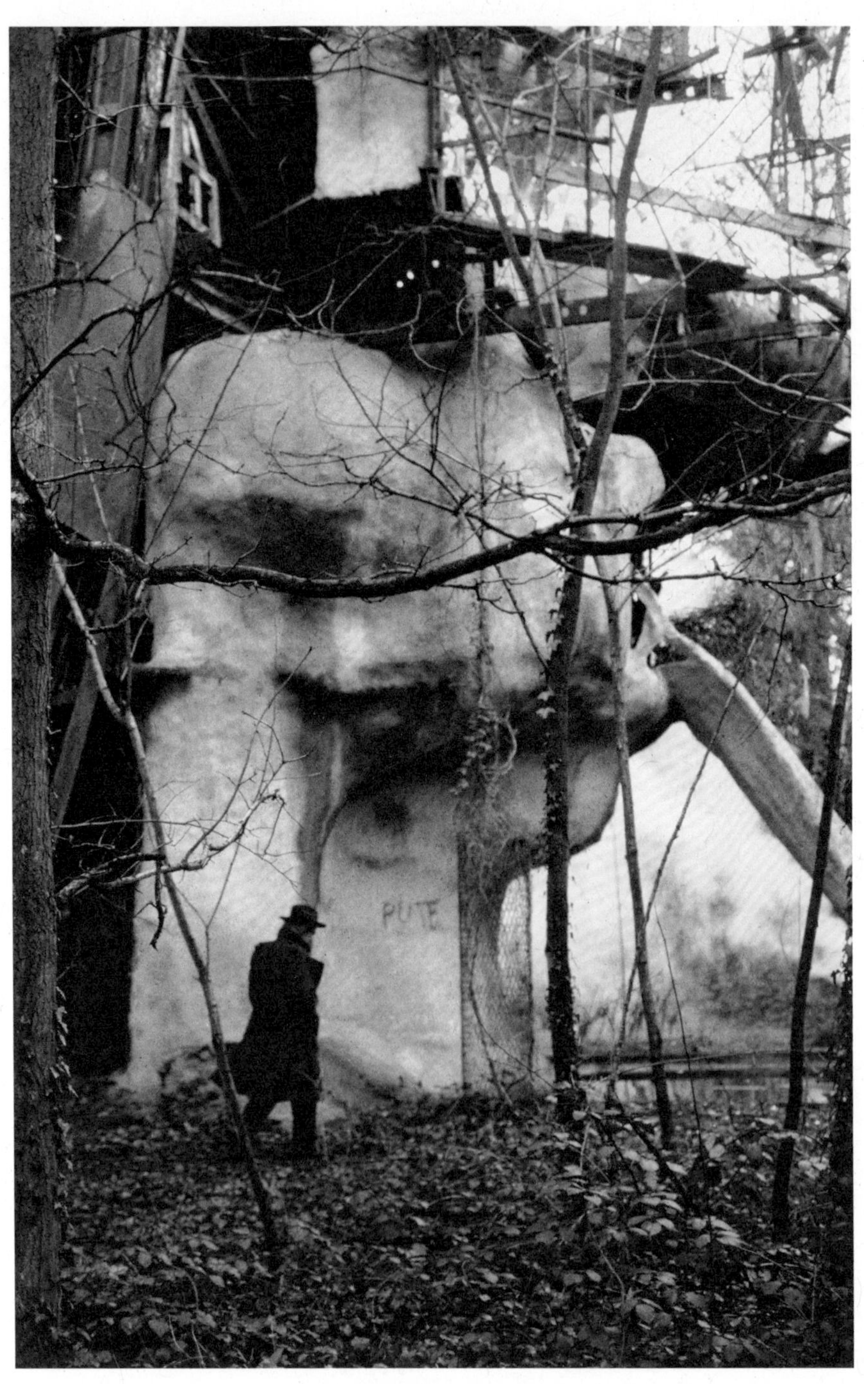

"Jeano rings the doorbell and asks for a cup of coffee before leaving for
Zurich for his catalogue things. The latest harebrained idea is to cut
the head in the forest into pieces and send it to the USA by ship. Sepp and
Jeano's new game. The rusty cargo ship was already waiting in Le Havre
to pick up the THING. Jeano moans about the vandals who cause ever
greater damage to the HEAD."

Bernhard Luginbühl, diary, April 24, 1982, n.p.

"There was so much vandalism. Once it was even set on fire. I gave the
order to concrete it over and sow it full of weeds. I wanted to 'Angkor
Watify' it, like in Cambodia. I put pockets of soil in the Head for the weeds
to grow. We wanted to concrete it all over and make a secret entrance
from underneath."

Jean Tinguely, in *Tinguely et le mystère de la roue manquante*, p. 80

1985 **Dismantling and moving *Le Cyclop*?**

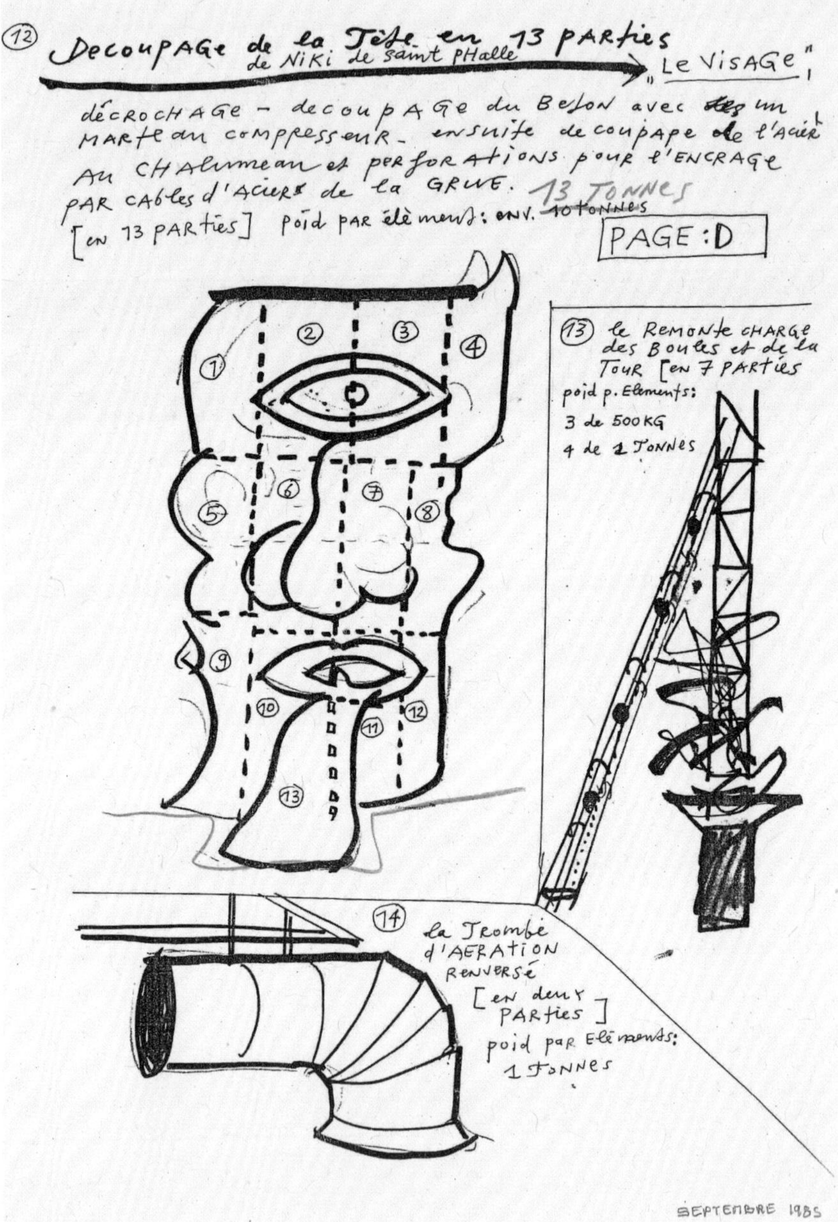

Jean Tinguely
Petite documentation pour le démontage-transport et reconstruction de Jean Tinguely, September 1985 (excerpt)
Xerox, two pages
Centre National des Arts Plastiques Archives, Paris

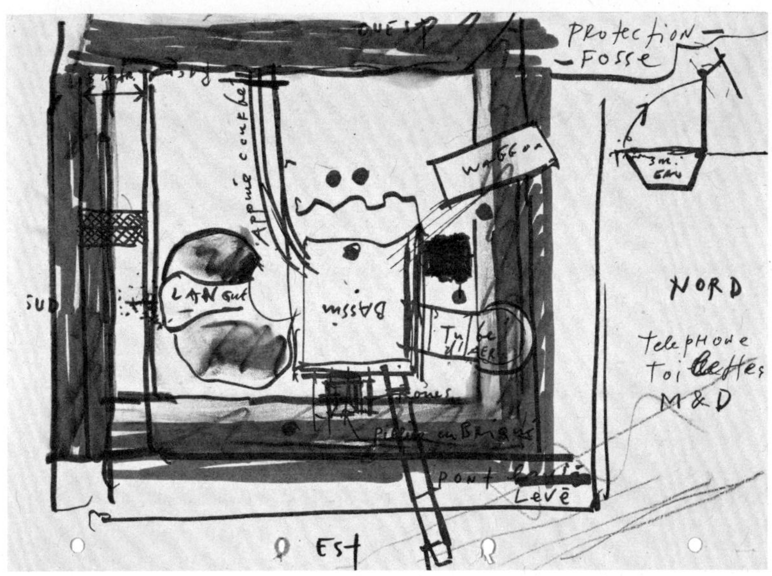

Jean Tinguely
Proposed location for *Le Cyclop* in the Parc de Saint-Cloud, 1983–1986
Felt-tip on paper
Collection Museum Tinguely, Basel; bequest of Josef Imhof, 2021

"I was prepared to move it. I would have found that great fun and completely crazy: moving the only work I wanted, in a way, to be stable and to stay where it was. Though as you know, I am under no illusion on that score, I find everything is fleeting, whatever you do. But I was prepared to move it to the Parc de Saint-Cloud. The enthusiasm was underwhelming, even though I'd found a superb hole in the grounds and I would have especially had fun watching all the lorries drive off, it would have been completely crazy."

Jean Tinguely, in *Le Monstre de Tinguely*, 25'53"

"In 1985, I'd almost completely given up, I was dying. Niki heard me talking about *Le Cyclop* in my nightmares. She went to see President [François] Mitterrand and they decided to take charge of the Head."

Jean Tinguely, in *Tinguely et le mystère de la roue manquante*, p. 80

"Now, [the main thing] is a bit of peace so that Jean can keep going, because there's been a fair bit of vandalism. The Head has been rather like sleeping beauty, it's had a rest, it's been asleep in the forest for several years."

Niki de Saint Phalle, in *Le Monstre de Tinguely*, 32'53"

1987   *Le Cyclop* is gifted to France.

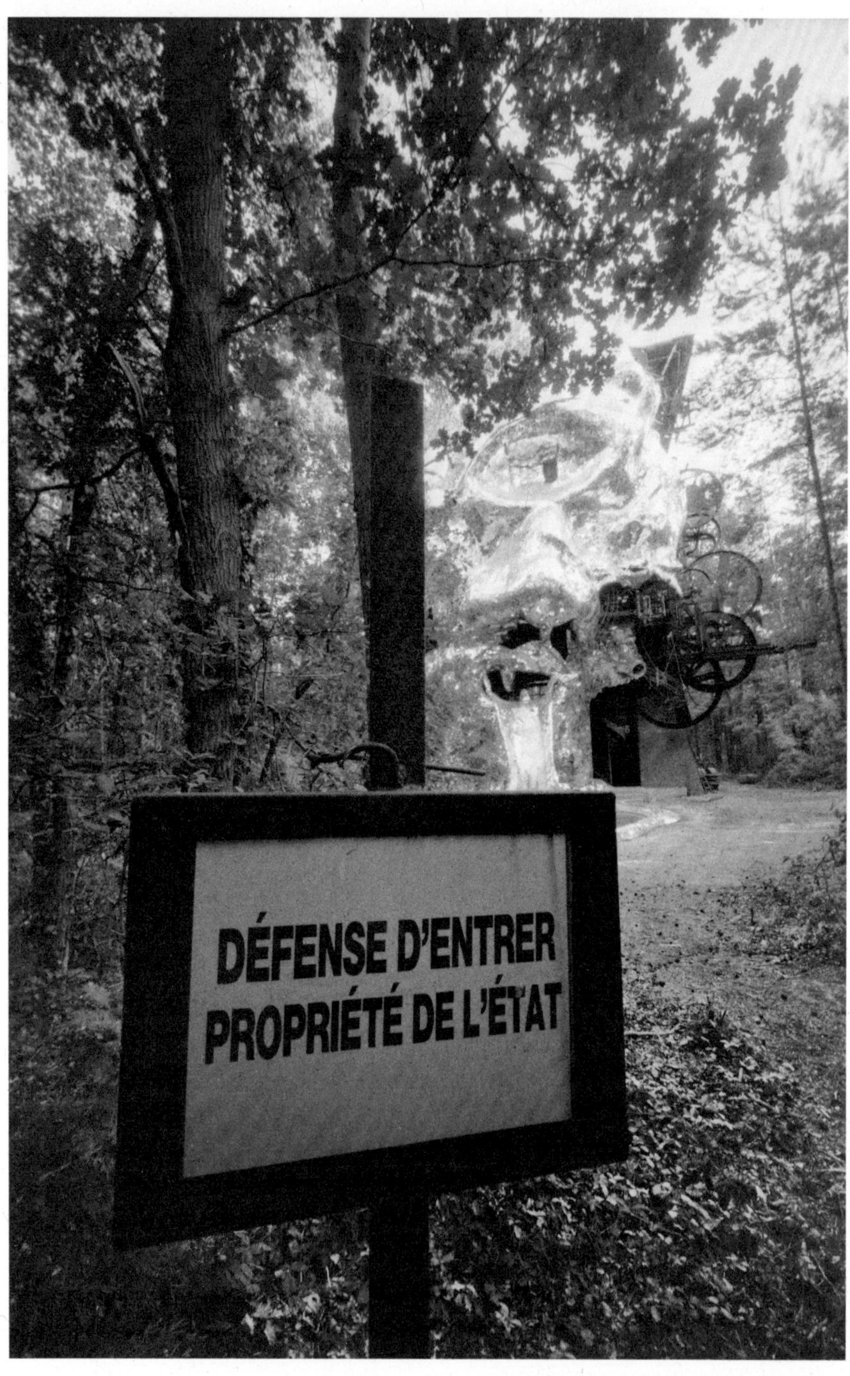

"Today, the cabinet secretary and Minister [François] Léotard are visiting, and I am going to try and palm the Head off on them. The Head was a mistake, *Le Cyclop* we made in the forest, we got it wrong and we want to be rid of it. I've tried to sell it, I haven't managed to sell it. I don't want to give it away to Australia. I've had an offer from Australia and another from California—I don't see what it would do over there in San Diego. When it comes down to it, I want the Head to be open to people, to public opinion, and to keep its link to the town of Milly-la-Forêt."

Jean Tinguely, in *Le Monstre de Tinguely*, 17'41"

"Very little happened at the Head for several years, just the bare minimum for its upkeep. Every suggestion we made to Jean to protect the Head so the work could keep going, he found an excuse to turn down. I had to face facts. Jean was not interested in finishing the Head at that point. Something new had to happen, something unexpected, to waken the sleeping beauty and make Jean want to finish it. Fortunately, the Head was officially accepted by France in the autumn of 1987."

Niki de Saint Phalle, in *Le Monstre dans la forêt*, 32'53"

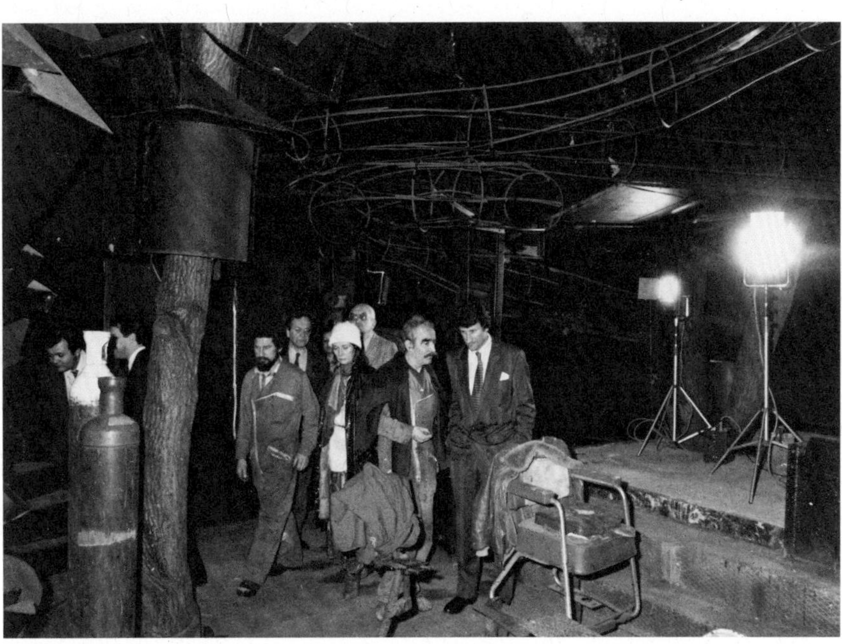

Official visit during the process of the donation, 1987
From left to right: Seppi Imhof, Dominique Bozo, Niki de Saint Phalle, Jean Tinguely, and Philippe de Villiers

1987   Work begins on Niki de Saint Phalle's *La Face aux miroirs*.

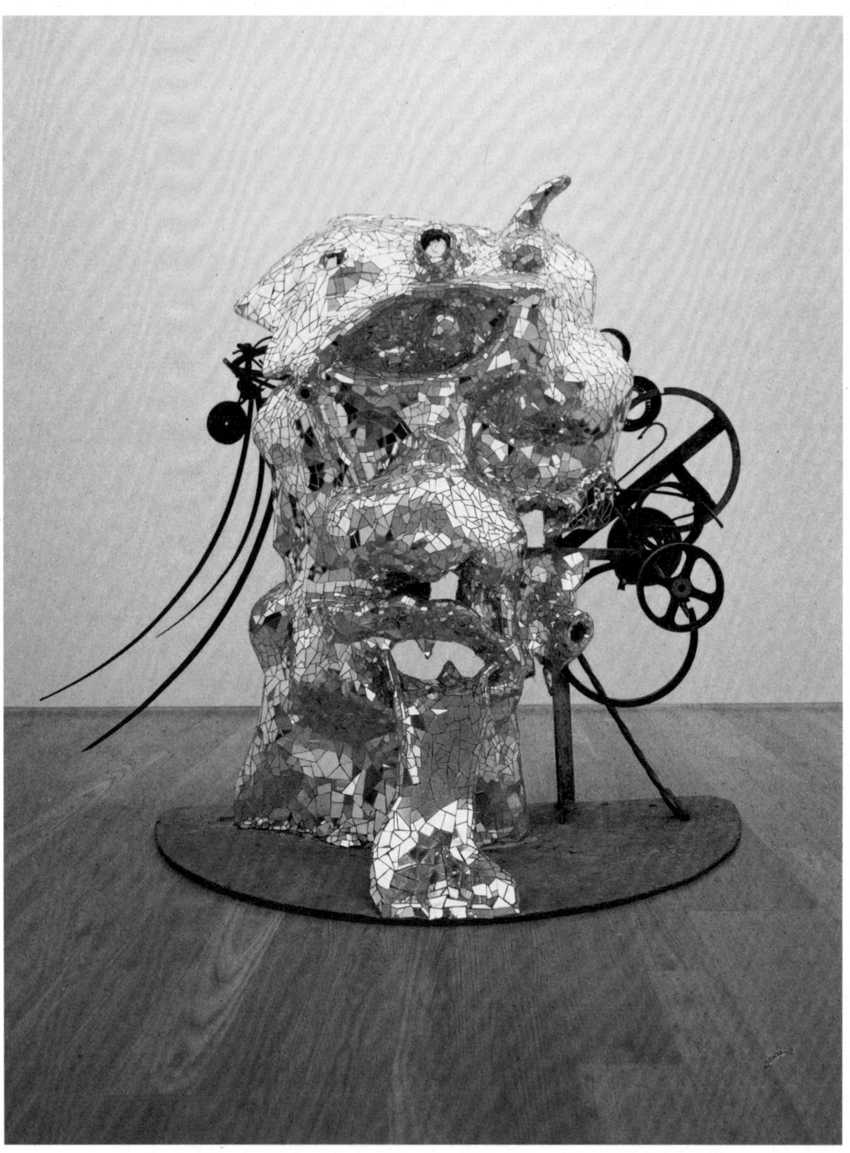

Niki de Saint Phalle and Jean Tinguely
Le Cyclop – La Tête, 1986
Metalwork and mirrors, 180 × 240 × 110 cm
Collection Museum Tinguely, Basel; bequest of Niki de Saint Phalle

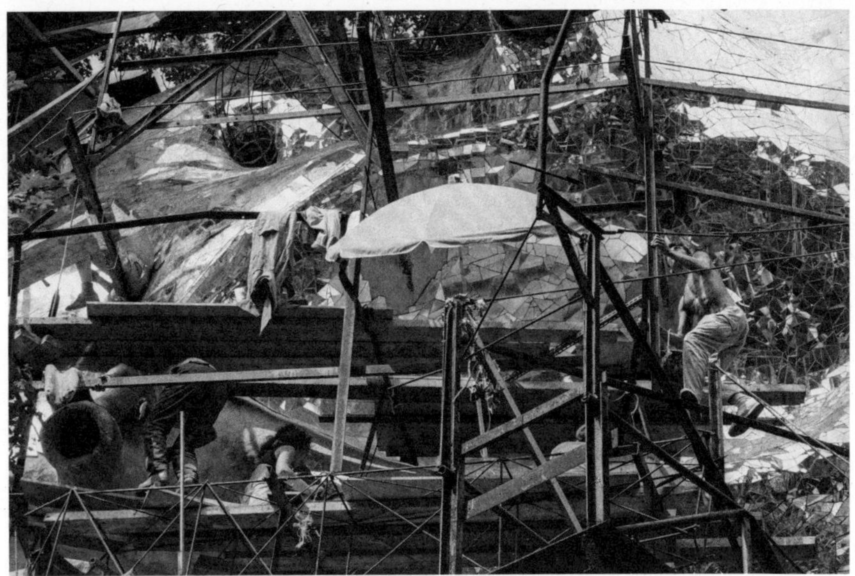

"It took me eight or ten years to come up with the idea of the mirrors. I could never decide how to approach my part of the Head. The problem was I worried that very bright colors might not look good in the forest, in nature. So for a while I thought about covering it all in moss, which would be very beautiful, but then moss eats away at concrete. So I could never make up my mind, and then suddenly, EUREKA! The idea came to me of my project in Italy where I used mirrors a lot, and I said to myself, mirrors!"

Niki de Saint Phalle, in *Le Monstre de Tinguely*, 30'06"

1988 Delivery of the skull for *L'Incitation au suicide* by Niki de Saint Phalle and Jean Tinguely.

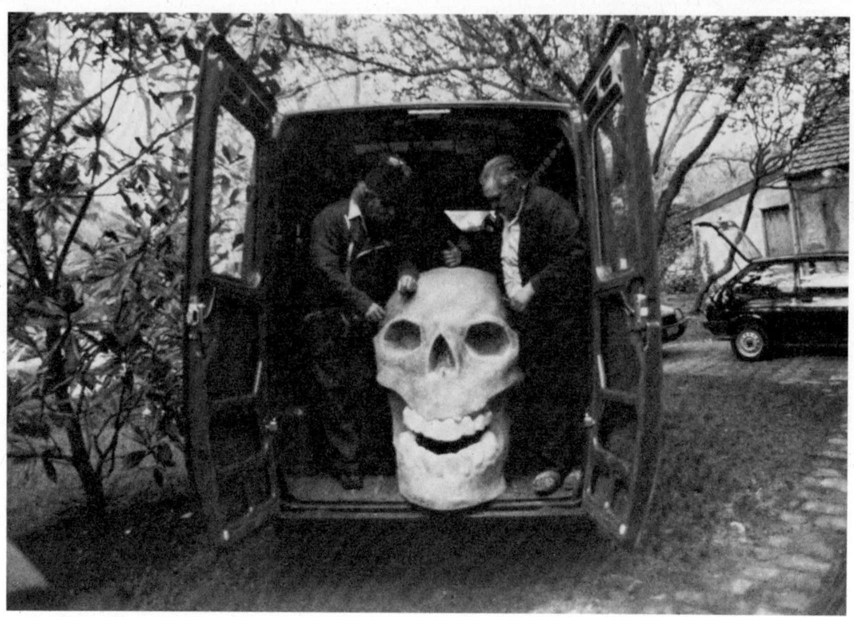

Bernhard Luginbühl and Jean Tinguely take delivery of Niki de Saint Phalle's skull at Soisy-sur-École.

1990   Jean Pierre Raynaud's *La Jauge* is reinstalled.

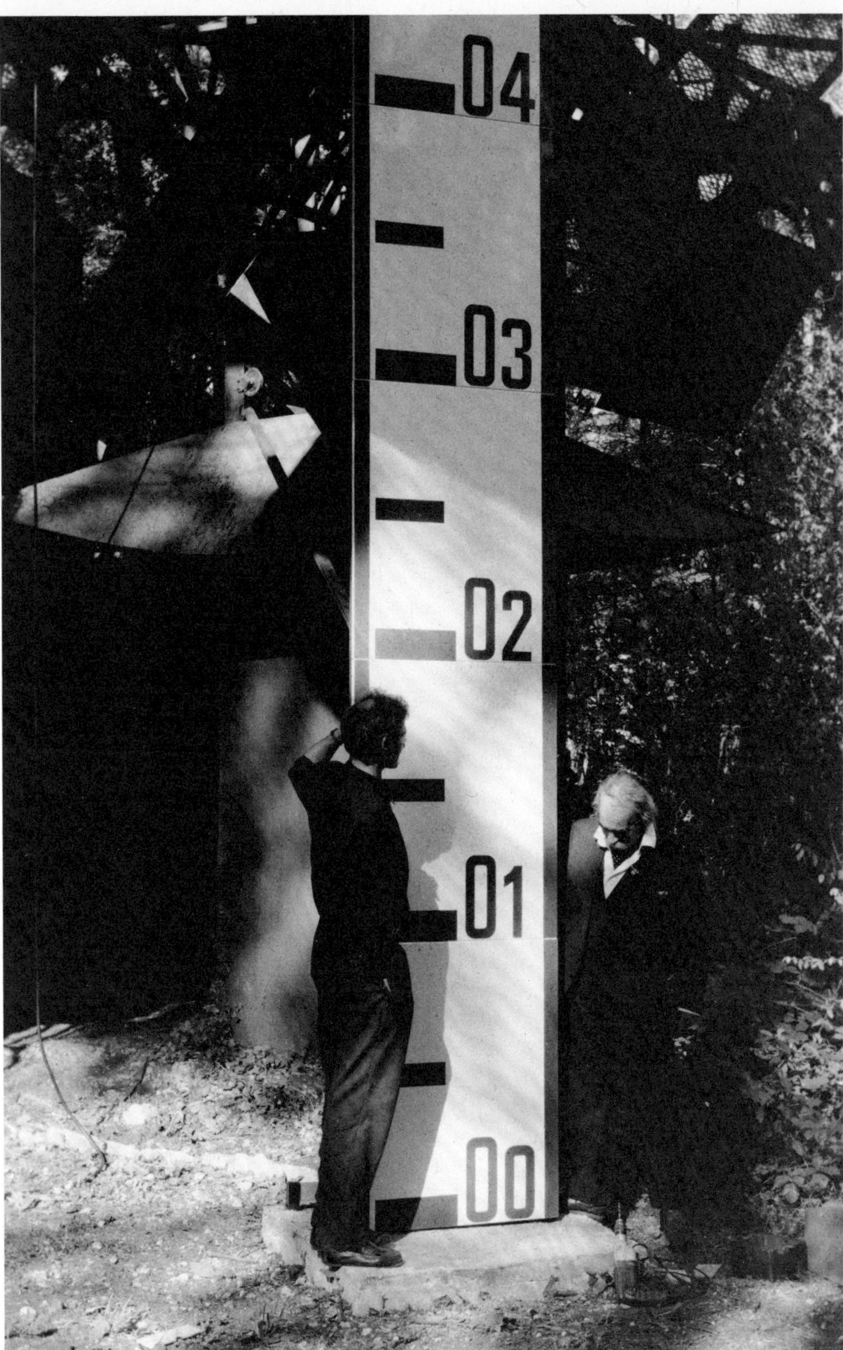

1991–1994
Niki Continues Jean's Dream

1991   Jean Tinguely dies in Bern on August 30, aged 66.
His funeral takes place on September 4 in Fribourg.

Arman's *L'Accumulation de gants* is created.

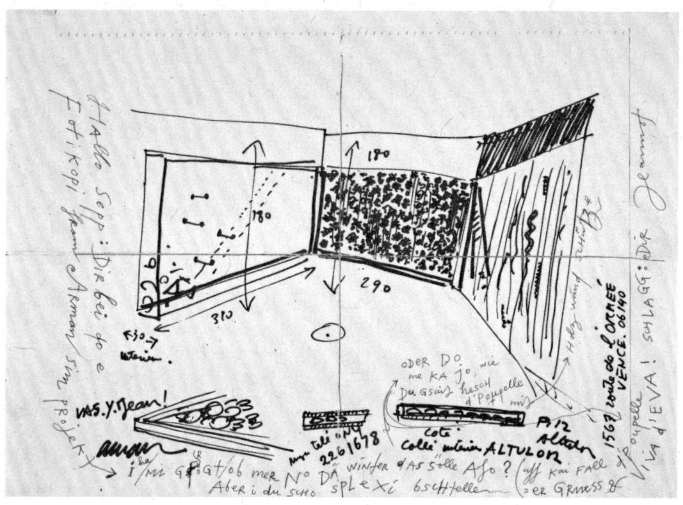

Arman and Jean Tinguely
Sketch for *L'Accumulation de gants*, n. d.
Ballpoint pen on Xerox
Collection Museum Tinguely, Basel; bequest of Josef Imhof

"We went into the shelves and [Jean Tinguely] told me, 'Here you go, if you like, I have a spot for you, there, there, and there, you can do whatever you like.' So I had a think. One day I said, 'I want to make gloves.' I saw that there was a lot of welding going on and welding gloves galore in boxes. He sent me two big boxes of worn-out gloves, and I looked at the heavy gloves all smeared with oil, and I said to myself, 'That won't work in plastic.' I can still see Jean asking me, 'What about your panels?' because we'd settled on the size and everything … I told him, 'I'm getting down to it.' Time flies … Sadly, in the meantime, Jean died. I can still picture Niki telling me not to forget. I said no, I am getting down to it. I go back to the studio, look at the boxes of gloves, I say to myself I can't use that. I say, 'Bin the lot, I'll buy new ones,' but we couldn't buy them in bulk, the factories had closed. And I said, 'It's a shame that box of gloves got thrown out because I think I'm going to have to get on with it and find another solution.' My assistant in Vence said, 'But we didn't throw them out, I forgot to do it.' The solution for the gloves I could not enclose in plastic was to sandwich them between layers of plastic board."

Arman, in *Le Cyclop de Jean Tinguely*, 43'26"

1991 The eye is installed on Niki de Saint Phalle's *La Face aux miroirs*.

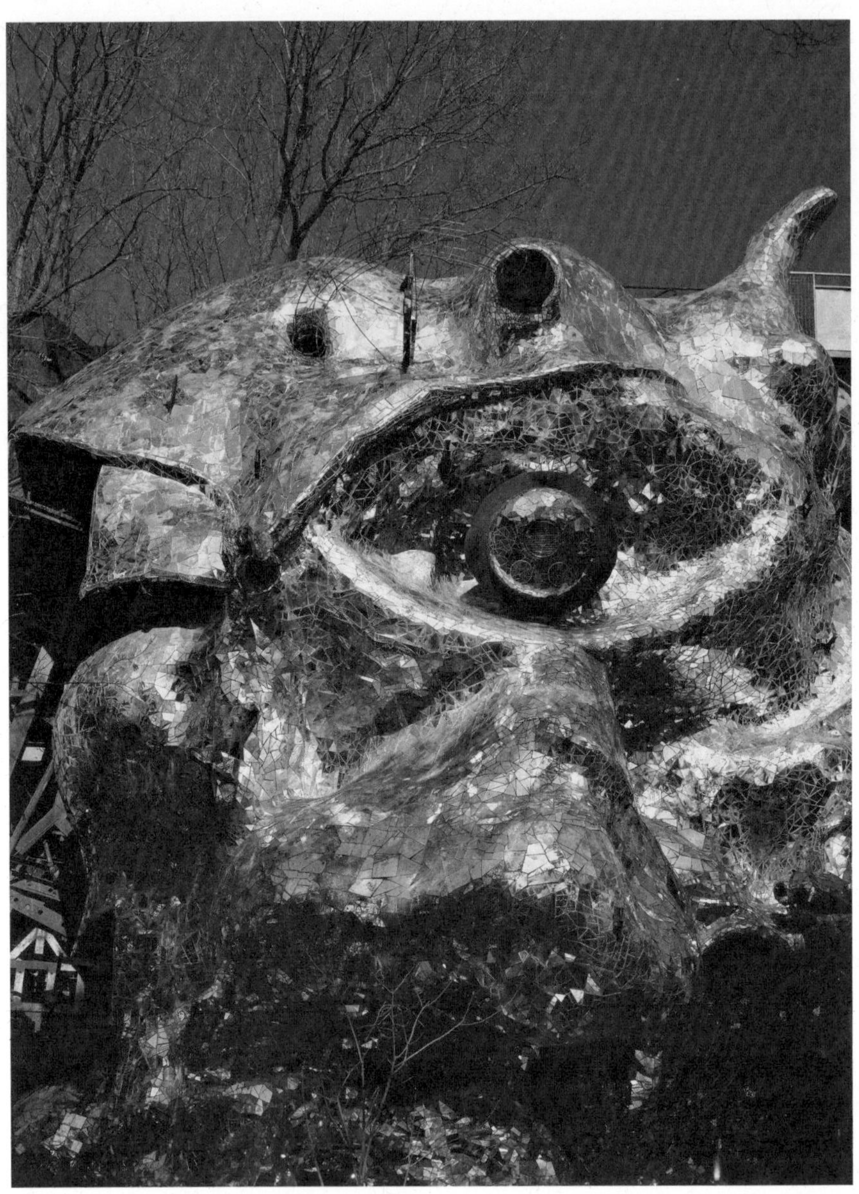

"A moving plastic eye with a projector, a direct pantograph, the axis of which (the projector) should of course squint into the darkness of the forest."

Bernhard Luginbühl, diary, August 6, 1976, n.p.

1992–1993 The skull is installed on *L'Incitation au suicide* by Niki de Saint Phalle and Jean Tinguely.

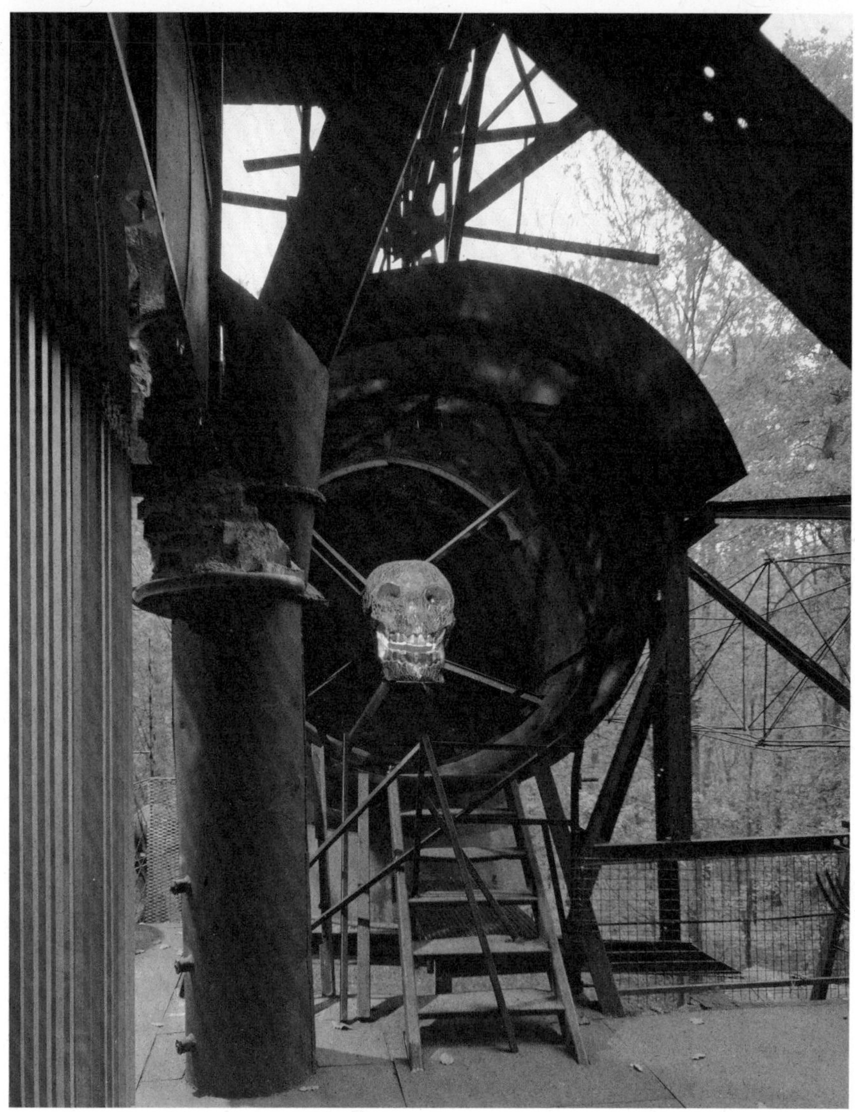

1992–1993 Niki de Saint Phalle's *Le Carrelage au damier* is created.

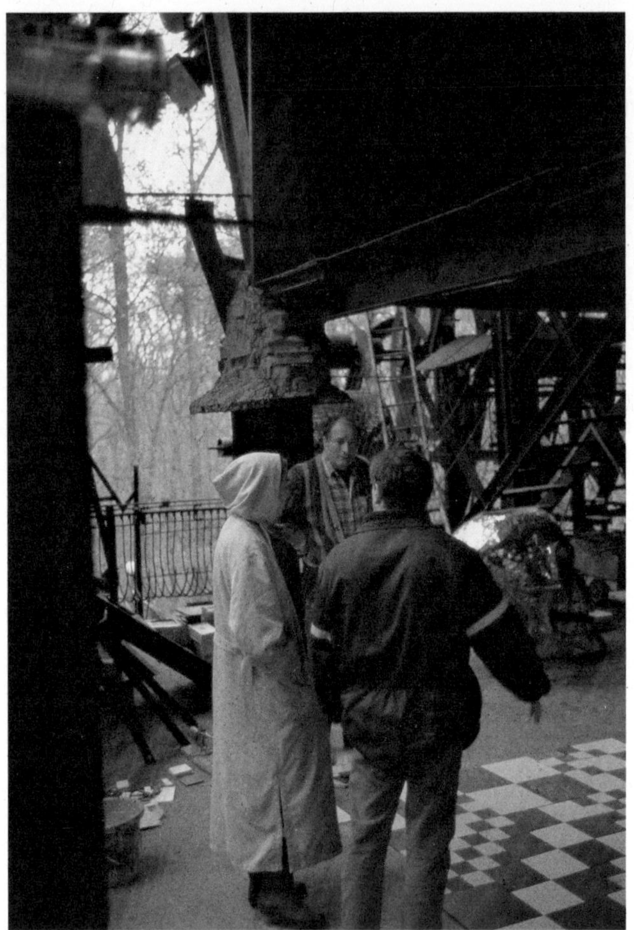

"For example, when Jeano said we were going to Madrid to see Goya's superb paintings, the main reason for the trip was actually to watch the Spanish Grand Prix. Tinguely often planned his appointments, visits, stays, and even exhibitions around the Formula 1 season. Tinguely also told me the only reason he attended the Osaka symposium was because Seppi Siffert was due to race on the Fujiyama track and he wanted to lend him moral support. We went to the Indy 500 together and when we were working on the Milly monster, we went to the 24 Hours of Le Mans and Clermont, and the first thing Tinguely wanted to show me in Columbus was a stock car race."

Bernhard Luginbühl, "Letter to Margrit Hahnloser," p. 316

The sculptures are installed in the train carriage in Eva Aeppli's
Hommage aux déportés.

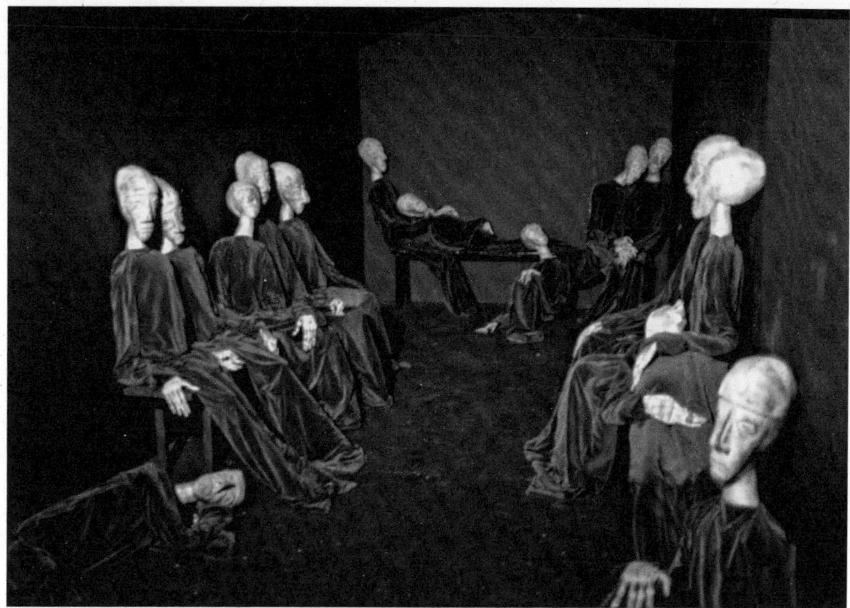

"I used blue silk, as it was all I had, and I soaked it in very strong Ceylon
tea (not bleach at all); the stains are deliberate, when you get beaten up,
it leaves marks on your face. It was a way of saying they'd been through
the wringer, as it were."

Eva Aeppli interviewed by Aude Bodet, 2009

1992–1993 Niki de Saint Phalle's *La Colonne* is created.

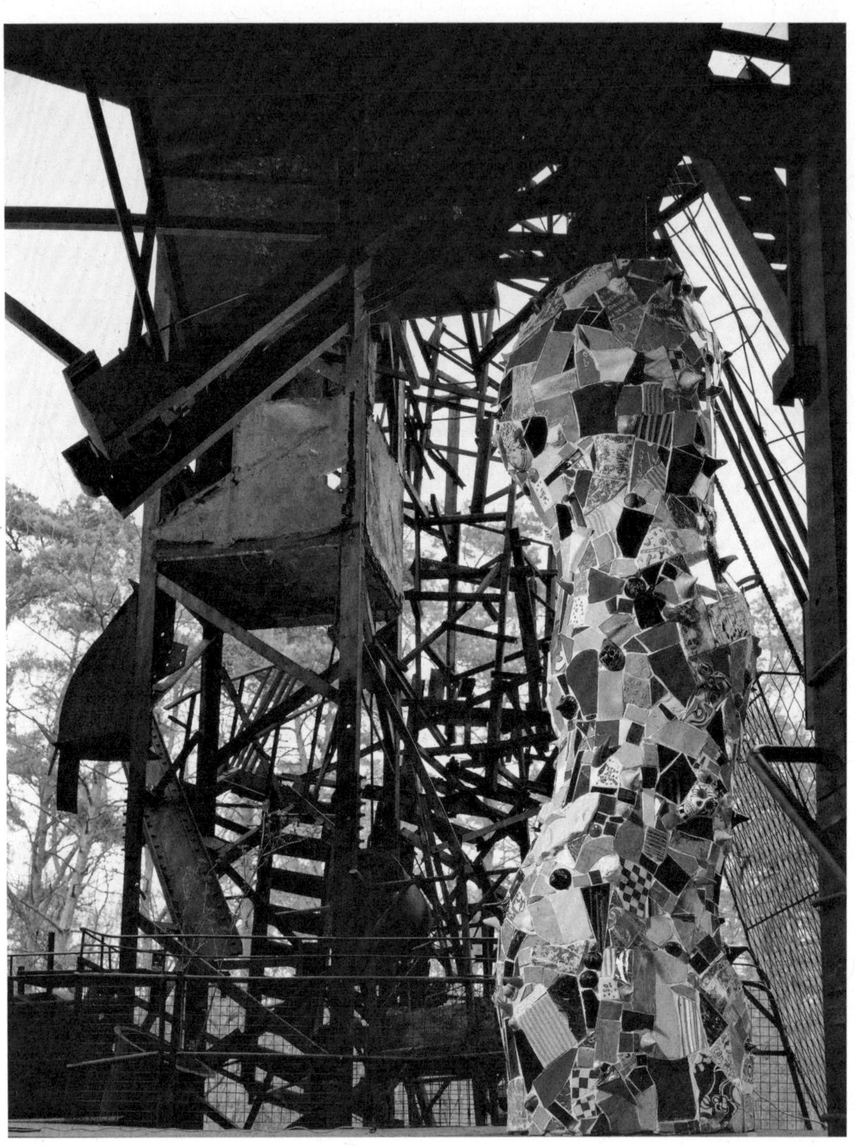

Pierre Marie Lejeune's *Le Siège-rameur du Petit Théâtre* is installed.

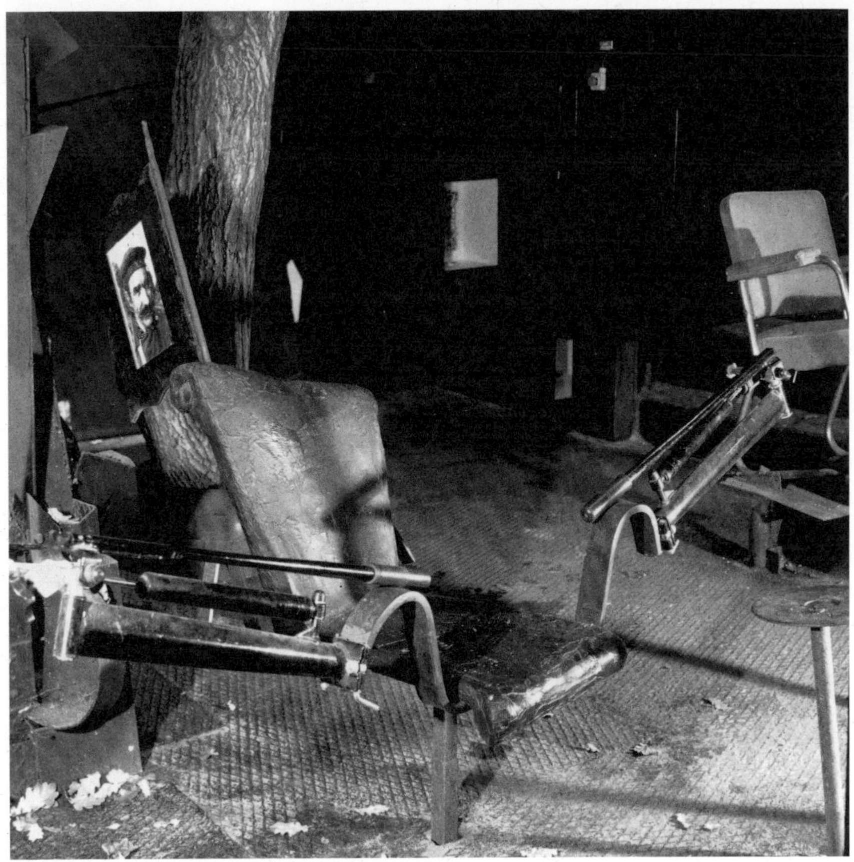

"Pierre Marie Lejeune started with a piece of gym equipment, a rowing machine. It is placed facing the stage and visitors are invited to row a bit while watching the performance. The rowing machine rises and falls, powered by the *Méta-Harmonie*. On each side of a metal flag on the back of the seat is a photograph of Jean Tinguely by Laurent Condominas."

Virginie Canal, in *Jean Tinguely. Le Cyclop*, p. 166

1992–1993 The *Piccolo Museo* is installed, featuring works by
Giovanni Battista Podestà.

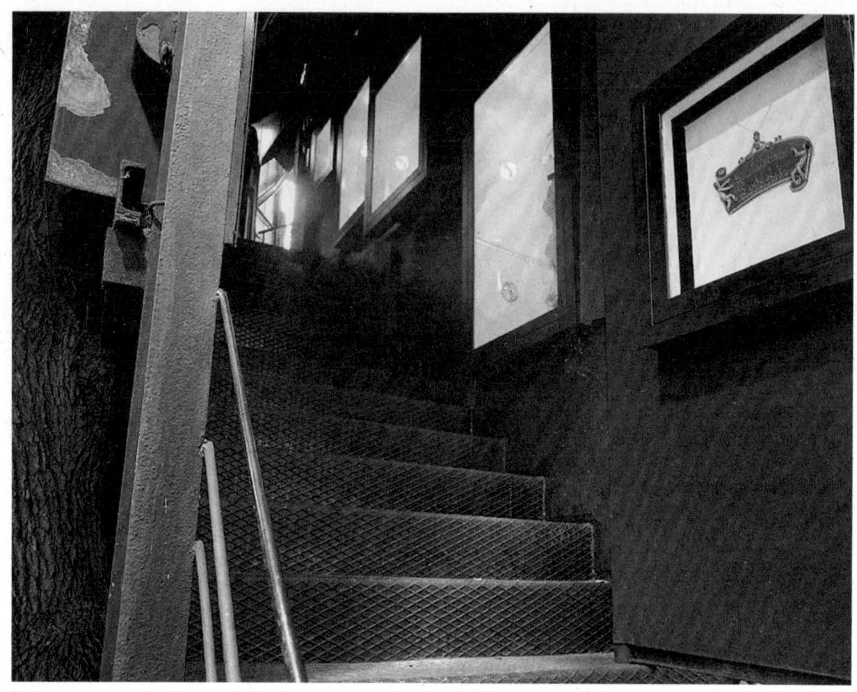

"Jeano arrived from Basel with figures by the naive artist Giovanni Podestá.
He wants to equip Soisy-sur-École with solar energy, and create a museum
site for Podestà in the head, using a background and mysterious matte
black stones."

Bernhard Luginbühl, diary, September 10, 1976, n.p.

Jesús Rafael Soto's *Le Pénétrable sonore* is installed.

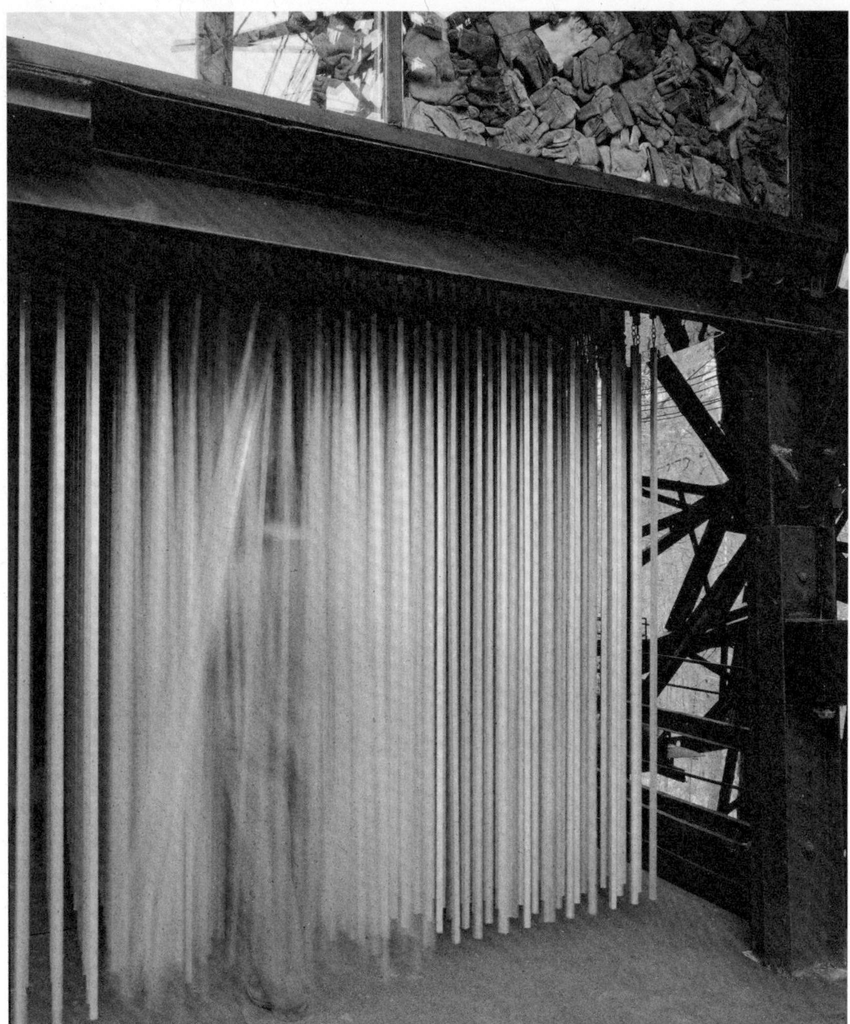

"He [Jean Tinguely] asked me to keep the penetrable for his idea, for his Head. I put out in the countryside and they recently came to fetch it, and there it was, waiting. Everything I did—and will do, I hope, until I can work—is connected to space-time and the idea of vibration and movement. The penetrable has all that, and sound as well. It's a work built to strict specifications but when someone goes inside, it becomes rather random, you never know exactly what will happen."

Jesús Rafael Soto, in *Le Cyclop de Jean Tinguely*, 25'44"

1994 Rico Weber's *Le Tableau électrique* is created.

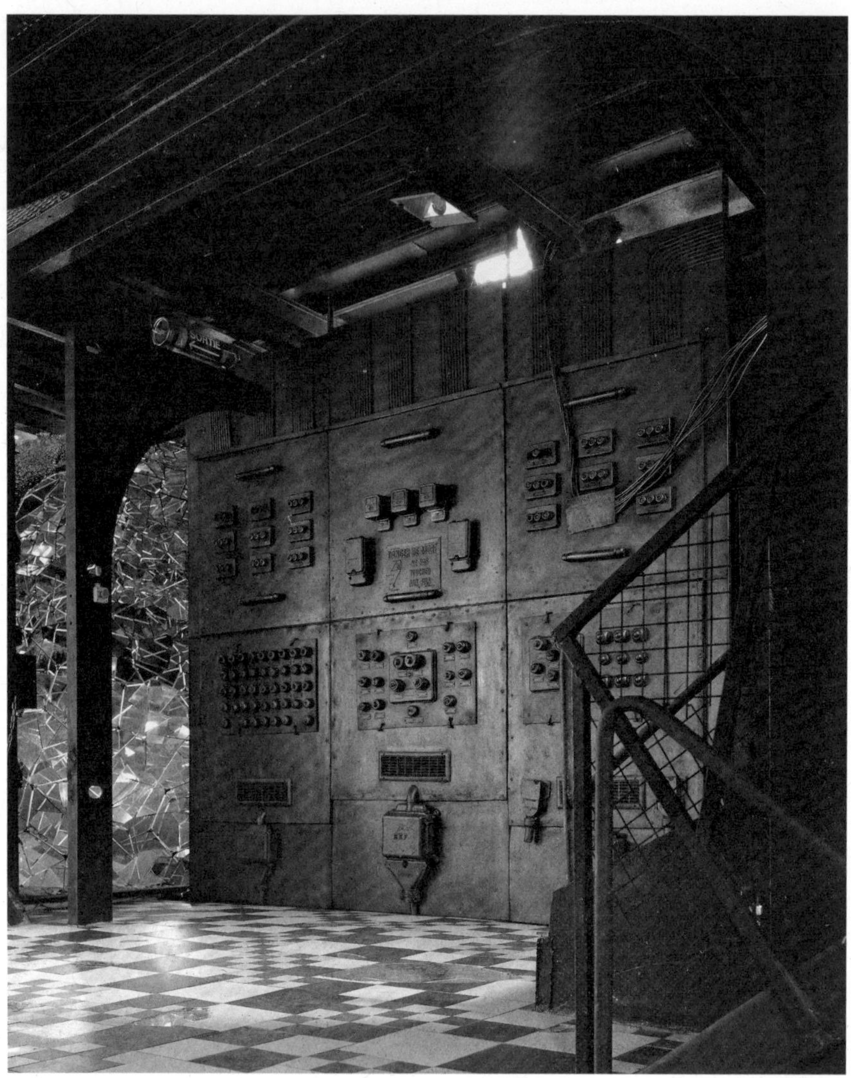

"The idea is for each participant to have a little acknowledgment, a switch with their name on. Jean loved the idea, so I turned it into a homage. This is where it begins: in the center are Jean, Niki, Seppi, and me, first. Then around us are the other artists who took part. And there's Duperche, the scrap-metal dealer, who supplied us with all the scrap: in the end, he's the Head's real owner."

Rico Weber, in *Le Monstre dans la forêt*, 45'29"

**Jean Tinguely's *La Molécule RU 486: Hommage à Étienne-Émile Baulieu*
is created.**

"I do think that putting the model in the Head, in *Le Cyclop*, is a provoca-
tion in the sense of provoking a positive reaction, of course, not stupid.
And I'm sure Jean would be thrilled with the sort of aggression that then
took place, with people sending us a tract saying it was bad and shameful
to do things like that. The conjunction of the women's cause and science
scares them. Well, this time, a sort of conjunction between the worlds of art
and science scares them too, because they see that our view of things,
which is simultaneously free, bold, realistic, and positive for people, is now
winning out, and that their old prejudices—often the product of ignorance,
for that matter—are crumbling."

Étienne-Émile Baulieu, in *Le Cyclop de Jean Tinguely*, 46'36"

1994   Daniel Spoerri's *Restaurant Spoerri* is installed.

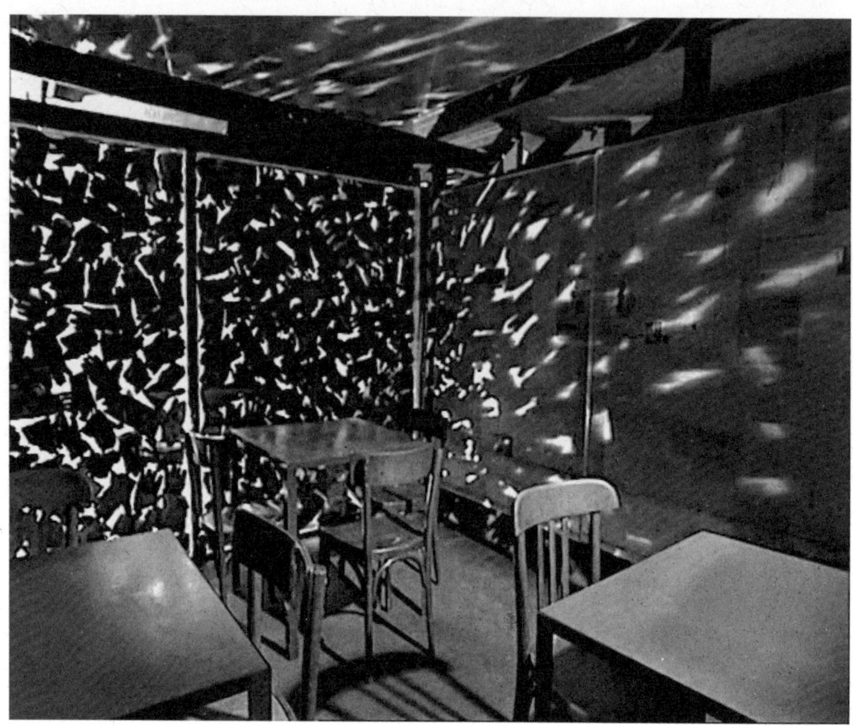

Niki de Saint Phalle's *Le Banc* is installed.

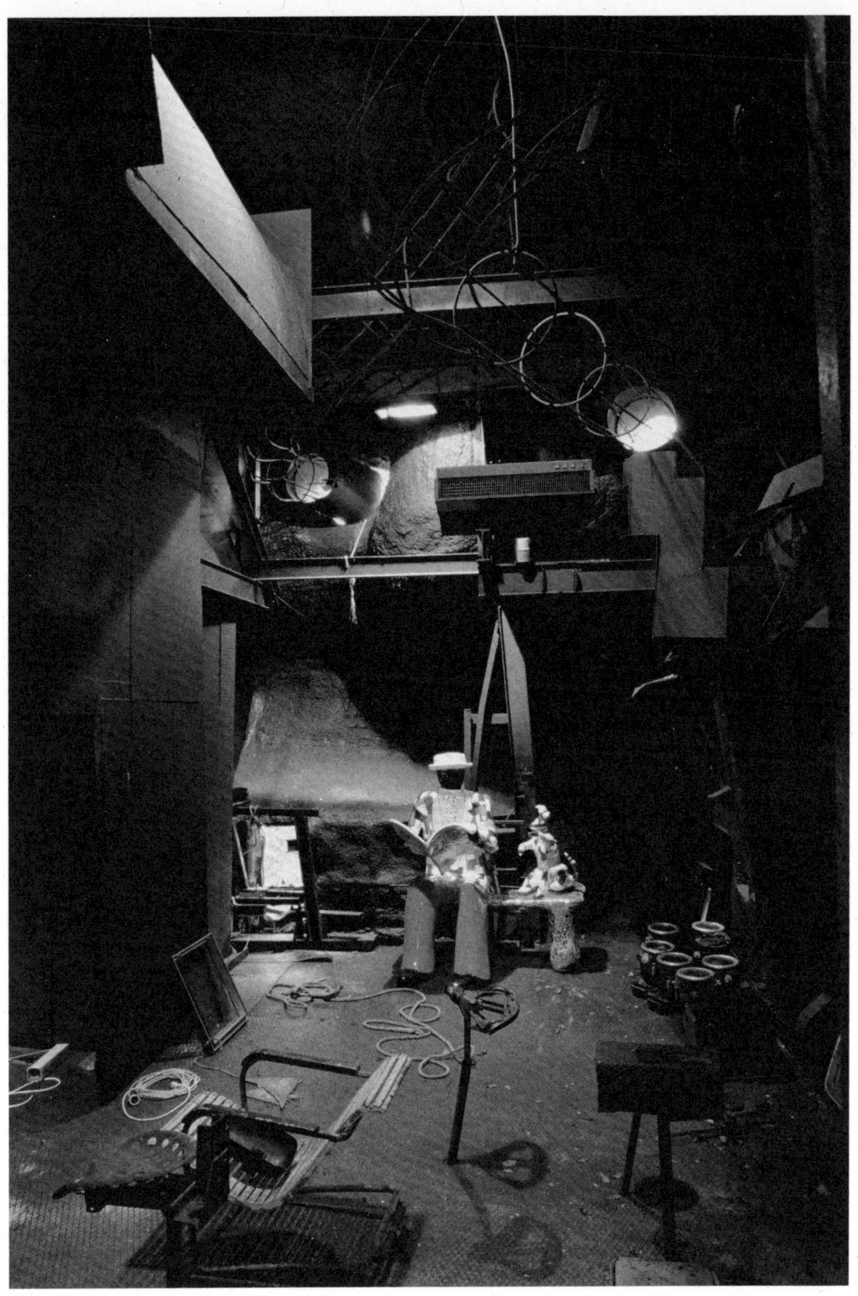

1994 · Philippe Bouveret adds the finishing touches to the stage for Jean Tinguely's *Le Petit Théâtre*.

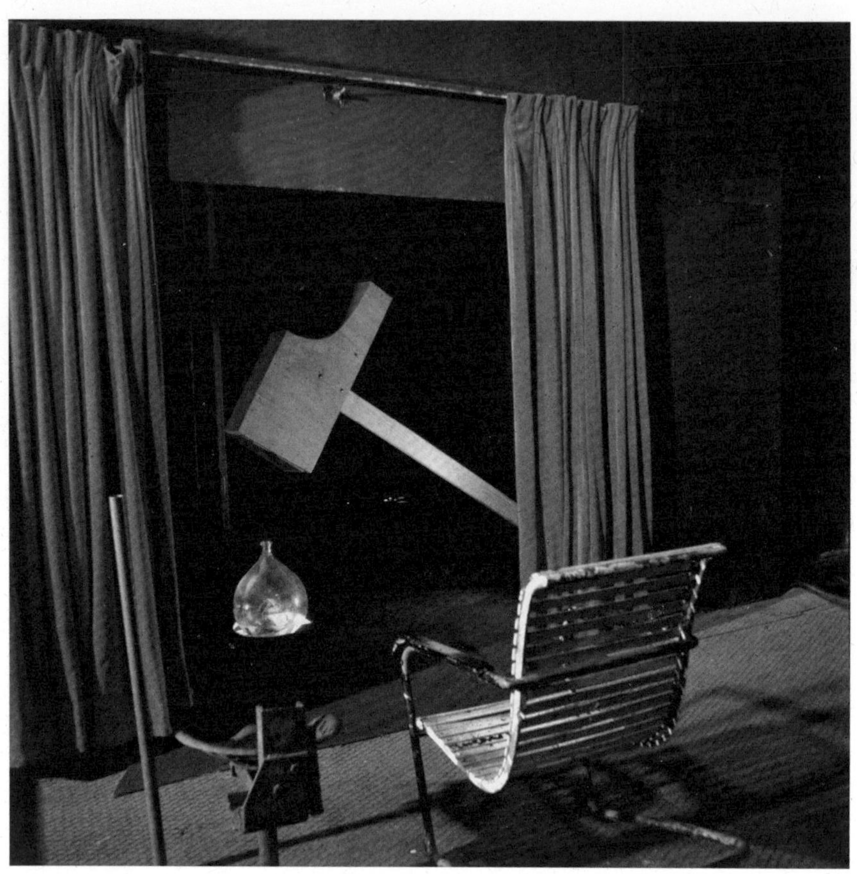

Philippe Bouveret's *Le Tableau générique* is installed.

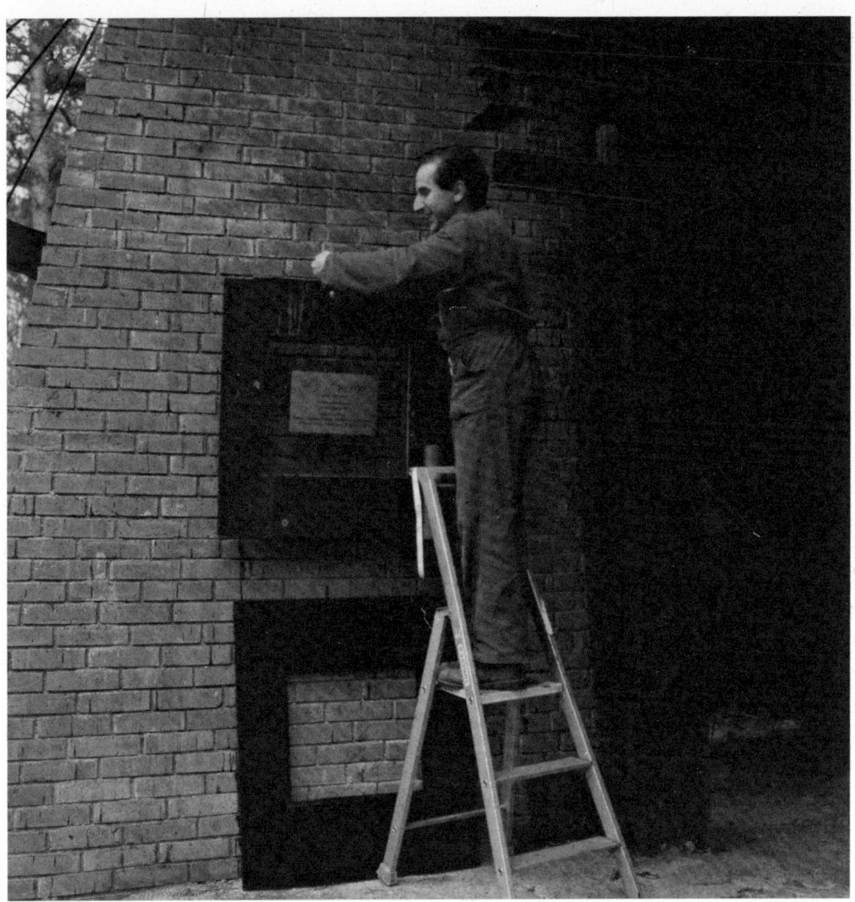

"The *Tableau générique* is a 'flat aquarium,' set in a metal box into
which an aspirin is dropped. Once the tablet has dissolved, as if by magic,
a plaque slowly appears bearing the following words: 'Le Cyclop.
Jean Tinguely. Sculpture commencée en 1969. Donnée à l'Etat en 1987.
Inaugurée en 1994 par Monsieur François Mitterrand, président de
la République, et Monsieur Jacques Toubon, ministre de la Culture'
[Le Cyclop. Jean Tinguely. Sculpture begun in 1969. Gifted to the State
in 1987. Inaugurated in 1994 by Monsieur François Mitterrand, president
of the Republic, and Monsieur Jacques Toubon, Minister for Culture]."

Virginie Canal, in *Jean Tinguely. Le Cyclop*, p. 158

1994 **President François Mitterrand officially inaugurates *Le Cyclop* on May 24, 1994.**

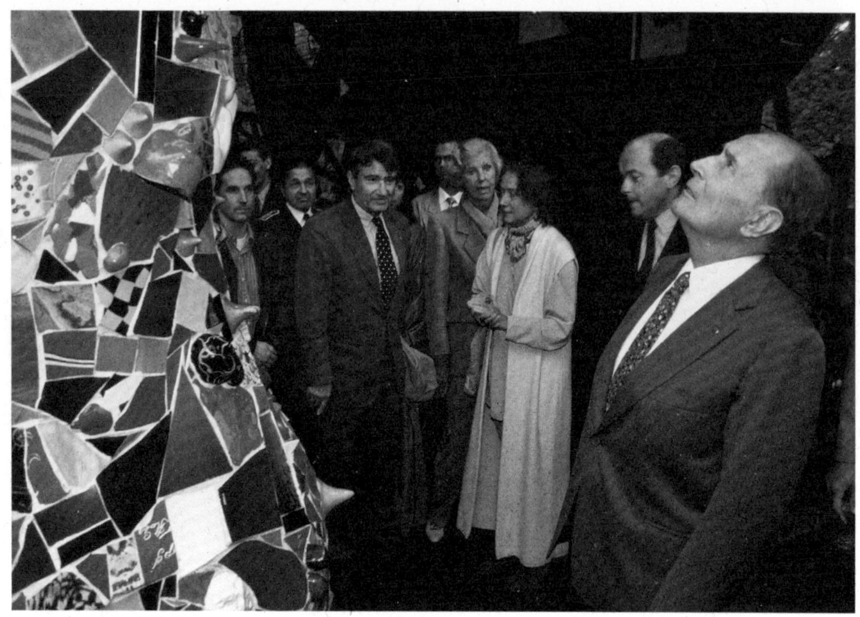

"'Those who love Tinguely will find here the essence of his work. This is my third visit,' François Mitterrand said, adding that he had only ever had 'one disagreement' with the artist, who died three years ago, about the possibility of moving *Le Cyclop*. Pointing to a hundred-year-old oak whose leaves form *Le Cyclop's* head of hair, he continued, 'Tinguely told me: "I didn't want the tree cut down."'"

François Mitterrand, AFP press release, May 24, 1994

Rico Weber's *Les Gisants* are installed.

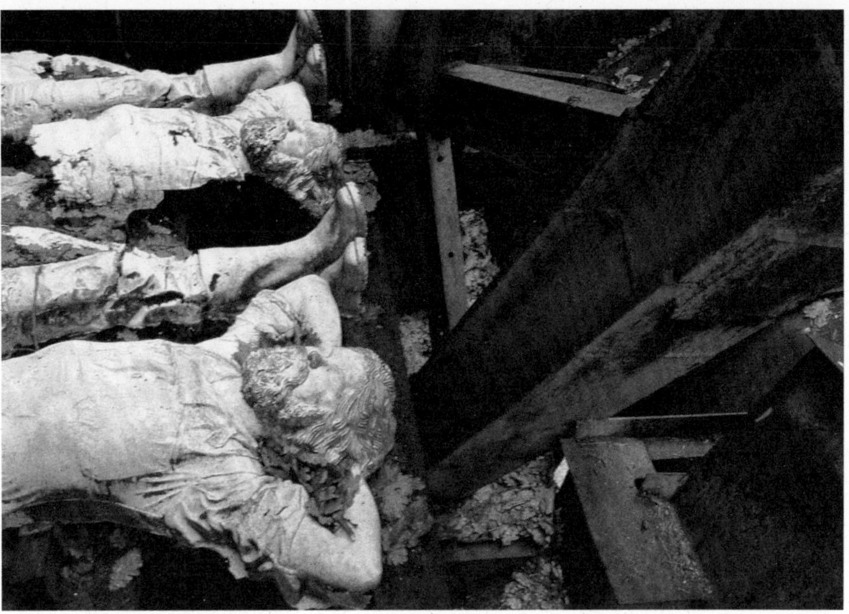

"His work is influenced by photo-realism. His earliest public presentations
were on the theme of himself. That was at the 1978 Hammer-Austellung
[Galerie Handschin]. He produced a series of plaster casts of himself.
He added a new cast every day during the exhibition. It was held in
a disused factory. Rico's aim was to use the reproductions of himself
to illustrate industrial production."

Yvonne Lehner, in *Rico Weber. Voyage au cabinet magique*, 21'08"

 César's *Compressions* are installed.

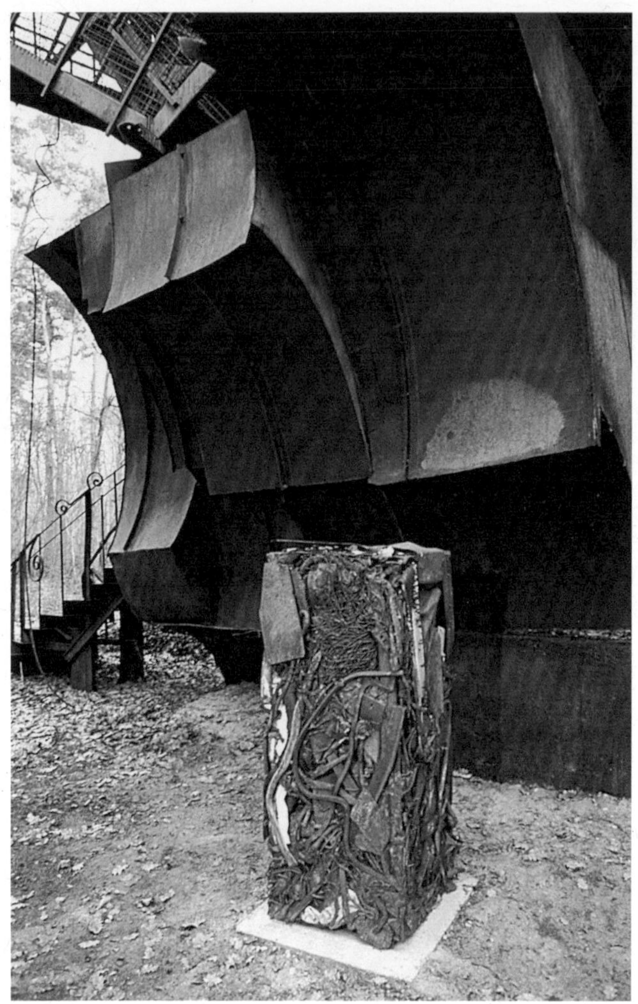

"Jean said, 'César, I'd like you to join us on *Le Cyclop*.' I replied, 'Of course!' If Jean Tinguely had asked me to climb up a tree, I would have done it! Because I liked him, I mean because I liked his work. I don't know who had the idea, him or me, but it was interesting to collect the leftover materials and scrap. Then I thought about the big welding station I had, the sort you only find in businesses. I said to myself, 'Hey, why don't I use the station and bring it into the project with the materials Jean Tinguely left behind?' He left scrap—the scrap he used to make the scrap mountain."

César, in *Le Cyclop de Jean Tinguely*, 39'56"

Larry Rivers's *Hommage à Mai 68* paintings are installed.

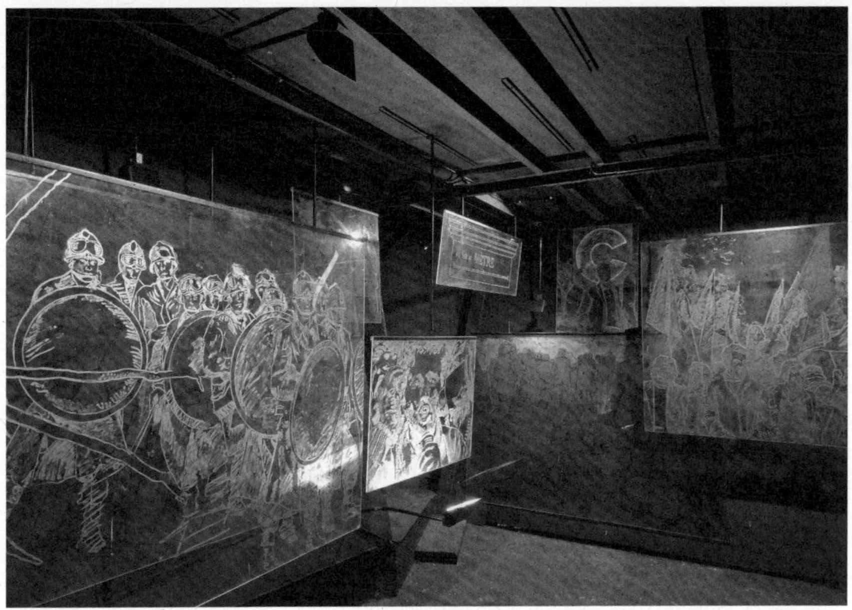

"I was working on my own project, looking at what happened in France ten years after May '68. I arrived with a team, we mainly went to Paris, but also other parts of France, to talk to people and film sites. I found lots of photos of that time, of police and students, and made drawings of them."

Larry Rivers, in *Le Cyclop de Jean Tinguely*, 49'03"

"Larry Rivers came and produced a magnificent painting that we will be installing, but it is very fragile since it plays with effects of light, video and Plexiglas, so it's very complicated. We are waiting for the Head to evolve further before installing it inside."

Jean Tinguely, in *Le Monstre de Tinguely*, 37'59"

In conclusion

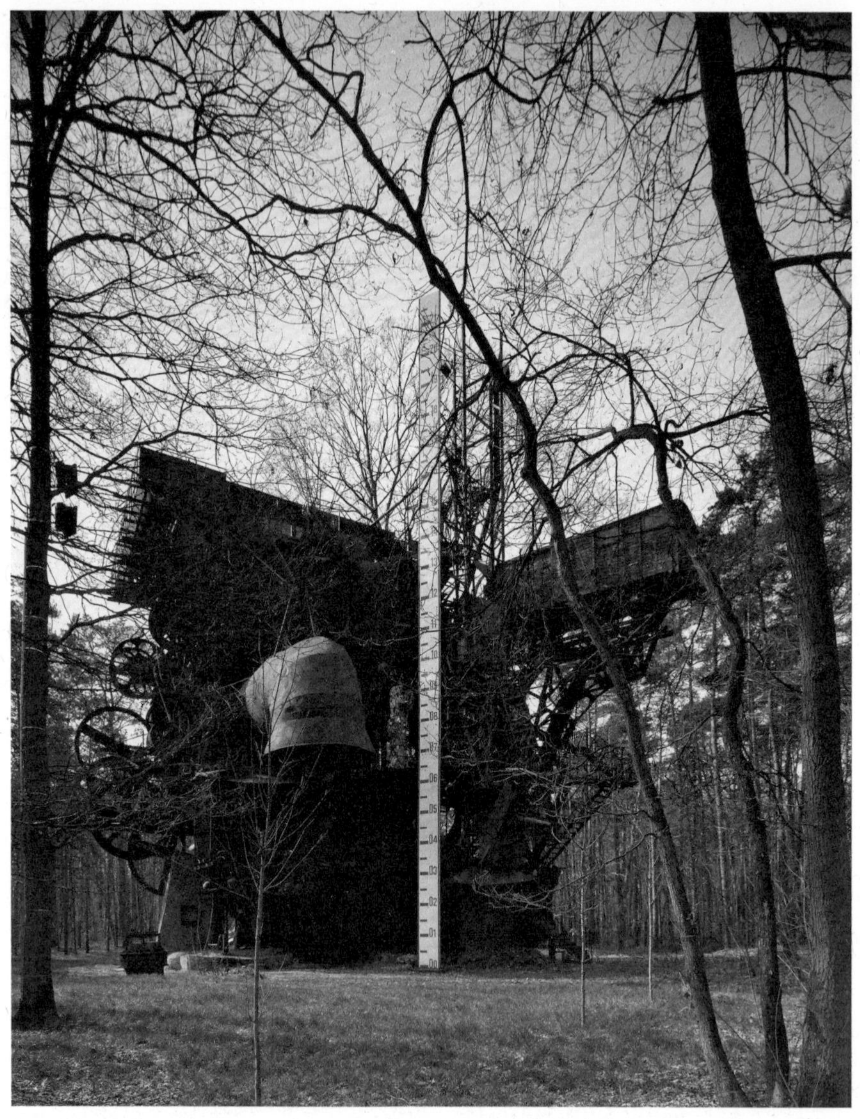

Le Cyclop, 1994

"We had the burning urge to work and succeed. Difficulties stimulated us, we worked for years and years … Really, when it comes down to it, I find the Head is a strange old thing. I don't know why I made it … Maybe to counteract the disastrous effect that can be triggered in me by always moving everything and by being constantly forced into all sorts of repairs, because it's all always movement, constant movement, in my world, motors burning out, fanbelts snapping. So maybe here I am seeking a body of work, or my idea was to seek a definitive body of work. Although it's ridiculous, I don't want anything definitive."

Jean Tinguely, in *Le Monstre dans la forêt*, 53'55"

"Deep down, for me, *Le Cyclop* will always be Jean's work, that he invited other friends to join him on. We all stimulated each other enormously. There was even a certain rivalry: Jean told me he made the Head one day because I admired the Facteur Cheval and he wanted to show me he was even greater. And perhaps my *Jardin des Tarots* was also a response to the Head: in other words, we stimulated each other enormously."

Niki de Saint Phalle, in *Jean Tinguely & Cie*, p. 60–61

Chronology Documentation Sources

Jacques Huwiler (journalist) and Jaroslav Vizner (director), *Le Monstre de Tinguely*, episode in the series *Viva*, Radio-Télévision Suisse, 1989, 52'

Bernhard Luginbühl, "Lettre à Margrit Hahnloser," in Margrit Hahnloser-Ingold (ed.), Leonardo Bezzola (photographs), *Pandémonium – Jean Tinguely*, Ex Libris, Lausanne/Zurich 1990

Pontus Hultén, *Jean Tinguely* [1988], Éditions du Centre Pompidou, Paris 1992

Jean-Pierre Keller, Véronique Revaz, *Tinguely et le mystère de la roue manquante*, Éditions Zoé, Geneva 1992

AFP press release, press coverage of *Le Cyclop* inauguration, May 24, 1994, Centre National des Arts Plastiques Archives, Paris

Arne Steckmest, *Le Cyclop de Jean Tinguely*, Artik Films, Paris 1996, 52'

Jocelyn Daynes, Pierre Restany, Jean Tinguely, *Jean Tinguely & Cie. Collaborations artistiques Eva Aeppli, Niki de Saint Phalle, Milena Palakarkina*, Musée de l'Hôtel-Dieu, Mantes-La-Jolie 2002

Louise Faure and Anne Julien, *Le Monstre dans la forêt* (57') in *Le Rêve de Jean*, DVD, Quatre à Quatre films, Paris 2005, 134'

Stefan Hugentobler, *Rico Weber. Voyage au cabinet magique*, CIP Productions, Tramelan 2006, 60'

Virginie Canal, *Jean Tinguely. Le Cyclop*, National des Arts Plastiques/Isthme Éditions, Paris 2007

Transcript of a telephone interview between Eva Aeppli and Aude Bodet, April 2009, Centre National des Arts Plastiques Archives, Paris

Extracts from Bernhard Luginbühl's diary about Jean Tinguely, self-published, Mötschwil, n. d. [after 1991]

Centre National des Arts Plastiques Archives, Paris

Most quotations have been adapted for legibility in the chronology, with silent correction of language errors, elisions, punctuation, and so on, particularly when taken from audiovisual sources. Nevertheless, the choice was made to respect, as far as possible, the spoken language of the statements and the diaristic aspect of Bernhard Luginbühl's self-published diary entries.

Photographs taken in 2023–2024

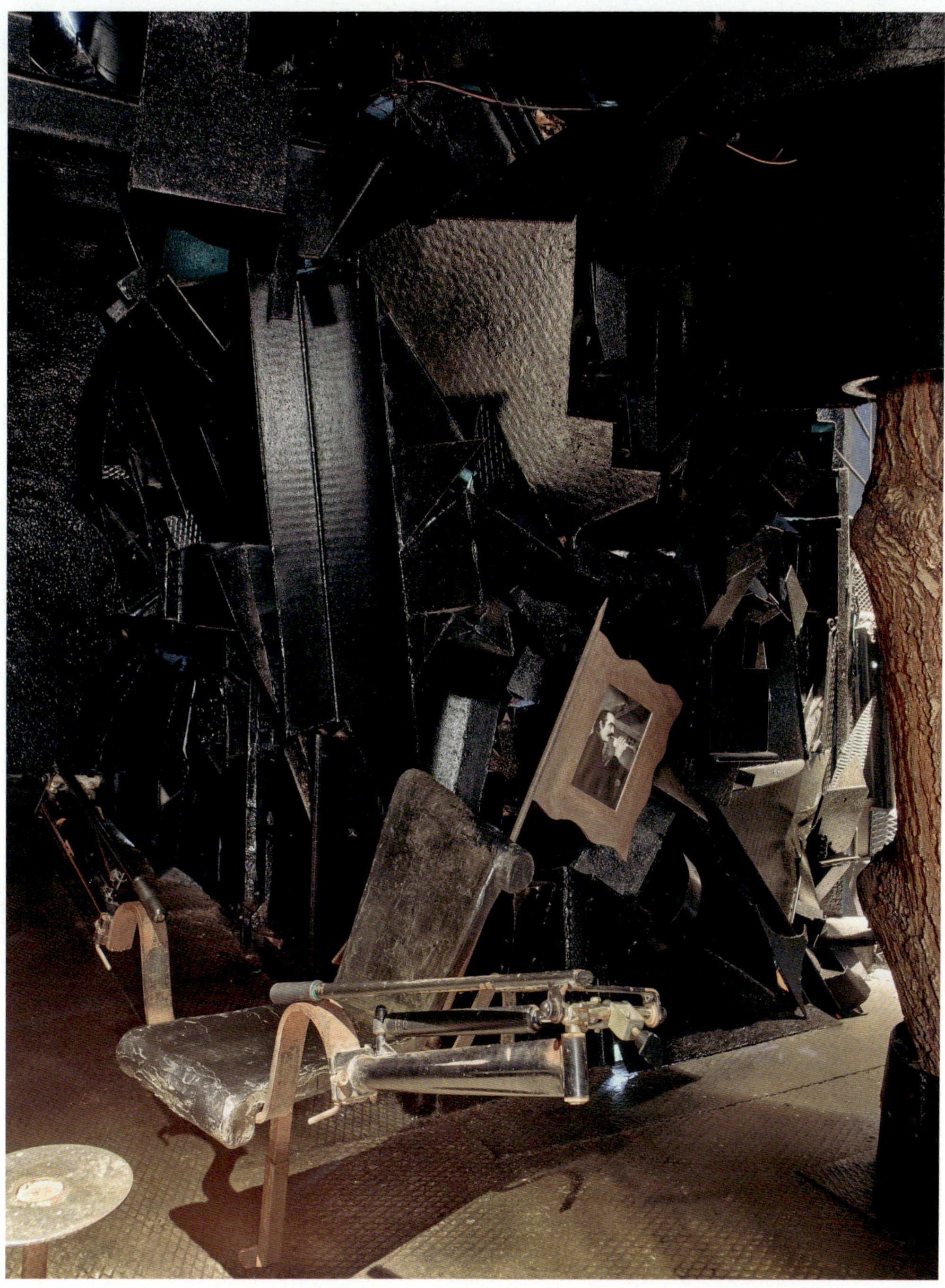

Pierre Marie Lejeune, *Le Siège-rameur du Petit Théâtre*, 1992 (installed 1993); Jean Tinguely, *Le Méta-Merzbau: Hommage à Kurt Schwitters*, 1976–1981
→   Jean Tinguely, *Le Petit Théâtre*, 1981/1994, *Les Sièges du Petit Théâtre*, 1980–1981; Niki de Saint Phalle, *Le Banc*, 1989 (installed 1994); Pierre Marie Lejeune, *Le Siège-rameur du Petit Théâtre*, 1992 (installed 1993)

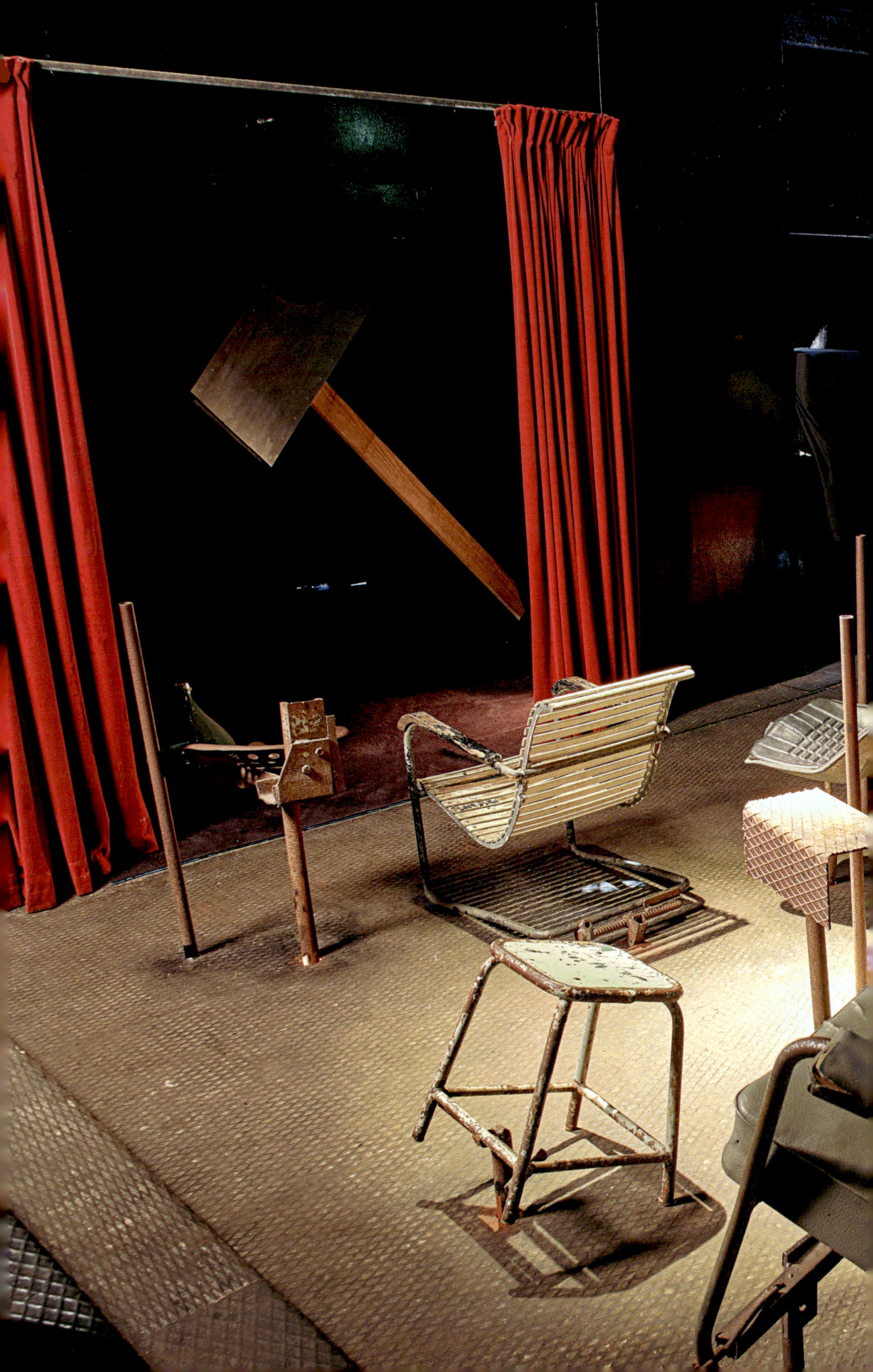

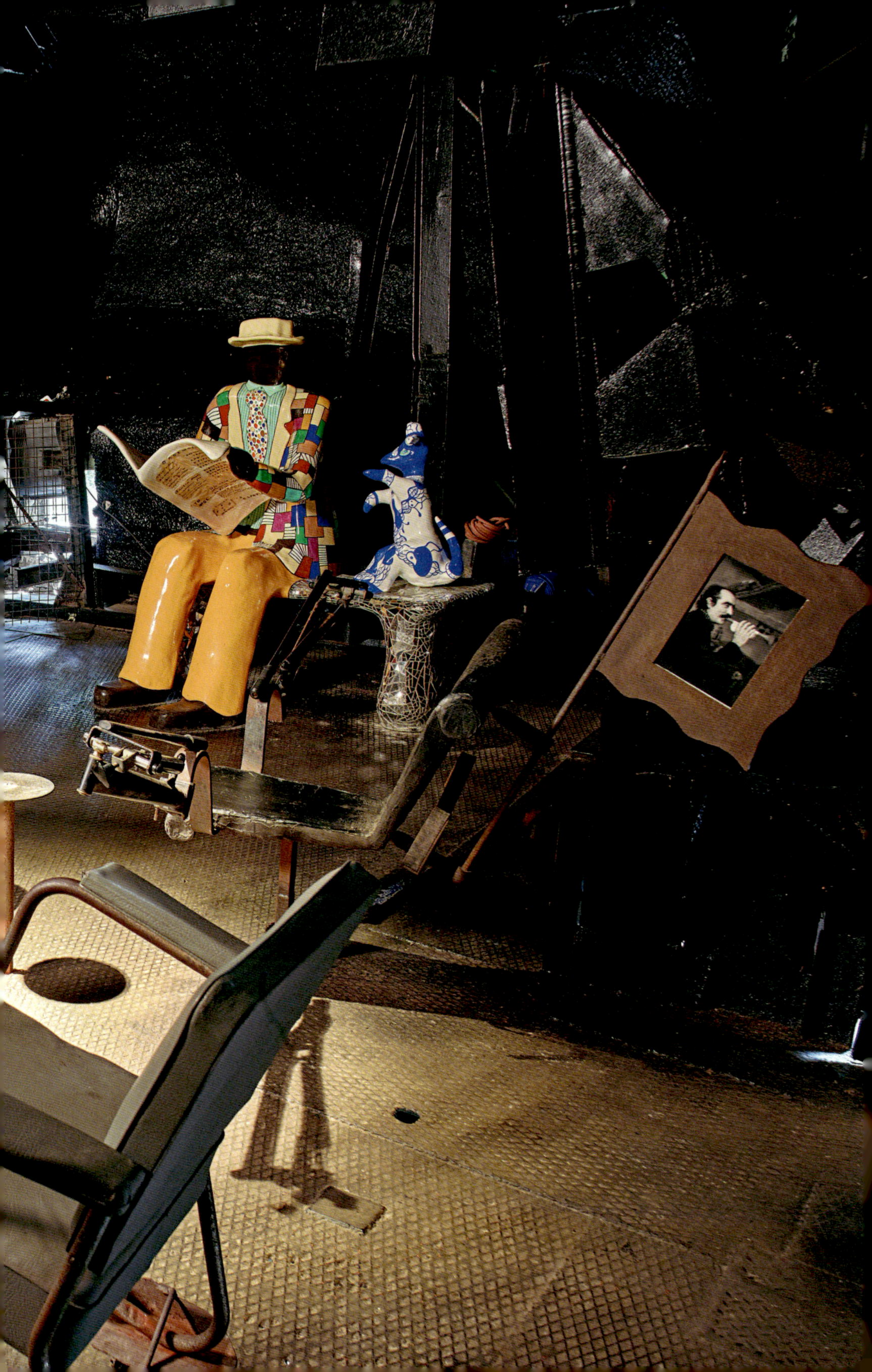

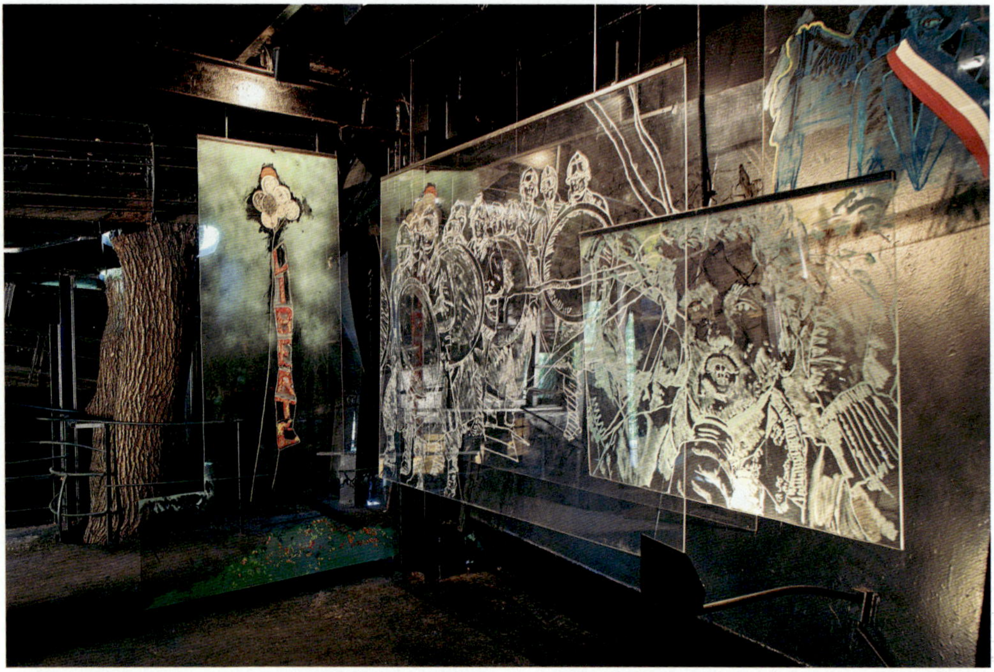

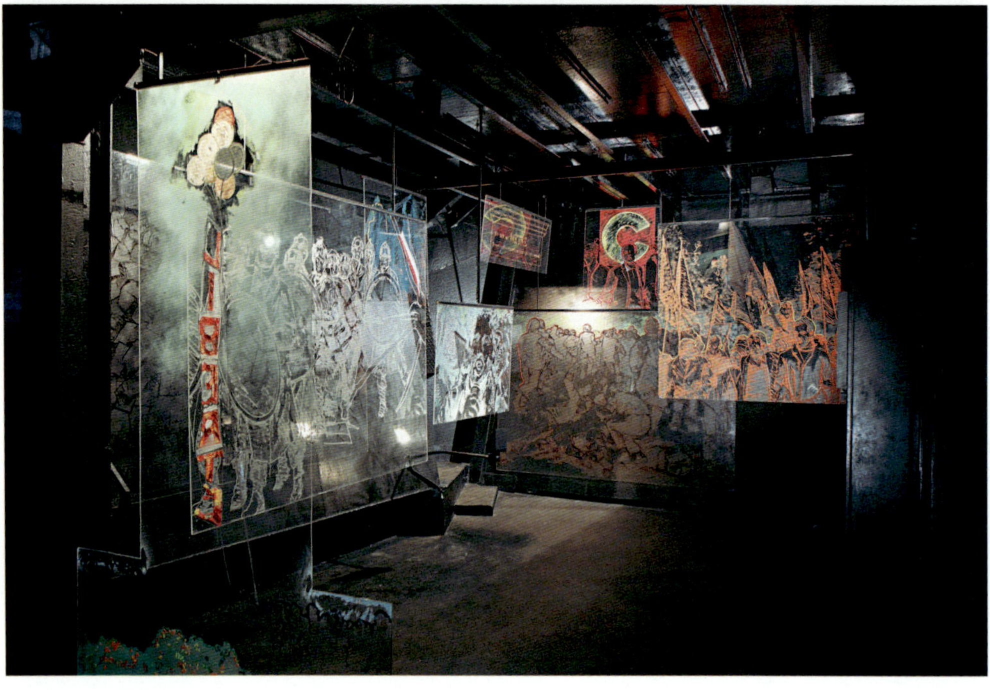

Larry Rivers, *Hommage à Mai 68*, 1978–1979 (installed 1994)

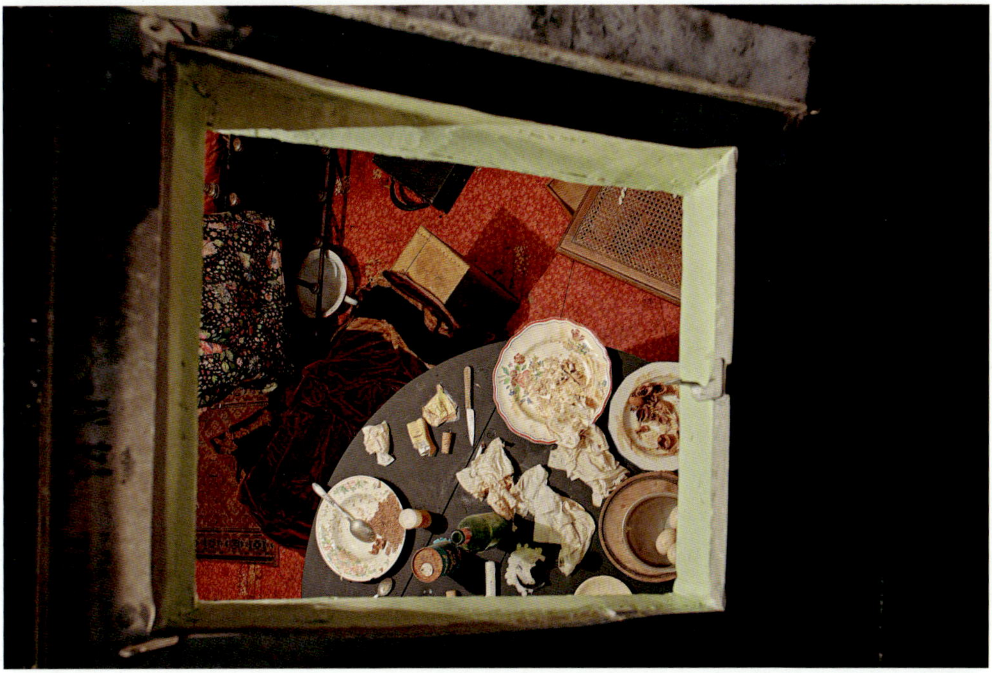

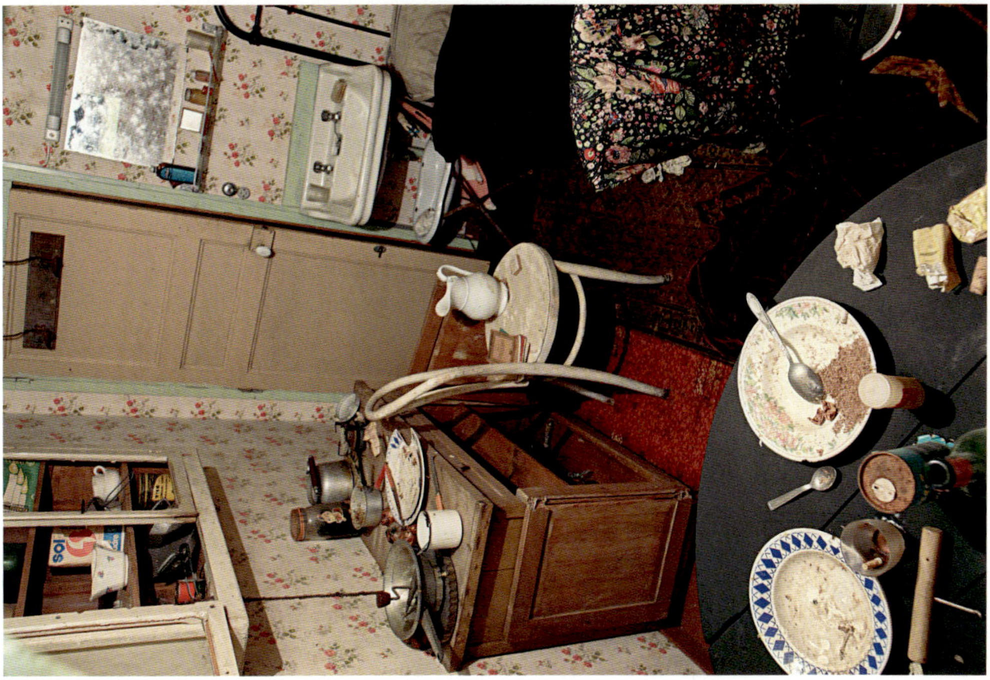

Daniel Spoerri, *La Chambre renversée de l'hôtel de l'Étoile*, 1976

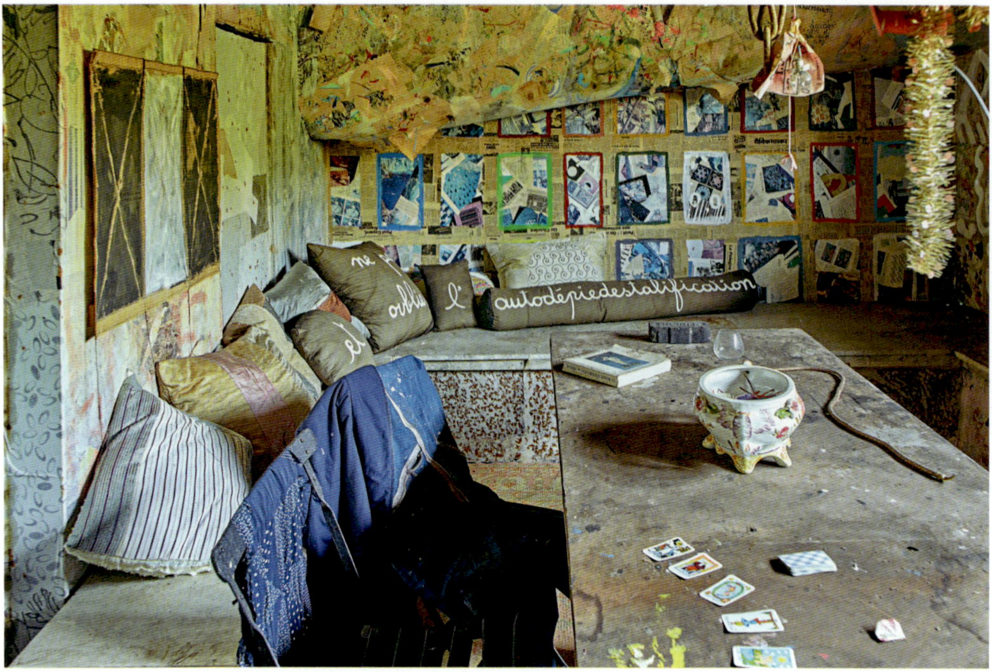

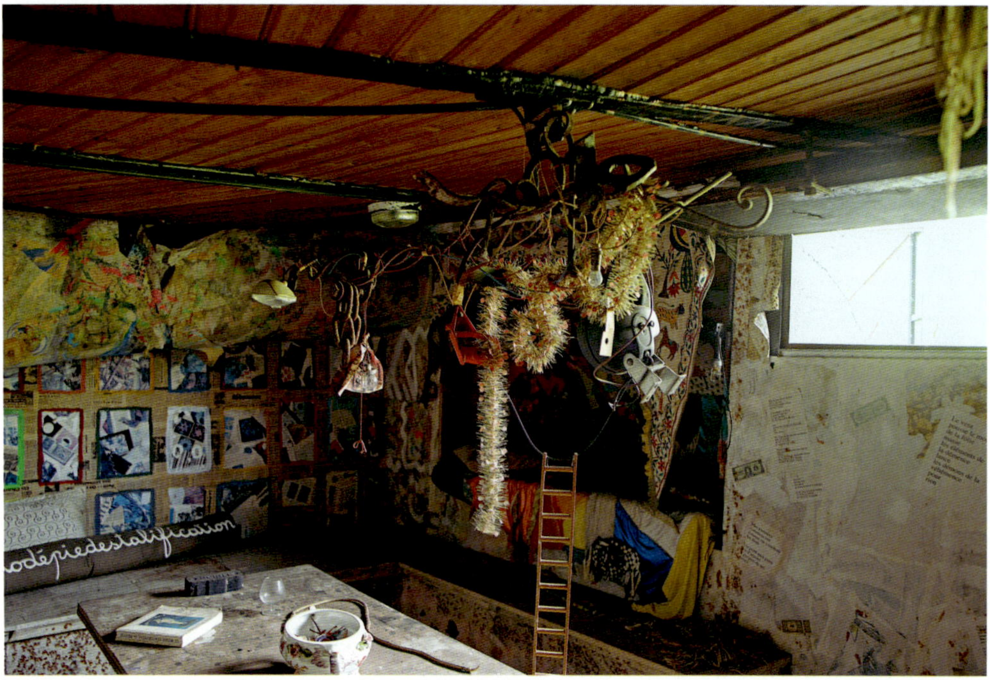

L'appartement, 1980; left wall, top image: Pierre Joly, Sans titre, n. d.; hanging from the ceiling: Jean Tinguely, *La Lampe*, n. d.

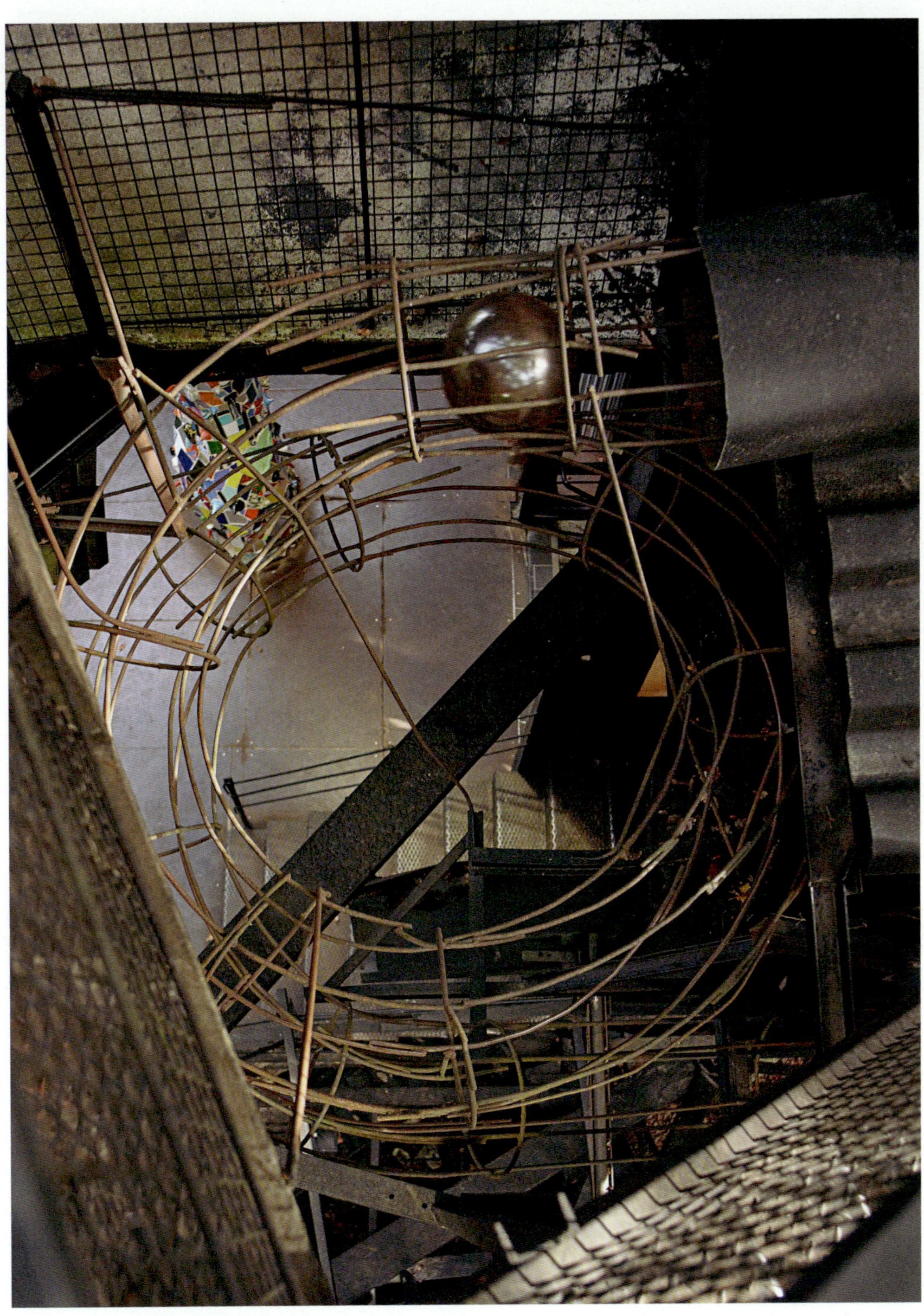

Jean Tinguely, *La Dégringolade*, 1975–1976
→   Eva Aeppli, *Hommage aux déportés*, 1976/1993

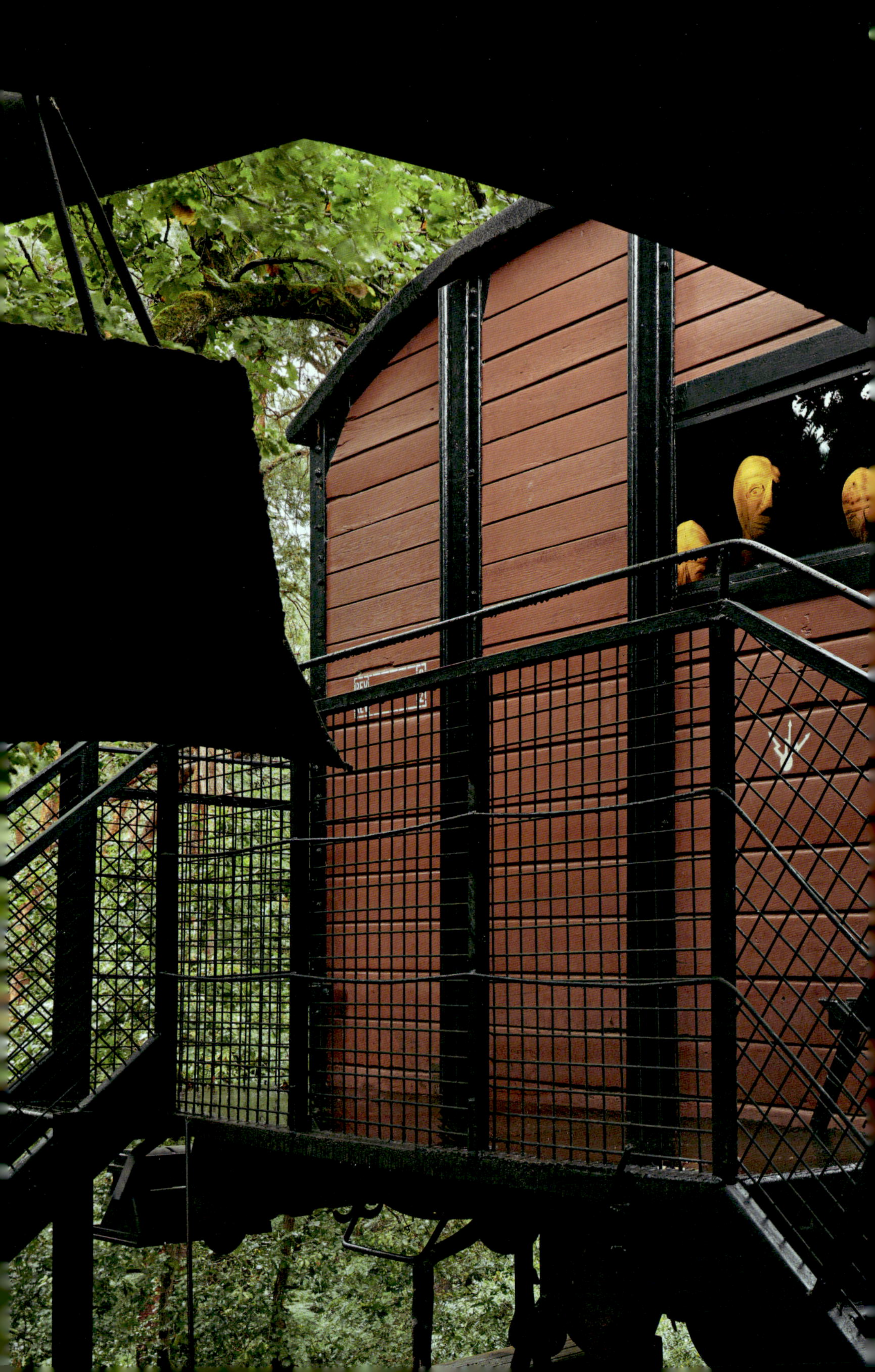

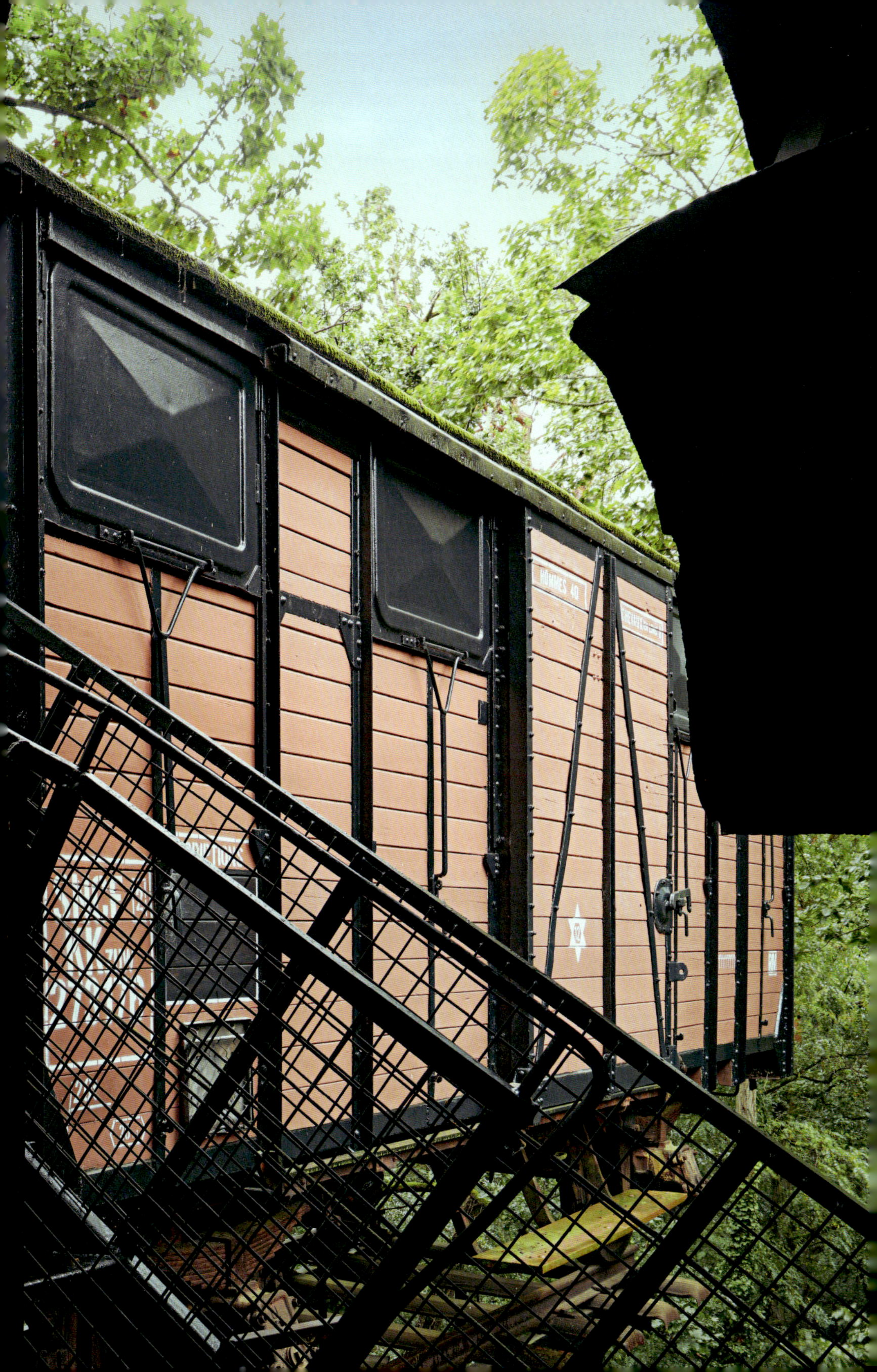

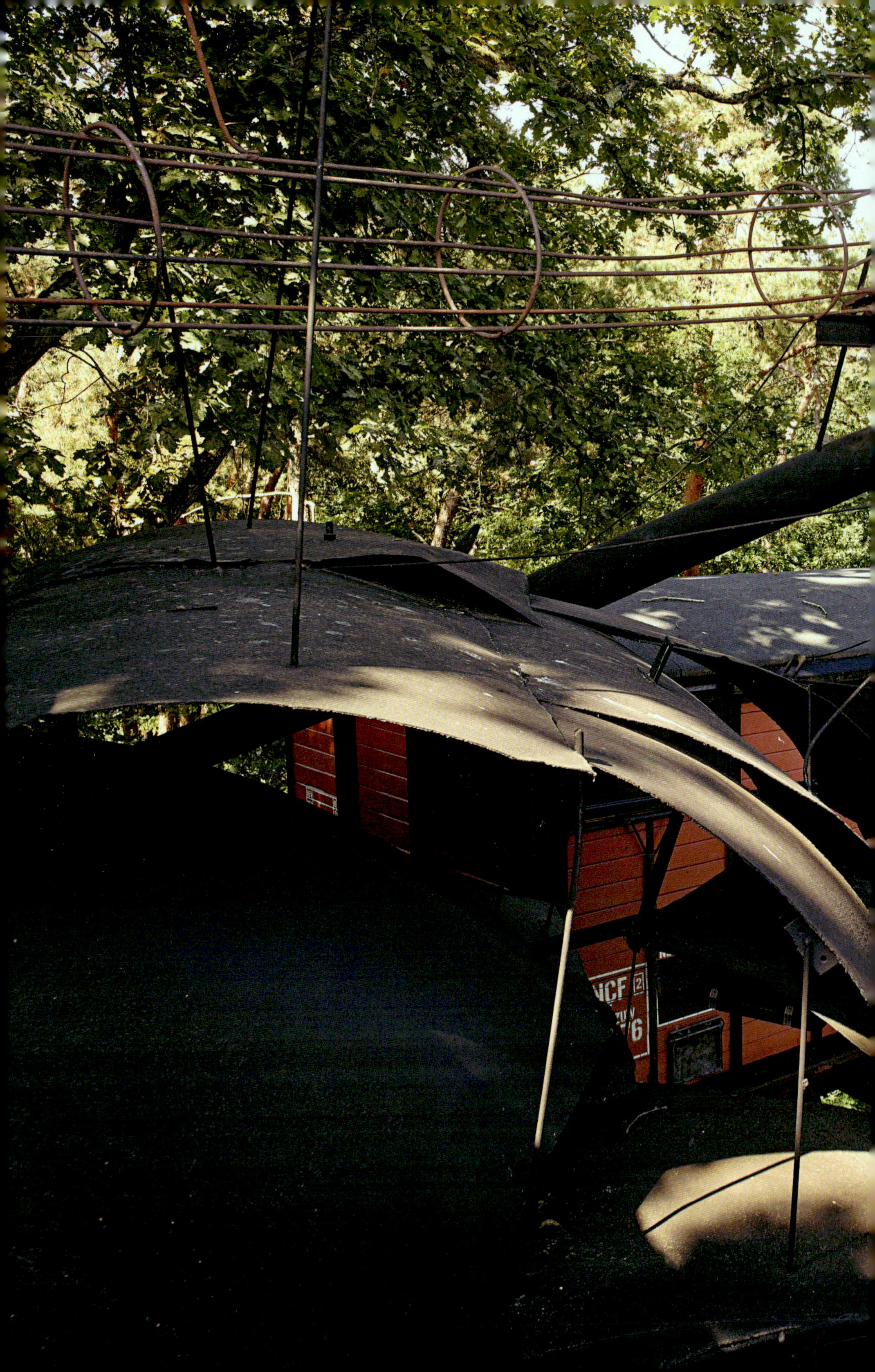

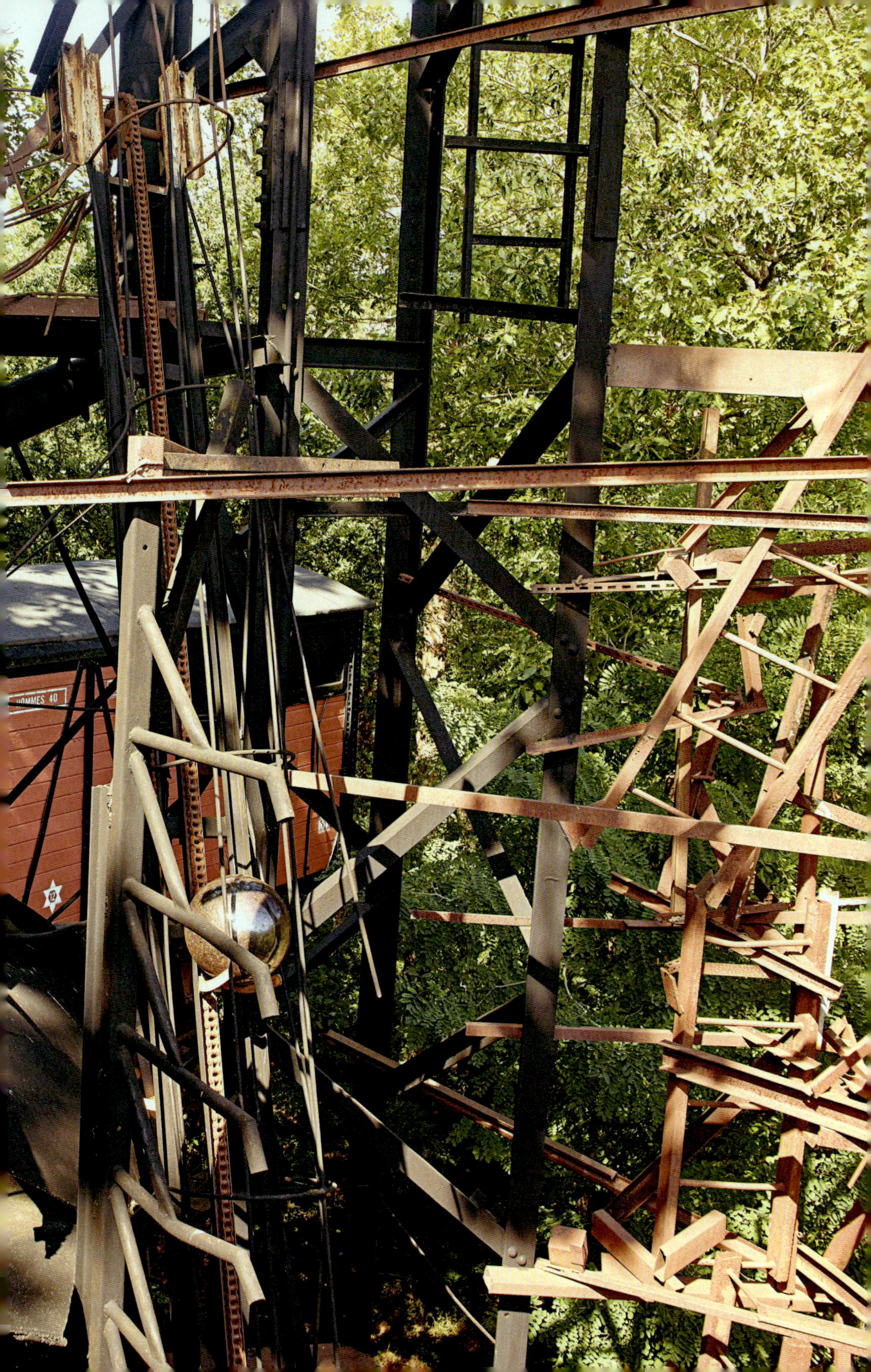

HOMMES 40
112

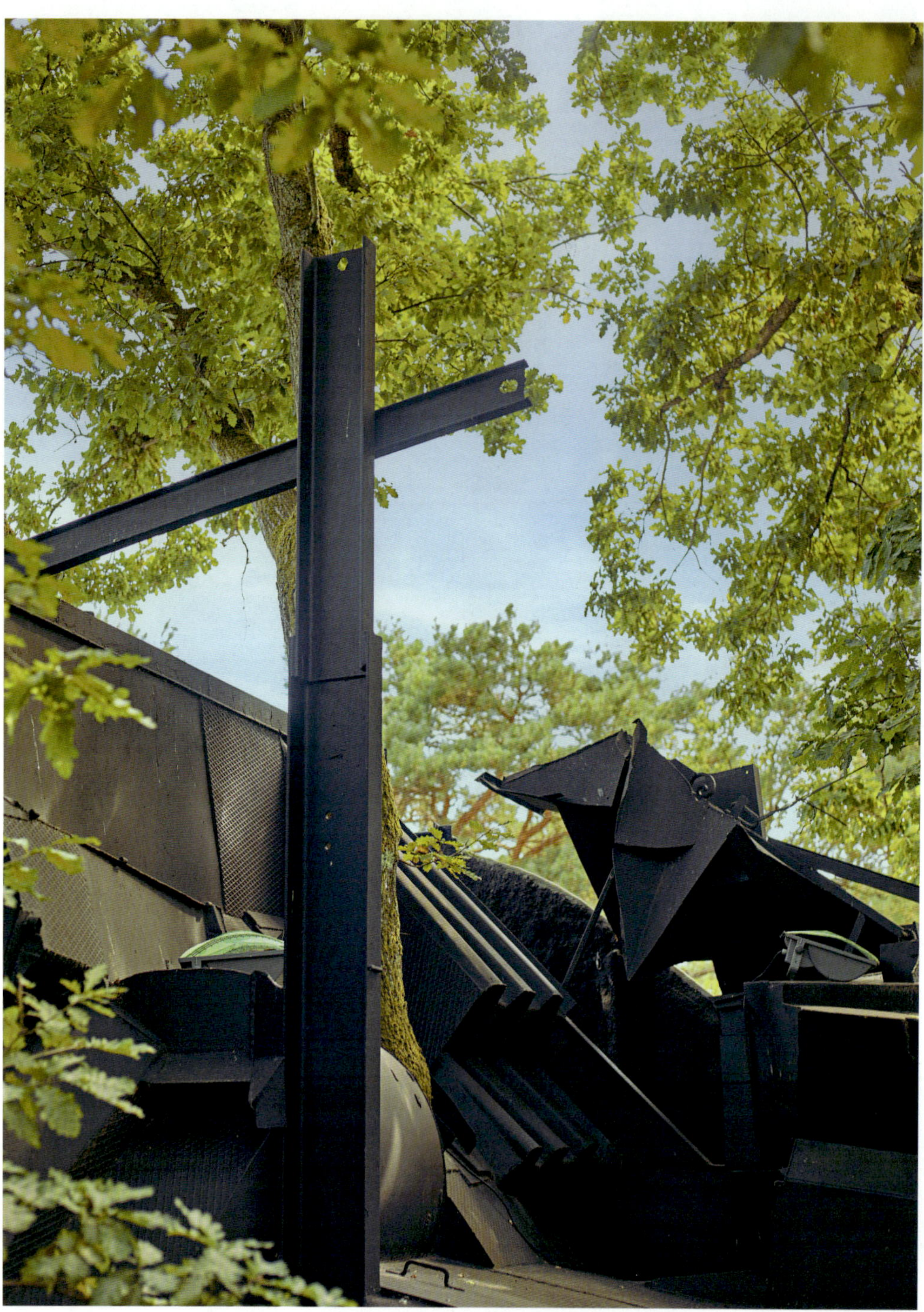

Jean Tinguely, *Le toit ouest cubiste*, 1978
← Eva Aeppli, *Hommage aux déportés*, 1976/1993; Jean Tinguely, *La Tour éphémère*, 1973–1989; *La Dégringolade*, 1975–1976

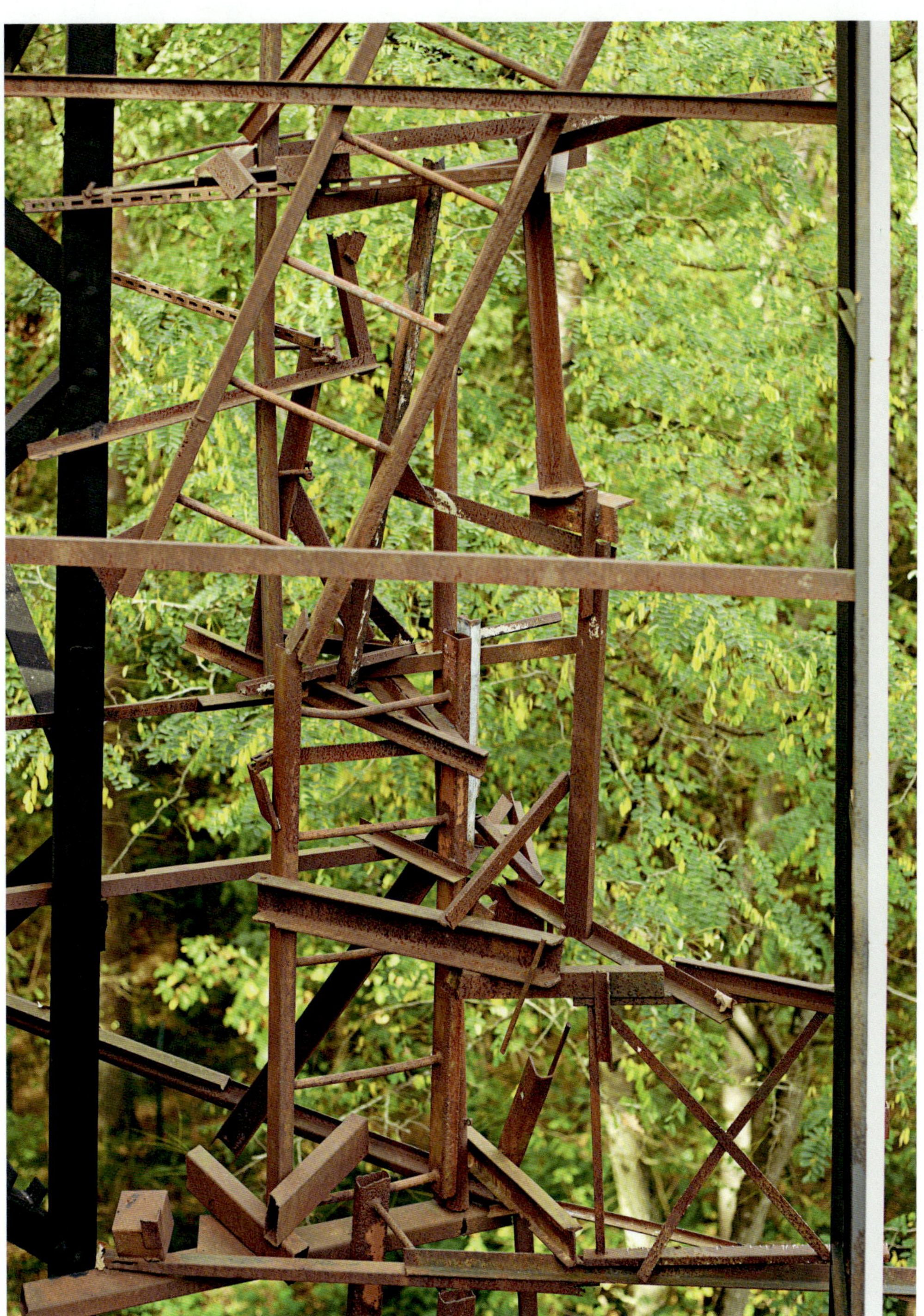

Jean Tinguely, *La Tour éphémère*, 1973–1989

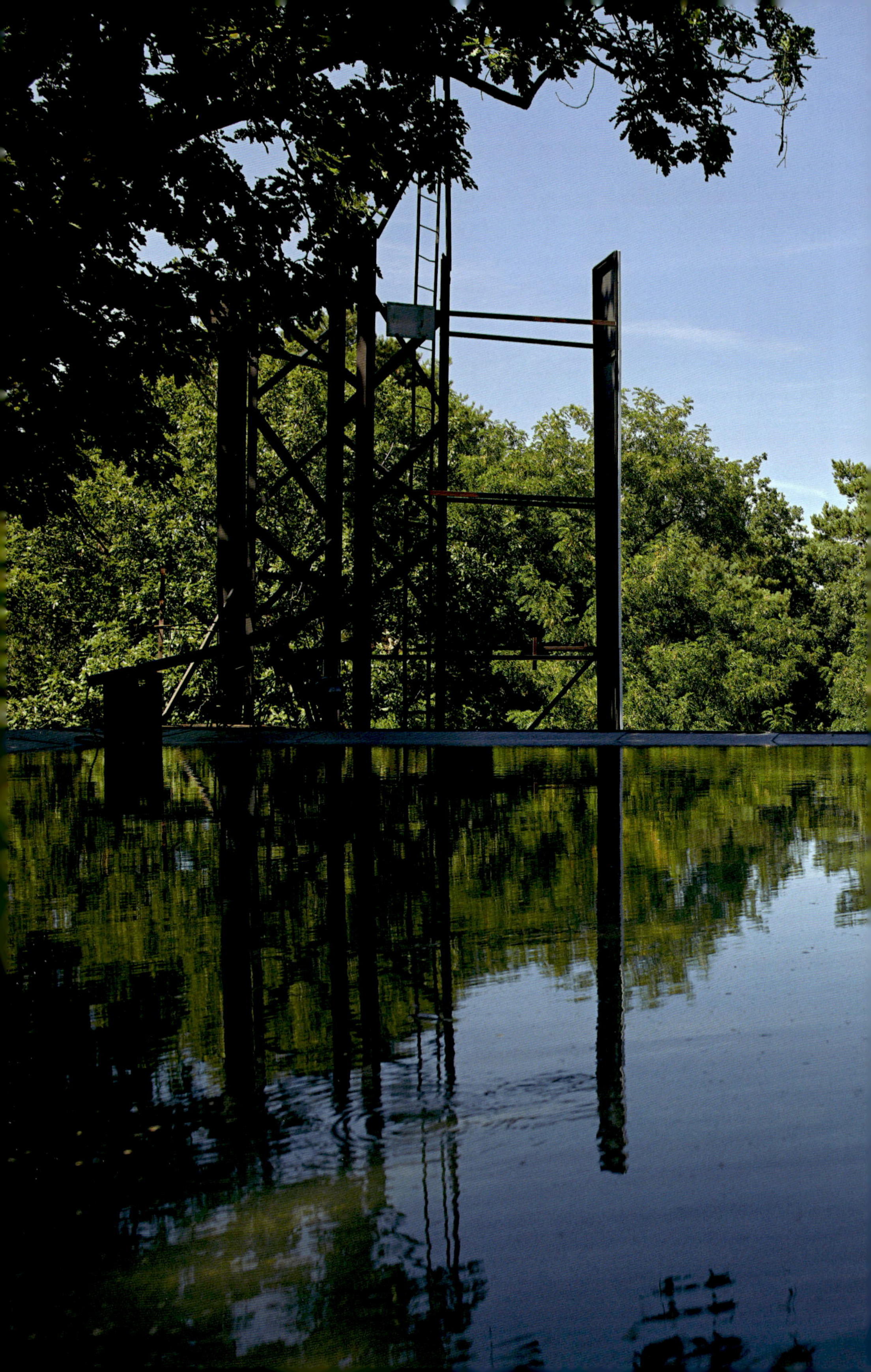

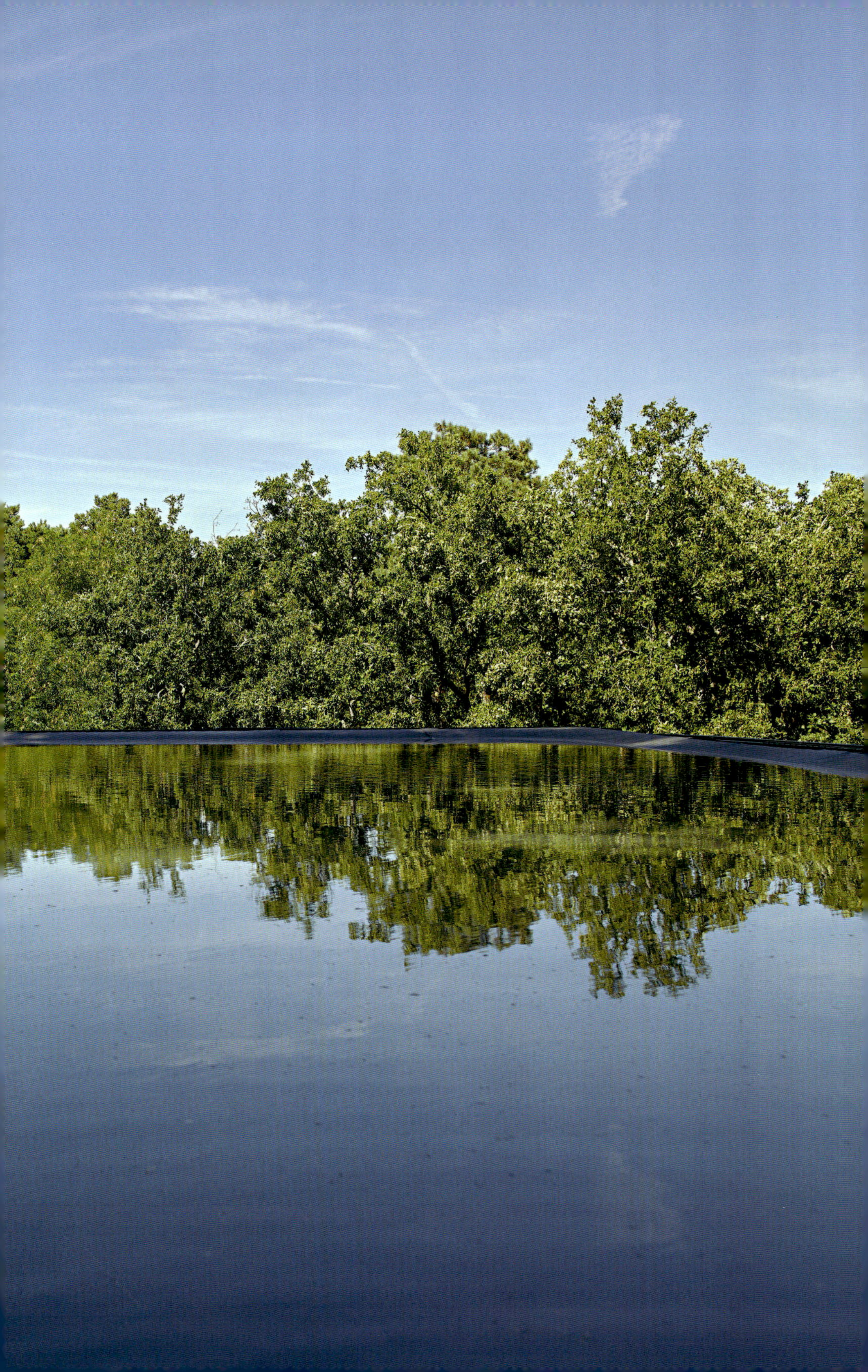

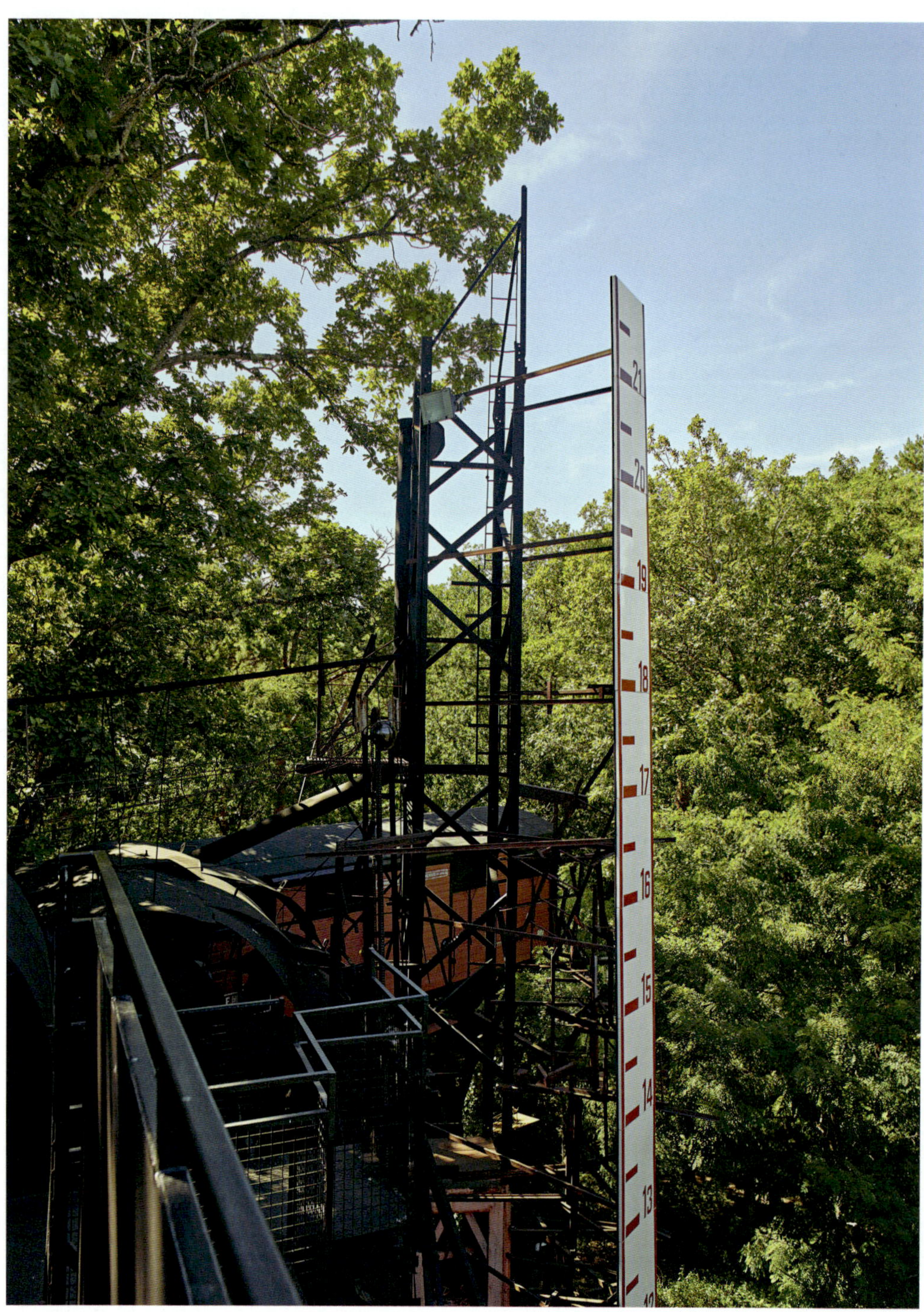

Jean Pierre Raynaud, *La Jauge*, 1975–1976/1990
← Jean Tinguely, *Hommage à Yves Klein*, 1976–1979

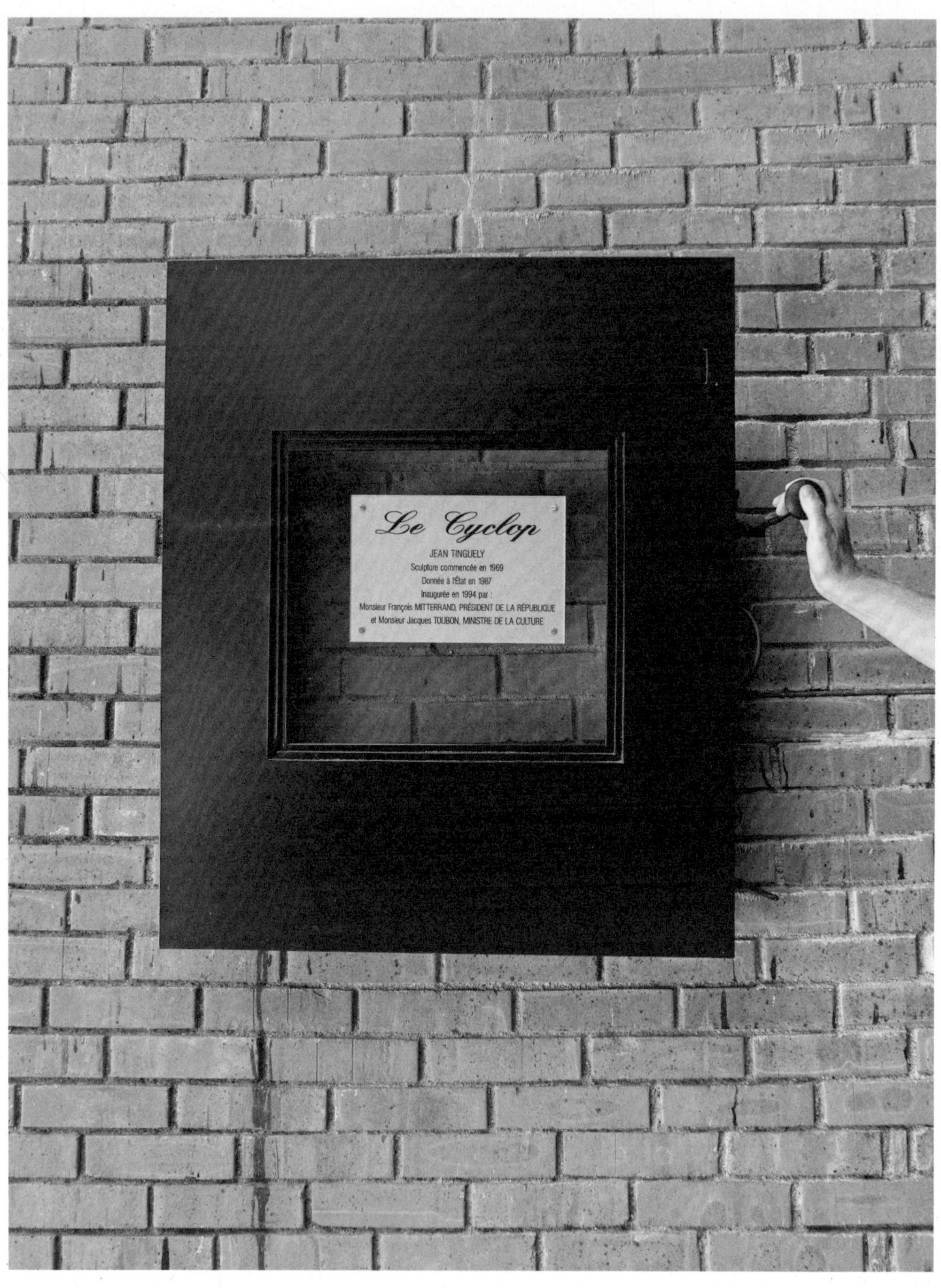

Philippe Bouveret
Le Tableau générique, 1994

Editors
Béatrice Salmon, Director, Centre National des Arts
Plastiques (Cnap)
Clément Dirié, Editorial Director, JRP|Editions

Contents Editor
Aude Bodet, Curator and Collection Deparment Head
(Cnap)

Writers (Essays)
Aude Bodet, Baptiste Brun, Jill Carrick, Dominik Müller,
Camille Paulhan, Denys Riout

Writers (Chronology)
Stéphanie Fargier-Demergès, Documentation and
Research Department Head (Cnap)
Gaëlle Guérin, Multimedia Documentalist (Cnap)
François Taillade, Director, Association Le Cyclop

Editorial Coordination
Clément Dirié
Bénédicte Godin, Head of Publications, Cnap

Documentation and Iconography
Stéphanie Fargier-Demergès, Gaëlle Guérin

Translations
Jean-François Allain, Anna Brailovsky, Deke Dusinberre,
Sandra Reid, Marie-Liesse Zambeaux

Graphic Design
current matters

Photographs of *Le Cyclop* taken in 2023–2024
Marc Domage

Typeface
Sabon LT

Color Separation and Print
Musumeci S.p.A, Quart (Aosta)

Printed in Europe

Authors' Biographies

Baptiste Brun

Baptiste Brun is an art historian who teaches at the University of Rennes 2. His work focuses on the interactions between art, art history, and the humanities and social sciences, artifacts associated with Art Brut, Outsider Art, and Folk Art, and 20th- and 21st-century artistic primitivism. He is the author of *Jean Dubuffet et la besogne de l'Art Brut. Critique du primitivisme* (Les presses du réel, 2019). He also works as an exhibition curator.

Jill Carrick

Jill Carrick is Associate Professor at Carleton University (Ottawa) in the department of Art and Architectural History and the Institute for Comparative Studies in Literature, Art, and Culture. Her current research focuses on Neo-Dada in 1960s France and Europe, with particular emphasis on the work of Daniel Spoerri and François Dufrêne. She is the author of *Nouveau Réalisme, 1960s France, and the Neo-avant-garde* (Ashgate Press, 2010; Routledge, 2024). She is the coeditor of *Daniel Spoerri: Topographies. Networks of Exchange* (arthistoricum.net, 2022) and *Dimensions de l'art brut: une histoire des matérialités* (Presses universitaires de Paris Nanterre, 2017).

Dominik Müller

Art historian Dominik Müller was a curator at the Basel Museum Tinguely for many years, and has published a reference biography on Jean Tinguely entitled *Jean Tinguely. Motor der Kunst* (Christoph Merian Verlag, 2015; new edition in 2024).

Camille Paulhan

Camille Paulhan is an art historian, art critic, and professor at the École Nationale Supérieure des Beaux-Arts in Lyon. She has published *Couper à travers les ronces* (Sombres torrents, 2021) and a book of interviews with Esther Ferrer (Manuella Éditions, 2021). She is currently preparing an essay on the art scene in Châteauroux, another on homonyms, and an exhibition at LAAC (Dunkerque) on feminist humor. Research in progress: exhibition visitors' books, the vagaries of art criticism, Basque haunted houses, artists' studios, anecdotal art history …

Denys Riout

An art historian, Denys Riout's books, all published by Gallimard, include *Qu'est-ce que l'art moderne* (2000), *Yves Klein. Manifester l'immatériel* (2004), *La Peinture monochrome. Histoire et archéologie d'un genre* (2006) and *Portes closes et œuvres invisibles* (2019). He is also the author of essays on *Arts incohérents*, Bodhan Litnianski, and graffiti.

Acknowledgments

The editors would like to thank all those who contributed to the publication's valuable iconography, in particular Laurent Condominas, Sheila Lanham, Pierre Marie Lejeune, the Leonardo Bezzola Estate, and the Museum Tinguely, Basel.

The Centre national des arts plastiques would like to sincerely thank Bloum Cardenas and Jean-Sébastien Tinguely, the rights holders of Niki de Saint Phalle and Jean Tinguely, the rights holders of Bernard Luginbühl, and the curators of the Museum Tinguely in Basel and the Musée d'Art et d'Histoire & Espace Jean Tinguely–Niki de Saint Phalle in Fribourg, for their generous support of *Le Cyclop*.

Aude Bodet would like to thank the artists she had the good fortune to meet who participated in the construction of *Le Cyclop*: Eva Aeppli, who confided to her in 2009, "All the faces must be parallel; it's stronger, more serious. No dialogue between the sculptures must be possible."; Daniel Spoerri, who visited *Le Cyclop* in 2013, and recalled the construction of *La Chambre renversée*: "Tinguely had made a large wooden crate in which I installed the furniture and all the objects over three months. When it was finished, we had a meal there with Tinguely, Niki, Seppi, and one of my art students from Cologne. Then everyone left and I started gluing and fixing all the objects. It took me a whole week, and then we turned it 90°!"; and finally Jean Pierre Raynaud, who recently was kind enough to talk about his contribution to *Le Cyclop*, "Jean asked me what I wanted to do […] Those were the days when I was 'gauging.' I used to call it 'reality by the meter.' I replied 'I'm going to measure the Head,' a way of teasing him and saying 'I'm as big as you are.' Jean immediately replied, 'Wonderful!'" And let us not forget Seppi Imhof, Tinguely's assistant, collaborator, and friend, as well as the artists—notably Philippe Bouveret and Pierre Marie Lejeune—who were present during the final years of the construction, and the opening of *Le Cyclop* to the public.

Bodet would also like to thank all the students who, over the past few years, often as interns at the Centre National des Arts Plastiques, have devoted a considerable amount of time to the countless research projects linked to the restoration of *Le Cyclop*, in particular Iris Baus-Lagarde, Pauline Fleury, Maria Claudia Gamboa, Eloïse Labie, Florence Macagno, Violette Morisseau, Raphaëlle Romain, Balqis Tandjaoui, and Marine Troadec.

Photo Credits

AKG-Images/CDA/Guillemot/St-Genès: p. 274, 278, 282, 291, 292; AKG-Images/CDA/Guillemot: p. 275, 281, 285; Association Les Amis de l'Abbé Fouré: p. 186; Leonardo Bezzola: cover (tr, tl), p. 14, 63, 77, 91, 96t, 161, 217, 219, 222, 225b, 226t, 227, 229, 230, 231, 232, 233, 235, 237, 238, 239, 240, 241t, 242, 243, 244, 245, 246, 247, 249, 250, 251, 252, 253, 254, 255, 256, 257, 260, 264, 269; René Burri: p. 226b; Centre National des Arts Plastiques, Paris: p. 117; Centre National des Arts Plastiques/Photo Stanislas de Grailly: p. 265; Centre Pompidou, MNAM-CCI, Dist. RMN-Grand Palais/Image Centre Pompidou, MNAM-CCI: p. 125; Yves Chenot: p. 34, 164–167; John Cox/Courtesy Museum Tinguely, Basel: p. 50; Cécil Mathieu Dubourg: p. 105t; Collection de l'Art Brut, Lausanne: p. 150; Laurent Condominas: p. 96b, 168, 223, 224, 225t, 241b, 267, 276, 277; Digital Image, The Museum of Modern Art, New York/Scala, Florence: p. 47, 55t, 156; Marc Domage: cover (br), backcover, p. 129–144, 193–208, 297–312, 314; R. R.: p. 111b, 112b, 146, 157, 173, 174, 185, 188; R. R./Collection de l'Art Brut, Lausanne: p. 152–153; D. R./Courtesy Museum Tinguely, Basel: p. 70; R. R./ Galerie Denise René, Paris: p. 45t; Robert Doisneau/ Courtesy Gamma Rapho: p. 46, 80, 218; Johannes Edberg; © Fredrik Ultvedt: p. 228; Ed van der Elsken/Courtesy Nederlands Fotomuseum: p. 56, 66–67, 87t, 159; Hans Erixon/Scanpix Sweden/AFP: p. 87b; David Gahr/ Courtesy Digital Image, The Museum of Modern Art, New York/Scala, Florence: p. 51b; Raphaël Gaillarde/ Courtesy Gamma Rapho: p. 184; The Estate of Gianfranco Gorgoni: p. 172; Allan Grant/Courtesy The LIFE Picture Collection/Shutterstock: p. 60b, 61; Otto Hahn: p. 268; Keystone-France/Gamma Rapho: p. 102; Monique Jacot/ Courtesy Museum Tinguely, Basel: p. 72; Laurent Jacquy: p. 178; Sheila Lanham: p. 98; Patricia Lecomte: p. 10; Bertrand Leroy: p. 112t, 286, 289, 290; Sophie Loubaton: p. 182; Allan Moe/Ritzau Scanpix/Ritzau Scanpix via AFP: p. 58b; Musée d'Art et d'Histoire, Geneva: p. 33; Museum Tinguely, Basel: cover (tl), p. 35, 36, 37, 38, 39, 40, 60h, 68, 69, 73, 75, 115, 122, 212, 220–221, 236, 248, 262, 263, 266, 273; The Niki Charitable Art Foundation: p. 159; Ad Petersen: p. 216; Erik Petersen/Ritzau Scanpix/ Ritzau Scanpix via AFP: p. 58t; Philadelphia Museum of Art, Philadelphia: p. 105b, 109; Julio Pietromarchi: p. 279, 280, 287; Clovis Prévost: p. 177; Wilhelm Redemann; BPK, Berlin, Dist. RMN-Grand Palais: p. 124; Frédéric Reglain/Courtesy Gamma Rapho: p. 288; Martha Rocher: p. 84tl; John D. Schiff/Courtesy Museum Tinguely, Basel & Leo Baeck Institute: p. 51t; Arne Steckmest/Artik Films, Paris: p. 284; Courtesy Stedelijk Museum, Amsterdam: p. 64–65; Hansjörg Stoecklin/ Courtesy Museum Tinguely, Basel: p. 84tr, 84b, 111t; Soichi Sunami; Digital Image, The Museum of Modern Art, New York/Scala, Florence: p. 55b; Succession Yves Klein: p. 45b; Telimage, Paris: p. 107; Rico Weber: p. 99; Rico Weber/Courtesy Musée d'Art et d'Histoire Fribourg: p. 234; Charles Paul Wilp/BPK, Berlin, Dist. Grand Palais RMN/Image BPK: p. 42

Copyright

Archives Cyclop
https://archivescyclop.fr

Archives Cyclop is a digital platform created by the
Centre National des Arts Plastiques, dedicated to
Jean Tinguely's *Cyclop* and its archives. Aimed at
amateurs and specialists alike, it brings documents
together virtually, allowing different ways of exploring
and (re)discovering *Le Cyclop* through the archives.
Designed to encourage users to move from archive to
archive as if wandering through *Le Cyclop*'s memory
and history, the platform also offers a number of features:
a database with a simple and advanced search engine,
data visualization modules for archive documents with
a chronological frieze, and an interactive map. It presents
an invaluable tool for understanding *Le Cyclop*, its
uniqueness, its history, and its protagonists, by providing
access to a wide range of resources, regularly collected
from and expanded by the many contributors who hold
archive material on *Le Cyclop*. The ongoing development
of the Archives Cyclop aims to make it a reference tool
through which the public can acquire more knowledge
about this extraordinary work.

Design and development (2022):
Center National des Arts Plastiques
(Stéphanie Fargier-Demergès, Documentation and
Research Department Head, and Gaëlle Guérin,
Multimedia Documentalist), Matter of Fact, Marie
Onillon (Cultural Projects Consultant)

Published by

JRP|Editions
Rue des Bains, 39
1205 Geneva
Switzerland
www.jrp-editions.com

and

Centre National des Arts Plastiques
CAP 18
189, rue d'Aubervilliers
75018 Paris
www.cnap.fr

ISBN 978-3-03764-606-9

A French edition is available under the
ISBN 978-3-03764-605-2.

JRP|Editions publications are available internationally
at selected bookstores and from the following distribution
partners:

Switzerland
AVA Verlagsauslieferung AG
www.ava.ch

Germany and Austria
JRP|Editions
books@jrp-editions.com

France
Les presses du réel
www.lespressesdureel.com

UK and other European countries, USA, Canada,
Asia and Australia
ARTBOOK|D.A.P.
www.artbook.com